The
Social Welfare Institution

The
Social Welfare Institution

AN INTRODUCTION

Second Edition

Ronald C. Federico
UNIVERSITY OF NORTH CAROLINA *at* GREENSBORO

D. C. HEATH AND COMPANY
Lexington, Massachusetts   Toronto   London

International Standard Book Number: 0-669-97287-8

Library of Congress Catalog Card Number: 75-16616

This book is dedicated to
Eleanor Vosburgh
in fond and grateful memory.

Preface

An early point in a social welfare, social work, or human services undergraduate curriculum is the intended place for this book. It attempts to lay the foundation for later more detailed and sophisticated study of basic policy and practice issues. Although it is assumed that it will be supplemented with other materials, this revised edition incorporates a considerable amount of additional readings not included in the original edition, especially material not readily available to students in school libraries and bookstores. Most of this material is included in the greatly expanded exhibits. In addition, new areas are now covered, including comparative social welfare programs and social policy. Other areas are expanded and rewritten, including social systems, economic and political theory, interventive methods, contexts of practice, and the future of social welfare. A new appendix provides case studies, while most of the material in the previous appendixes has been updated and incorporated as exhibits. Study questions have been added at the end of each chapter to assist students in their review of pertinent material, and a glossary has been included at the end of the book.

As in the original edition, no single "theory" of social welfare is proposed, and the objective continues to be as a stimulus, guide, and source of basic factual material to students, rather than a scholarly study. Although this revision is substantially rewritten and expanded, the conception of the original edition remains intact. It has now simply been elaborated upon and made more relevant to the rapidly changing social welfare institution in the mid-1970s.

Those persons and groups acknowledged in the original edition helped to make the basic outline of the book possible. In further developing the book in this revised edition, Mareb Mossman, Virginia Stephens, and Wilburn Hayden have been especially stimulating colleagues. Judy Vetock, Teresa Walker, Helen Taylor, Betty Deskins, and Alice Tillman always provided help cheerfully and unstintingly as the manuscript was being prepared. Ralph Dolgoff and Paul Schwartz made insightful suggestions for changes in content, many of which have been incorporated into this revision. Mary Ellen Elwell was uniquely helpful in patiently reviewing the manuscript and suggesting stylistic and content changes that have greatly enriched the book. To these people, and to the countless other colleagues, students, and friends who helped formulate and prepare the present revised edition, I am deeply grateful. Despite all the assistance provided by these and other people, errors and omissions will no doubt occur in the book. For these I take full responsibility.

Contents

Exhibits

THE EFFECTIVENESS of the American social welfare system has been undergoing increasingly critical examination in the past few years. The questioning of the system has resulted from changes in American society as well as from evidence that the welfare structure has not always been successful in implementing its societal mandate. The changes occurring in society and their effects on the welfare system have created a period of flux in the welfare professions. We are in the midst of a shift from the traditions of the past to new values and behavior patterns that will be more effective in the society of the future.

Any transitional period creates anxiety and uncertainty. Possessing advanced degrees or professional certification does not necessarily avoid the common reluctance to step out of the past, or the honest perplexity in looking to the future. Social welfare practitioners have felt the anxieties, and many have reacted quite normally in trying to deny the need for change. Others accept the fact that the traditional order was indeed ripe for reexamination. Uncertainty is being faced and will be an issue in social welfare for many years, since the building of a new social order takes time and experimentation.

One of the responses to the critical examination of social welfare has been a concerted effort by the major social welfare professions to specify their goals more clearly, and identify the personnel required to attain these goals. For example, the National Association of Social Workers (NASW) recently published their "Standards for Social Service Manpower," excerpts from which appear in Exhibit I-1. In this document, the profession attempts to specify the kinds of skills social workers must have to function effectively at various levels of professional activity. Associated with this are the recent NASW guidelines for licensing bills, the purpose of which is to protect legally the title and practice of social work just as the title and practice of a medical doctor is protected. Excerpts from this document are also included in Exhibit I-1. Both of these documents attest to the social work profession's effort to clearly specify the competencies that social workers must have. As this becomes clearer, professional social workers will be accountable for those activities that are called social work, and they will disassociate themselves from persons calling themselves social workers but who have not had social work training that meets professional standards. Not incidentally, such specification and licensing will also give professional social workers better hiring and salary benefits. The main point is, though, that all of the major social welfare professions seek to strengthen their practice by more closely controlling channels of professional training and certification. By so doing, it is believed that these professions will reflect current scientific and practice knowledge, as well as the highest contemporary standards of professional practice.

From this process of codifying knowledge, skills, and professional identity have emerged several issues related to the meaning of professional competence. Among the issues are the following:

1. The helping process entails the use of existing resources. However, it also includes the identification of inadequate or missing resources. This may require the professional helping person to seek change in various parts of the social system, which may in turn involve the helping person in situations of confrontation and conflict. Do contemporary societal views of appropriate professional helping behavior include the mandate to engage in conflict when necessary to achieve change? Are there inconsistencies between helping a person solve his problems and engaging in social-change activities? What are the risks involved in engaging in social-change activities, for the individual professional as well as for the profession itself?

2. The process of strengthening a professional organization and its ability to control professional access and behavior is necessary to improve practice and obtain stronger societal support. To what extent may it also insulate the profession from healthy input from other professionals or nonprofessionals? To what extent does greater professional autonomy work counter to greater client autonomy? Should there be a lessening of professional boundaries rather than a strengthening of them, so that there is less division between the various helping professions, and between professionals and those who use their services?

3. It is believed that competent professional training includes knowledge, value, and skill components. Is there at present a codified body of knowledge that can be clearly identified as necessary for each of the helping professions—social work, for example? Is the behavioral science knowledge that forms an important part of much professional training really scientific, verified, and reliable? Are the practice skills taught in the human service professions really effective?

There are no easy answers to these questions, and they are raised at this point to introduce the beginning student to the fact that becoming a social welfare professional is fraught with uncertainties and the need to make important personal professional decisions based on careful, informed thought. The social welfare professional of today must be a widely informed, sensitive, analytical person who can use a professional problem-solving approach at the individual, group, and societal levels. Studying social welfare as a social institution means developing an awareness that, although one deals with individuals in identifying and solving problems, those problems exist in a social context and may in fact be caused by that context. It also means understanding that resources usable in the change process range anywhere from federal, state, and local legislative chambers to the most intimate relationships between individuals. It means understanding that social and economic forces operate differently for different groups in society, and that behaviors that appear strange or even pathological may be attempts to deal with a reality that the professional has never directly experienced and may only dimly understand. It means a knowledge of the forces that led to earlier attempts to deal with human and social need, the legacy of these attempts in our own day, and ways in which other societies have grappled with the same problems this society now faces.

There is no more fascinating study than of the social welfare institution, and there are no more fascinating jobs than social welfare jobs. This book may leave serious students shaking their heads with astonishment as they examine in detail the study of social welfare, constantly amazed by the fads, foibles, and successes of the helping professions. Throughout, it will be emphasized that there is no substitute for an analytical approach: Why does the system operate as it does? Who benefits and who suffers? What changes are possible? What do we know and what don't we know? What do we assume and what do we accept on someone else's say-so? Social welfare is an important area of study and a meaningful arena in which to spend one's adult life.

PLAN OF
THE BOOK

The transitional period of the sixties and seventies has created many exciting and promising changes and challenges. Social welfare objectives, methods, and task allocations are being reevaluated, and social welfare education has felt the impact. At the undergraduate level, courses are closely tied to a behavioral and biological science base. Undergraduate social welfare education has become more formalized with the help of the Council on Social Work Education (CSWE), which now accredits undergraduate as well as graduate social work programs. The complex relationship of social welfare to social work will be examined in more detail in Chapter 1. CSWE's attempts to codify appropriate content at the undergraduate level led to the identification of four major objectives for undergraduate social welfare education.[1]

1. Preparation for social welfare practice—enabling the undergraduate social welfare major to fit into appropriate work contexts with basic but minimal on-the-job training.

2. Preparation for informed citizenship—enabling the college graduate to understand the social welfare issues of our time and to be active citizens regarding them (at the polls, as volunteers in the community, and so on).

3. Preparation to enter graduate programs in social welfare areas.

4. Preparation for employment or graduate training in a variety of fields related to social welfare.

Some believe these tasks cannot all be met in any given undergraduate program, but I believe they can. The heart of the program lies in the first objective, with the others following from its attainment. The attempt to meet these CSWE objectives seems most logically to begin with the study of social welfare as a social institution, in which the broad foundation knowledge of the liberal arts can be joined with specialized knowledge relating to professional means and goals.[2]

This book is written as an introduction to the issues and knowledge upon which social welfare and social work curricula are built. It examines the scope of social welfare as a concept, the structures that have grown out of the concept, and the theory and practice techniques enabling the structures to function. The attainment of the CSWE objectives requires this breadth and this essentially interdisciplinary approach. An attempt is made to provide a reasonably objective picture of the subject, while openly recognizing that we are in a transitional period. The reader should have an elementary background in sociology, psychology, economics, and political science so that major theories can be introduced and analyzed with minimal foundation material. This is not a "how-to" manual. Becoming a social welfare professional requires mastery of basic social science and social welfare concepts, as well as direct practical experience. Sometimes theory seems very far removed from practice; actually it simply helps us to organize what we know so that we can use our knowledge more effectively as practitioners. At the beginning level for which this book is intended, mastery of social welfare's theoretical, conceptual, and factual foundations is essential so that later practice-oriented courses can build upon these foundations.

EXHIBIT I-1

Licensing and Manpower Standards in Social Work

Two recent publications of the National Association of Social Workers (NASW) illustrate the current focus on clearer specification of professional standards for training and practice. In "Standards for Social Service Manpower" (1973), NASW has attempted to specify professional levels of practice in social work, relating these to appropriate social work tasks and education or training for each level. This attempt illustrates the increasing formalization occurring in the social welfare professions in an attempt to protect professional autonomy and improve service delivery.

From "Standards for Social Service Manpower" (Policy Statement 4; Washington: NASW, 1973), pp. 5–19.

In "Legal Regulation of Social Work Practice" (NASW, 1973), the formalization developed in the professional standards is carried further. In suggesting that social work titles be protected through legal regulation that prohibits their use by anyone other than persons meeting established professional criteria, and that practice be similarly protected through licensure, the profession is attempting to assure that persons calling themselves social workers and engaging in social work practice be competent to do so. Such legal regulation protects the consumer from incompetent practitioners, and protects the profession's claim to set standards of professional practice. Professionals themselves are protected from competition with persons calling themselves professionals but who are untrained to provide professionally competent services. Professionals are also provided with a career continuum that provides them with incentive and flexibility.

While there is little question that a clearly specified and closely integrated system of training, practice, and legal regulation of standards can be expected to have desirable effects on the level of service offered to clients, there are other less obvious issues involved in the strengthening of professional autonomy. As training procedures become more formalized, it is increasingly difficult for persons who have skill—but who lack the formally specified training—to receive professional certification. This can be of particular importance to members of minority groups who may have had very valuable life experiences, but who may not have had the opportunity to pursue their formal education beyond grade school or high school. Women, too, may be affected, since they often have to drop out of school to raise families, or may only be able to study or work part-time. Having pre-professional levels of professional recognition helps, but still does not altogether overcome the rigidity imposed by formalized standards of training and practice.

Another potential problem with increased formalization is the potential isolation of the profession from those it serves. Users of services frequently lack the training that would qualify them for input into professional decision-making as formally structured. Yet clients have a perspective on services that the professional cannot have, no matter how much training and experience the individual practitioner might have. Once standards are established, especially when established by professional organizations that never have direct contact with users of services, there is a tendency for them to become rigid. Behavior tends to be molded around the standard, rather than the standard remaining flexible to the needs of practitioners and users of services. The result is a potential for professional standards to become increasingly unrelated to practice realities, so that professionals have the power to control practice in spite of beliefs by users and other non-professionals (or even some dissenting professionals) that the standards being used are irrelevant to people's needs.

This exhibit concludes with excerpts from pages 8–15 of the "Standards for Social Service Manpower: Professional Standards" referred to above. Try to maintain a balanced analytical perspective when reading these standards. How do they help to strengthen social work practice? How might they serve to isolate the profession from its clients? How might they serve to isolate professionals from each other? Can you suggest any alternative standards or approaches to standards? On the whole, would you support the standards? Why or why not?

LEVELS OF PERSONNEL

This classification plan recognizes six levels of competence. There are two preprofessional levels, as follows:

Social service aide. Entry is based on an assessment of the individual's maturity, appropriate life experiences, motivation, and skills required by the specific task or function.

Social service technician. Entry is based on completion of (1) a two-year educational program in one of the social services, usually granting an associate of arts degree; or (2) a baccalaureate degree in another field.

There are four professional levels, as follows:

Social worker. Entry requires a baccalaureate degree from an accredited social work program.

Graduate social worker. Entry requires a master's degree from an accredited graduate school of social work.

Certified social worker. Entry requires certification by (1) the Academy of Certified Social Workers (ACSW) as being capable of autonomous, self-directed practice; or (2) licensure by the state in which the person practices.

Social work fellow. Entry requires completion of a doctoral program or substantial practice in the field of specialization following certification by ACSW.

PREPROFESSIONAL SOCIAL WORK

The two levels of preprofessional social work practice have distinct levels of competence:

Social service aide. Under professionally guided supervision or as part of a team, the social service aide performs various specified duties to help clients obtain and use social and related services, including obtaining information, providing specific basic information, aiding clients in agency procedures and services, and other sup-

portive functions. The aide classification may cover a variety of specific service-related functions other than social service, but should be integrated with the performance of duties by other social service personnel.

Responsibilities require an ability to communicate freely, to understand and describe program procedures, to interpret the concerns and needs of clients, and to provide defined, concrete assistance with the needs of living. The aide must have knowledge derived from accumulated life experiences paralleling those of the consumer community, a capacity to learn specific skills taught through on-the-job training, and motivation to serve others. The minimum educational requirement for this classification is the ability to read and count, in addition to other individual skills necessary to carry out the tasks of the particular position.

Social service technician. As part of a team or under the direction of and close supervision by a professional social worker, the social service technician performs a wide variety of duties to facilitate the knowledge and use of social services. These involve disseminating information, obtaining information from clients, assisting clients in the use of community resources, obtaining information about assessing the impact and coverage of programs, carrying out specific program activities and tasks, and in other ways applying life experiences and knowledge derived from training in working with individuals or groups.

In carrying out these responsibilities, the social service technician must be able to make inquiries discreetly, provide clear information, understand and describe agency programs, recognize general levels of anxiety or reactions of fear, maintain emotional self-control, retain values, and provide services to assist clients with defined environmental problems.

The technician must have knowledge of the

fundamentals of human behavior, specific agency operations, and specific communities and their social service programs and have skills in working with people, including the ability to communicate and empathize, attitudes of respect for individual and group differences, appreciation for the capacity to change, and the ability to use social institutions on behalf of consumers. The educational requirement is an associate of arts degree in a technical program of social services or its equivalent.

PROFESSIONAL SOCIAL WORK

The four levels of professional social work practice also have distinct levels of practice and preparation:

Social worker. Under supervision, the social worker is responsible for professional service designed to sustain and encourage the social functioning of individuals or groups. He assists them to appraise their situation, to identify problems and alternative solutions, and to anticipate social and environmental consequences.

The social worker is guided by professional social work values, purposes of the service, prevailing organized knowledge, societal sanctions, and social work methodology. In carrying out his responsibilities, the social worker uses methods of disciplined inquiry based on interpersonal relationships involving cause and effect; interpretation of resources and their limits; intervention with related individuals or groups, colleagues, and other disciplines and organizations; direct counseling and services; and other related activities.

The social worker must have a beginning knowledge of human behavior and development, the social and economic environment, the social service system, and the factors that contribute to normal development and social and individual abnormalities, including symptomatology. He must be able to demonstrate a conscious use of social work methods, for example, skill in the use of specific techniques, such as interviewing, diagnosis, use of self-discipline, and use of social resources. The educational prerequisites for this classification are a baccalaureate degree from an undergraduate college or university with a social welfare program accredited by the Council on Social Work Education (CSWE).

Graduate social worker. The graduate social worker is responsible for providing professional, skilled social work services to individuals, groups, or larger social contexts and is capable of providing supervisory assistance to less advanced workers. Although he works under professional supervision, a significant portion of his work activity involves independent judgment and initiative.

The graduate social worker is guided by professional social work values, the purposes of the service involved, accepted theoretical and organized knowledge, societal sanctions, and social work methodology. In providing services, the graduate social worker uses methods appropriate to the situation, including a disciplined interaction based on a knowledge of interpersonal relationships of cause and effect, relevant professional literature and research to obtain necessary additional professional knowledge, the conduct of social research regarding the service or broad professional concerns, the interpretation of community resources and advocacy needed to assure the availability of resources, intervention with related individuals and organizations, the provision of therapeutic counseling directed toward clear goals, social action to increase awareness and to work toward the resolution of professional concerns, as well as other related activities.

The graduate social worker must have a theoretical and a beginning empirical knowledge of human behavior and development, a working understanding of social and economic realities and forces, a critical knowledge of social service systems, a familiarity with the nature and causation of individual and social abnormalities and an awareness of relevant community and professional organizations and related institutions. He must have demonstrated competence in at least one of the specialized social work methods and a knowledge of others. The educational prerequisite for this classification is the master's of social work degree from a graduate school of social work accredited by CSWE.

Certified social worker. The certified social worker is responsible for a wide range of independent social work activities requiring individual accountability for the outcome of service, including direct services to individuals, groups, or organizations; supervision of social workers and social service technicians; consultation at key points of decision-making in the social services; interdisciplinary coordination; education and in-service training; improvement and development of services; and other activities requiring sensitivity and expert judgment.

Guided by the values of professional social work, purposes of the service, prevailing organized knowledge, societal sanctions, and social work methodology, the certified social worker uses methods of basic social research and planning, interpersonal therapeutic techniques, group and social organizational relationships, education and administration, and others as required by the clients or groups served.

The certified social worker must have both theoretical and empirical knowledge of human behavior and development and be familiar with the social and economic processes, the philosophy and operations of social services systems, the nature and causation of individual and social abnormalities, and the different relationships and responsibilities of professions, organizations, and societal institutions. The educational prerequisites for this classification are a master's degree from a graduate school of social work accredited by CSWE and certification by the ACSW as being capable of autonomous, self-directed practice.

Social work fellow. The social work fellow is capable of a wide range of independent social work activities requiring individual accountability for the outcome of service and special expertise in intensive services to individuals, groups, and organizations; administration and direction of programs and organizations; specialized consultation, planning, education, and decision-making; and other activities requiring special combinations of education and experience. Having mastered the integration of social work values, the delineation of the purposes and policies of service, the integration of organized knowledge and practice, the testing of societal sanctions, and the incorporation of social work methodology, the social work fellow utilizes combinations of knowledge and skills in the following areas:

1. The direction and conduct of major research and planning efforts.

2. The application and extension of interpersonal therapeutic techniques.

3. The study and implementation of the objectives of groups or social organizations.

4. The expansion of educational and administrative theory and practice.

5. Other specialized endeavors based on social work expertise.

The social work fellow is required to have a broad knowledge of the field, with concentrations in specific areas. These areas include advanced knowledge of theories of and research in human behavior and development; the social and economic processes and their interrelationships; the nature and causation of individual and social abnormalities; and the planning of services involving the integration of professional, organizational, and institutional activities. In addition, he provides leadership in the planning, development and administration of social service agencies; analysis and formulation of social policy; research and the evaluation of social service delivery systems; advanced clinical practice, and education for social service.

The educational prerequisite for this classification is (1) a doctoral degree in social work or a related social science discipline, with at least two years of experience in an area of social work specialization; or (2) certification by ACSW and two years of experience in an area of social work specialization.

GUIDELINES

The standards have been prepared by NASW to provide a basis on which local and state NASW bodies, educators of social service manpower, administrators planning for or employing social workers, personnel specialists, and individual social workers may evaluate job classifications for social work and social service personnel.

Such evaluations should have two objectives: (1) to assure that classifications of existing job functions are related to the appropriate level of competence and educational preparation; and (2) to clarify and strengthen relationships among job classifications actually used to maximize the career potential in a setting or organization.

It is important to restate that the simple classification plan provided in these standards is not a substitute for the detailed and rational analysis of specific tasks required to establish accurately and professionally a staffing plan for social work manpower in an agency. It should, however, provide a means by which various staffing plans can be contrasted and interrelated for purposes of career planning and staff development.

A major purpose of these standards will be to assist in the development of curricula for social work programs appropriate to each of the defined levels. It is axiomatic that effective education requires definite educational goals. Both short-term training programs and more substantial educational programs should be directed toward specific vocational levels. Similarly, curriculum-building requires well-defined concepts of skills and competence. These standards are seen as a beginning step toward the more technically complete definitions required by educational planning. They should be adequate for general usage by personnel and staffing planners and for the administrative purposes of most agencies.

As a tool, it is hoped these standards will (1) achieve maximum effectiveness of and accountability in social service programs; (2) assure the appropriate use of qualified manpower; (3) provide opportunities for advancement in individual agencies; (4) facilitate the adaptation of workers transferring to other agencies; and (5) provide clear goals for the development of educational curricula.

DIFFERENTIAL USE OF MANPOWER

In applying these standards, the community social service system should be the initial focus of attention. For a comprehensive range of services to be provided in a community, a complete and appropriate use of manpower must be available. The combination of social worker classifications needed by an individual agency will be determined by the agency's size, functions, and technological development and by the available manpower. For example, in some agencies the nature of the functions would allow the use of social worker, technician, and aide levels, while in others the need for high discretionary or technical judgments might require a greater use of the certified social worker or graduate social worker levels.

In planning for the use of all social service

manpower, emphasis should be placed on permitting individual employees to contribute as much as they can, according to their ability to practice. The opportunity to make meaningful contributions to the achievement of social service goals makes the difference between motivation for professional services and mere existence on a job.

To accomplish a differential use of manpower will require individual agencies, which comprise the community social service system, to cooperate formally in implementing a career ladder. Such a ladder must have two essential characteristics: (1) it should open doors to persons wishing to find a career in the social services and provide entry at each level of competence; and (2) it should provide the opportunity for career advancement, as well as for horizontal mobility. These characteristics will require programs of career recruitment, counseling, and meaningful staff development.

JOB LEVELS

Because of the ordinal nature of this classification plan, several concepts concerning its application must be highlighted. As a general rule, a complexity-scale concept has been used. This means that an employee at any given level of competence should be capable of performing less complex functions but not be able to perform effectively those that are more complex.

Further, it should be recognized that there are qualitative differences among abilities at different levels. A social worker should be able to complete a survey schedule or interview clients for data to determine their need for agency services, while a certified social worker should be able to develop a survey design or to conduct counseling interviews involving complex marital adjustment problems. And there will be different performance levels within classifications that are dictated by such factors as length of service and demonstration of special abilities.

For a variety of reasons, agencies may find it necessary to define several grade levels within each classification level, primarily as a result of the differential activities within the agency. That is, certain clusters of work responsibilities might require unique abilities. However, additional levels should reflect two characteristics: (1) there should be a continuum of logical steps from one level to another, if possible, so that both responsibilities and opportunities for career advancement are clearly perceived; and (2) opportunity for advancement to a higher level should be possible for employees who can demonstrate an ability to perform such functions and who meet the prescribed qualifications.

Finally, all classification levels should provide salary levels commensurate with the functions performed and with the employee's performance. The salary structure should be commensurate with the standards for the field and reviewed annually for equity and for comparability both within the field and to the labor market generally.

SUMMARY OF FUNCTIONS

Social Service Aide

Functions. As part of a team or other professionally guided supervision,

Interviews applicants for services to obtain basic data and to provide information on available services.

Interprets programs or services to ethnic or cultural groups and helps such groups or individuals express their needs.

Assists people in determining their eligibility for services and in assembling or obtaining required data or documentation.

Participates in neighborhood surveys, obtaining data from families or individuals.

Provides specific information and referral services to people seeking help.

Conducts case-finding activities in the community, encouraging people to use available services.

Provides specific instructions or directions concerning the location of services or procedures involved in obtaining help.

Serves as a liaison between an agency and defined groups or organizations in the community.

Qualifications. Life experiences and knowledge of the community or special groups are the primary abilities required.

Although high school graduation is not always required and may be irrelevant, basic skills in reading, writing, and computation are important. A high school diploma may be required for certain positions.

A concern for people and a willingness to learn on the job are essential attitudes.

Social Service Technician

Functions. As part of a team or under close professional supervision,

Conducts fact-finding and referral interviews based on an awareness of generally available community resources.

Assists in helping individuals or groups with difficult day-to-day problems, such as finding jobs, locating sources of assistance, or organizing community groups to work on specific problems.

Contributes to special planning studies from knowledge of a client's problems and viewpoints, as part of a project or planning unit.

Helps assess the suitability or effectiveness of services by understanding and relating to the experiences and specific needs of a group.

Provides coaching and special supportive role assistance to help groups or individuals use services.

Provides specific instruction or direction to persons seeking services, as part of an outreach or orientation activity.

Records data and helps collect information for research studies.

Works with local agencies or workers regarding specific problems and needs for clients and agencies.

Does emergency evaluations and provides emotional support in crises.

Qualifications. Completion of an organized social welfare program leading to an associate of arts degree or a bachelor of arts degree in another field.

Motivation to help people.

Social Worker

Functions. Using social work supervision,

Provides social work services directed to specific, limited goals.

Conducts workshops to promote and interpret programs or services.

Organizes local community groups and coordinates their efforts to alleviate social problems.

Consults with other agencies on problems of cases served in common and coordinates services among agencies helping multiproblem families.

Conducts basic data-gathering or statistical analysis of data on social problems.

Develops information to assist legislators and other decision-makers to understand problems and community needs.

Serves as an advocate of those clients or groups of clients whose needs are not being met by available programs or by a specific agency.

Works with groups to assist them in defining their needs or interests and in deciding on a course of action.

Administers units of a program within an overall structure.

Qualifications. Completion of an approved social work program awarding a baccalaureate degree.

Graduate Social Worker

Functions. Using consultative or routine supervision,

Provides therapeutic intervention under supervision.

Organizes a coalition of community groups to work on broad-scale problems.

Is the social work component on a multidisciplinary team.

Conducts group therapy sessions in a clinic setting.

Provides consultative assistance with social services to a community.

Develops and conducts research involving basic statistical techniques.

Works on program planning for a major public agency providing social services.

Is an instructor on a faculty of a school of social work.

Administers a social service program.

Serves as a team leader in a service unit.

Works in a program planning section of a social service agency.

Qualifications. Completion of a master's of social work program in an institution accredited by CSWE.

Certified Social Worker

Functions. Using consultation, when appropriate,

Serves as a team leader in a multidisciplinary therapy group.

Provides psychotherapy to individuals and groups on an independent basis.

Serves as a consultant to major social service and community action programs.

Administers a social service program or agency.

Teaches on the faculty of a school of social work.

Plans and conducts research projects.

Conducts program evaluation studies.

Works as an independent consultant with industrial organizations to provide social work-oriented direction to employee service programs.

Works as a community organizer or planner for a metropolitan coordinating body.

Provides teaching supervision in a program providing intensive casework services.

Qualifications. Completion of a master's degree program in social work and certification by ACSW.

Social Work Fellow

Functions. In accordance with professional standards,

Administers a major social service agency or program.

Works as an independent consultant in private practice.

Works as a psychotherapist in private practice.

Is a professor on the faculty of a school of social work.

Develops and directs a research program for a consultant firm specializing in social problems.

Conducts independent research.

Qualifications. Completion of a doctoral program at an accredited school of social work or in a related discipline, with two years of specialization in an area of social work or certification by ACSW and two years of social work experience in the field of specialization.

STUDY QUESTIONS

1. What does becoming a professional mean to you? Do you perceive the training and certification or licensing procedures as having practical benefits or as arbitrary obstacles and screening devices? What personal rewards do you anticipate you will receive by becoming a professional?

2. What are the advantages and disadvantages of licensing both for professionals and the people they serve? Do you believe that professionals should be licensed? What are the reasons for your beliefs?

3. Before you go any further in using this book, write a definition of social welfare. Then make a list of the things you think you will need to know if you decide to enter a social welfare profession. Put your definition and list aside and refer back to it after each chapter. This will help you to evaluate your progress as you go along, and identify those areas you still need to explore at the end of the course. Remember that what *you* want to learn deserves your time as much as the things your instructor wants you to learn.

REFERENCES

1. The basic guide to objectives is the Council on Social Work Education, *Undergraduate Programs in Social Welfare: A Guide to Objectives, Content, Field Experience, and Organization* (New York: The Council, 1967), esp. pp. 5–6.

2. A concise, interesting statement of the general perspective being adopted here is Verl Lewis, "The Relevance of Social Welfare to the Liberal Arts," in Margaret Long and Edward Protz, eds., *Issues in Planning for Undergraduate Social Welfare Education* (Atlanta: Southern Regional Education Board, 1969), pp. 1–8.

PART I

An Overview of Social Welfare

1

Basic Concepts

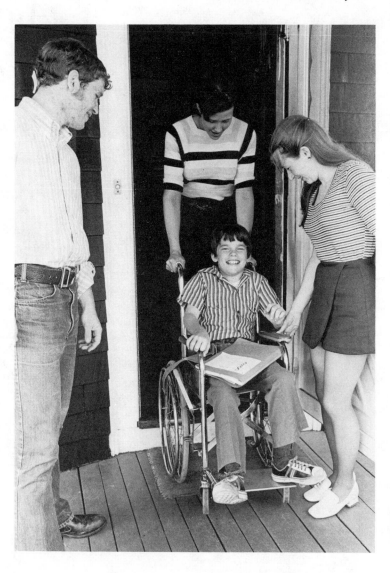

SOCIAL WELFARE is a concept that is made operational through the interaction of a number of separate but related professions. For example, vocational rehabilitation counseling is a profession that helps individuals overcome handicaps and develop appropriate job skills, while social work helps individuals and groups develop skill in the procurement and use of emotional, social, and financial resources. Each profession is a means to attain one or more social welfare goals, and as such forms part of a societal social welfare structure. However, each social welfare profession has its own distinctive concerns and techniques that distinguish it from others. Undergraduate social welfare education, then, must begin by identifying and clarifying several important points: (1) the meaning of social welfare as a concept; (2) the ways in which social welfare professions operationalize this concept through the provision of concrete resources and services; and (3) the range of social welfare professions and their interrelationships. Because all of the social welfare professions spring from the same conceptual base, they share major concepts, practice techniques, and organizational characteristics. These common elements make up the core content of undergraduate social welfare education, and subsequent specialized professional education is built on this base.

The number of distinct professions and subprofessions that the social welfare institution is composed of are too numerous for each to be discussed in detail. Instead, social work will be used to exemplify the ways in which social welfare professions translate the concept of social welfare into concrete resources and services. Of the many professions that might have been selected for illustrative purposes, social work suggests itself because of the integrative position it occupies among the many specialized social welfare professions. (Social work will be explored in more detail later in this chapter, but briefly it may be defined as the profession that helps individuals and groups to develop and utilize personal and societal resources to attain goals.) Also, the fact that social work as a profession has commonly been confused with social welfare as a concept provides the opportunity to clarify the distinction between this concept and its practical operation in various specialized but interrelated professional contexts.[1]

THE SOCIAL
WELFARE
SYSTEM

There have been many attempts to define social welfare. A sampling of the diversity of these definitions, reflecting the breadth of the concept itself, is presented in Exhibit 1-1. Social welfare will be defined in this book as *im-*

proving social functioning and minimizing suffering through a system of socially approved financial and social services at all levels in the social structure. The focus of the social welfare system may be on solving existing problems (curative), preventing the future occurrence of problems (preventive), or rehabilitating those with problems to prevent future problems (rehabilitative).

EXHIBIT **1-1**

Defining Social Welfare

There have been many attempts to formally define social welfare. As stated in the *Encyclopedia of Social Work*:

> "Social welfare" generally denotes the full range of organized activities of voluntary and governmental agencies that seek to prevent, alleviate, or contribute to the solution of recognized social problems, or to improve the well-being of individuals, groups, or communities. Such activities use a wide variety of professional personnel such as physicians, nurses, lawyers, educators, engineers, ministers, social workers, and paraprofessional counterparts of each.[a]

Philip Klein refers to social welfare as "the administration of certain services to individuals and families who find it difficult or impossible to maintain themselves and their dependents in material solvency and in health by their own efforts."[b] Crampton and Keiser "define social welfare operationally as a system that embodies a multifaceted approach to social and economic problems, reflecting social values and using the expertise of interrelated disciplines for the collective good."[c] Friedlander defines social welfare as "the organized system of social services and institutions, designed to aid individuals and groups to attain satisfying standards of life and health, and personal and social relationships which permit them to develop their full capacities and to promote their well-being in harmony with the needs of their families and the community."[d] Wilensky and Lebeaux define welfare by distinguishing traits of the contemporary social welfare structure. These are: (1) formal organization; (2) social sponsorship and accountability; (3) absence of a profit motive as a dominant program purpose; (4) an integrated view of human needs; and (5) direct focus on human consumption needs.[e] Finally, Smith and Zeitz say simply that "the social services institutionalize, as public policy, the philanthropic impulse."[f]

The United States Committee Report at the 1974 International Conference on Social Welfare, authored by John Turner, uses the term social welfare to include:

> (1) the wide range of services designed to attain ways of life acceptable to individuals and the community, sometimes thought of collectively as the "social aspects of development" and including services designed to strengthen the individual confronted with economic, physical, mental or social disabilities, together with (2) those aimed at

[a]National Association of Social Workers, *Encyclopedia of Social Work* (New York, 1971), Vol. II, p. 1446.
[b]Philip Klein, *From Philanthropy to Social Welfare* (San Francisco: Jossey-Bass, 1968), p. 7.
[c]Helen Crampton and Kenneth Keiser, *Social Welfare: Institution and Process* (New York: Random House, 1970).

[d]Walter A. Friedlander, *Introduction to Social Welfare* (Englewood Cliffs, N.J.: Prentice-Hall, 1961), p. 4.
[e]Harold Wilensky and Charles Lebeaux, *Industrial Society and Social Welfare* (New York: Russell Sage Foundation, 1958), pp. 140–47.
[f]Russell Smith and Dorothy Zeitz, *American Social Welfare Institutions* (New York: John Wiley, 1970), p. 3.

influencing the remedy of conditions leading to dependency.

Realistically evaluating its theoretical definition of social welfare, the Report continues:

The scope of social welfare in the U.S. is not as broad as social work professionals concerned with the question would like it to be. While the preferred definition suggests improvements in social conditions for all, [and] support and enhancement of the social well-being of the total population, in actual practice the scope of social welfare has a narrower more residual orientation. . . . The principal targets of social welfare are then, in spite of our preferences for a broader view, special groups in the population whose social situation is problematic [i.e.] . . . the poor, the handicapped, the dependent, the deprived, the deviant, the disadvantaged, the alienated.[g]

[g]John Turner, *Development and Participation: Operational Implications for Social Welfare* (New York: United States Committee, International Council on Social Welfare, 1974), p. 19.

The scope of the social welfare system may include only those who have already experienced need or problems (a residual system), or provide services to all as a normal part of the social environment (an institutional system). Considerations of scope and focus form two continua along which a specific social welfare system can be measured. Exhibit 1-2 (pp. 20–21) illustrates this process in more detail.

By defining social welfare as improving social functioning and minimizing suffering we are attributing social functions to this system. By also including socially approved financial and social services in our definition, we are saying that social welfare is structured in some way. It is these characteristics of social welfare that allow us to talk about it as a social institution, meaning that it embodies a set of norms clustered around a societal function and operationalized by a social structure of positions and roles.[2] As a social institution, social welfare has three important characteristics: (1) it is an organized structure of activities; (2) it develops from the effort to meet societal needs; and (3) it grows out of the normative (value) system that characterizes a society. It is apparent that social welfare as a social institution exists as one part of a large, complex societal structure and that it must operate within a given set of values.

A useful contemporary perspective on the social welfare institution as an organized structure of activities is the systems approach. Brill defines a system as "a whole made up of interrelated and interdependent parts. The parts exist in a state of balance, and when change takes place within one, there is compensatory change within the others."[3] She goes on to note that the consequences are that a change within one system will affect the other parts of that system, and a change within one system will affect other contiguous systems. For example, if a social work agency has one worker that quits and hires another to fill his place, a series of effects result that are felt within the agency and by the agency's users. The caseload of the leaving worker must be redistributed among other workers so that service is ongoing. The workers receiving these reallocated cases must then contact the clients

EXHIBIT 1-2

The Scope and Focus of Social Welfare

The magnitude and complexity of the American social welfare system can make it a difficult one to comprehend. This exhibit illustrates the kinds of social welfare services that would exist in various types of systems using the framework presented in the text. Concrete examples of existing services are provided for illustrative purposes. Further analysis of the distinction between residual and institutional social welfare systems may be found in Harold Wilensky and Charles Lebeaux, *Industrial Society and Social Welfare* (New York: Free Press, 1958).

AN INSTITUTIONALIZED SOCIAL WELFARE SYSTEM

Social welfare services are built into the normal functioning of the social system. They are available as a matter of course to the participants in the social system. The American social welfare system has some institutionalized segments, such as public education, but most social welfare services are available only upon evidence of need and qualification for the service.

1. *Curative Institutionalized Services.* Institutionalized services to help when a problem arises. Free hospital care would be an example of such a service, since it would provide needed care for all in the event of illness. Few curative institutionalized services actually exist in contemporary North America. The legal system is one of the closest approximations of such an existing service, since it is available to all in times of need. This includes the police as a social service resource available to handle an extremely wide range of personal and social problems.

2. *Preventive Institutionalized Services.* Such institutionalized services prevent the future occurrences of personal and social problems. Free medical care would be an example of such a service, since it would enable everyone to enjoy the benefits of preventive medicine. Preventive institutionalized services are not common in our society, but free public education is one example of such an existing service. It is intended to guarantee an education to a certain level, helping to prepare the

individual for a satisfying and productive life in the social system of which that person is a part.

3. *Rehabilitative Institutionalized Services.* Institutionalized social welfare services that help those with an existing problem overcome it and avoid similar problems in the future. An example would be free marital counseling, whereby those experiencing marital problems could be helped to solve these problems and develop the skills to avoid similar problems in the future. One of the very few rehabilitative institutionalized services available in our society is the United States Employment Service. It assists the unemployed to find work, as well as providing job training to try to avoid unemployment in the future.

A RESIDUAL SOCIAL WELFARE SYSTEM

Residual social welfare services are provided only to those in crisis who also qualify for the service. Therefore, residual social welfare services are only selectively available. The majority of the United States social welfare system is of the residual type.

1. *Curative Residual Services.* These services help those who qualify when a problem arises. Medical care is an excellent example, since medical services are available only to those sick persons who can afford it (either by paying cash, by having health insurance, or by being on public assistance). Disaster victims (floods, tornados, fires, etc.) generally qualify for services to meet their basic needs, another example of a curative residual service.

2. *Preventive Residual Services.* These services help prevent the future occurrence of personal and social problems. Prevention and residual are almost by definition exclusive, but nevertheless, some preventive services do exist for selected groups in American society. Social Security is an example, in that eligible individuals contribute to a fund that will provide income when they are no longer able to work, thereby helping to prevent poverty in old age.

3. *Rehabilitative Residual Services.* These services help selected persons with an existing problem overcome the problem and avoid similar problems in the future. Here again there is a certain inconsistency between rehabilitation and residual, but programs that are both do exist. The WIN (Work Incentive) program for public assistance mothers is an example. The purpose of the program is to help financially needy unemployed mothers obtain job training so that they can hopefully become self-supporting, thereby improving their own self-image as well as their family's standard of living.

The above analytical framework is not completely comprehensive or mutually exclusive. For example, the line between prevention and rehabilitation is not always clearcut, and residual services shade into institutionalized services in some cases. Even so, it is helpful when trying to disentangle some of the complex characteristics of the social welfare system in the United States, since it is such a mixture of all parts of the framework.

---

involved and start to develop a meaningful relationship with each. The clients in turn must find ways of continuing their problem-solving activities with minimal disruption or setback. Meanwhile, all members of the agency must help the newly hired person to learn agency procedures and establish professionally and personally meaningful relationships within the agency. This includes agency administrators, who must try to help the new worker become productive as quickly as possible; other workers, who may try to help their new colleague; and other support personnel, such as secretaries, who need to train the new person in the use of forms and other agency procedures. In a systems approach, any change must be analyzed in terms of its effects on the internal and external social positions that interrelate with the changed component of the system. Rarely will a change occur without creating adjustments in related systems or system components.

Systems are organized in such a way that there is a clear distinction between those activities that fall within the system boundary and those that fall outside it. However, as was noted above, activities within the system boundary may have an effect on activities of other systems outside that boundary. Any system, then, must solve two problems. One is the attainment of an equilibrium within itself, and the other is establishing feedback channels through which it is aware of pertinent activities that are occurring in external systems that in turn may affect its own cohesion. A system must be concerned with self-maintenance if it is to endure, and must find some level at which the social processes operating within and outside itself can be accommodated without system disintegration.

Feedback is very pertinent to this, since input from other systems can have a considerable influence on the forces operating within a system, as well as the system's ability to control those forces. Exhibit 1-3 analyzes how a variety of social welfare agencies impinge on each other in attempting to manage their own resources. Wiseman, whose work forms the basis of this exhibit, notes that the skid-row alcoholic is subject to very different forces in each of the social welfare agencies he uses, reflecting the fact that each agency is part of a system (which Wiseman calls the "loop") composed of many forces, of which the skid-row alcoholic is only one—and a pitifully minor one at that (see Exhibit 1-3, pp. 23–25).

Pincus and Minahan further elaborate on the relevant systems in the social welfare institution by identifying four major systems in the change effort.

1. *Change agent system:* The change agent and the people who are part of his agency or employing organization.
2. *Client system:* People who sanction or ask for the change agent's services, who are the expected beneficiaries of services, and who have a working agreement or contract with the change agent.
3. *Target system:* People who need to be changed to accomplish the goals of the change agent.
4. *Action system:* The change agent and the people he works with and through to accomplish his goals and influence the target system.[4]

In the above framework, one can see that the social welfare institution is actually a network of systems that overlap and interrelate. One can also begin to see that social welfare as an institution pervades our society. Agency systems interact with family systems, community systems, and political and economic systems in the course of identifying needs and recognizing the obstacles and resources through which the helping process will occur.

This interlocking structure of systems includes three major components. First there are professional helping persons operating in organizational contexts. Professional helping behavior typically occurs within agencies, which suggests that there are several structural determinants of the helping process. There are professional standards, which guide the kind of activities professionals perform among themselves and toward clients and nonprofessionals. These professionally sanctioned behaviors are influenced by the rules of the organizations within which the professionals function (keeping case records, caseload size, whether fees are charged, and the like). The helping person, then, finds considerable structure in her work before confronting a first client, and before confronting structures outside the agency —a client's family structure, community structures, decision-making structures, and so on.

Second, there are the social contexts of the users of services. The users of social welfare services exist within the total societal institutional network, and their experiences in the social welfare institution are affected by their other group memberships. This is one of the reasons why professional helping persons cannot concentrate exclusively on the individual needing or requesting help. It is difficult to help an individual without being aware that the social environment in which he lives impinges greatly on that person's life, sometimes causing problems and sometimes providing resources to solve problems. An excellent example of the complex web of institutional structures and their effects on users of social welfare services is found in institutional racism. Institutional racism has been defined as

> ... the operating policies, properties, and functions of an on-going system of normative patterns which serve to subjugate, oppress, and force dependence of individuals or groups by (1) establishing and sanctioning unequal goals, objectives, and priorities for blacks and whites, and (2) sanctioning inequality in status as well as in access to goods and services.[5]

The effect of these on-going normative patterns is to structure everyday behavior in such institutional structures as schools and sources of employment so that racial minority groups are systematically deprived of opportunities and benefits available to nonminority-group members. It is known that educational standards in poor schools located in racial ghettos are low, for example, and that poor children are more likely to suffer from a variety of physical and social handicaps that impede their learning. This educational disadvantage in turn reflects patterns of discriminatory housing, and results in limited employment opportunities, all conspiring to perpetuate racial inequality and its effects. Given an institutional structure that functions to maintain inequality, it is foolish for a professional helping person to concentrate exclusively on a racial minority-group member's specific problems, since his problems reflect problems built into the societal institutional structure. Using an institutional approach, effective intervention would include a combination of individual assistance and advocacy for social change.

EXHIBIT 1-3

The Social Welfare System in Action: Skid-Row Alcoholics

Jacqueline Wiseman, in *Stations of the Lost: The Treatment of Skid-Row Alcoholics*, takes an in-depth look at the organization and operation of the major social welfare agencies that serve skid-row alcoholics. She notes that there is a variety of agencies that serve such alcoholics, ranging from specialized agencies (missions, alcoholism schools) to multipurpose agencies that serve many other types of persons along with alcoholics (hospitals, jails, welfare homes). She also notes that a variety of professions is involved in the provision of services—medical, corrections, social work, religious, and the like. These many agencies and professions are interrelated in a system that contains the alcoholic, and which Wiseman calls the "loop."

Wiseman's general conclusion, supported through extensive interview data, is that the loop is ineffective in meeting the needs of the skid-row alcoholic. The various agencies and professions in the system are so concerned with meeting their own organizational and professional needs that they are frequently insensitive to the needs of the alcoholic. For example, two value approaches determine the services offered: (1) "Punitive-Correctional Strategies," focusing on control and containment when alcoholism is seen as "sheer self-indulgence"; and (2) "Strategies of Therapy," when alcoholism is seen as the result of psychological and physiological problems, or moral and spiritual problems. The use of these approaches bears little relationship to the feelings and preferences of the alcoholic—the agency simply offers service as it sees fit, and the alcoholic must take it or leave it (except when it is actually forced upon him, as when he is arrested).

Another example of the way agency needs dominate in the provision of services is in the selection of services provided. While there are many agencies and services, they are for the most part unrelated to each other. Each agency decides on its services and offers them as it wishes. There may be overlap with other agencies, and some needs may not be met by any agency. The alcoholic has no control over these decisions. He simply has the loop as the professionals decide to structure it. The result is that alcoholics tend to go from agency to agency, getting what they can at each, but nowhere having the multi-faceted totality of their needs met.

As a system, the loop is essentially oriented toward achieving its own equilibrium, in this case each of the agencies involved maintaining its own autonomy in policy-making and service delivery. Alcoholics are part of the system in that they provide the rationale for the existence of many of the agencies and their services, but within the system they have no power they could use to make it more responsive to their needs. In striving to justify their own existence, the agencies are responding to external systems as well, since they depend on public and private sources of funds, and the good-will and mandate of the public (who, among other things, are sources of referrals). In describing the loop, Wiseman clearly illustrates a system, its structure, and its attempt to maintain internal cohesion and external support. She also illustrates some of the dilemmas of professional autonomy referred to in Exhibit I-1. While the social welfare agencies described by Wiseman are generally successful in maintaining their own autonomy in policy-making and service delivery, they are generally unsuccessful in meeting the needs of those they serve. At the same time, those being served have no power to affect policy or services. What is the solution?

To illustrate the points above, two diagrams based on Wiseman's work are shown on the opposite page. In the first, the professional contexts in which social welfare services are offered to skid-row alcoholics are shown and briefly described. In the second, the operation of the loop is illustrated—it is easy to see the hapless and powerless alcoholic making the rounds of the agencies.

Table and figure (opposite) from Jacqueline P. Wiseman, *Stations of the Lost: The Treatment of Skid-Row Alcoholics*, © 1970, pp. 51 and 55. By permission of Prentice-Hall, Inc., Englewood Cliffs, N.J.

Professional Contexts in which Social Welfare Service to Skid-Row Alcoholics is Offered:	Official Goal is Rehabilitation of the Alcoholic. Means Used in Goal Attainment:
City jail	Place to sober up and dry out; context in which alcoholic is punished for public drunkenness (norm violation).
Alcoholism school	Education on the evils of alcoholism.
County jail	Same as city jail, except more severe (longer sentences) for repeaters (chronic norm violators).
State mental hospital	Drying out and psychological therapy (emphasis on alcoholism as an illness).
Jail branch clinic	Same as state mental hospital.
Out-patient therapy center	Psychological therapy.
Welfare home for homeless men	Drying out; informal therapy; food and shelter provided.
Clinics and hospitals	Detoxification; treatment for physical problems caused by alcoholism or skid-row life.
Christian missionaries	Spiritual renewal; food and shelter provided; employment.

ROUTES BY WHICH SKID-ROW ALCOHOLICS ENTER TREATMENT CONTEXTS

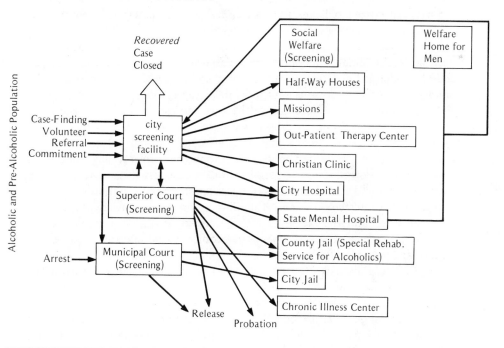

An institutional approach to social welfare concerns also helps to understand the role that persons who are neither professional helping persons nor users of services play in social welfare services. These nonusers can be divided into two categories. The first includes those in a position to directly affect decisions about social welfare services, such as legislators. These persons include the full spectrum of their societal experiences and beliefs, so that social welfare decisions reflect societal beliefs and structures as much as specific social welfare concerns. The Social Security Act, discussed in the next chapter, illustrates how most social welfare legislation emerges as a compromise between need as defined by social welfare professionals and the needs and interests of various other social institutions, especially the economic and political institutions. The second group of nonusers is composed of the average citizens who do not directly participate in social welfare decision-making, but who nevertheless have an impact on those decisions. For one thing, all citizens have the right to participate in the political process and thus to affect public policy, even if only by going to the polls to vote for a pro- or anti-welfare candidate. But citizens participate in a variety of other ways as well—humiliating someone using food stamps in a supermarket, teaching one's children not to play with minority-group children, making sure a school PTA is responsive only to the needs of middle-class children, refusing to hire ex-convicts in one's business, lamenting over the state of a nation that allows welfare "chiselers" to drive Cadillacs. Individually, any of these acts may seem trivial, yet each of them reflects and in turn has an impact on the societal mandate that legitimates a social welfare system. When the average citizen believes that social welfare promotes unacceptable behavior, the social welfare institution is in trouble.

Third, there are societal value systems. Any part of society depends on a basic societal mandate sanctioning its existence. Without such a mandate, an activity is defined as irrelevant or deviant, and in either case it is practically impossible to secure societal resources in a stable, enduring manner. A social institution is a structure created by a society to meet a perceived need. In the case of social welfare, there is a perceived need for dealing with individual and social problems that interfere with normal patterns of functioning. Chapter 2 goes into more detail about how society has come to its current perception of existing social welfare needs. At this point it is sufficient to note that social definitions of normal patterns of functioning, and the problems that interfere with such functioning, are many, varied, and changeable. On one hand the fact that such a concern exists is desirable, but on the other, the lack of specificity about problems and solutions creates ambiguity and uncertainty.

Keith-Lucas discusses three value bases commonly used in United States society: the capitalist-puritan, the humanist-positivist-utopian, and the Judeo-Christian. His analysis of the tenets of each and their implications for social welfare beliefs and values is presented in Exhibit 1-4. In spite of the diversity of societal values related to helping, Keith-Lucas sees an identifiable core of professional helping values:

1. People should be free to choose [including the choice of failure].

2. The individual matters, and his interests cannot be wholly subjected to those of the community.

3. Man has neither the right nor the ability to judge his fellows in terms of what they deserve.

4. Helping people find their own way is better than controlling them, however subtly.

5. Feelings, and personal relationships, matter.

6. People should be treated as "subjects" and not as "objects."[6]

EXHIBIT 1-4

Value Systems Underlying Social Welfare's Societal Mandate

The following discussion of major value systems underlying society's approach to social welfare is taken from Alan Keith-Lucas, *Giving and Taking Help* (1972). In this discussion, the complexity of societal values is illustrated, as well as the difficulty encountered in trying to define a coherent social welfare system based on such opposing values. Yet Keith-Lucas makes it clear that whatever the problems, values form the base upon which our social welfare institution is built.

There are in our culture three . . . more or less logical [value] systems. There are variations on these, and perversions of them, which may be held by some to be distinct belief systems, but for the purposes of this discussion these three may be sufficient.

The first such system, and possibly the most powerful among people as a whole, might be called capitalist-puritan or CP for short. Its basic assumptions might be summarized as follows:

1. Man is responsible for his own success or failure.

2. Human nature is basically evil, but can be overcome by an act or will.

3. Man's primary purpose is the acquisition of material prosperity, which he achieves through hard work.

From Alan Keith-Lucas, *Giving and Taking Help* (Chapel Hill: University of North Carolina Press, 1972), pp. 138–43. Used by permission.

4. The primary purpose of society is the maintenance of law and order in which this acquisition is possible.

5. The unsuccessful, or deviant, person is not deserving of help, although efforts should be made, up to a point, to rehabilitate him or to spur him to greater efforts on his own behalf.

6. The primary incentives to change are to be found in economic or physical rewards and punishments.

The prevalance of these assumptions needs no emphasis at this time. The 1968 election in the United States is ample evidence of it. It is the creed popularly thought of as "American" or even common sense, and as such is part of the heritage of most of us. . . .

So closely have God's favor and worldly success become identified that the successful are thought of as "good" and the unsuccessful as "bad" or inferior. Man takes over what was originally

God's prerogatives of judgment and chastisement and those who do not exercise sufficient ambition or will are shamed, exhorted, punished, or left to the workings of the economic system.

Where the CP system of beliefs is associated with certain other religious values it has strong ethical content, in which success and failure to achieve certain ethical goals is thought of in almost exactly the same way as are material achievement and its opposite. The two systems meet in the matter of work, which has both a material and an ethical value, and in statements applying ethical standards to business enterprise, such as the statement, "Honesty is the best policy," or emphasis on the "service" motive in business. . . .

Almost diametrically opposed to this system is the one that can be called humanist-positivist-utopian, or HPU for short. This is the belief of most social scientists and many liberals, but is also held to some degree by people who profess CP views and by many religious people, despite some inherent contradiction. Summarized its basic assumptions can be presented as follows:

1. The primary purpose of society is to fulfill man's needs both material and emotional.

2. If man's needs were fulfilled, then he would attain a state that is variously described, according to the vocabulary used by the specific HPU system, as that of goodness, maturity, adjustment, or productivity, in which most of his and society's problems would be solved.

3. What hampers him from attaining this state is external circumstance, not in general under his individual control. This, in various HPU systems, has been ascribed to lack of education, economic circumstance, his childhood relationships, and his social environment.

4. These circumstances are subject to manipulation by those possessed of sufficient technical and scientific knowledge, using, in general, what is known as "the scientific method," and consequently

5. Man, and society, are ultimately perfectible.

HPU-ism is perhaps difficult to see as a unitary theory, since many of its devotees have relied on a single specific for creating the utopia it envisages. Dewey, for instance, a strong HPU-ist, saw education as the answer; Marx, reform of the economic system; and Freud, the early Freud at least, the removal of repressions. . . .

The sources of this system are to be found in the Enlightenment and its first prophets were Rousseau and Comte. Today it is most obvious in the Poverty program, but many of its assumptions are inherent in modern materialism, at which point it joins hands with and lives somewhat uneasily with CP thought.

Behind, and yet parallel with these two systems is a third, for which it is harder to find a name. Perhaps the best that can be devised is the familiar "Judeo-Christian" tradition. . . .

Yet the system is essentially the system of assumptions about man and the universe that are inherent in the Jewish and Christian Scriptures, and is accepted, at least officially, although not always acted upon by the mainstream religious bodies, Catholic, Protestant, and Jewish.

Summarizing its basic assumptions in the same way as we have done for the CP and HPU systems, these might be presented as follows:

1. Man is a created being one of whose major problems is that he acts as if he were not and tries to be autonomous.

2. Man is fallible, but at the same time capable of acts of great courage or unselfishness.

3. The difference between men, in terms of good and bad, is insignificant compared with the standard demanded by their creator, and, as a consequence, man cannot judge his fellow in such terms.

4. Man's greatest good lies in terms of his relationship with his fellows and with his creator.

5. Man is capable of choice, in the "active and willing" sense, but may need help in making his choice.

6. Love is always the ultimate victor over force.

The position of this ethic vis-à-vis the others is a complicated one. In one sense it lies parallel to them and is a viable alternative, or a middle ground, especially in item 2, its recognition of man's simultaneous fallibility and potential. In another, it lies behind them and makes both of them possible. . . .

Probably most people are influenced to some extent by all three of these sets of assumptions. All have some value and it is not so much a matter of saying that one is good and another bad as it is of taking a position nearer or further from one or another extreme. Yet we do need to explore which set of assumptions is more likely to preserve the kind of values we see as important in helping, and which is most compatible with what we can observe in the process of helping as we know it.

Quite obviously the CP position is in general the least likely to lead to help. If man is totally responsible for his own actions, if he can better his condition by an act of will, if he can be induced to change by punishment or reward, then helping becomes a simple matter of us arranging the appropriate rewards and punishments. There is no room for relationships, or concern for another, except in a highly condescending and judgmental way.

This is the view of man that created the workhouse and the pauper's oath, which demands of children in Children's Homes or welfare clients that they work harder and behave better than other people, and which is terrified of any welfare measure that would make the receipt of relief in any way bearable or dignified. It assumes without question that welfare clients will "naturally" lie, cheat, or steal if given the chance, prefer laziness to work, and feign sickness in order to shirk working. And typically it is much more concerned to punish the few who may do such things than help the many who do not.

Yet it is not without some positive features. It does at least recognize that it is the person in trouble who must bear the final responsibility for his own betterment, and as such it has moderated some of the extreme implications of the HPU set of assumptions which, for many helping people, have appeared to supersede it.

In its initial impact on helping theory and practice HPU thought produced a tremendous outpouring of love and understanding. The helped person was freed from the total responsibility he had borne up till then for his own condition. He was no longer a second-class citizen, judged by his fellows. He was valued for his own sake. The particular social science which became the model for helping in the 1930s—analytical psychology—also stressed certain things which, if not strictly HPU—and indeed I shall argue that they are basically Judeo-Christian and not HPU at all—were at least acceptable to those who claimed to be humanists and utopians. These were in general:

1. A sense of man's common vulnerability. There were, and this is one of Freud's greatest contributions to helping, no longer "sick" and "well" people, but people who were in greater or less difficulty with problems that trouble us all.

2. A habit of looking at problems from the point of view of the helped person rather than from the outside, that is, treating him as subject rather than as object.

3. An emphasis on relationship as the principal means of help.

4. At least in the earlier stages a degree of awe in the face of new knowledge of a somewhat mysterious nature. . . .

One of the most important insights of the Judeo-Christian tradition is the nature of man himself. He is neither the evil being of capitalist-puritan belief, nor is he as good as many HPU-ists believe. But it is not so much a matter of steering between an over- and an underestimation of his nature as it is of recognizing two different factors in his makeup. The first is his fallibility and the second his ability, in certain circumstances, to work out for himself something somewhat better than his fallibility would suggest. This is far from saying that he has in him a potential which needs only some triggering, or some favorable circumstance, to tap. It means rather that with help, or where he is put to it, or from the depths of despair, he can sometimes transcend his own fallibility. Moreover this ability is found in the most unlikely places. It is often demonstrated by those whom objectively one would be forced to believe are unequipped or incapable. This is the constant surprise one comes up against in helping. Not infrequently it tends to have the air of the miraculous about it.

Part of the professional helping person's task is to attempt to bring societal values into congruence with professional values so that professional helping behavior has the ideological and material support essential to its success. Here again the interrelationships between the social welfare institution and other social institutions become important, since the values espoused by social welfare professionals may conflict with values embraced in other institutions—e.g., economic values of free enterprise and a market economy.

Social welfare, then, can be seen as having both input and output. Its output is primarily the concrete social services that are provided to individuals and groups, are focused on improving social functioning and minimizing suffering in the social system, thereby also helping to maintain the system itself. However, given the interlocking institutional nature of social welfare, its output must also include attempts to interpret its goals effectively enough to achieve changes in the total institutional structure that are essential to its successful operation. This output is in turn dependent on input—the support of society, both ideologically and materially—without which there could be no institutionalized social welfare system. It becomes, then, a delicate process of generating resources within the existing society, and then using those resources to change society so that more resources are available to support social welfare goals. The Johnson administration's War on Poverty was the most recent example of the difficulty of succeeding at this difficult and delicate task.

SOCIAL WORK AS A SOCIAL WELFARE PROFESSION

Social welfare as a social institution covers a broad range of helping services, including individual counseling, physical therapy and vocational rehabilitation, corrections, homemaker services, physical and mental health services, child welfare services, and education, to name a few. Some of these services require highly specialized physical professional skills, such as those needed by the medical doctor and the physical therapist or nurse. Others require a set of relationship-oriented skills that may be used in a range of helping situations, such as those used by the social worker and the community planner. There are many tasks to do, and there is a variety of separate professional groups that claim special competence in dealing with various of these tasks. All of these professionals need to have a basic understanding of social welfare as a social institution to recognize the nature of their ultimate objectives. They also share basic skills needed by anyone dealing with people in helping situations. Even the medical doctor, one of the most specialized social welfare professionals, should be able to understand and deal appropriately with the fact that the body that is his primary concern belongs to a unique human being existing in a specific social environment.

While it is impossible to deal with all the social welfare professions at once in a book such as this, there are some very basic commonalities in the knowledge, values, and skills which all social welfare professionals should have. So it is possible to study social welfare as a social institution in a manner useable by all of the many professions involved. The problem comes in illustrations and specific examples where a concrete, real-life approach is needed. In order to have such a source for examples, social work will be used throughout as an example of a specific social welfare profession at work. Social work is perhaps the most general and wide-ranging of the social welfare professions, so illustrations from it touch on most of the other professions at various points. It provides a specific and yet sufficiently generalized example to use throughout the study of the social welfare institution.

Social work, like social welfare, has been defined in many ways by many people. Some of these definitions are summarized in Exhibit 1-5. Whichever definition one chooses, we can see that it is a socially legitimated profession that uses a body of methods that are tied to specific knowledge bases and utilizes the resources of the social welfare system. Its methods and resources are focused on the solution of individual, group, and community problems, interacting with other social welfare professions as each attempts to bring its specific competencies to bear on complex and often overlapping problems. As has already been noted, the social welfare institution is an interrelated web of structures and behaviors, making it inevitable that different specialized professional groups will frequently be dealing with parts of the same problem. This can create problems of coordination, as will be seen in Chapter 3. On the other hand, each profession can monitor its members' behavior and enrich professional practice through member identification and interaction.

EXHIBIT 1-5

Defining Social Work

Social work concerns itself with making social relationships more effective and rewarding, an enormously broad area which cuts across the specific concerns of many other professions in the social welfare system. This has made it difficult to concisely define the profession. Yet, the following thoughtful attempts at definition give a flavor of what social work is all about.

The National Association of Social Workers' Board of Directors adopted the following definition in 1970:

Social work is the professional activity of helping individuals, groups, or communities enhance or restore their capacity for social functioning and creating societal conditions favorable to this goal. Social work practice consists of the professional application of social work values, principles, and techniques to one or more of the following ends: helping people obtain tangible services; counseling and psychotherapy with individuals, families, and groups; helping communities or groups provide or improve social and health services; and participating in relevant legislative processes. The practice of social work requires knowledge of human development and behavior; of social, economic, and cultural institutions; and of the interaction of all these factors.[a]

Ruth Smalley has written:

The underlying purpose of all social work effort is to release human power in individuals for personal fulfillment and social good, and to release social power for the creation of the kinds of society, social institutions, and social policy which make self-realization most possible for all men.[b]

Elizabeth Ferguson cites a definition of social work, formulated by a committee of the National Association of Social Workers, that "social work practice, like the practice of all professions, is recognized by a constellation of value, purpose, sanction, knowledge, and method."[c] Skidmore and Thackery assert that "social work may be defined as an art, a science, a profession which helps people to solve personal, group (especially family), and community problems and to attain satisfying personal, group, and community relationships through use of certain methods including casework, group work, community organization, and the enabling processes of research and administration. Social work not only helps people to solve problems, but also assists them to prevent problems and enrich daily living."[d]

[a]National Association of Social Workers, "Standards of Social Services Manpower," Washington, D.C., 1974, pp. 4–5.
[b]Ruth E. Smalley, *Theory for Social Work Practice* (New York: Columbia University Press, 1967), p. 1.

[c]Elizabeth Ferguson, *Social Work: An Introduction* (Philadelphia, J. B. Lippincott, 1969), p. 7.
[d]Rex Skidmore and Milton Thackery, *Introduction to Social Work* (New York: Appleton-Century-Crofts, 1964), p. 8.

To conclude this discussion of social work as a social welfare profession, Exhibit 1-6 discusses some issues facing social work in its continuing attempt to clarify its own boundaries and its relationships with other social welfare professions. To a greater or lesser extent, practically every other social welfare profession faces many of the same issues in looking to the future.

EXHIBIT 1-6

Social Work Seeks Its Future

In an article entitled "Social Work: A Profession Confounded by Contradictions," Natalie Davis Spingarn discusses some of the issues facing social work as it seeks its place in the social welfare system of the future. As Ms. Spingarn points out in her article, social work shares many of these issues with the other social welfare professions. This exhibit is also a clear illustration of social welfare input and output—the relationship of a societal mandate and social resources to effective, change-oriented social services.

Surely no profession dedicated to the alleviation of human suffering suffers as much as social work—or tries as hard to solve as many human problems. Young, hampered by an image that links it both to the establishment and to the welfare poor, powerless to control that establishment or to strike at the roots of poverty, it goes about its business. The problem of the moment is to define precisely what that business is. . . . Over 240,000 "social workers," as defined by the U.S. Census (60,000 of them belong to the professional National Association of Social Workers), stand ready to do that work. . . .

The questions which have plagued social work as it has sought to broaden its domain with shrinking funds in a chilly national climate, confound those trained, like doctors, lawyers, nurses, or clergymen, to accomplish specific tasks for others. For example:

1. Should social work aim to help people adjust to the vagaries of an unjust society,

From Natalie Davis Spingarn, "Social Work: A Profession Confounded by Contradictions," *The Chronicle of Higher Education* 8 (May 20, 1974): 8. Used by permission.

or should it work with them to change that society? In so doing, should it concentrate its efforts directly on its clients, or indirectly through the more equitable and efficient distribution of community resources? And should its loyalties be primarily to those clients, or to the agencies that serve them?

2. Should it develop substantive expertise in fields affecting the quality of life, like housing, aging, health care, or the economics of income maintenance, or should it concentrate more intensively on refining its methods of dealing with human behavior, like casework or community organization?

3. Should it open the profession wide, welcoming under its official umbrella the thousands of workers, especially those in public welfare agencies, who consider themselves "social workers" but who have never set foot inside a social-work classroom? How should it approach its newest rivals, the other "helping" professionals and paraprofessionals, be they vocational counselors, community psychologists, psycho-social nurses, or mental health, recreation, and child-development aides?

STUDY QUESTIONS

1. Make a chart that shows as many of the relationships you can think of between the social welfare institution and the other major social institutions in our society. Do certain institutions have more of an impact on the social welfare institution than others? Be sure to include the impact the social welfare institution has on other institutions. After you have finished, compare your chart with someone else's chart, and discuss the differences between the two with that person.

2. Write down an example of each of the following: a curative, preventive, and rehabilitative institutional and residual social welfare service in your community (six in all). If you don't know one of each, use available resources to find an example of any missing links—interview a social worker, consult a community service directory if available, etc. Which kinds of services are most common and which are least common? What does this tell you about the social welfare structure of your community?

3. Visit a social welfare agency and record your impressions. Who works there and who goes there to get service? What does the agency look like—is it attractive? Modern? Does it seem well run? How do you think you would feel if you needed to use the services of the agency? Why? Do you think others would be likely to feel as you do? Why or why not?

4. Try writing down your personal value system. How much freedom and responsibility do you think each individual should have? What rights and responsibilities do you think society has? What do you think is an appropriate way to deal with people who are poorly able to care for themselves? How about people who break the law? Try to project the kind of social welfare system that would result if it were created on the basis of your values.

REFERENCES

1. A good discussion of some of the confusion in the use of social welfare as a concept may be found in Philip Klein, *From Philanthropy to Social Welfare* (San Francisco: Jossey-Bass, 1968), p. 7.
2. The student not familiar with the sociological definition of this term should refer to the Dushkin Publishing Group's *Encyclopedia of Sociology* (Guilford, Conn., 1974), pp. 141 and 273.
3. Naomi Brill, *Working with People: The Helping Process* (Philadelphia: J. B. Lippincott, 1973), p. 63.
4. Allen Pincus and Anne Minahan, *Social Work Practice: Model and Method* (Itasca, Ill.: F. E. Peacock Publishers, 1973), p. 63. Reprinted by permission of the publisher.
5. Quoted in Terry Jones, "Institutional Racism in the United States," *Social Work* 19 (March 1974): 219.
6. Alan Keith-Lucas, *Giving and Taking Help* (Chapel Hill: University of North Carolina Press, 1972), p. 136.

SELECTED READINGS

Dolbeare, Kenneth, and Patricia Dolbeare. *American Ideologies*. Chicago: Markham, 1971.

Goodman, James. *Dynamics of Racism in Social Work Practice*. Washington, D.C.: National Association of Social Workers, n.d.

Howard, Donald. *Social Welfare: Values, Means, and Ends*. New York: Random House, 1969.

Keith-Lucas, Alan. *Giving and Taking Help*. Chapel Hill: University of North Carolina Press, 1972.

Romanyshyn, John. *Social Welfare: Charity to Justice*. New York: Random House, 1971.

Towle, Charlotte. *Common Human Needs*. New York: Family Service Association of America, 1952.

Wilensky, Harold, and Charles Lebeaux. *Industrial Society and Social Welfare*. New York: Free Press, 1958.

2

A Brief History

THE PRESENT SOCIAL WELFARE INSTITUTION cannot be understood adequately without an awareness of the historical experiences that have led up to it. This history is characterized by attempts to develop social welfare structures in response to social needs, much as our own structure continues to develop to meet the needs of our time. It is the nature of human culture to accumulate and build on the experiences of the past, and many of the values and services that are part of our contemporary social welfare system have their roots in earlier times. Whether or not these traditional approaches to social problems continue to be appropriate is a difficult question to answer, but a knowledge of the sources of these approaches is essential to an intelligent decision about their current applicability.

There are two characteristics of the human condition that make social welfare an integral part of our humanity. The first is that compared to most other animals, human beings are poorly equipped instinctually. They are helpless at birth and for a relatively long period thereafter, depending on others for the nurturance necessary for their physical survival. The most characteristic feature of the human organism is its ability to learn and adapt. We learn our behavior, making it possible for us to learn the ways of whatever culture we happen to be born into, and allowing us to move from one culture to another if necessary. This creates the second important characteristic of human beings; namely, that our humanity resides in our interaction. We become human, meaning participants in an ongoing social unit, by interacting with others and learning appropriate behavior. This interaction not only teaches us what to do, but ultimately gives us a sense of ourselves— we acquire a group identity and a position within that group on the basis of our interaction with others.

Our need for nurturance and for social interaction makes us dependent on others. In social welfare terms, if we are going to talk about improving social functioning and minimizing pain, this can only be accomplished socially. Ultimately our dependence on others can itself be a source of personal breakdown and suffering, but even in those cases the cure lies within the social network. Human groups are functional for their members and no doubt always have been. By banding together, human beings insure their basic survival in terms of protection and reproduction. Beyond that, the group makes possible the highly complex social patterns we take for granted today.

The first human group to emerge was probably the family, a group reflecting man's sexuality and need for protection. The family can be considered the earliest social welfare unit, and it continues to be a basic welfare resource. Most societies have had extended family units, that is, families made up of three or more generations and a variety of kin members. The family form dominant in the United States today, the nuclear family, is made up of two generations, adults and their children. Compared to the extended family, which has many family members who can work together to provide for each other's needs, the nuclear family's human resources are limited. In a later chapter we will see why the nuclear family is an important family form in America today, but the early extended family provided a more useful social unit that identified rights and responsibilities within a fairly large unit. In later societies, tribes were sometimes equated with the family concept, providing a way of extending the network of responsibility for the needs of others to a larger unit. Originally the family was the only social welfare unit, but gradually it was supplemented with other social structural resources until today a society like our own is a complex network of social welfare services of which the family is only one. However, even today the family holds a special place in the social welfare system, and families have the right to make decisions that other social welfare units are legally prevented from counteracting (see Exhibit 3-3, "Battered Freddy," in the next chapter).

EARLY SOCIAL WELFARE SERVICES OUTSIDE THE FAMILY

The church was perhaps the earliest formalization beyond the family of a concern for the poor, the sick, and the aged.[1] The Judeo-Christian beliefs expressed in the Old and New Testaments, which commanded that the needy be served, were instrumental in early church-provided social welfare services through its network of parishes and monastaries. Only as the development of national governments gradually broke the power of feudal and church landholdings were these services substantially reduced in importance. Today the church continues to be instrumental in providing social welfare services, informally through its church helping programs, and more formally through social agencies with religious affiliations.

In the 1500s early attempts were made to formalize and unify social welfare services beyond churches, monasteries, guilds, and other benevolent groups.[2] In the Tudor period, the parish (the local governmental unit most analogous to contemporary counties) organized the provision of charity by parceling out responsibility for the poor to both religious and secular organizations. Gradually a series of societal changes related to the beginnings of the Industrial Revolution created a strain on existing systems of private charity, and eventually led to their modification. Three of the most significant changes associated with the early roots of the Industrial Revolution were the breakdown of the medieval feudal system, the centralization of political power in national governments, and the displacement of church power by secular government. As church funds available to meet the needs of persons displaced from feudal estates declined, the power of local and ultimately national governmental units to care for the poor increased.[3]

As England became the world's greatest wool-producing nation, the wool trade became more productive than farming, with much land being removed from cultivation and given over to grazing. This displaced many workers from the land, and was a force breaking the economic feasibility of the feudal manorial system. This in turn decreased the need for men previously in the service of nobles. These dislocations occurred at the same time that monasteries were broken up and their resources confiscated, thereby greatly weakening one of the earliest welfare resources in a period of increasing need. By 1518 the swelling ranks of the unemployed was a serious enough problem to generate efforts to block migrants and the unemployed from wandering around the countryside in search of work or aid. Although later in the sixteenth century the English commission responsible for studying unemployment noted that the societal conditions of grazing enclosures and erratic commerce were the main causes of unemployment, thereby removing the blame from personal shiftlessness, the large numbers of persons displaced were considered a problem in their own day.[4]

In an attempt to protect themselves against these vagrant and starving people, the more affluent passed legislation to control the moral and social order.[5] The Elizabethan Poor Law of 1601 was an important early piece of such legislation.[6] This legislation established three categories of the poor: the helpless, the involuntarily unemployed, and the vagrant. The helpless, or needy by impotency of defect, were the aged, decrepit, orphaned, lunatic, blind, lame, or diseased. The involuntarily unemployed, including those made poor by misfortunes such as fire, robbery, or being "overcharged with children," were set to work or sent to a house of correction.[7] The vagrant, including drifters, strangers, squatters, and beggars, were ostracized. Each parish felt responsible only for its own members. Since the social dislocations of the time created forced vagrancy for many people, the fact that the Poor Law encouraged parishes to ostracize nonmembers tended to create a group of the poor who belonged nowhere. This has led some later observers to blame the Poor Law for having caused many of the poor to remain vagrant.[8] The Settlement Act of 1662 further legitimated the concept of a residence requirement, a carryover of which was one of the qualifications for public assistance in the United States until the Supreme Court decision of 1969 (Shapiro v. Thompson) that declared it unconstitutional.[9]

The parish welfare structure legitimated by the Poor Law consisted of three main parts. Almshouses, sometimes called indoor relief because assistance was provided in a facility established for that purpose, were provided for the helpless, a group considered legitimately needy. Outdoor relief— assistance provided in the recipient's own home—was provided for the aged and handicapped helpless, also a group considered legitimately needy. Workhouses or houses of correction were provided for the ablebodied needy, a group bearing the stigma of being shiftless.[10] Children of destitute families were indentured, being removed from their own homes and placed with a family in the community that agreed to provide room and board in return for the child's work. Although indenture seems cruel by contemporary standards, and it was true that many children were exploited by the families that agreed to support them, at the time it was believed that removing children from destitute families would both provide for their physical needs as well as give them appropriate role models. The legacy of these practices remains in our current social welfare structure in outdoor relief, which forms the major part of our public assistance system, and prisons and other total institutions, which carry on the traditions of ostracism, stigma, and forced work of the houses of correction. Whatever the social conditions of the time that created widespread need, the service structure established by the Poor Law indicated that poor peoples' needs were at least partly their own fault.

The Elizabethan Poor Law of 1601 had several other significant components. It recognized the desirability of national coverage and administration of public welfare, a feature of many contemporary public programs. It never accomplished total national coverage, however, and the parish continued to be the local unit through which the legislation was administered. Each parish had an Overseer of the Poor appointed every Easter by the Justice of the Peace. Social welfare funds were obtained through voluntary contributions and a public land tax. The Poor Law tried to strengthen the family unit, which was felt to be the foundation of the community. It made parents and grandparents responsible for their children (unless married) up to the age of twenty-four for boys and twenty-one for girls. If relatives could not care for orphaned or abandoned children, they were apprenticed or indentured. Finally, ablebodied individuals were set to work in special public factories, establishing the principle still used today that the more people working, the less tax burden on the affluent. If the ablebodied refused to work, they were sent to a house of correction. Ultimately the competition between private and public factories led to the demise of the latter, but the work ethic for the poor has remained in many other guises.

As the number of needy increased, attitudes changed, and by the 1700s harsher laws and the narrowing of poor relief occurred. The attitude in workhouses became more punitive. Virtue was tied to thrift, industry, sobriety, and wealth, and poverty and dependency were further stigmatized. Amendments to the 1601 law went so far as to evict anyone from the parish who might "become" dependent. In 1776, Adam Smith published *The Wealth of Nations,* in which he advocated the amassing of wealth. People should operate to the best of their ability with minimal societal restraints—laissez-faire capitalism. Though he did not call for the end of the poor laws, he felt that giving freely to people would only result in dependency and misery.[11] Others followed in pointing out the evils of supporting those in need, with Thomas Malthus in 1798 arguing that population growth would soon outrun food production. Further impetus for the making of relief more punitive was the rise of Protestantism in Europe and England. It stressed the importance of individual effort, rather than the charity and the help-your-neighbor attitude of the Judeo-Christian tradition. Gradually the punitive aspects of the poor laws came to be stressed over their rehabilitative components.[12]

Social conditions worsened between 1740 and 1850 as the Industrial Revolution gained momentum. The shift from agriculture to technology continued; the population greatly expanded and the numbers needing to be clothed and fed shot up rapidly. The uncontrolled growth of towns and factories created many new social problems. In response to increasing need, the Speenhamland Act was passed in 1796. It broadened relief by making aid available when one's wages fell below a subsistence level. This subsistence level was based on family size and food costs, and was called the "bread scale." The Speenhamland Act was probably ahead of its time in trying to establish an approximation of a guaranteed income, but the direct cause of its failure turned out to be the greed of the law-abiding citizens. Since employers knew that workers would get at least the bread scale no matter what wages they were paid, the Speenhamland Act had the effect of driving wages down, thereby increasing welfare costs. This unfortunate situation is an early example of how well-meaning and humane social legislation is sometimes abused and exploited by the affluent so that it benefits them rather than those in need. College students' abuse of food stamps and industry contractors' exploitation of Office of Economic Opportunity contracts are two recent examples of this same process.

After the postwar depression of 1815, poverty was widespread and it became apparent that broader political changes were essential.[13] Taxes to support the Poor Law had tripled by 1832, and the law was called "a bounty of indolence and vice" and "a universal system of pauperism."[14] In the New Poor Law of 1834, the ablebodied poor were to receive no relief except for employment in workhouses. Outdoor relief was sometimes granted in an attempt to maintain the family at home, but relief payments were usually meager because they were supposed to supplement income rather than replace it. Widows and the aged constituted the two groups receiving the majority of aid. Despite the lower payments provided, the New Poor Law was praised for its more orderly, firm guidelines, which were open to less misuse, and for speeding up special reforms in the medical, housing, and sanitation areas.[15] Nevertheless, its restrictive and punitive features were evident.

To summarize the development of social welfare in England from 1601 to 1834, we have seen that the poor laws sought to stem disorder during rapid economic and social changes that made many members of society dysfunctional. The legitimately needy were distinguished from the shiftless and criminal, and involuntary unemployment was grudgingly accepted as a necessary outcome of industrialization. Only in the 1700s, when wealth became a virtue, was poverty considered a sin and a vice. The Industrial Revolution brought insecurity to many while others achieved wealth; but those who had prospered because of the economic changes were reluctant to take a charitable attitude toward those who had not. The poor were a burden with whom few wanted to contend.

THE COLONIAL
SOCIAL
WELFARE
SYSTEM IN
AMERICA

Considering the conditions of life in the colonies, it was not at all surprising to find many people in the 1600s and 1700s in need of public assistance and charity. Some of the original settlers were paupers, criminals, and indentured servants of whom England was trying to dispose, while others were seeking religious freedom, adventure, fortunes, or a new life. The colonists often landed in America in poor financial condition. They turned to subsistence farming as a livelihood or sought work in the early cities, such as Boston, Philadelphia, and Charleston.

Since the value system and conditions of life in the new country were compatible with the negative attitudes toward dependency that had been developing in England, the English Poor Law of 1601 and the Law of Settlement and Removal of 1662 were adopted. The public did acknowledge its responsibility to protect and care for the needy, but this did not mean that the needy were accepted or understood.[16] Throughout its history the United States has reaffirmed this responsibility to care for the needy, but along with it the fear has persisted that public care of the needy fosters dependence.[17] Carried over with the Poor Law were the practices of residence requirements, parental responsibility, classification of the needy, and indoor and outdoor relief. Residence requirements in the colonies included the practices of "warning out"—the turning away of persons who might become dependent— and "passing on," whereby a person was transported to his legal residence if he became dependent.[18] Assistance was provided in four ways: private citizens could be paid to house the destitute (similar to foster-care today); the destitute could be auctioned to the lowest bidder; the needy could be placed in almshouses; or they could obtain outdoor relief. The ablebodied were required to work, a practice finding increasing popularity in our contemporary assistance systems (see Exhibit 2-1).

Though originally the concept of self-help was strong, two major events helped to modify these early beliefs. Between 1760 and 1820, the French and Indian Wars left many families fatherless and drove frontier people to seek safety along the coast. Unemployment increased and wages fell as a result, while bad crop years, low yields, and other natural catastrophies made costs skyrocket. These conditions created need under circumstances that called into question the New England Puritan values of self-sufficiency, the goodness of work, piety, and the strength of the family.

A series of bloody revolutions at the end of the eighteenth century, of which the American and French were the most famous, created societies more equalitarian than ever before. The greater power of the common man over the social institutions that governed his life generated the rise of Romanticism. Romantic ideals countered ascetic Puritan beliefs with a faith in the goodness, uniqueness, and value of each individual, thereby supporting attempts to increase individual autonomy and provide basic social welfare services to all. The depression after the Napoleonic Wars (1815–1821), the growing population, and the arrival of over six million immigrants between 1820 and 1860 were all factors that supported the adoption of some of the practical implications of Romanticism.

EXHIBIT 2-1

Progress?

The following editorial and pictorial comment appeared on p. 37 of the June 22, 1971 issue of the New York *Daily News*. It does seem to support the old adage that history has a way of repeating itself, and illustrates the perennial tendency to seek simplistic, individually focused solutions to complex, socially generated problems. Notice also the implied stigma—persons needing financial help are not people, they are "reliefers."

AND SO, TO WORK

A new state law requiring able-bodied reliefers to get to work goes into effect July 1.

There are an estimated 60,000 employables on the local welfare rolls. They are being directed to pick up their semi-monthly relief checks after July 1 at state employment offices.

From there, it should be a short hop in most cases to paying jobs, or to public work that needs to be done in hospitals, parks, schools, etc. Failure without good reason, to appear at the state employment office to which a reliefer has been assigned is to result in removal from the welfare rolls.

We hope the new system may get a fair tryout here, as a small measure of relief (no pun intended) for taxpayers. . . .

Reprinted by permission of The New York News.

These effects were first felt in prison reforms, starting with the opening of the Walnut Street Prison in Philadelphia in 1790, followed by greatly improved conditions in almshouses. Almshouses became important as poor men's hospitals, a development fostered by the large number of immigrants who arrived destitute, ill, with language barriers, and encountering difficulty finding work. These immigrants were highly motivated and usually needed temporary care until they could regain their health and become somewhat acclimated to their new society. In response to such needs, medical care in almshouses was usually excellent, with some of the greatest physicians in the country working in them. Manhattan's Bellevue Hospital, Philadelphia's General Hospital, and Baltimore City Hospital were all originally almshouses.

Though many thought the residents of almshouses were capable of work, studies showed this to be false. In Philadelphia's Blockley Almshouse in 1848, only 12 percent of the men and women were ablebodied. Nevertheless, there was growing criticism that almshouses were too costly, too crowded, had unhealthy conditions, and were ineffective in reaching the needy whose pride would not let them be confined in an almshouse. These criticisms stimulated a period of vigorous social reform from 1830 to 1860. Thoreau, Emerson, and other intellectuals recognized the need for social reform, and stimulated attempts to establish experimental social communities to find better ways of life. Brook Farm and the Oneida Community were two examples of their day, while the communes of our day continue the search for more satisfying community contexts.

In the Jacksonian era, 1830–1846, movements to correct the social ills of industry, eliminate religious intolerance, and provide better treatment of the insane increased.[19] Education, women's suffrage, temperance, trade unionism, and slavery were other important issues of the time that reflected society's struggles with early industrialization and the values of freedom and democracy. There continued to be conflicting views on welfare. Some felt that hard-working individuals should not have to pay taxes to support the idle, while others felt that those people who had once contributed to society should be aided in troubled times. Some felt volunteer charities should be the only source of aid, while others believed that volunteer charities were too limited and unstable to bear the sole responsibility for aiding those in need. While these issues were being debated, the evidence of need included antirent wars staged in New York; constant looting and burning in opposition to depressed economic conditions in Baltimore; and Boston's need to cope with a massive influx of Irish immigrants.

NEW PATTERNS
OF HELPING:
THE LEGACY OF
THE 1800s

From 1860 to 1900, the population of the United States rose from 31.5 million to 76 million, with 13.7 million being immigrants. The Industrial Revolution was having a profound effect on the United States during this period, and the nation was rapidly becoming a large, urban society increasingly cognizant of its many problems. During the 1800s, social welfare progress occurred in three major spheres: public social welfare services; private social welfare services; and services for special groups.

Progress in Public Social Welfare.   Starting in 1857, outdoor relief became more generally accepted and replaced many almshouses. This resulted from studies that showed it to be less costly than help provided in almshouses, as well as an increasingly prevalent belief that those temporarily in need should not be subjected to the degrading conditions of almshouse life. Outdoor relief payments were small, however, since many continued to believe that low payment levels would encourage recipients to seek work in spite of evidence indicating that the majority of the needy could not work.[20] Relief payments in cities were usually in cash, but in rural areas relief was usually given "in kind" (giving the actual products, such as food and clothing, instead of money to buy these items).[21]

The Civil War and its aftermath led to other changes in the public welfare system. In this period of intellectual and social upheaval, the equality of all men and the struggle between competing political and economic systems became issues of high priority, with profound moral consequences. Congressional response to these issues included the passage of the Morrill Act and the establishment of the Freedman's Bureau in 1865. The former gave states land grants to build colleges and other public facilities. The latter was created to help the needy, especially ex-slaves, by providing financial assistance and free education in the South.[22] It was supported by the first federal tax legislation to care for the poor, a clear governmental declaration of its responsibility for citizens who were the pawns of the political and economic dislocations of the Civil War.

Progress in Private Social Welfare: The Charity Organization Society. In spite of progress in the public sphere, the limited help provided in the 1880s was strained to the limit by such events as the depressions of 1815–1821 and 1837–1843, as well as the panics of 1847 and 1857. Soup kitchens, collections through newspapers, and old clothing and bread funds were used to supplement public relief channels, but it became clear that more organized procedures would be more effective. An early attempt at such organization appeared in 1817. The New York Society for the Prevention of Pauperism stressed prevention and rehabilitation within a rather moralistic framework for dealing with problems. The New York Association for Improving the Condition of the Poor (AICP), founded in 1843 and subsequently copied in several other cities, was modeled after the New York Society for the Prevention of Pauperism, and superseded it. This association developed a classification for the needy: those who were needy by "unavoidable causes," by "own improvidence and vices," or by laziness. Like the society on which it was modeled, the AICP felt intemperance was a main cause of poverty. However, it realized that social reform was as important as moral reform, so in addition to moral preaching, attempts were made to improve sanitation and housing, and to lessen alcoholism, promiscuity, and child neglect.

The associations were in turn superseded by the development of the Charity Organization Society (COS). Begun in England in 1869, COS opened its first United States affiliate in Buffalo in 1877. By 1892, America had ninety-two COS's. Care in investigating claims, meeting individual needs, and providing minimal relief payments was stressed. COS also sought to coordinate private social welfare services to avoid costly duplication. Help was to be provided only to the "truly needy."[23] Case records were taken, and agents increasingly found education helpful in preparing such records. The workers kept accounts of all persons receiving aid and made regular visits to recipients. Paid agents were used to check up on welfare recipients. The COS's followed the teaching of Josephine Shaw Lowell as espoused in her book *Public Relief and Private Charity.* She believed that all relief should be voluntary, and made unpleasant enough so that few would stoop to ask for aid. Lowell believed that almshouses and workhouses should be rehabilitative, with those working there finding moral regeneration.

Lowell's relief system was based on some insidious values. Her underlying belief was that most needy people were capable of work, a belief no truer then than it had been earlier or is today. She also continued to distinguish between deserving and undeserving poor, and used a means test to determine eligibility for aid. Such values and practices continue to undermine contemporary efforts to formulate an adequate social welfare system, and as such were unfortunate parts of Lowell's work. However, she did make some beneficial changes to the practices then existing. The individual was considered for relief according to that person's personal set of circumstances, although if a person was found worthy of aid, the charity of relatives, the church, and others was sought first. A scarcity of other resources eventually led the COS organizations to have their own relief funds, and since few people volunteered to visit relief recipients, both the investigation of claims and the visiting of relief recipients became the job of a paid agent. These agents formed what might be called the first social workers in our current use of that name, being paid helping persons using a specified set of procedures to investigate need and provide resources to meet that need. This development was greatly aided by the work of Mary Richmond, a major figure in the COS in the United States. In 1897 she called for the establishment of a training school for professional social workers, and she subsequently formulated the first statement of the principles of social casework.

The COS also played an important role in the development of welfare in the United States in other ways. It countered the harshness of Social Darwinism* by focusing on individual circumstances that might create need. It influenced and enlisted the support of scholars from university campuses, and set standards of case evaluation by which all charity and relief organizations could

---

*Social Darwinism was an extension of Darwin's biological concept of the survival of the fittest to the social world. The theory asserted that the poor and helpless were inferior to those not in need, and therefore to help them would be to perpetuate weakness. This idea completely ignored the social system as the cause of need.

be measured. COS also offered auxiliary services: an employment bureau; a savings and thrift class; a loan office; a workroom; legal aid; a day nursery for working mothers; and visiting nurses. The establishment of the first State Board of Charities in Massachusetts in 1863 established a trend that resulted in sixteen states having such boards by 1897. These were public agencies modeled after the private Charity Organization Societies. They improved conditions in facilities for the needy, and created special services for children, the handicapped, and the mentally disturbed.[24] They also tried to counteract the excessively moralistic and restrictive aspects of COS practices, supporting outdoor relief as the most effective and humane way to provide help. However, the battle over the effects of outdoor relief continued into the new century, as Lowell continued to contend that it would lead to shiftlessness and dependence, and many states vacillated between outdoor relief and almshouse care.

Other Private Social Welfare Developments. In response to continued assertions by some groups that outdoor relief did not properly discourage the temptation to take help instead of trying to improve one's condition, other solutions to the relief problem were sought. The settlement house movement caught on as a possible alternative, and in 1887, Neighborhood House in New York, Hull House and the Northwestern University Settlement in Chicago, and the South End Settlement in Boston, were opened. They were community centers that met special community needs for practical education, recreation, and social cohesion. They were especially helpful in helping immigrants get a foothold in America. They formed ties with universities and the community in which they existed, and proved more understanding of the causes of poverty than the COS. In addition, Hull House, under Jane Addams's leadership, was able to offer auxiliary services, such as a free kindergarten, a day nursery, a playground, clubs, lectures, a library, a boarding house, and meeting rooms. Settlement houses, then, exemplified a community approach to problem-solving.

We are just emerging from a long period in which a psychological approach was thought to be the most effective one to adopt in the solution of human problems. The limitations of such an approach in terms of problem abstraction, loss of client power, reduced quantity of services, and inequitable distribution of services have led many contemporary social welfare practitioners back to a more community-focused approach. Contemporary indigenous movements to reduce inequality and improve the quality of life in society are logical successors to the principles established in the settlement house movement. Today we speak of consumer advocacy, participation of the poor, community organization, and the like. While the terminology may be contemporary, the ideas were sown in the earlier community settlement house movement.

Progress in the provision of services for special groups moved ahead in several areas during the 1800s. As American society industrialized, distinctions between the laborer and the industrial manager were becoming more apparent. It became increasingly evident that the old moral code of an individualistic, agrarian society was being applied to the practices of a corporate and industrial society.[25] Social Darwinism was the philosophy of the time, and it discouraged governmental intervention in the realm of business. The formation of groups such as the National Labor Union in 1866, the Knights of Labor in 1878, and the American Federation of Labor in 1886, was the result of workers' attempts to organize to protect themselves against such beliefs and their results. These organizational attempts were vigorously and often violently opposed by managerial and entrepreneurial groups. Recent efforts of Cesar Chavez to organize migrant farm workers in spite of economic and social reprisals by the food industry as well as other union groups gives some flavor of what early organizational efforts were like.

The needs of the physically and mentally ill were also issues at mid-century. The American Medical Association (AMA) was founded in 1847, giving powerful support to early attempts to improve standards of medical care and practice. Movement of mentally ill prisoners from houses of correction to mental hospitals in 1844 improved their chances for receiving humane treatment. However, President Pierce vetoed legislation in 1854 that would have provided federal money to build homes for the mentally ill, in spite of Dorothea Dix's eloquent appeals. From our contemporary perspective, the AMA may be seen as maintaining professional privilege as much as supporting standards of medical practice, and the wisdom of Dorothea Dix's attempts to remove the mentally ill from the community into isolated mental hospitals may be questioned. However, at the time, the formation of the AMA was seen as a positive act, and the refutation of Dorothea Dix's goals slowed reform considerably.

Children and prisoners were two final groups for which services were improved during this period. Legislation passed in 1878 prohibited the removal of children from their homes solely because of poverty, while legislation in 1887 and 1890 improved the procedures used when children had to be placed in foster homes or large residential facilities. Reform schools to rehabilitate youthful delinquents were developed, and juvenile courts were established in 1899. Related to these changes were more general prison reforms resulting in the separation of male and female prisoners, and attempts to eliminate political influences in jails and prisons. In 1891, the National Conference of Charities and Correction (now the National Conference on Social Welfare)[26] recommended maximum and minimum sentences, a reformatory system, encouraging prisoners to learn a trade, letting the disabled practice their trade within the institutions, rewarding good behavior, keeping total records of each prisoner, giving classroom instruction, and allowing prisoners to attend regular religious services. As can be seen, more humane care was slowly being attempted for additional groups in society. Events like the atrocities documented in the Arkansas prison system and the spectacular Attica prison disaster in New York State serve as periodic reminders of the as yet inadequate nature of attempts to deal more humanely with all human beings regardless of their problems or offenses.

SOCIAL
WELFARE IN THE
TWENTIETH
CENTURY IN
THE UNITED
STATES
Before 1900 the stigma of poverty was keenly felt, a result of Social Darwinism and the COS blaming dependency on personal failure. In spite of the progress toward an adequate social welfare system, substantial challenges remained as America moved into the twentieth century.[27] After 1900 the developing social and biological sciences helped people realize that social, economic, and other environmental factors played large roles in people's lives.

Between 1900 and 1925 the population of the United States reached 100 million, with 50 percent of the people living in cities. The United States had become an important industrial nation and world power, attaining unique prosperity and wealth; the gross national product (GNP) reached $104.4 billion just before the stock market crash of 1929. The publication of Robert Hunter's *Poverty* in 1904 showed that the growing society was developing a new regard for the poor. Hunter's statistics on the prevalence of unemployed men, low wages, and poor working conditions showed the poor to be victims of unfortunate circumstances rather than moral inadequacy. After John A. Ryan published *A Living Wage* in 1906, the value of more than a minimum standard of living became more accepted. He and other economists calculated what a family needed to live comfortably, and the discrepancy between the then-current wage scale and the estimated living wage was enormous.

Immigrants, though they did not comprise the entire group of unemployed, continued to form the majority of them. The communication problem, slum conditions caused by overcrowding, and the fear of a great number of men flooding the labor force caused much adverse feeling toward the new arrivals. The pressure became so great that in 1921 legislation was passed that set strict quotas on further immigration.[28] The 1924 Immigration Act further restricted and controlled immigration.[29] Unfortunately, such legislation did not raise wages, and did not stem the increasing migration of impoverished farm families to the cities in search of work.

In the period from 1900 to World War I, a group of concerned citizens called Progressives sought to expose the evils of low wages, long hours, bossism, health hazards, and other problems facing the poor in the cities. Social workers also tried to help, and at the 1912 Conference on Charities and Correction, the Committee on Standards of Living and Labor recommended a liberal list of much needed reforms. Among them were the eight-hour workday for women, children, and some men; a six-day workweek; and an end to work hours at night.[30] In 1912, Woodrow Wilson took office on the platform of New Freedom, and before the outbreak of World War I he pushed strongly for reform. He encouraged the passage of the Federal Reserve Act and the Sixteenth Amendment (which established the federal income tax), the setting up of the Federal Trade Commission, legislation creating an eight-hour workday for railroad workers, laws against interstate transportation of goods made by child labor, and the Clayton Antitrust Act of 1914.

Children were of prime concern in the early 1900s. Theodore Roosevelt held the first White House Conference on Children in 1909. It dealt with the care of dependent children, and one of its outcomes was the formation of the Children's Bureau in the Department of Labor in 1912.[31] The bureau, in the capable hands of Julia Lathrop and Grace Abbott, carefully regulated the laws and reforms concerning children's rights in this country.[32] President Wilson held the second White House Conference on Children in 1919, which resulted in the Maternity and Infancy Act of 1921 (Sheppard-Turner Act).[33] In 1930, President Hoover held the third conference, which produced the Children's Charter. The charter emphasized the child's need for love, security, and understanding, as well as for protection, recreation, proper schooling, and preparation for adulthood. The fourth conference was held in 1940 by President Roosevelt. The topic was children in a democracy, and concern was for economic and social security for each child.[34] In 1918, the Children's Bureau identified another gap in services to children in its study of the existing juvenile courts. It found only a few acceptable. Reforms that resulted included hearings held in the judge's private chambers under informal conditions (i.e., no warrants or indictments); the provision of probation services; and special detention centers and psychiatric services.[35] Unfortunately, the unintended effect of these well-meaning reforms was to deprive juveniles of their basic legal rights, and many of these practices have since been abolished by the courts. Special health services for children were also sought, and by 1934 thirty-seven states had developed programs for diagnostic services, medical treatment, and convalescent care for crippled children.[36]

By the 1920s reformers had generated a greater awareness of the need that often resulted from such factors as poor sanitation facilities, low wages, poor safety precautions in industry, and various other occupational hazards. Unemployment, illness or incapacity, death of the breadwinner, and old age were also accepted as legitimate causes of need. Work-related problems were especially obvious in early factory systems, and by 1920 forty-three states had passed workmen's compensation laws.[37] However, many of these laws were ineffective and there was no uniformity in coverage or administrative structure from state to state.[38] This legislation was especially important for being an early form of social insurance, a type of social welfare program that was to be used widely in the Social Security Act of 1935.

Workmen's Compensation is a program to cover work-connected injury. Each state is required to develop its own program, as does the federal government to cover federal employees. The program is considered a cost to an employer of doing business, and employers are required to have a plan with a private insurance company, a state-run plan, or be self-insured. Although the scope of coverage, benefit provisions, and administrative procedures vary by state, in all states covered workers injured on the job receive benefits from the employer's insurance plan. Workmen's compensation is a plan that does not entail a direct cash grant out of public monies. Instead, employers have paid into a fund from which workers are paid in the event of injury on the job. As with any insurance, some employers pay in more than their workers ever collect, while others have workers collecting more than the employer paid. This sharing of risk is characteristic of any insurance plan. It is easy to see how a particularly salient problem of the time, industrial safety, combined with a social welfare program that did not disrupt societal values of self-reliance, resulted in a workable solution to the problem. When the need for the Social Security Act was recognized in the 1930s, it is little wonder that the Congress turned first to the social insurance concept.

Workmen's compensation is a good program to use to examine some characteristics of the relationship between the states and the federal government with respect to social welfare policy. In recognition of state's rights, a basic principle of the society's political structure, each state has developed its own workmen's compensation plan within broad federal guidelines. This has led to variations in coverage among states that results in unequal benefits: residents of different states get different benefits. This trade-off of nonuniform and therefore inequitable programs in return for maintaining state autonomy is one that characterizes several other important programs, Aid to Families with Dependent Children being another major example.

State autonomy in welfare policy also makes it possible for some states to have programs that others do not, creating another type of inequality among states. In the Aid to Families with Dependent Children program, for example, some states allow families with an unemployed father to be living in the family, while others will not provide benefits if there is an employable adult male present, unemployed or not. The effect of this difference in programs is that in some states families can remain together while receiving AFDC benefits, while in others men must abandon their families in order for the family to receive help.

On the other hand, state autonomy often has a beneficial impact on national programs by allowing for state experimentation that may ultimately result in national legislation. Workmen's compensation is a case in point, since it was the recognition by individual states of the need for compensation for work-related accidents that finally led to the legislation requiring all states to have such programs. Once again the close interaction between the social welfare institution and the other major social institutions is illustrated.

Social welfare programs were gradually developed to aid various special groups in addition to those already mentioned. By 1920 forty states had passed acts to aid needy mothers, and soon after, similar aid was made available to the aged. Lobbies were formed to improve facilities for the destitute aged, and by the Depression this was one of the most powerful groups pushing for social security.[39] Unfortunately, other needy groups were not as successful in organizing to protect against the low level of aid and geographically variable coverage.

The early 1900s saw the continued growth of voluntary organizations financed by dues, donations, and subscriptions. Some of the best-known groups were the Boy Scouts, Girl Scouts, National Tuberculosis Association, American Cancer Society, Camp Fire Girls, Goodwill Industries, the National Association for the Advancement of Colored People (NAACP), and the National Child Labor Committee.[40] Another voluntary organization, the Red Cross, performed important functions under the directorship of Harry

Hopkins during World War I. It provided a communications link between servicemen and their families and assistance to needy dependents of servicemen. It also advanced money to families that had not received their allowance from the Soldier's and Sailor's Insurance Law of 1919, which was supposed to protect the enlisted man's family from hardship due to his military service.[41] Charitable trust funds were also growing during the early 1900s. Some of the best known were the Rockefeller and Carnegie Foundations, the Rockefeller Institute for Medical Research (1901), the General Education Board (1902), the Carnegie Foundation for the Advancement of Teaching (1905), and the Russell Sage Foundation (1907).[42]

THE IMPACT OF THE GREAT DEPRESSION

The Great Depression of the thirties forced a change in the nation's thinking about social welfare and related values. The developing society had carefully nurtured values of self-reliance, initiative, hard work, and thrift, and was proud of its reputation as the land of opportunity where an individual could make a personal fortune—the classical rags-to-riches philosophy. It followed that anyone who had not been successful had not worked well or wisely enough, or had been improvident. Although there had been increasing recognition of some of the social causes of personal misfortune, there was still a very basic belief that for most people work and thrift would lead to success. The Great Depression shattered this dream. For the first time, people who had worked and saved, who had been proud of their accomplishments and were recognized in their communities as being fine citizens, had their savings wiped out. People who had always worked and who desperately wanted to work could no longer find jobs. It became painfully clear that there was something wrong with a value system that said that anyone who tried hard enough could work and prosper. It was no longer a situation in which individuals were in control. Social events were preventing people from working and were generating massive need. The American value system would never be the same again, and it was this change that made possible the sweeping changes enacted during Franklin D. Roosevelt's New Deal.

The Depression also answered once and for all the question of whether relief should be primarily public or private. The crisis was so widespread that private agencies could not hope to alleviate the unemployment and resulting need.[43] It was this impetus that finally made the federal government assume the major responsibility for economic stability and personal security. As it became clear that the private sector could not control business cycles, the government had to step in. No longer was the government that governed least necessarily the best; strict laissez-faire capitalism had failed. The lack of economic opportunity and resources were clearly responsible for poverty and unemployment, particularly in the cases of youth, the aged, women, minority groups, and farmers,[44] and only the federal government had the power to step in to stem the rising tide of business and banking failures. The Great Depression was the major reason for poverty coming to be seen as a societal rather than an individual problem.[45]

Early Social Welfare Responses to the Great Depression. The Great Depression encouraged many changes in the administration and financing of outdoor relief. It stimulated increased public works and work-relief programs, an expanded categorical approach to relief, and eventually a new program of social insurance and social assistance.[46] To help with unemployment relief, some state governments established emergency relief administrations,[47] while the Wagner-Rainey bill of 1932 authorized the Reconstruction Finance Corporation to make loans to states for public works and unemployment relief.[48] In 1933 President Roosevelt established the Federal Emergency Relief Act (FERA), appropriating $500 million for grants-in-aid to states for work relief and unemployment relief. When FERA was abolished in 1936, it had allocated over $3 billion to assisting states.[49] In November of 1935 President Roosevelt created the Civil Works Agency, administered by FERA, "to give work to able-bodied poor."[50] The Public Works Administration was also formed, with goals to increase the demand for heavy or durable goods and to stimulate purchasing power. In spite of their good intent, the flurry of such experimental and often hotly contested legislation ultimately proved incapable of dealing with the need for a new approach to social welfare in the United States.

Legislation following the Great Depression constituted what was termed the New Deal, and it accelerated the increase in the amount of public control imposed on the nation's economy. "The New Deal, however, was more concerned with the social repercussions of industralization, rather than with more narrowly economic problems."[51] While much of the early legislation passed in immediate response to the Great Depression was at least partially successful in alleviating need, it soon became clear that a more fundamental and enduring change in the nation's economic and social welfare structures was necessary. Such a plan, the Social Security Act, was proposed by President Roosevelt and was passed by the Congress in 1935. Two social insurance programs were established on the national level to meet need created by old age and unemployment: Old Age and Survivor's Insurance (OASI, or Social Security), a federal system of old-age benefits for retired workers; and a federal-state system of unemployment insurance. The program also provided for federal grants to states to help them provide financial assistance to the aged, the blind, and dependent children. Some health services and vocational rehabilitation were also included. "The creation of a foundation of social insurance was laid, and areas previously considered the exclusive province of the private sector were brought under the scrutiny of a democratic government."[52]

The Social Security Act of 1935: The Enduring Legacy of the Great Depression. The Social Security Act laid the foundation of the present public welfare system in the United States. Its major significance lay in two major categories of programs that it established: (1) social insurances; and (2) grant programs. The social insurance programs were seen as much more desirable than the grant programs, since as in all insurances the recipients of the benefits had contributed to them, while in the grant programs recipients received money taken from general revenues (obtained from tax revenues). In a society still trying to encourage self-sufficiency, hard work, and thrift, much less stigma was attached to a social welfare program in which an individual could be seen as simply receiving his own money back. Receiving a direct grant from noncontributed money carried the stigma of receiving something for nothing, something which one had not earned. Since the current structure of social welfare services is still built on these programs, and apparently will be until some form of guaranteed income is legislated, it is worthwhile to take a closer look at the Social Security program and the grant programs that accompanied it.

Social Security was intended to provide for need during old age when earning capacity was minimal. Payment levels were never intended to be sufficient to meet living costs in and of themselves, but were to be supplemented by personal savings—a direct attempt to maintain values of self-reliance and thrift. Although social security payments have steadily risen, they remain low enough to require some supplementation. (See Exhibit 2-2, on pages 54 through 58, for a detailed examination of how the current Social Security system operates).

Social Security was intended to provide for need during old age and for the survivors (widows and children) of workers. Since it would take some years for the Social Security trust fund to be developed from the contributions of workers, the grant programs (which used current tax revenues) were included in the Social Security Act to meet the needs of those who were already aged, disabled, or dependent at the time of the passage of the legislation. It was assumed that these grant programs would decrease in importance as more and more persons were covered by the new Social Security program. Social phenomena, such as rural to urban migration, family disintegration, and regional pockets of poverty (Appalachia and native American areas especially) created an enduring need for these programs that was not originally anticipated.

Social Security has since been expanded to include disabled workers and their dependents, and certain health benefits for recipients. This is why the program is now called the Old Age, Survivors, Disability and Health Insurance Program (OASDHI).

It should be emphasized once again, however, that the intent of the Social Security Act was to supplement people's incomes and savings when they reached retirement age, rather than to provide enough for them to survive solely on the benefits.

Social Security, being an insurance program, requires that working persons who are covered in the program contribute part of their salary to the Social Security trust fund. Employers also contribute to this fund for each employee. The fund is then used to pay benefits when an individual qualifies. Note that Social Security is work-related (only persons working can contribute, and they have to have worked for a specified period of time in an approved work context before they or their dependents qualify to receive benefits). Exhibit 2-2 provides data on Social Security contribution rates, benefit levels, and beneficiaries.

EXHIBIT 2-2

Social Security in Operation

The following data give a picture of current levels of Social Security operation. Table 1 shows the contributions paid by employers and employees on the specified taxable earnings. Note that both employee and employer contributions are only made on earnings as shown—any earnings above this level have no Social Security contributions taken out. It is for this reason that Social Security is called a regressive tax, since lower-income groups pay a larger *percentage* of their income in the tax than do higher-income groups. For example, in 1973 a person earning $10,000 in taxable income would have Social Security contributions withheld on all of his taxable income, whereas a person earning $50,000 would have Social Security contributions withheld from only the first $10,800. Table 2 shows the number and percent of persons covered by Social Security (coverage is determined by length of work in a job in which Social Security contributions have been made). Table 3 shows the number of beneficiaries receiving Social Security payments, and the average amount of payments. A final section discusses some of the current issues raised by the Social Security program.

TABLE 1 Employer and Employee Contributions to Social Security

Year	1960	1965	1970	1973
Taxable Earnings Base[a]	$4,800	$4,800	$7,800	$10,800
Percent of Base Paid by Each —For OASDI	3.0%	3.625%	4.2%	4.9%
—For Medicare Hospital Insurance	NA[b]	NA[b]	0.6%	1.0%
Total	3.0%	3.625%	4.8%	5.9%

[a]The taxable earnings base in 1974 was $13,200, and $14,100 in 1975.
[b]NA—Not available.

TABLE 2 Social Security Coverage (in millions of persons)

Year	1960	1965	1970	1971
Covered Persons	59.4	65.6	72.1	72.9
Percent of paid employed	88.0%	89.1%	89.5%	89.4%
Not covered	8.1	8.0	8.5	8.6

Data for tables 1–3 from U.S. Bureau of the Census, *Pocket Data Book: USA 1973* (Washington: Government Printing Office, 1973), pp. 183–84. The final section from the *Washington Bulletin* 23 (October 14, 1974): 173–76. Used by permission.

TABLE 3   Social Security Beneficiaries and Benefit Levels

Year	1960	1965	1970	1972
Number of beneficiaries (in millions)	14.8	20.9	26.2	28.3
Average monthly benefits (in 1972 dollars) for:				
—Retired workers	$106	$112	$126	$162
—Disabled workers	127	130	140	179
—Wives/ husbands of deceased beneficiaries	55	57	63	81
—Widowed mothers	84	87	92	115
—Widows/ widowers without children	82	98	109	138

ISSUES IN THE SOCIAL SECURITY PROGRAM

Social Security provides the bulwark of income for 30 million people: the retired, the disabled, and survivors. It provides assurance of protection to 95 percent of children in the event the family provider should die. Nearly all of the aged are receiving or are eligible for benefits, and 80 percent of the population between 21 and 64 are covered in the event they should become seriously disabled. It is a matter of deep concern if the system supporting this structure of protection should be deficient. While even the most ardent supporters recognize gaps and deficiencies and have proposals for improvement, the Social Security "problem" is not as serious as many of its critics profess. The program is sufficiently complex that few people are able to evaluate the criticisms and to distinguish between legitimate concerns and the destructive criticisms

which, in some instances, are aimed at liquidating the program.

Fiscal Solvency of the System.   Critics of the system and many of its friends have noted that the "trust fund" is not the basic source of paying benefits. Social Security is different from some private insurance plans. The trust fund has funds to pay benefits for a period of less than a year. This time period has been diminishing. In 1957 it had the capability of paying benefits for a period in excess of 3 years. It is evident that the trust fund is a contingency fund and that current income is used to pay current obligations. There is nothing wrong with this for the income is tax revenue and its collection on a regular basis is assured by the authority of the U.S. government. Misleading Social Security literature has used the term "trust fund" in a manner which suggests something more than this.

Although critics have made much of this point, conventional economic thought is that it is not only impractical but dangerous for the Social Security trust fund to be fully funded. If it were, the government would have immense sums to invest, more than the entire national debt and enough to dominate the private security market. The trust fund or contingent fund is composed of U.S. government securities. This has led some critics to say that the trust fund is composed of worthless "I.O.U.'s." The trust fund holds such securities just as any bank or private fund would and receives interest on the securities at a fair rate. The trust fund is not the basic source of payments to beneficiaries, and such payments are not endangered.

The long-term trend is in the direction of a fiscal problem. Social Security's tax system and benefit structure are premised upon a birth rate higher than is evident and upon a growth in real wages which has not materialized. The low birth rates for the past ten years suggest that in the next century the ratio of workers to retired persons will be reduced problematically. Since the currently employed support the retired there must be a sufficient number of workers for every retired person to make the system secure. In 1947 there were 22 workers for every beneficiary. By 1972 there were only 3. Also the many benefit increases provided to compensate for price increases have been financed in a manner which creates increasing obligations to pay higher benefits to many of those currently employed. Benefit increases have been financed by increasing the wage base and requiring higher wage-earners to pay taxes on more income. Currently the law provides that when benefits are increased in the future (and the law assures that benefits will keep up with prices) there will be automatic increases in the level of wages subject to tax. . . . This will require a continued increase in the tax base, and this is dependent upon a growth in real wages. The entire matter is now under study by the Advisory Council on Social Security which will report later this year [1974] and may recommend a higher social security tax rate or contribution from general revenue or both.

Equity of the Retirement Test. This test which has been subject to severe criticism is one of the ways Social Security determines who is to receive benefits. Social Security is not a program of assured annuities. It is a program of protection for those among the aged who are not employed. Since this is a "social" security system it is appropriate to skew the system to achieve certain social objectives. The test of whether an individual is working is a substitute for a means test. It identifies those who are most likely to be in need. A true means test would also have to include a test of resources and this is avoided because studies of the income and resources of the aged show that those who are not working are the least likely to have sufficient resources to support themselves. While there are older people who have significant resources but are not employed, to ferret them out would require a full means test for everyone.

The law has established that the amount of money which an individual has earned shall be the test of retirement. Currently the test figure is $2,400 a year, and this represents liberalization. In the past criticism of the retirement test has been blunted by raising the amount of earnings the individual may have and still be considered out of the work force. The amount of additional earnings which reduce benefits has been liberalized also. Now each $2 of earnings above the $2,400 reduces benefits by only $1. This has not stilled the attack on this particular provision. Some people want the test removed entirely. That is possible but could be accomplished only by a general reduction in benefits or an increase in taxes or some combina-

tion of the two. The people who would benefit by the abolishing of the test are those who are least in need.

In the criticism of the retirement test some unfair comparisons are made. It has been stated that the test figure is below the poverty level. It is true that $2,400 is below the poverty level, but an individual who is earning $2,400 can receive a full Social Security benefit which currently cannot be less than about $100 a month. The retirement test when applied to an individual who has $250 a month in earnings means that he can receive his full benefit minus only $300 a year. Many critics of this provision are people who want to retire from their regular employment and supplement their Social Security by part-time employment. If earnings from such employment run over the retirement test level, they are not eligible for benefits. Thus the group most affected are highly skilled workers, those with a relatively high standard of living, whose needs and expectations are legitimate but whose claim on a "social" security system cannot be equal to the claims of the lower-income group.

Inequities in the Social Security Tax. It is generally recognized that the Social Security tax is inequitable. It is a tax on "the first dollar" of earnings. It taxes earnings no matter how small. It does not take into account family size or how many wage-earners there are in the household. It differs from the income tax which does take into account these items plus excessive medical expenses and other factors. Since the Social Security payroll tax is less equitable, why is it used? Taxes have to be imposed in an acceptable way. The payroll tax was acceptable in 1935 because Social Security was conceived as a worker-employer investment in the worker's retirement. At that time the trust fund concept was conceived as the mechanism for payment of benefits. The trust fund was shifted to a contingency fund some years after the program started. This method of taxing is also easier to administer.

A more basic consideration is the feeling that the program is more secure if taxes collected are used for benefits. While it is true that Social Security "contributions" are really taxes and go into the general treasury and are appropriated to pay benefits, nevertheless the relationship between the amount of the taxes and the amount of the benefits is maintained. For a shift to a more equitable tax system one would have to assume the risk that Congress might not consider the Social Security obligation inviolate and might fail to appropriate enough to pay full benefits. This concern has permeated Social Security planning. It is this provision which distinguishes Social Security from welfare in the public eye. The worker has been willing to accept the Social Security payroll tax because he feels it promises future security.

An unwillingness to risk loss of public support keeps the inequitable Social Security tax in place. There are many proposals to correct this. One ... would provide for an adjustment in the 1040 tax form for low-income workers. They would receive a refund for Social Security taxes. Another ... bill would reduce the payroll tax from 5.8 percent to 3.9 percent and have a general revenue contribution make up the loss. This would make the tax less inequitable but would not eliminate the problem. The ... report of the Social Security Advisory Council may have some impact for it will focus on the entire problem of financing.

Other Inequities. Critics have identified other inequities. Some of these are not reasonable and tend to overlook the fact that Social Security is an insurance program. Instances are cited of individuals who made contributions and received no benefits. Illustrations include the situation of someone who works for a year and pays taxes and then dies with no resultant beneficiary rights for his wife and dependents. This occurs because he has a marginal relationship to the work force and the law requires 6 quarters of coverage before survivor benefits will be paid. Another illustration is the individual who works his lifetime and dies before retirement without dependents. His contribution is "lost" inasmuch as he cannot include any of his rights in his will. The amounts he contributed are used in the system to help finance benefits for others. Illustrations are given of individuals who contribute little but receive a great deal. The best examples are the older persons who made small contributions because much of their work experience was during the period when the tax rate was low. A retiree who started work in 1937 and worked at full taxable wages would have paid in a maximum of $5,200. This is contrasted with someone

who is now working at a wage equal to the current taxable wage base ($13,200) and continues in that status for 30 years who will have paid in about $21,660 and will receive benefits less generous as related to his contribution than the already retired worker.

There is no doubt that these are valid examples of inequities in contribution vs. benefits. The justification for the "grandfathering in" of the older worker is that the alternative was to have a large welfare program. The available mechanism was the State operated Old Age Assistance program which was not able to carry the responsibility. It can be argued that those already old should not be penalized for the failure of the nation to have anticipated their needs by broadening the Social Security program while they were working and could have contributed to its cost.

Criticism has also focused on some of the provisions which tend to exclude or delay potential benefits. Among these obstacles is the requirement that a disabled applicant must wait 5 months before receiving benefits. Congress determined that the program was for the permanently and totally disabled. The waiting period is one of the ways of establishing that fact. This is a serious problem for disabled persons. It can be eased but at a cost.

Married vs. Unmarried Beneficiaries. A longstanding source of complaint is the different status of married and unmarried beneficiaries. This seems to discriminate against working wives. The problem arises because of a provision which offers especially generous treatment for the wives of retired workers. The wife of a retired worker is recognized in the benefit payment for that worker by a 50 percent addendum. If a woman is unmarried and has worked or if she is married and has worked, she may receive no more in benefits than a nonworking wife, although she has contributed to the system. Under the law the wife with a separate Social Security account has her benefits compared under both provisions of the law (addendum to husband's benefits and independent beneficiary), and she receives the amount of the larger benefit. The married woman who did not work is in a favored position in the receipt of retirement benefits. However, the employed woman received protection against disability in her working years while her counterpart who stayed home did not. The employed woman was also assured of benefits for her children in the event of her death which the unemployed woman was not. Critics have made proposals to combine in some fashion the benefits accruing to the woman who worked with the benefits she is entitled to as a spouse. This proposal has some validity but would involve additional cost.

While the law makes an assumption of wifely dependence upon the husband, it does not make a similar assumption about the dependence of the husband on the wife. For a wife's benefits to be increased 50 percent for a dependent husband proof must be submitted. No proof is necessary for the husband's benefits to be increased for his wife. A similar situation prevails in the event of the death of a spouse. The Equal Rights Amendment (now [1975] only 5 States short of approval) would undoubtedly have an effect on this situation. The many intricate provisions of the Social Security Act would be subject to examination against the criteria of equal treatment of men and women, and some changes would be required.

Level of Benefits. A persistent criticism is that for many people, especially those in the lower wage level, the Social Security system cannot promise enough retirement income for a decent level of living. Benefits are related to level of earnings. The minimum primary insurance amount is now $94 a month. A recently enacted provision assures a somewhat larger amount for low-paid workers who have a record of many years of covered employment. That special minimum can be as high as $170 a month. The average benefits paid are reflective of the many people who retired years ago and whose benefit calculation was based on low earnings characteristic of the times. The many increases which Congress has voted have been motivated by a desire to help these people. Although the benefit level is constantly rising, prices also continue to rise, and the situation of many beneficiaries remain critical.

A factor which aggravates this situation is the increasing proportion of applicants who retire at an earlier age with reduced benefits. Currently more than half of the applications for benefits are made by persons who are below the specified retirement age of 65 (62 for widows). Men and women workers may apply at age 62 and widows at 60 with benefits reduced 20 percent. Studies show that it is the workers with the poorest work records, lowest earnings, and poorest health who apply for early retirement. Even if they had postponed retirement to avoid the 20 percent reduction they would still have had a low benefit because their wage records were below average. "Retirement" is perhaps the wrong term to use with respect to such individuals. They are generally out of work and without resources. For them Social Security is a form of unemployment relief. The employment market has increasingly discriminated against older workers, especially those with marginal skills.

No provision is made for this situation. Early retirement at reduced benefits costs the system nothing, for the reduction of 20 percent is actuarially calculated to assess the cost to the beneficiary. Should retirement without benefit reduction be offered to all at an earlier age? Strong arguments can be made to support that point of view, but if this is done there remains the question of the effect on the composition of the work force and the further erosion of the ratio of retired workers to employed workers. One possibility is to consider early retirees a part of the unemployed group and offer some coverage under unemployment insurance, relieving the Social Security system of a responsibility it is not equipped to handle.

General Considerations. Some of the possibilities for changing and improving the Social Security system have been identified, and there are many others. Few improvements can be made without costing money. Since there is no general tax revenue in the Social Security program, any additional cost would have to be assessed to employed persons. It is difficult to determine which of the proposed changes is the most urgent and which should be enacted with a tax increase. Many of those impatient with the slowness of change have urged the introduction of general revenue money in Social Security. The arguments against this have been presented. The pressures are so great that some breach in the position held for the past 39 years is likely.

The second social insurance established by the Social Security Act of 1935, unemployment insurance, was intended to be a temporary income-maintenance program during periods of temporary, involuntary unemployment. Each state has its own unemployment insurance program, established with federal guidelines, and has established its own methods of computation of benefits, maximum benefit amounts, and maximum benefit duration. The program is supported by a payroll tax paid by employers on a specified amount of earnings per employee. It is administered by the federal government, which collects part of the tax (through the Internal Revenue Service) for administrative expenses and to support the U.S. Employment Service. The remainder of the funds are held in trust for each state to use in paying benefits. Benefits are based on earnings or employment experience during a recent, specified base period, which varies by state. Recipients must register at the state employment office, seek work, and be available for work. Since each state has its own program, there is variability between states, and not all persons are covered, especially many low-income, unskilled, marginal participants in the work force whose work history is often too unstable to qualify them for coverage. Nevertheless, the program has been subject to minimal criticism, and has proved somewhat flexible in adapting to fluctuating economic conditions, with states being especially hard hit by depressed economic circumstances able to extend the duration of benefits and the level of benefit payments.

By far the most controversial programs in the Social Security Act were those providing the nucleus of the present public assistance programs. These were direct grant programs for the blind, dependent children, and aged persons not covered by Social Security. These programs were controversial because recipients received direct cash grants from tax revenues rather than the money they had previously paid into a fund, as was the case with the social insurances. Because the public assistance programs were so controversial, they were restricted to helpless groups with obvious need: the destitute aged or blind, and needy dependent children. A program of grants to the partially and totally disabled was added later. These grant programs involved complex federal-state cooperative arrangements in an attempt to support a governmental system that sought to leave as much power as possible at the local level, where it is assumed that the needs of the people can be more easily expressed and assessed. The federal government established certain broad guidelines governing these grant programs, which all states had to meet. For example, any program had to be offered uniformly to all citizens throughout a state. In general these federal guidelines sought to assure that there would be some level of uniformity and equity within and between programs, but specific characteristics of the programs, including major eligibility requirements and benefit levels, were left to the discretion of each state. We have already seen that this results in inequitable benefits among states.

Funds supporting these grant programs came from a combination of federal, state, and local general revenues. In 1968 an average of 66.1 percent of the total cost (payments and administrative costs) was federal money, 28.8 percent was from the state, and 5.1 percent was local money. The amount of federal funds is determined according to the characteristics of the state's program, the state's ability to meet the costs, and the general economic condition of the state. Withholding federal funds is one of the major ways in which the federal government can attempt to convince a state to comply with federal guidelines, but this power is limited by the ability of states to threaten to eliminate altogether one or more of the programs.

It has already been noted that the Social Security Act emphasized social insurances as a more acceptable way of providing for peoples' needs, since they are compatible with values of self-reliance and thrift. The grant programs were always minimal in scope and benefit levels, and concentrated on groups that were obviously helpless. The minimal nature of these programs also reflected the original belief that they would be temporary, and that persons receiving benefits from them would gradually be covered by OASDHI instead. To emphasize clearly the difference between the desirability of insurances and grants, the latter always had a "means test," requiring recipients to prove that they had no other resources or source of support. Recipients of social insurances did not have to do this. The only requirement was that they fell into the appropriate category; for example, that they be over 65 and retired, in order to collect Social Security. The difference was obviously one of entitlement and stigma, since the means test made it clear that the recipient was receiving a handout because of his inability to provide for himself, whereas the recipient of an insurance benefit had simply claimed his rightful benefit.

In January 1974, the programs for the blind, disabled, and aged were transferred to a completely federally funded and administered program called Supplemental Security Income (SSI), leaving the Aid to Families with Dependent Children (AFDC) as the only major federal-state grant program for public assistance recipients. This action illustrates once again societal values at work, reflecting society's continued struggle with the work ethic and a belief in personal responsibility. Although AFDC dealt with a helpless group—dependent children—it also had to contend with the adults caring for the children. This created a host of potentially difficult value issues —mothers having children out of wedlock, fathers who abandoned their legitimate or illegitimate children, mothers staying home to care for the children rather than working, and so on. Society has tried to deal with these issues by imposing a variety of restrictions on AFDC recipients at one time or another. The program still remains a federal-state one with variable eligibility requirements and benefit levels, indicating that the value issues are still troublesome. Transferring the grant programs for the aged, blind, and disabled to a federal program with less restrictive eligibility requirements and higher benefit levels suggests that some criterion of worthiness continues to operate in our social welfare system. The aged, blind, and disabled can be clearly defined as helpless, and are therefore helped with a minimum degree of stigma. Dependent children and their guardians, however, mix helplessness with an assortment of other less acceptable values and behaviors, and society's assistance to them comes grudgingly and minimally. Only when a guaranteed income is provided for all will the issue have been resolved once and for all. Exhibits 2-3 (pp. 62–64) and 2-4 (pp. 65–68) may help to illustrate the differences between SSI and AFDC.

Although the programs established by the Social Security Act in 1935 have been gradually expanded in scope and benefit levels, the basic structure of the Social Security Act has not been changed. As the number of recipients and program components have grown, so has the unwieldiness of the structure. This has been especially true of the one remaining public assistance program where federal-state sharing is involved—AFDC. The current administrative costs of public assistance are very high, as are the costs of the benefits themselves. Yet it is obvious that in spite of high costs, need is being inadequately met both financially and socially. The Social Security Act established the social acceptability of a national attack on need, but contemporary needs are probably too different from those in 1935 to be served adequately by legislation formulated and enacted forty years ago.

There are several areas in which the Social Security Act is presently inadequate:

1. It was limited in scope, reflecting the political and social realities of 1935. By its very passage, it paved the way for a more comprehensive view of needed social welfare legislation. New legislation will no doubt continue some parts of the 1935 act (such as Social Security and unemployment insurance), but it will probably change the whole basis for handling other social welfare needs (health care, financial assistance, social services, and so on). The Supplemental Security Income program is a step in this direction.

2. Contemporary society is vastly different from what it was in 1935. Rural-to-urban migration, civil rights progress, automation, and changes in educational opportunity have each had a significant impact on the nature of social life and the definition of social problems. New legislation must take account of these changes.

3. Funding and political realities have changed. The crisis in local and state fiscal affairs has shifted the burden of funding needs to the federal government. Patterns of cooperation and funding established in 1935 will have to be reexamined and altered. Revenue sharing is an attempt to deal with this issue.

4. National priorities have changed. Minority groups are more vocal and more powerful. Domestic and foreign priorities are being reexamined. Affluence and its effects are being reevaluated. All of these priority adjustments must be reflected in national social welfare policy.

In summary, the Social Security Act of 1935 marked the recognition of governmental responsibility for needs in a new and creative manner. The act continues to support the basic framework of the social welfare system in the United States, but will probably continue to be supplemented or replaced by more contemporary legislation.

EXHIBIT 2-3

AFDC and Supplemental Security Income Compared

Some of the differences between AFDC and the Supplemental Security Income program are illustrated in the following data, which look at eligibility requirements and benefit levels, as well as administrative procedures. The stigma against AFDC recipients turns out to be a costly one for them, and illustrates the importance of values in the determination of social welfare programs, a fact as true today as it has been throughout the development of social welfare concepts and programs.

	AFDC	SSI
Eligibility Requirements		
Age	Under 21 years. If 16 or 17, must be regularly enrolled in and attending school; if 18 or over and under 21, must be regularly and successfully attending high school, college or university, or a course of vocational or technical training.	None, except for the aged category (age 65+)
Residence	Child is making his home in the state.	U.S.A.
Need	Deprived of parental support or care by reason of death, continued absence from home, or physical or mental incapacity of one or both parents, and living with relatives listed in federal act as interpreted, or in foster care as permitted under the federal act.	65 or older Blind Disabled

The data on Supplemental Security Income is taken from U.S. Department of Health, Education, and Welfare pamphlet No. SSA 74-11000 (January 1974), and the data on AFDC in North Carolina is taken from pages 76 and 77 of *Characteristics of State Public Assistance Plans—January 31, 1973* (Washington: Government Printing Office, 1973). North Carolina data are illustrative, since each state's plan is somewhat different. Data on comparative payments by state are taken from *Public Assistance Statistics—April 1974* (Department of Health, Education, and Welfare Publication No. SRS 75-03100), Table 4 (unpaginated).

	AFDC	SSI
Financial/Property Eligibility	Ownership of real property used as a home does not of itself disqualify. However, in determining need and amount of payment, resources (shelter, rent, etc.) from such property are taken into account. Real property not used as a home and all personal property (savings, cash value of insurance, bonds, and any other cash reserves) are limited to $1,100 for adult and one child, plus $50 for needy spouse and for each eligible child up to $2,000 maximum. When application or budget does not include needy adult, limitation on reserve for one child is $1,000; for two children, $1,100; with $50 for each additional child in family unit up to $2,000 maximum. (Administrative) May have equity in essential motor vehicle not to exceed $1,000; excess equity plus equity in the loan value of non-essential motor vehicles and non-essential personal property such as cameras, television sets, etc. are treated as reserve. Transfers of property must be made at fair market value; the proceeds are treated as a reserve.	Assets of $1,500 for single person. $2,250 for couple excluding house with market value under $25,000. Household goods, personal effects, insurances, car. Nonwage income over $20 a month reduces benefits. Wage income over $65 a month reduces benefit $1 for each $2 earned. Living in someone else's home usually reduces benefits.
Administration		
State	State Board of Social Services[a] (policy-making), for aged and disabled.—Seven members appointed by Governor for 6 years, overlapping terms, one to be a woman. Commissioner appointed by Board, with Governor's approval and serves at pleasure of Board. State-supervised program.	None. Administered by the Social Security Administration (federal), and checks sent directly to recipient. Apply at Social Security offices.
Local	County Department of Social Services (100). County Board of Social Services—usually 3 members, 1 appointed by Board of Commissioners, 1 by State Board, and 1 by the other two for 3-year overlapping terms; in 51 counties, 5-member boards. County Director appointed by County Board of Social Services.	None (see above)
Financing	Assistance costs: State and local funds. Source of state funds: general fund. Of nonfederal share, state not less than 50 percent, local not more than 50 percent.	General funds of the U.S. Treasury (Social Security funds are not used to pay SSI).

[a]Operated within Department of Human Resources.

	AFDC			SSI

Financing (*cont.*)

Administrative costs: Nonfederal share, state and local funds. State's participation varies according to county's financial ability (on an equalizing basis) from a small percent to 50 percent of the balance after having deducted federal participation.

Average Benefit Payments (per month)

	Family	Recipient	One Person	Married Couple
North Carolina	$130.24	$41.55	Uniform throughout U.S.A.[b]	
Mississippi	51.08	14.37	$146	$219
New York	294.38	85.37		
California	215.27	67.01		
Montana	145.63	48.59		
Indiana	136.27	42.09		
Arizona	125.43	35.31		

[b]May be higher if state supplements federal SSI payments, or lower if has other income as noted above.

The period directly following the passage of the Social Security Act of 1935 focused mostly on World War II and its effects. As Russell Smith and Dorothy Zeitz put it in their book, *American Social Welfare Institutions* (1970), "The road to social change from F. D. Roosevelt's third inauguration in 1940 until the election of President John F. Kennedy in 1960 was circuitous at best and impassable at times."[53] The volunteer and public agencies were concerned with providing for the needs of men and women in the military, and their dependents, leaving postwar plans for the economy somewhat undirected. The Servicemen Readjustment Act of 1944 (better known as the G.I. Bill), which provided for medical benefits and a maintenance allowance for education, was the major social welfare legislation of the forties. During this period government support of social welfare was continued with few major changes. Foreign-policy concerns and ideological questions continued to be dominant in the fifties. As Smith and Zeitz point out, "Many social insurance measures and programs involving social spending were defeated in a rising tide of reaction against social legislation and a virulent anticommunist hysteria that convulsed the nation at midcentury."[54] Although revisions in the Social Security programs were made during both the Truman and Eisenhower administrations, radical innovations were rejected.

EXHIBIT 2-4

Welfare Myths

A good indication of the value conflicts involved in AFDC can be seen by the fact that the federal government feels it necessary to distribute brochures about welfare "myths" in an attempt to minimize resistance to the AFDC program. One such leaflet, "Welfare Myths vs. Facts" (Department of Health, Education and Welfare pamphlet SRS-72-02009, undated and unpaginated), is reproduced below, and each of its myths embodies a societal value which is threatened by the AFDC grant program. Can you translate the myths into their underlying values?

Myth. Welfare people are cheats.

Fact. Statistics reported by states indicate that four-tenths of one percent of welfare cases are referred for prosecution for fraud. The number of cases where fraud is established is even smaller. However, the states do not have a comprehensive means of detecting fraud, and some fraud undoubtedly is undetected. Nevertheless, the direct evidence available indicates that the amount of deliberate misrepresentation by welfare recipients is small. Errors due to other factors are a larger problem in the present welfare system.

Early results of a new reporting system on eligibility and payments show that about 5 percent of the nation's welfare recipients were ineligible for benefits received. Most of the errors were identified as honest mistakes by state and local welfare agencies or by recipients, operating under complex rules that vary with each jurisdiction. More than half the errors were by agencies. State and local agencies seek to minimize errors but are handicapped by lack of staff in the face of rising welfare caseloads and costs.

The first report covers about half the national caseload and thus is preliminary. It shows about 5.6 percent of welfare families as ineligible. It also reveals that 14.6 percent of welfare families received overpayments and 9.7 percent received underpayments. . . .

Under welfare reform, new rules regarding both eligibility and payments would be applied uniformly across the country. Use of modern, high-speed computers would provide an advanced system for preventing most incorrect payments and would use Social Security numbers to cross-check for duplicate applications and unreported income.

Myth. Give them more money and they'll spend it on drink and big cars.

Fact. Most welfare families report that if they received any extra money it would go for essentials. A survey of welfare mothers showed that almost half would spend it primarily for food. Another 28 percent said they would spend any additional money on clothing and shoes. The survey found that 42 percent of mothers bought used clothing or relied on donated clothing to make ends meet. Seventeen percent of the mothers said their children occasionally stayed home from school because they lacked decent clothes and shoes.

Nearly 10 percent of the mothers in the survey said they would spend extra money on rent for better housing, and 13 percent said they would spend it on a combination of food, clothes, and rent.

Myth. Most welfare children are illegitimate.

Fact. A sizable majority—68.6 percent—of the more than 7 million children in welfare families are legitimate, according to data compiled by the Social and Rehabilitation Service.

To help welfare families avoid unwanted pregnancies, the government in recent years has made family planning services available to those who wish it.

Myth. Once on welfare, always on welfare.

Fact. Half the families on welfare have been receiving assistance for 20 months or less. Two-thirds of families have been on the rolls less than three years. About one in five families (17.7 percent) have been on welfare for five years or more, and about one in sixteen families (6.1 percent) have been on the rolls ten years or more.

Current figures show that about 65 percent of cases are on welfare for the first time; about one-third of cases have been on the rolls before.

Proposed welfare reforms are designed to strengthen work incentives, eliminate barriers to employment, and thus help present recipients rejoin the work force as soon as possible.

Length of Time on Welfare

Less than six months	17.4%
Six months to one year	17.8%
One to two years	20.8%
Two to three years	12.2%
Three to five years	13.7%
Five to ten years	11.6%
Ten years or more	6.1%

Myth. Welfare families are loaded with kids —and have more just to get more money.

Fact. The latest statistics for welfare families indicate that over half—54.2 percent—are comprised of one- and two-child families. This is a slight decline in two years: according to statistics gathered in 1969, only 49.6 percent of welfare families had one or two children and slightly more than half the welfare families had three or more children.

The typical payment for an additional child is $35 a month, hardly enough to cover the cost of rearing an additional child. A few states impose payment limits; families reaching that ceiling— usually a five- to six-person family—get no additional money for another child.

Myth. Welfare's just a dole, a money hand-out.

Fact. Money is necessary to a family lacking subsistence, but it usually takes more than just cash to help the typical welfare family get on its feet and back into the mainstream of society.

The Social and Rehabilitation Service asked welfare agencies what social services they had

Children per Welfare Family

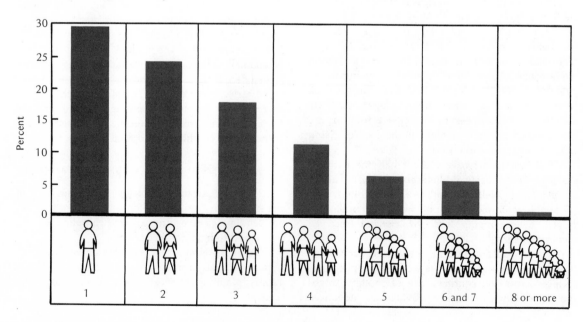

given to welfare families besides money. Here's what the agencies recently reported and the percentage of families receiving each kind of service (most families received at least one service):

- Health care advice and referrals (including Medicaid): 38.9 percent

- Counseling on financial and home management: 37.1 percent

- Employment counseling: 40.8 percent

- Services to secure child support: 28.4 percent

- Services to improve housing conditions: 27.2 percent

- Services to enable children to continue school: 17.5 percent

Other services which many agencies provide include those related to child welfare, vocational rehabilitation, and youth development. This range of social services has been found essential in helping disadvantaged people move toward independence and constructive living.

Welfare reform, among other things, would separate the administration of cash payments from the delivery of social services. The goal is improved social and rehabilitation services, more accessible services, and more coordinated services to those in need.

Myth. Most welfare families are black.

Fact. The largest racial group among welfare families—48.3 percent—is white.

Blacks represent 43.3 percent. Most of the remaining 8.4 percent are American Indians, Orientals, and other racial minorities.

Statistics show blacks comprise about 11 percent of the U.S. population, but 34 percent of the black population have incomes below the established poverty level, compared to 13 percent of the white population with incomes below the poverty level.

Myth. Why work when you can live it up on welfare?

Fact. The largest payment for basic needs that can be made to a welfare family of four (the typical family aided on AFDC) with no other income varies among states, from a low of $60 per month in Mississippi to a high of $372 per month in Alaska.

In July 1971, in all but four states, welfare payments, excluding payments for special needs, were below the established poverty level of $331 per month, or $3,972 per year, for a family of four. Unfortunately, some of the nation's working poor —ineligible for assistance under the present welfare system—earn less than the poverty level, too.

Each state establishes its own "need standard" —the amount required for the necessities of family living. A state standard may be below or above the poverty line. A state will use its "need standard" as a base for determining eligibility. However, 39 states pay less—some much less— than their own established standard of need. The federal government shares the cost of payments made by the states.

Welfare reform proposals—establishing a federal income floor nationally for welfare families— would provide an even base for payments. The working poor would get a cash assist as well, insuring that a family head would always be better off by working. Under welfare reform, family heads who are able to work would be required to make themselves available for jobs or job training. Penalties are provided if they fail to accept suitable jobs or training.

Myth. The welfare rolls are full of ablebodied loafers.

Fact. Less than 1 percent of welfare recipients are ablebodied unemployed males: some 126,000 of the more than 13.6 million Americans on federal/state-supported welfare (October 1971 statistics). All these individuals are required by law to sign up for work or work training in order to continue to be eligible for benefits. Prior to enactment of the new work-training law, government studies in three cities (Los Angeles, Milwaukee, and Camden) indicated that 80 percent of the ablebodied unemployed males on welfare did want to work. Nationally, among the fathers in this group, one in three was already enrolled in work training.

The largest group of working-age adults on welfare are 2.5 million mothers of welfare families, most of whom head families with no ablebodied male present. About 15 percent of these mothers

**Federally Assisted Welfare Population
(as of October 1971)**

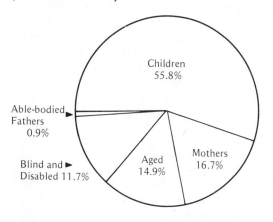

work, and 7 percent are in work training. Many of the other mothers confront serious barriers to employment under the existing welfare system, such as lack of child care facilities, transportation, etc. With additional day care service and job training available, it is estimated that another 34 percent

would be potential employees. About 4 percent of welfare mothers require extensive social and rehabilitative services to prepare them for employment.

The remaining 40 percent have little or no employment potential because they care for small children at home, have major physical or mental incapacities, or other insurmountable work barriers.

**Factors in the Employability of Welfare Mothers
(From a 1969 study)**

Needed at home to care for small children, have a long-term disability, etc.	40%
Employable if job training, jobs, and day care were made available	34%
Already employed full- or part-time	15%
In work-training programs or waiting to be accepted	7%
Need extensive medical or rehabilitative services before becoming employable	4%

In 1953 Congress reorganized the welfare structure with the hope of gaining administrative efficiency and more coordinated planning. Modifications of the Social Security Act in 1954 and 1956 brought into the system many members of the labor force left out of the original act. Unemployment insurance coverage was broadened, and the amount of assistance and the duration of coverage were increased. The Social Security amendments of 1962 made significant funds available for the training of public assistance workers, and social services were added to financial aid in public assistance programs. The concept of public welfare as a rehabilitative program was stressed, maintaining the view of welfare as temporary until people could once again independently participate in a competitive society.

THE
DEVELOPMENT
OF THE
CONTEMPORARY
SOCIAL
WELFARE
SCENE

A new dimension of welfare began to come into focus in the fifties. In 1954, the Supreme Court found school segregation unconstitutional on grounds that "separate but equal" is inherently unequal, and ordered desegregation of the public school system "with all deliberate speed." President Eisenhower ordered federal troops to Arkansas to enforce integration of Little Rock Central High School in defiance of Governor Orval Faubus in 1957. The same year, Eisenhower signed the Civil Rights Act authorizing the Justice Department to bring to federal courts cases involving discrimination in voting. The Civil Rights Act of 1960 made legal action against state and local officials possible. These events ushered in a significant new period of social welfare growth. The Supreme Court's action established its role as a powerful force for social change and social justice. It has the power to mandate the enforcement of civil rights legislation and strike down legislation and interpretations of legislation that violate human rights. The use of this power has made it possible for progressive legislators and law enforcement officials to act to preserve social justice when it has been threatened by persons motivated by bigotry, ignorance, or greed.

As the Supreme Court's actions changed the climate for social justice, courageous members of groups traditionally discriminated against were encouraged to accelerate their on-going quest for justice and equality. The blacks were the first to make major assaults against institutional inequality. Under the leadership of people like Martin Luther King and his associates, the 1950s and 1960s witnessed a series of nonviolent confrontations to demonstrate the existence of inequality and the need for social change. Blacks, often joined by white college students, carried out planned sit-ins at places of business that practiced discrimination. They organized peaceful protest marches to Washington, D.C., state capitols, and local power centers. They also carried out voter registration drives to help persons denied their legal voting rights through fraud and intimidation to exercise this right. These nonviolent attempts to enforce existing laws and to seek the passage of needed nondiscriminatory legislation were frequently met with harassment, intimidation, and physical violence (including murder) from law-enforcement officials and others. In spite of this, these courageous groups succeeded in gaining new legislation and widespread public support for their goals. By their successes, blacks stimulated similar attempts by other repressed groups, especially Chicanos, native Americans, and women.

At the onset of the decade of the 1960s, President Kennedy gave social problems the perspective of his New Frontier policies, and put problem-solving authority in the hands of concerned intellectuals. Social Security revisions were liberal; the Redevelopment Act was passed in 1961; and in 1962 the Manpower Development and Training Act was enacted. Food stamps were initiated as a new method of helping to meet the nutritional needs of welfare recipients. Kennedy's assassination burdened the American conscience, and enabled President Johnson to pass numerous pieces of social legislation. "The Great Society was envisioned as a perfectable society in which social justice can be created by the development of institutions to meet the needs of the citizens."[55] Under the Johnson administration the following legislation was passed: in 1963, the Mental Retardation and Community Mental Health Centers Construction Act; in 1964, the Economic Opportunity Act (the plan to mobilize the War on Poverty), and a civil rights act; in 1965, Medicare, Appalachia Regional Development Act, Department of Housing and Urban Development legislation, and another civil rights act; in 1966, a housing act; and in 1967, legislation further revising the Social Security Act.

The Economic Opportunity Act, which established the Office of Economic

Opportunity (OEO) with its Vista, Job Corps, and Head Start programs to name a few of the better known ones, was one of the most significant acts of the times. For the first time the "participation of the poor" in the power structure of the war on poverty was attempted in the form of community-action agencies. This new direction for welfare threatened local political structures and entrenched welfare organizations whose structures were poorly adapted to include client participation. The American dilemma of private versus common good arose again under the guise of federal and state funding conflicts, and in the shocking exploitation of OEO contracts by private contractors. Many communities had little experience in organizing to obtain grants, and they often deteriorated into many squabbling groups competing for resources to end their own deprivation. The lack of success of many programs reflected inadequate funding, inadequate planning, inadequate knowledge of needs, and inadequate client participation in planning.

The ultimate failure of most of the programs established by the Economic Opportunity Act underlined the need for more adequately conceptualized and implemented legislative solutions to the nation's welfare needs, the entrenched complexity of most social problems, and the obstacles created by the welfare bureaucracy itself. In spite of these problems, the Economic Opportunity Act succeeded in creating a new focus on community organization and planning, and a lasting involvement of users of social welfare services in decision-making about those services. It also proved the enduring value of some of the programs established on an experimental basis, such as Head Start. Exhibit 2-5 looks at some of the problems, failures, and accomplishments of the Economic Opportunity Act and the War on Poverty in more detail.

EXHIBIT 2-5

The Legacy of the Economic Opportunity Act

The War on Poverty, and the Economic Opportunity Act which formed its foundation, was a massive and complex attempt to deal more adequately with poverty and a variety of other social needs. From its inception, the War on Poverty was mired in political and bureaucratic structures and problems that ultimately led to the dismantling of the Office of Economic Opportunity, created by the Economic Opportunity Act. Even so, the legacy of the War on Poverty is substantial. The following excerpts are from "The Good War that Might Have Been," by Mark R. Arnold, and appeared in *The New York Times Magazine*, September 29, 1974. The selection provides a good summary of the importance of politics in the public decision-making arena, as well as the many and often conflicting influences on public social welfare programs.

Ten years after President Johnson signed the Economic Opportunity Act on August 20, 1964, declaring it "the policy of the United States to eliminate the paradox of poverty in the midst of plenty," poverty is in much less danger than the Office of Economic Opportunity. The House voted in May to repeal the act and transfer remaining OEO programs to other agencies, and the matter is now before the Senate. . . .

It is clear now in 1974 that the original antipoverty strategy was based on a number of misapprehensions or beliefs that weakened its impact. One was that a class of Americans—the poor—could be singled out for special treatment without arousing deep resentment among others. . . .

This was, in fact, done with surprising success in many areas. But it was a mistake to have supposed that the system could be used to change the system—without arousing the system.

Yet, despite its difficulties, the antipoverty program introduced new techniques for coping with neglected problems, such as neighborhood-oriented health and legal services, preschool education, cooperative business enterprises, paraprofessional jobs and training programs that screen the hardest cases in, not out. It created, through establishment of local community-action agencies, new self-help institutions in the slums, enabling the poor to exert leverage on governments at all levels. It provided food, transportation, job training, health care, legal representation, homemaker skills, compensatory education and other basic human services to millions of needy Americans. It established career ladders for hundreds of talented minority-group members, among them Representatives Ronald Dellums of California and Parren Mitchell of Maryland and Mayors Coleman Young of Detroit and Theodore Berry of Cincinnati. . . .

The Economic Opportunity Act was Johnson's first major legislative achievement as President. Its passage marked the beginning of one of the most prolific bursts of legislative activity in history. Within little more than a year after its passage, a historic civil-rights act, a voting rights act, the first omnibus program of aid to public schools and health insurance for the elderly all became law—

testimony to Johnson's skill, to the nation's remorse over President Kennedy's death and to Congress's determination to bring to fruition the seeds of social policy planted in the New Deal. . . .

Behind the [proposed OEO legislation] message lay a titanic bureaucratic struggle involving almost a dozen agencies—Agriculture, Commerce, HEW and Labor among them—each eager to have its pet projects included in the poverty package sent to Congress. The basic choice was between a jobs-and-training approach, favored by Labor, and social services stressing community self-help, urged by HEW. The eventual compromise put primary reliance on community self-help, but with a strong youth-oriented employment component. A companion question—who was to run the new federal effort?—was harder to resolve. To settle conflicting claims, and take command of planning, Johnson turned to Shriver, director of the popular Peace Corps and a man whose links to the Kennedy family underlined Johnson's pledge of continuity. . . .

Johnson knew the agency would stir some trouble; it was to be an advocate for the poor within government, a prodder and goader of the great bureaucracies. At his insistence, it was set up in the executive branch and Shriver was made a Presidential Assistant as well as OEO director. "Sarge," the President said, putting a protective arm around him, "this thing can't survive less'n everybody knows when they're hitting it, they're hitting me. I'm your protection."

The Economic Opportunity Act gave the new OEO responsibility for operating some of the programs itself and for coordinating the often competing activities of the other agencies. Some of the major ones it ran were the community-action agencies, the Job Corps and VISTA (Volunteers in Service to America). The community-action groups, to be composed of all segments of a community, would attack local poverty with the help of $90 in federal funds put up for each $10 raised locally. The Job Corps established residential training centers, for youths 14 to 22, where school dropouts with poor job prospects could complete their education and learn a trade. VISTA was to be a domestic counterpart to the highly successful Peace Corps; enrollees would work in migrant camps, Indian reservations, urban slums and rural outposts, helping the poor overcome their poverty. The Economic

Opportunity Act also established a Neighborhood Youth Corps, within the Labor Department, to help keep youths in school, to provide help for migrant workers and small businessmen, to provide job-training for welfare mothers and to provide work-study grants to poor college students. New programs quickly joined the list: Head Start, a preschool program that emphasized attention to medical and nutritional as well as educational needs; legal services; and neighborhood health centers. . . .

Though prepared for some bureaucratic squabbling, Johnson was taken by surprise at adverse local reaction, and complained to Shriver: "Is OEO being run by a bunch of kooks, Communists and queers?"

Job Corps youths had been flown cross-country to camps without beds or programs. A half-million comic books were printed for recruitment purposes but were never distributed when it was discovered that earlier drives had generated 300,000 inquiries for only 1,000 job-training slots. Congressmen were fuming, by 1967, that the program was costing $8,000 per enrollee—more than it cost to send a young person to Harvard. . . . The trainees often clashed with local townspeople, indeed, rioted in some instances.

Community-action organizers, who had begun seeking to "strike down all the barriers," took aim at local merchants, slumlords, even Mayors. Local officials learned to their horror that they couldn't control community-action agencies. The act included the stipulation that such agencies should be public or private nonprofit enterprises, thus bypassing City Hall, and should be run with the "maximum feasible participation" of the people served.

There was another factor too. It was that many people took the rhetoric literally. Many of the tactics that drove Mayors and Governors to distraction—rent strikes, marches on City Hall, demands for more municipal jobs for minorities, even suits against welfare restrictions—were legitimate assaults on real sources of poverty. "I'll never forget the day in 1967 when the Supreme Court struck down state residency requirements for welfare eligibility," says Baker. The suit had been brought by OEO-supported legal services attorneys. "Many of our best friends on the Hill, in Governors' mansions, the Mayors' offices—they were all mad

at us. This would cost them millions. They might have to raise taxes. Yet here was a decision that did more to alleviate poverty than almost anything else we had done. And that was always our quandary: how could we alleviate poverty without hurting the people whose support we needed to alleviate poverty?"

In 1966 and 1967, Congress enacted a series of restrictions, limiting salaries of antipoverty officials, putting a $6,900 ceiling on per-enrollee costs in the Job Corps, and permitting local governments to take control of community-action programs. These actions, coupled with a number of changes within the OEO itself, took much of the sting out of its activities. . . .

Back in June, 1966, Shriver's people worked up a 410-page four-year plan: By a combination of expanded services, stepped-up income maintenance and economic growth, two-thirds of the 36 million poor would be lifted from poverty by 1972, the remainder over the next four years. There was only one catch: Government antipoverty outlays would have to grow by $6.4 billion, or 28 percent, the first year, and $3 billion a year thereafter; OEO's own budget would quadruple from $1.7 billion in 1967 to $6.8 billion in 1972. Yet, the report said, the recommended increases were "less than the normal annual increase in federal tax revenues" in a prosperous economy and "would provide a real start" in the all-out war on poverty.

What happened, of course was that the country got deeply involved in waging, and providing the funds, for another, hotter war. "Vietnam took it all away. . . ."

Charles Schultze, then L.B.J.'s budget chief adds: "Rather than relying on economic growth to provide more antipoverty funds, he [Johnson] would have to raise taxes. He wouldn't do that. He could say he was raising taxes to finance Vietnam, but he feared the conservatives would use it as a club to kill all the Great Society legislation. By the time he decided to ask Congress for a tax hike [in 1968] he was afraid chances of getting it would be killed if people thought it was for the war on poverty." Thus, the four-year plan was never begun, and the nation never really adopted a goal for eliminating poverty, or a realistic strategy for meeting it. . . .

Shriver and his successor, Bert Harding, had

already begun spinning OEO programs off to other agencies once such programs were deemed mature enough to survive in old-line bureaucratic settings without losing their poverty focus. OEO, after all, was to be experimental, not permanent. Nixon continued the process, sending Head Start to HEW, the Job Corps and other manpower programs to Labor. More transfers were to follow. . . .

In retrospect, it can be argued that if OEO had not pulled in its horns, it would not have survived as long as it has and many of its programs would not have survived at all. The showdown came in California, where Gov. Ronald Reagan compiled a report charging serious wrongdoing on the part of the statewide California Rural Legal Assistance and demanded that its funds be terminated.

CRLA was the prototype for dozens of the country's poverty law offices that served up occasional class-action suits along with a steady diet of routine divorce, housing and consumer cases. Acting on behalf of migratory and other poor farm workers in the state, it had brought one suit after another against state agencies and influential growers. Its legal victories had cost Reagan and his conservative supporters millions. The charges against CRLA were transparently politically motivated and were thoroughly discredited in 1971 by a panel of judges set up to investigate them, but the flap redoubled the Administration's determination to minimize controversy. It also provided a major push for detaching legal services from the OEO and placing them in a nonprofit government-chartered corporation where they could be better insulated from political attack. . . .

Richard Nixon's landslide reelection in November, 1972, affected OEO like no event since the escalation of the war in Vietnam. Federal outlays for the poor had doubled under Lyndon Johnson, rising from $7.9 billion in 1964 to $15.9 billion in 1969. They doubled again in the next six years, but virtually none of the increase went to programs authorized under the Economic Opportunity Act. Outlays for OEO programs in 1973 stood at the same level Nixon inherited in 1969: $1.9 billion. Most of the increase in funds for the poor under Nixon were not spent in training or service programs aimed at getting rid of poverty, but rather the funds took the form of direct financial assistance—in some cases available to nonpoor as

well—such as Social Security benefit increases mandated by Congress, Medicare-Medicaid, the new federalized Supplementary Security Insurance, which replaced the "adult welfare" categories: aid to the aged, blind and disabled. The major exception was food stamps, a program which will have reached 15 million people in 1974 as compared with 1 million in 1969, and on which federal outlays soared, under Nixon, from $1.6 billion to $5.1 billion. . . .

In fiscal 1975, again the Administration had asked for no community-action funds. If the Mayors and Governors—and local administrators —wanted community action to stay in business, Arnett (the director of OEO appointed in 1973) told them, they'd better make their voices heard in Washington. They did.

What happened between last October and May 29 [1974], when the House acted, was unprecedented in OEO's history. The two national organizations that represent CAP [Community Action Program] directors and other friends of the program hired a high-priced lobbying team in Washington, headed by former Representative William Cramer, a one-time OEO critic. Letters proclaiming the virtues of community action poured in from 32 Governors, dozens of Mayors, Chambers of Commerce and more than a few of the 185,000 Americans who owe their jobs to the program. . . .

By a vote of 331 to 53 the House approved the Community Services Act, which kills OEO but preserves all programs in other agencies. . . .

Martin LaVor, a House Republican staffer who has followed OEO from its inception, explains the shift in sentiment: "Community action keeps the poor off the Mayors' backs. Some of them provide useful services, some are largely job-creating enterprises. . . . They create a buffer between the local power structure and the poor. Take them away and a lot of public officials will have problems on their hands they'd prefer not to have to deal with."

"It was a perfect way to resolve the issue," says Representative Albert Quie of Minnesota, the committee's ranking Republican. "The people who hate OEO could say, 'Look, we're getting rid of it.' The people who like the individual programs could say 'Look, we're keeping them.' Very often they were the same people."

The real questions raised by the short, unhappy

life of the OEO transcend the fortunes of this or that program, this or that office. What indeed has it accomplished? What are its lessons? What does it take to eliminate poverty?

Certainly it has accomplished less than it initially promised. But it also seems clear that it achieved more than most Americans appreciate, changing city halls, welfare offices, housing officials and Congress in their treatment of the poor, bringing millions of poor into the political process and many of them into the decision-making process. It demonstrated that the public attention span is short and that, as Eli Ginzburg and Robert M. Solow put it in *The Public Interest:* "Social legislation needs a constituency larger than its direct beneficiaries" if it is to benefit the poor and the minorities, for they are, almost by definition, weak and powerless.

There were 23 million poor in 1973, according to the government's inflation-related price index ($4,540 for a nonfarm family of four); this is a third less than there were 10 years ago, when Johnson declared the poverty war. What's happened in the past decade has been a gradual maturing of often effective programs—accompanied by a diminished sense of national interest in the matter.

BOX SCORE

Community Action. 937 local "self-help" agencies . . . no longer organize rent strikes or city-hall marches as some did in the sixties, but provide a range of noncontroversial services to the poor: provide emergency assistance to the needy, channel welfare recipients into job training, find housing for the homeless, help for the homebound, run interference for the poor in dealing with local bureaucracies. . . . Employs a work force of 180,000, half of whom were formerly poor or on welfare. Cost: $330 million. Effectiveness: Mixed.

Head Start. Comprehensive health, nutritional, and educational assistance to 380,000 preschoolers from low-income families. . . . Politically popular program whose frequently imaginative teaching techniques have rarely gained a foothold in public schools into which "graduates" are fed. . . . Children attending Head Start and its sequel, Follow Through, grades 1–3, score higher on achievement tests than those who don't. . . . Program is concentrating increasingly on home environment as the key factor in educational attainment. Cost: $430 million. Effectiveness: High.

Job Corps. Schooling and job training in a new environment for teenage school dropouts; program has undergone drastic changes from the sixties, maintains a low profile . . . boasts a 93 percent placement rate—in jobs, school or military service. But half of each year's 43,000 enrollees drop out within 90 days, and expenses required for residential setting keeps costs per enrollee at more than $6,500 a year. Cost: $180 million. Effectiveness: Questionable.

Legal Services. Employs 2,500 lawyers in 900 "poverty law" offices . . . provides free legal advice to persons meeting income guidelines up to a third above the poverty level . . . handles domestic, housing and welfare problems, consumer grievances concerning faulty merchandise, repossession threats and the like. . . . A few successful class-action suits against government agencies—lowering barriers to qualify for welfare, for example—have enraged many officeholders, but benefited the poor. Cost: $71 million. Effectiveness: High.

Volunteers in Service to America (VISTA). 4,200 "domestic Peace Corps" volunteers spend two years working in health clinics, migrant camps, drug rehabilitation programs, senior citizens centers. . . . Well-established program now housed in ACTION, the conglomerate agency formed by the 1971 merger of all federal volunteer efforts, VISTA has shed its earlier controversial image, now gives its workers specific functions to perform. But program's inability to attract large numbers of volunteers with needed skills (plumbers, nurses) and $4,300-a-year cost of volunteer support has forced administrators to favor less expensive approaches to volunteerism. VISTA's cost: $22.8 million. Effectiveness: Mixed.

The first massive violence in the civil rights movement broke out in 1965 in Watts, a section of Los Angeles. Similar rioting later broke out in other cities. These riots reflected the accumulating frustrations with the steady but slow pace of progress achieved in civil rights. As greater social justice was attained, the remaining incidences of inequality and the poverty and humiliation associated with it were made even more visible—and perceived as even less tolerable. A period of conflict within the black civil rights movement developed. One side continued to argue for nonviolent protest, pointing to the real progress attained using this approach. Another view argued for a more activist—and, if necessary, violent—approach, pointing to the slow pace of progress and the high price blacks continued to pay in terms of poverty, illness, and discrimination. In April 1968, Martin Luther King was murdered in Memphis, Tennessee, weakening the forces pushing for nonviolence. Dissipation of the direct action through peaceful public protest phase of the civil rights movement was signaled by the ineffectiveness of the Poor People's Campaign in Washington, D.C. that same year. Thereafter, more militant and more politically sophisticated approaches were adopted, as exemplified by the National Welfare Rights Organization (NWRO). Formed primarily of public assistance recipients, it seeks changes in social welfare legislation to make benefits more adequate and equitable. It also seeks greater involvement of welfare recipients in social policy by organizing them as an effective political force. Unfortunately, by the early 1970s NWRO had lapsed into inactivity.

Students also had a period of militancy spurred by the escalation of the Vietnam War in 1966, the assassination of Robert Kennedy in the spring of 1968, and the invasion of Cambodia in 1970. "The SDS (Students for a Democratic Society), the leading group in campus unrest, in 1968 had only 250 chapters with 35,000 members, but could mobilize up to 300,000 supporters."[56] Not only the poor were organizing to demand a measure of influence in the nation's social policy.

The emerging new politics, social legislation, and living styles of the seventies seem to be seeking a way to make America a more just society. The New Left is a revolt against the bureaucracy of government, the depersonalization of universities, the inhumanities of war, the social and economic deprivation of minority groups and the poor, and the discrepancy in some areas between what America stands for and what it practices. The New Left has drawn its support mostly from college students, middle-class youth, and discontented blacks, and has emphasized community and social change.

Governmental responses to the problems posed by the Vietnam War, civil rights, and welfare reform have been slow and often ineffective. At present, "there is no clear definition of purpose, nor central direction in welfare effort as a whole. . . . Acceleration of programs toward the abolition of poverty seems unlikely."[57] President Nixon's resistance to school busing as an effective civil rights tool stimulated anti-busing legislation in 1972 that has seriously weakened school busing in concept and practice, a discouraging reversal of hard-won gains. Attempts to deal with the need for an overhaul of the nation's basic social welfare system have shown similar inconsistencies. Public assistance applicants must make themselves available for work as a condition for the receipt of aid, in spite of high unemployment rates, low wages, and the unsuitability of most assistance recipients for gainful employment.[58] The old question of welfare vs. workfare continues to live on in spite of centuries of experience that has repeatedly shown that most welfare recipients are unable to work because of age, illness, disability, or child-rearing responsibilities.

During the first half of the 1970s some significant legislation has been enacted that improves the social welfare service delivery system, while other legislation is more questionable, and some issues remain to be resolved through legislative action. As noted earlier, the Supplemental Security Income Program took effect in January 1974, and generally was a step forward in providing a uniform, federally administered guaranteed income program for the needy aged, blind, and disabled. The fact that the AFDC program was excluded from SSI is also to be regretted, however, since it continues to exhibit the many problems and inequities referred to earlier.

Other legislation has begun the difficult task of changing society's inadequate medical system. Although American medical practice includes the most sophisticated technology available anywhere, society has been relatively ineffective in insuring that all of its members have access to adequate medical care. Whereas most highly industrialized societies provide comprehensive medical care to all of their members, Americans must purchase health care on an individual basis. This seriously discriminates against lower-income groups. It also discourages people from utilizing preventive medicine, since medical check-ups tend to be costly and are often not covered by medical insurance (insurances tend to cover services only in the event of an illness). The first problem, making medical care available to all, will not be a reality until a national health insurance plan is enacted by Congress. The second problem, encouraging preventive medicine, has been addressed by legislation mandating the support of health maintenance organizations (HMO) as an alternative to health insurance, which is focused on the incidence of illness.

The HMO is an organization that contracts with individuals to provide comprehensive health services for a flat fee. This is thought to encourage persons to utilize services on a preventive basis since they are included in the fee paid the HMO, rather than utilizing services when an illness occurs as is the case with traditional health insurance plans. The HMO also has its own staff of medical practitioners (or contracts with such persons), enabling the HMO to exert more control over services and costs than is possible when an individual uses services provided by independent practitioners and organizations as is the case with traditional health insurance plans. It is important to note that the HMO is simply an alternative form of private health insurance; it is not a governmentally provided health insurance program.

Potentially significant legislation is Public Law 92-512, revenue sharing, passed in 1972. This legislation was part of Richard Nixon's so-called "New Federalism," an effort to transfer as much decision-making responsibility as possible back to the states from the federal government. "PL 92-512 provides for financial assistance to states and localities, one-third to the states, two-thirds to the localities. The localities are restricted in their use of funds to (1) 'ordinary and necessary capital expenditures' and (2) 'ordinary and necessary maintenance and operating expenses' in eight priority areas. These are public safety, environmental protection, public transportation, health, recreation, libraries, social services for the poor or aged, and financial administration."[59] Revenue sharing funds are not really new monies, since they are intended to replace, partially or totally, grants-in-aid, and funds for many grant-in-aid programs have been reduced with the advent of revenue sharing. Within the priority areas established by the federal government, the revenue sharing funds can be used at the discretion of the local and state decision-makers.

In theory, revenue sharing allows states and localities to allocate funds more wisely than is possible by the federal government, since these units of government are closer to the people and presumably more responsive to their wishes. However, Hardcastel notes the following:

> The trend represented by revenue sharing shows that nationally, a commitment to domestic programming, especially in social services, is simply not there. The political implications are clear. Federal protection for social services will be removed and they will have to compete with the entire array of fiscal demands for public funds. Mental health programs, for example, will have to compete for funds at the state and local level not only with child welfare services but also with street improvements.[60]

Revenue sharing marks a step backward in a process that had been developing for some time, namely increased federal planning and supervision of the social welfare system. An expanded role for the federal government in social welfare planning and supervision reflects the impact of large-scale social forces on individual and community functioning. The return to more local control opens up possibilities for less efficient and more inequitable use of funds, as well as an inability to see long-range human needs and plan appropriately for them. Social welfare has always been enmeshed in the societal need to set priorities in the use of relatively scarce resources. Revenue sharing reemphasizes the need for establishing priorities, but vests much of the decision-making power with those having perhaps the weakest grasp of the significance of their decisions.

It is still too early to know how effective revenue sharing will be in meeting America's social welfare needs, but preliminary data are not encouraging. A National Revenue Sharing Monitoring Project sponsored by a coalition of the League of Women Voters Education Fund, the Center for Community Change, the National Urban Coalition, and the Center for National Policy Review, reports the following in a 1974 interim report:

The general revenue sharing program intended to return "power to the people" to increase citizen influence and to make government more responsive to taxpayer pressure appears to be failing and failing miserably. Defenders of revenue sharing blame this failure on the narrowing flexibility in local budgets caused by increased costs of existing local government services. Many also cite concurrent federal categorical grant cutbacks or impoundments, and the pinch put on local budgets by spiraling inflation . . . but the widespread barriers to effective citizen participation which monitors reported are not explained by arguments about inflation or reduced federal spending. Citizen participation problems are built into the Revenue Sharing Act which does not specifically provide for such participation in local decision-making processes of allocation of these monies. The Act provides only that these monies be allocated in conformity with and through the same budgeting process established under local and state law. The assumption is that citizens participate in decisions as to how local revenues are spent and that this participation would be extended to revenue sharing expenditures as well. The assumption is erroneous. Citizens generally are not involved in complex local and state budgeting processes. Revenue sharing has not changed this fact of life.[61]

The result has been that "revenue sharing money was most often spent for the same purpose as local revenues have been spent in the past,"[62] yielding no particular benefit to social welfare services. Indeed, to the degree that grant-in-aid programs have been cut back, the net effect may be negative. While revenue sharing legislation is of great potential significance, perhaps the lesson from history it ignores is that we can't go backward. In the attempt to meet society's needs, it is rarely possible to resort to solutions that did or could have worked at an earlier point in society's history, because no society stands still.

Legislation which has not yet been passed, but which is very badly needed, includes some type of guaranteed annual income, and national health insurance (see Exhibit 2-6). Part of the significance of the Supplemental Security Income Program is that for the first time it does establish a federal guaranteed annual income, at least for a segment of the population. Proposals for such a guaranteed income for all Americans have covered a wide spectrum. Some of the major proposals have included the following:[63]

1. *Guaranteed Income.* A plan to supplement the income of individuals and families to insure that the annual income reaches a predetermined level. President Nixon proposed such a plan, the Family Assistance Plan, but it was not approved by Congress. There has been considerable debate about the level of income to be guaranteed, and whether all individuals and families would be included in the plan.

2. *Negative Income Tax.* A plan that again establishes a base income level, with those falling above it paying taxes and those falling below it being paid a supplement to reach that level. Somewhat similar to a guaranteed income, such a plan would also build in a work incentive

provision, but unlike the above plan, it would be administered by the Internal Revenue Service.

3. *Children's Allowances.* A plan that automatically pays parents a cash allowance for each child. It is used in several other industrialized countries, and, contrary to some fears in this country, it has not led to an increase in the birth rate. But this plan discriminates against those without children, and, by automatically paying money to all parents, would in effect subsidize those not in need.[64]

4. *Social Dividend.* The least likely of all the plans, it would provide a universal payment to all regardless of income or status. It is the most costly of all the plans, but insures equal treatment to all and has no work provisions.

EXHIBIT 2-6

National Health Insurance

In 1974, before the Watergate scandal reached such proportions that it paralyzed Congress and ultimately led to the resignation of President Nixon, there was considerable interest in and hope for national health insurance legislation. The events of the last part of the Nixon administration later helped to make action on the proposed legislation impossible, but it seems certain that that action will occur before long. In the April 8, 1974 edition of *The Washington Post,* the paper editorialized about the then-current health insurance proposals. This discussion is a concise presentation of the issues involved in such legislation.

Dissatisfaction with the way health care is financed in the United States has been building for years. As a result, pressure has been growing for some kind of federal health insurance that would give low-income people access to good quality medical care no matter where they lived, that would protect all families against the cost of catastrophic illness, and provide some incentives to hold down the mounting costs of medical care. Until recently, however, there was deep division over what the plan should be.

From *The Washington Post,* April 8, 1974, p. A22. © 1974 by The Washington Post. Used by permission.

On one side were the "incrementalists," who thought the current health insurance system could be patched up and improved by means of federal standards and federal money but that a role for private insurance companies should be preserved. On the opposite side were those who believed the present system had to be replaced in its entirety. Senator Kennedy was among the most vocal proponents of total replacement, advocating a federal system of compulsory national health insurance that would provide free medical care to everyone and replace the private insurance industry. This approach has strong labor union support but carried such a large price tag—variously estimated at between $60 billion and $100 billion—that it has not been seriously debated by a budget-conscious Congress.

The President's new proposal is clearly incrementalist in spirit: Preserving as much as possible of the current system and minimizing federal budget cost. The federal government would define a set of basic health insurance benefits to be made available to everyone. All employers would be required to offer this basic benefit package to their employees and to share the cost. Ultimately the employer would pay three-quarters and the employee one-quarter. The federal government would share the cost for low-income people, replacing the current state-run Medicaid program with a uniform federal program of health financing for the poor. A modified form of Medicare for the aged would be retained. Everyone would have a "health card"—a medical care credit card to be presented to doctors and hospitals. Care would not be entirely free, however. All except the poor would pay part of the cost of their care themselves unless their bills were very large. No family would pay more than $1,500 per year no matter how serious and costly their medical problem.

Since employers would negotiate directly with insurance companies and pay the premiums directly to the companies, this part of the plan would not appear in the federal budget at all. The federal cost (estimated at around $6 billion more than is currently being spent) would go only for underwriting the basic insurance package for the low-income population. It should not be imagined, however, that extending comprehensive health protection to all employed Americans is really "free," just because it does not appear in the federal budget. The premiums that employers would pay to private insurance companies would be very much like privately collected taxes. Moreover, a uniform premium is essentially a head tax—a highly regressive tax that takes a higher proportion of low earnings than high earnings.

The Kennedy-Mills Plan—unlike Senator Kennedy's former total replacement approach—is also incrementalist, but avoids some of the pitfalls and inequities of the administration's bill. Employers would also be required to offer a basic health insurance package and to pay three-quarters

of the cost. Those covered by the insurance would also pay part of their medical bill unless they were very poor but would be protected against all medical bills that exceeded $1,000 for one family in a year. The federal government would also aid those with low incomes.

The biggest difference, however, is that private employers would not negotiate with insurance companies nor pay premiums. Employers would simply collect a 4 percent tax on everyone's earnings (up to $20,000), of which 1 percent would be deducted from the employee's wages and the rest paid by the employer. The self-employed and even people with unearned income would also pay a tax. These taxes would go into a trust fund which would be used to finance the health insurance, with private companies playing a purely administrative role. The Kennedy-Mills Bill would augment the federal budget far more than the administration's plan, a fact which the Democratic legislators seek to disguise by proposing that the health insurance trust fund, and other social insurance trust funds, would not be counted in the regular federal budget.

Both of these efforts strike us as strongly constructive and realistic proposals for a national health insurance, and we hope the Congress will engage in serious debate leading to legislation before the end of the session. Of the two, in their present form, we prefer the Kennedy-Mills version for two reasons. A single federal health insurance plan seems likely to be more workable than one that would have individual employers negotiating with private insurance companies, perhaps leaving gaps in coverage for employees moving from job to job. More important, the Kennedy-Mills tax is less regressive than the disguised head tax of the administration plan, which would fall heavily on low-income workers. Financing health insurance out of a progressive tax, such as the income tax, would in our view, be still more desirable. In any case, all federal receipts and expenditures should appear in the budget so that the Congress and the public can make rational decisions about the federal government as a whole. Hiding a tax in a trust fund is no better than disguising it as a private "premium." There is no such thing as a free lunch. We need national health insurance and we must be prepared to pay for it.

Whatever guaranteed income approach ultimately selected, there is considerable feeling that America needs to move toward some such program. It will be a contemporary expression of the belief that has been developing throughout the history of social welfare that society has a responsibility for the basic well-being of its members. Meeting peoples' economic needs is by no means equivalent to meeting their social needs, but it is a major step in that direction.

The second legislation that seems destined to become reality in the not too distant future is national health insurance. The rising cost of health care has made it an increasing burden on Americans, yet it is a necessity that few can do without, and upon which many depend for their very survival. Private insurance plans, often in conjunction with one's place of work, have existed for some time, but they are expensive. As with all attempts to deal with societal need, there are many possible ways of structuring a national health insurance plan, some of which are discussed in Exhibit 2-6. Other industrialized societies have national health insurance plans, which have been very positive in terms of their value in preventing illness and improving individual functioning. Hopefully Americans will soon enjoy these benefits.

CONCLUSION Expansion on the only meaningful frontier, that of individual people and their relationships with each other, is essential. Strengthening police and corrections structures in the nation cannot hope to solve the problem of social disintegration and individual malfunction. While there is some reason to be proud of the nation's progress in conceptualizing and operationalizing social welfare as it celebrates its two hundredth anniversary in 1976, and while there is some optimism that current legislative trends are addressing basic needs, there is still much to be done. Millions continue to live in poverty. Inequality continues to be a way of life for many blacks, Chicanos, native Americans, and women. Social priorities continue to be questioned. Social welfare students and practitioners of today are living through a period of crucial importance to the future of social welfare in the United States. As is always the case, knowledge of the past will help all of us to make more intelligent decisions about the future. Exhibit 2-7 summarizes some of the major trends of social welfare history that will affect the shape of the social welfare institution of the future.

EXHIBIT 2-7

The Threads of History in Social Welfare

To summarize this chapter's review of the historical development of the concept of social welfare, the major stages of welfare growth are presented on the following pages, along with a brief discussion of their enduring effects on social welfare concepts and programs.

Informal Welfare Structures. The highly formalized and specialized welfare structures we take for granted have their roots in informal attempts to meet people's basic needs. The family was the earliest structure in which this occurred, and, in spite of the highly formalized and professional programs that exist today, informal attempts to help others continue to exist and be important—the family, friendship groups, mutual aid groups. As long as the magnitude of need was small, and the definition of who was responsible for helping whom was narrow, informal welfare structures were adequate. When need and responsibility grew beyond immediate kin or friendship groups, more formal structures became necessary.

The Causes of Need. The incidence of need has generally been related to social conditions. The Industrial Revolution, including its earliest phases that broke up the manorial system, generated need of many kinds—housing, food, illness, and others. During periods of economic depressions, or during periods of war, it is common for people to experience need. Institutionalized inequality in whatever form—slavery; child labor, and indenture; lack of women's rights; and religious persecution, to name a few—serves to make people helpless and dependent. Although there is always some need caused by willful neglect and deviance, the lessons of history demonstrate that need is most often a social phenomenon. It is remarkable how resistant to these lessons some societies can be.

Categorizing the Needy. With the formalization of welfare services came the desire to categorize the needy in order to determine who qualified for what services (formalized in eligibility requirements). The Elizabethan Poor Law established three categories of the needy, which have proven remarkably long-lived. These categories, the services provided in each, and the present-day forms of both, are summarized below:

The helpless were persons who could not be blamed for being needy because of age, illness, or disablement. These persons received outdoor relief or were placed in almshouses. The helpless are still with us (the aged, dependent children, and the physically and emotionally disabled), and they continue to be considered worthy of assistance. Such aid today is normally provided in their own homes rather than in almshouses (although there

are still some vestiges of almshouse-like residential facilities).

The involuntarily unemployed were persons who were the victims of misfortune, but who were generally ablebodied. They were usually sent to workhouses or houses of correction, where they were expected to work in return for help. The involuntarily unemployed are today generally helped through outdoor relief, although there is still a tendency to try to make receipt of aid dependent on going to work if at all possible.

The vagrant were persons without a stable place of residence. They were usually ostracized, or, if they had to be accepted by a community, placed in workhouses or houses of correction. They were considered willfully indigent, and despised as a result. Vagrancy today has a somewhat different connotation. Persons who exist outside the normative structure are our contemporary vagrants, whether or not they are physically mobile—skidrow alcoholics, drug users, persons who have committed a crime, sexual deviants, etc. They are likely to inhabit the modern-day houses of correction—prisons and mental hospitals—and they continue to carry the scorn of their society.

Public and Private Responsibility for the Needy. The enduring dislocations of industrialism created need on a scale beyond the resources of the informal welfare system. The result was the development of two types of structured social welfare: public and private. Publicly supported social welfare has always been the more important of the two because it is societal recognition of its responsibility to its members. Private social welfare depends on the personal sense of responsibility of individuals, and requires that they voluntarily forego some of their own resources to help others. In some this sense of responsibility does not exist, while in others available resources are too limited to allow any to be contributed to help others. Private contributions are also heavily dependent on societal economic health. On the other hand, until the 1930s private social welfare often met people's needs more adequately and comprehensively than did the then-minimal public system. Private services also served to stimulate the development of more adequate public services. However, public services have always been the barometer of societal attitudes toward the needy. Especially since 1935, public social services have come to dominate the society's social welfare system, reflecting changed attitudes toward helping.

Financial Aid, Social Services, and Special Groups. Two of the enduring issues in the provision of social welfare services have been deciding for whom society is responsible, and what needs should be met. Beginning with a focus on basic survival needs (food, money, shelter, health care) there has been a gradual expansion to include more socially oriented services—marital counseling, job skills, mental health, recreation, group participation, and the like. One way in which this has occurred is by focusing on special groups—children, the aged, the handicapped, the mentally ill, and prisoners—and developing a comprehensive network of services to meet their needs. This has generally led to a fragmented service delivery network (the aged are helped by programs different from those for children, or veterans, or the retarded), but still a gradually expanding network of increasingly comprehensive services has developed. Part of the reason for the initial focus on just one type of service (such as financial aid) or a special group whose needs seem so obvious (dependent children, for example) lies in society's struggle to define those who are deserving of need. Another part of the reason lies in changing and developing awareness of the causes of and solutions to need. And a third factor lies in historical accident—the existence of a Dorothea Dix, Jane Addams, or Michael Harrington to document need in a particular group, and often to fight for the development of services to meet identified need.

Professionalizing Social Welfare. There has been a progression in social welfare from informal services, to structured services, to structured professional services. Several factors have contributed to this progression: the increasing numbers of services provided and users served; the growth of the social sciences, making the measurement of social behavior possible and demonstrating the complexity of social behavior; and the expansion of the concept of social welfare beyond mere survival to include complex social behaviors. Although some other societies have well-developed social welfare systems that are informal in structure, in contemporary Western, industrialized societies the professionalization of social welfare is an indication of the society's commitment to social welfare goals.

The Quest for Social Justice. The very concept of social welfare suggests a concern with social justice in its attempt to share social resources with those in need. Early attempts to meet need were focused on physical needs for food, shelter, and nurturance. Gradually individual autonomy became another right recognized by society, and was reflected in a concern with adequate psychological functioning and personal care in such places as prisons and mental hospitals. The professionalizing of social welfare emphasized individualizing people and problems, so that services were adapted to individual needs. A much later development has been recognition of a need for social participation, the right of people to have input into social policy-making and service delivery. Paternalistic views of minority groups by majority groups are increasingly repudiated as unjust. Racial, ethnic, age, and sex groups are all being seen as having the right to determine their own destinies. Social justice means the right to equal participation in societal decision-making, and equal access to social resources. As the survival needs of people as physical beings have been more adequately met, society has been able to turn to the survival of people as social beings. Much of the future of social welfare will be in the development of a society characterized by higher levels of social justice.

STUDY QUESTIONS
1. What impact did the Industrial Revolution (including its earliest manifestations) have on the development of the social welfare institution? How did it affect the social welfare institution by affecting other institutions, such as the family? What type of new needs were created by such effects of the Industrial Revolution as new work patterns, new community structures, and new political forms?

2. Why was the Social Security Act such a significant piece of legislation when passed in 1935? Do you consider the Economic Opportunity Act as significant a piece of legislation in terms of its effects on the services provided and its impact on the way in which services are structured? Why or why not?

3. Taking a broad historical perspective, would you say that we have reason to be optimistic or pessimistic about the future of the social welfare institution? Do you think it will ever meet all the major needs people experience? Do you think it is now or will ever be an accepted part of the American social structure? Support your argument with specific historical references.

REFERENCES

1. Philip Klein, *From Philanthropy to Social Welfare* (San Francisco: Jossey-Bass, 1968), p. 10.
2. S. H. Steinberg, ed., *A New Dictionary of British History* (New York: St. Martin's Press, 1963), p. 280.
3. Blanche D. Coll, *Perspectives in Public Welfare* (Washington, D.C.: Government Printing Office, 1969), p. 2; Wallace Notestein, *The English People on the Eve of Colonization* (New York: Harper & Row, 1954), p. 245.
4. Samuel Mencher, *Poor Law to Poverty Program* (Pittsburgh: University of Pittsburgh Press, 1967), p. 11.
5. Klein, op. cit., p. 11.
6. Actually the Statute of Labourers of 1349 is sometimes regarded as the first poor law in England. For a good summary discussion of the breakup of feudal organization, and the replacing of church authority by secular power, see Paul A. Kurzman, "Poor Relief in Medieval England: The Forgotten Chapter in the History of Social Welfare," *Child Welfare* 49 (November 1970): 459–501.
7. E. M. Leonard, *The Early History of the English Poor Relief* (New York: Barnes & Noble, 1965), p. 16.
8. Mencher, op. cit., p. 12.
9. Russell Smith and Dorothy Zeitz, *American Social Welfare Institutions* (New York: John Wiley, 1970), p. 14.
10. Leonard, op. cit., p. 137.
11. Coll, op. cit., p. 9.
12. Mencher, op. cit., p. 27.
13. Steinberg, op. cit., pp. 174–75.
14. Coll, op. cit., p. 10.
15. Ibid., p. 14.
16. Ibid., p. 18.
17. Mencher, op. cit., p. 144.
18. Coll, op. cit., p. 20.
19. Nathan E. Cohen, *Social Work in the American Tradition* (New York: Dryden Press, 1958), p. 49.
20. Coll, op. cit., p. 30.
21. Ibid., pp. 36–37.
22. Smith and Zeitz, op. cit., p. 43.
23. Ibid.
24. Frank Bruno, *Trends in Social Work* (New York: Columbia University Press, 1957), p. 108.

25. Cohen, loc. cit.
26. Ibid., p. 7.
27. Coll, op. cit., p. 60.
28. Ibid., p. 63.
29. Walter Friedlander, *Introduction to Social Welfare* (Englewood Cliffs, N.J.: Prentice-Hall, 1961), p. 107.
30. Coll, op. cit., p. 63.
31. Friedlander, op. cit., p. 113.
32. Coll, op. cit., p. 72.
33. Friedlander, op. cit., p. 114.
34. Ibid., p. 116.
35. Arthur P. Miles, *An Introduction to Social Welfare* (Boston: D.C. Heath and Company, 1949), p. 200.
36. Ibid., p. 200.
37. Coll, op. cit., p. 74.
38. Miles, op. cit., p. 175.
39. Coll, op. cit., p. 81.
40. Richard H. Bremner, *American Philanthropy* (Chicago: University of Chicago Press, 1960), p. 117.
41. Bruno, op. cit., p. 232.
42. Bremner, loc. cit.
43. Coll, loc. cit.
44. Mencher, op. cit., p. 363.
45. Ibid.
46. Duncan M. MacIntyre, *Public Assistance—Too Much or Too Little?* (Ithaca: New York State School of Industrial and Labor Relations, Cornell University, 1964), p. 14.
47. Mencher, loc. cit.
48. Miles, op. cit., p. 219.
49. MacIntyre, op. cit., p. 15.
50. Miles, op. cit., p. 224.
51. Daniel Bell, ed., *The Radical Right* (New York: Anchor, 1964), p. 213.
52. Smith and Zeitz, op. cit., p. 101.
53. Ibid., p. 107.
54. Ibid., p. 108.
55. Ibid., p. 200.
56. Ibid., p. 151.
57. Clair Wilcox, *Toward Social Welfare* (Homewood: Richard D. Irwin, 1969), pp. 360–77.
58. John Romanyshyn, *Social Welfare: Charity to Justice* (New York: Random House, 1971), pp. 173–75, 219–22, 231–32.
59. David Hardcastle, "General Revenue Sharing and Social Work," *Social Work* 18 (September 1973): 3–4. Reprinted by permission of the National Association of Social Workers.
60. Ibid., p. 7.
61. "Monitoring Revenue Sharing," *Washington Bulletin*, Vol. 23, Issue 42, September 23, 1974, p. 170.
62. Ibid., p. 172.
63. A more complete summary may be found in Romanyshyn, op. cit., 258–90; and the President's Commission on Income Maintenance Programs, *Working*

Papers (Washington, D.C.: Government Printing Office, 1969), Part III, pp. 407–55.

64. A clear comparison of children's allowances and the negative income tax is in Irwin Garfinkel, "Negative Income Tax and Children's Allowance Programs: A Comparison," *Social Work* (October 1968): 33–39.

SELECTED READINGS The history of social welfare is an area that is exceedingly well-covered in published materials. These works give a good overview, and the more recent books are thorough yet concise.

Coll, Blanche. *Perspectives in Public Welfare: A History.* Washington, D.C.: Government Printing Office, 1969.

Feagin, Joe. *Subordinating the Poor: Welfare and American Beliefs.* Englewood Cliffs, N.J.: Prentice-Hall, 1975.

Kershaw, Joseph. *Government against Poverty.* Chicago: Markham, 1970.

Komisar, Lucy. *Down and Out in the USA: A History of Social Welfare.* New York: New Viewpoints, 1974.

Lubove, Roy. *The Professional Altruist.* New York: Atheneum, 1969.

Schottland, Charles. "The Changing Roles of Government and Family," in Paul Weinberger, ed., *Perspectives on Social Welfare.* 2nd ed. New York: Macmillan, 1974, pp. 120–35.

Smith, Russell, and Dorothy Zeitz. *American Social Welfare Institutions.* New York: Wiley, 1970.

Steiner, Gilbert. *The State of Welfare.* Washington, D.C.: Brookings Institution, 1971.

Trattner, Walter. *From Poor Law to Welfare State: A History of Social Welfare in America.* New York: Free Press, 1974.

3

Planning, Structuring, and Evaluating Social Welfare Services

SOCIAL WELFARE as a concept is only as good as its implementation. The concept is fundamental to the creation of a service delivery system, yet the way in which services are structured has an enormous impact on the effectiveness of those services. Remembering that social welfare is an institution existing within a larger societal institutional network, we can expect that the way in which social welfare services are structured will reflect societal values and practices concerning the organization of activities. The Industrial Revolution began the process of work specialization and mass production, events that have led to the highly complex and centralized bureaucratic structures with which we are all familiar today. These massive but impersonal forms of organizing workers and their activities have been adopted by most social welfare service delivery systems, in part because of their success in obtaining and expanding their societal mandate to provide a growing range of services. When over one million persons receive public assistance in New York City alone,[1] a highly sophisticated service delivery system is necessary. Consequently the social welfare practitioner has become a professional, a paid person working in an organizational setting with specialized training and a codified set of professional values and skills.

The use of specialized large-scale forms of work organization is pervasive in contemporary American society. The society takes pride in the standard of living its citizens enjoy through mass production techniques. There have been problems in the use of these techniques in delivering services to people, however. When shopping it can be annoying to have to go to several salespersons and check-out counters to obtain all of the items one needs, although this system allows the store to maximize its sales and distribution efficiency. Dealing with a set of salespersons who are only trained in the sale of one particular item can also be frustrating, although it again permits the efficiency of in-depth specialized knowledge. While these situations are only annoyances to most of us, their prevalence in social welfare service delivery contexts can be serious obstacles to effective service delivery. Peoples' problems tend to come in groups, making it difficult to provide specialized services, each of which deals with one problem or one aspect of a problem. (The case studies in the Appendix to this book provide examples of this point.) The values of social welfare professionals also create problems within highly specialized service delivery systems, since they emphasize meaningful relationships with users and a commitment to solving peoples' problems—not part of them. It becomes evident that the interaction of the bureaucratic form of organization and social welfare professions is an area of considerable importance for the student of social welfare.

BUREAUCRATIC MODEL OF ORGANIZATION

The bureaucracy is a way to formally organize a variety of people and activities into "a system of control based on rational rules."[2] When organizational goals and means can be specified, when tasks can be broken into their component parts and rationally organized, and when tasks can be organized into hierarchical spheres of control, a bureaucracy can be an extremely effective form of social organization. For example, the calculation and payment of Social Security benefits is relatively straightforward, and is generally conceded to be effectively accomplished by the Social Security Administration bureaucracy. Because the bureaucratic form of organization is the major one in contemporary American society, its pervasiveness encourages its use in all organizational contexts. Its appropriateness in social welfare contexts, however, depends on the nature of social welfare tasks to be performed and their suitability for the organizational characteristics of bureaucracies.

The formal characteristics of bureaucracies may be summarized as follows: (1) a high degree of specialization; (2) hierarchical authority structure with specified areas of command and responsibility; (3) impersonal relations between members; (4) recruitment of members on the basis of ability; and (5) differentiation of personal and official resources.[3] In the ideal bureaucracy, rational rules govern behavior, and individuals are expected to interact as organizational role occupants rather than as unique individuals. Given the above characteristics, a bureaucracy has several potential advantages: efficiency in the performance of set tasks in set ways by trained bureaucrats; predictable behavior; behavior that stresses competence more than personal feelings; and the possibility of rapid goal attainment given the trained personnel and routinized activity.

On the other hand, the bureaucracy has several potential disadvantages. It can become quite inefficient when its highly formalized structure must be changed. It can be inhuman in responding to the human needs of those within it, which can seriously affect the motivation of workers and in turn impair both the quantity and quality of productivity. Workers can become so highly specialized that they may be unable to adapt to new working conditions and tasks (trained incapacity), as well as losing sight of goals by focusing so intensively on the means (technicism). Finally, in an attempt to gain personal satisfaction and power from the basically impersonal, rational structure, various types of informal organization may arise.[4] Such organization may either supplement the formal organization and increase productivity,[5] or it may conflict with the formal organization and disrupt or restrict productivity.[6] Exhibit 3-1 illustrates two aspects of bureaucratic organization.

PROFESSIONAL MODEL OF ORGANIZATION

In contrast to the formal, hierarchical structure and emphasis on predetermined goals and means, which characterize bureaucracies, professions have rather different characteristics. Hall identifies the following five characteristics of professions: (1) the use of the professional organization as a major reference; (2) a belief in service to the public; (3) belief in self-regulation; (4) a sense of calling to the field; and (5) professional autonomy.[7] Using the profession as a major reference can be seen in the various professional social welfare organizations, such as the National Association of Social Workers. They usually have local chapters that offer their members a full range of services and activities, including meetings to exchange information and plan professional activities, group life insurance, professional publications, certification, and group travel arrangements. It is through such mechanisms that the professional's identity is reinforced and maintained.

EXHIBIT 3-1

Aspects of Bureaucratic Organization

There are two aspects of bureaucratic organization illustrated in this exhibit. Table 1 illustrates the structure within one organization, in this case the National Association of Social Workers. In the organizational chart of the staff organization of this professional association, the specialization and complex interrelationships between positions is evident. This chart is taken from NASW's "Educational Legislative Action Network—Operations Manual" (1972). Table 2 illustrates the magnitude of the effort at the federal level to organize a vast range of services occurring within many different specialized structures. While the Department of Health, Education, and Welfare encompasses the major social welfare planning and service programs at the federal level, a variety of other agencies perform some aspect of the social welfare task. Note that each of these agencies would have a complex organizational chart such as the one illustrated in Table 1, and that there is no agency that has as its primary responsibility coordinating the various tasks of all of these agencies. Specialization and division of labor may be necessary, but when a service delivery and planning structure becomes as elaborate as many of those currently existing, the problem of coordination is a major and often ignored part of the structure. Table 2 is abstracted from information provided in NASW's *Encyclopedia of Social Work* (1971). The information is not intended to be a complete description of the federal social welfare structure; it is simply illustrative.

Table 1 from "Educational Legislative Action Network—Operations Manual" (Washington: NASW, 1972), following p. 37. Table 2 (shown on p. 92, below) from *Encyclopedia of Social Work*, Vol. 16 (New York: NASW, 1971), pp. 1440–45. Both tables used by permission.

TABLE 1 Staff Organization of the National Association of Social Workers as of September 1, 1971

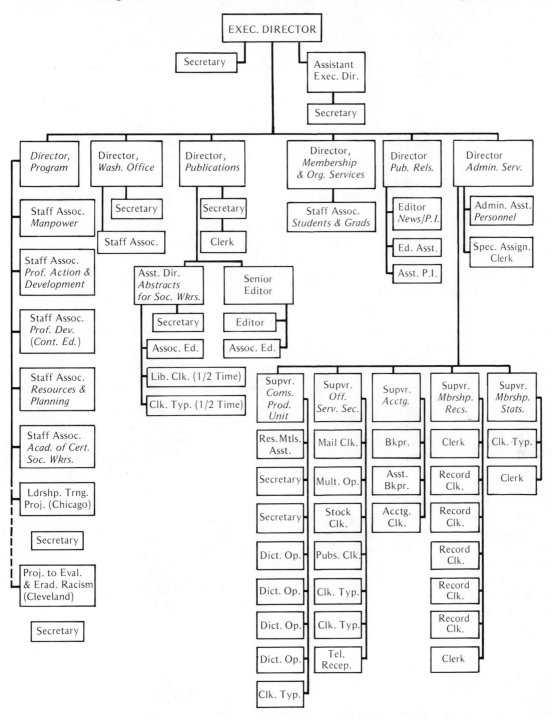

TABLE 2 An Overview of Federal Social Welfare Programs

Dept. of Health, Education, and Welfare
  Social Security Administration—
    OASDHI, SSI
  Social & Rehabilitation Service
    Administration of the Aging—
      services to the aged
    Assistance Payments administration—
      public assistance payments
    Medical Services Administration—Medicaid
    Rehabilitation Services Administration—
      makes rehabilitation grants, promotes
      research activities
    Community Services Administration—
      public assistance services and community
      action programs
    Cuban Refugee Program
    Office of Urban Development (Model Cities)
    Office of Citizen Participation—
      volunteer services
  Office of Education
    Bureau of Elementary and Secondary
      Education—special education
    Teacher Corps
    College student loans, adult education services,
      education for the handicapped, guidance,
      counseling & testing grants, etc.
  Public Health Service
    Health Services and Mental Health
      Administration—comprehensive health
      planning services, grants, research, training
    Consumer Protection and Environmental
      Health Service—food & drugs, pollution
    National Institutes of Health—
      research programs
  Howard University
  Gallaudet College (for the deaf)
  American Printing House for the Blind

Department of Agriculture—school lunch, school
  milk, food stamp programs, home economist
  services to rural areas & farmers

Department of Commerce
  Area Redevelopment Administration—
    chronic unemployment area assistance

Department of Labor
  Bureau of Apprenticeship and Training—
    improve skills of the work force
  Bureau of Employee's Compensation—
    for special groups, establishing general
    guidelines

Bureau of Employment Security
  Unemployment
    Insurance
    Service   state-run under
  U.S. Employment   federal guidance
    Service

Bureau of Labor Standards—industrial safety

Bureau of Labor Statistics—research

Women's Bureau—welfare of
  wage-earning women

Bureau of Veterans' Reemployment Rights

Office of Manpower Administration—
  development and training

Department of the Interior
  Bureau of Indian Affairs

  Bureau of Outdoor Recreation—research grants

  National Park Service—outdoor
    recreation services and facilities

Department of Justice
  Bureau of Prisons—runs federal prisons

  Immigration and Naturalization Service

  Board of Parole

  Halfway houses and other services

Department of Defense—armed
  forces social services

  Office of Civil Defense—social
    welfare services in national emergencies

Department of Housing and Urban Development
  Federal Housing Administration—
    insures mortgage loans and has
    rent-supplement program

  Urban renewal, housing for poor and
    handicapped, Model Cities, etc.

Department of State
  Agency for International Development (AID)—
    grants and assistance to foreign countries
    for national development; participates in
    welfare work of various international
    organizations

  Organization of American States
    Pan-American Health Organization
    Inter-American Indian Institute
    Inter-American Children's Institute

Using the profession as a reference combines with a belief in service to the public to make the specific organization in which a professional works less important than his professional mission. Dunbar and Jackson, talking about social workers working in free clinics, express the ideal of professional commitment: "Accomplishing a job and delivering a service are more important to them than hours, pay, professional status, recognition, or conventional agency procedures."[8] So, while a bureaucracy concentrates on procedures to help it most efficiently attain its objectives, professionals concentrate on meeting human needs within the framework of professional values, and the two are not always compatible.

A belief in self-regulation and professional autonomy results from the specialized knowledge bases and socialization procedures that characterize professions. For example, physical therapists have specialized knowledge of the human anatomy and technical skills derived from that knowledge. Both are learned through a well-documented socialization process.[9] Professionals maintain that nonprofessionals are not equipped to evaluate their competence, since the nonprofessional has not mastered the specialized knowledge base. It follows that professionals must be trusted to evaluate each other, and impose necessary sanctions when appropriate. This in turn makes it difficult for the consumer to sanction the professional. However, professional organizations are sometimes too weak to be effective regulating bodies (social work, for example). In some rare instances, gross incompetence may be overlooked to protect the professional image from potentially intrusive legal action (medicine is a case in point). In these unusual situations, professional autonomy may interfere with service delivery.

A belief in service to the public and a calling to the field are important in creating a professional value system. Such values are often codified by the professional organization, and these set the standard for professional behavior. In the social service professions, such values usually emphasize the value of human life and personal integrity, the significance of knowledge, judgment, and self-awareness to help others in a professional way, and the equal accessibility of service to all who need it. For example, medicine has its Hippocratic Oath, and social work values emphasize client self-determination, confidentiality, and impartiality. Exhibit 3-2 looks at social work values in some detail.

There are several problems that emerge from the bureaucratization of professional behavior. One is the need for bureaucratic structure versus the need for professional autonomy. A bureaucracy attempts to structure its positions in such a way that authority and responsibility are clearly specified. In this way, the organization has control over the behavior of its members, and intervention points are specified in the event that something goes wrong. This kind of structure automatically creates differences between participants in the organization. Since some have more power than others, there is an implicit or explicit assertion that some are more knowledgeable and skilled than others. This type of structure makes it very difficult to have the sharing between equals that a profession assumes. A profession recognizes that some of its members are more skilled than others, but the assumption is that all are at least minimally skilled, and that a continual process of member communication will serve to increase the skills of all. When professionals are forced to work in a superior-inferior relationship, as happens in many agencies using a supervisor-worker system, there is a real danger that there will be a loss of motivation in workers who have been trained to think autonomously. Barriers to innovation may also be created. This problem often surfaces in settings where one professional group is a minority in relationship to one or more others. John Wax's article exploring social work's power in a medical organization is an excellent example of this issue.[10]

EXHIBIT 3-2

Social Work Professional Values

The following is the Code of Ethics of the National Association of Social Workers (NASW), the social work professional association. Until 1969 only social workers holding the Master of Social Work degree were eligible for membership. In that year a membership category was created for graduates of B.A. social work programs approved (now accredited) by the Council on Social Work Education, reflecting the increasing differential use of manpower in the social welfare professions. This NASW Code of Ethics is a good example of the codification of professional values, although naturally in practice there may be some deviation from such values. This Code of Ethics was provided by the National Office of NASW in Washington, D.C.

Social work is based on humanitarian ideals. Professional social workers are dedicated to service for the welfare of mankind; to the disciplined use of a recognized body of knowledge about human beings and their interactions; and to the marshaling of community resources to promote the well-being of all without discrimination.

Social work practice is a public trust that requires of its practitioners integrity, compassion, belief in the dignity and worth of human beings, respect for individual differences, a commitment to service, and a dedication to truth. It requires mastery of a body of knowledge and skill gained through professional education and experience. It requires

Reprinted by permission of the National Association of Social Workers.

also recognition of the limitations of present knowledge and skill and of the services we are now equipped to give. The end sought is the performance of a service with integrity and competence.

Each member of the profession carries responsibility to maintain and improve social work service; constantly to examine, use, and increase the knowledge upon which practice and social policy are based; and to develop further the philosophy and skills of the profession.

This Code of Ethics embodies certain standards of behavior for the social worker in his professional relationships with those he serves, with his colleagues, with his employing agency, with other professions, and with the community. In abiding by the code, the social worker views his obligations in as wide a context as the situation requires, takes all of the principles into consideration, and chooses a course of action consistent with the code's spirit and intent.

As a member of the National Association of Social Workers I commit myself to conduct my professional relationships in accord with the code and subscribe to the following statements:

- I regard as my primary obligation the welfare of the individual or group which includes action for improving social conditions.

- I give precedence to my professional responsibility over my personal interests.

- I hold myself responsible for the quality and extent of the service I perform.

- I respect the privacy of the people I serve.

- I use in a responsible manner information gained in professional relationships.

- I treat with respect the findings, views, and actions of colleagues, and use appropriate channels to express judgment on these matters.

- I practice social work within the recognized knowledge and competence of the profession.

- I recognize my professional responsibility to add my ideas and findings to the body of social work knowledge and practice.

- I accept responsibility to help protect the community against unethical practice by an individual or organization engaged in social welfare activities.

- I stand ready to give appropriate professional service in public emergencies.

- I distinguish clearly, in public, between my statements and actions as an individual and as a representative of an organization.

- I support the principle that professional practice requires professional education.

- I accept responsibility for working toward the creation and maintenance of conditions within agencies which enable social workers to conduct themselves in keeping with this code.

- I contribute my knowledge, skills and support to programs of human welfare.

- I will not discriminate because of race, color, religion, age, sex or national ancestry, and in my job capacity will work to prevent and eliminate such discrimination in rendering service, in work assignments and in employment practices.

A second problem is the need for bureaucratic structure versus the need for professional flexibility. The use of the profession as a major reference, belief in service to the public, and a sense of calling all demand a commitment to helping others on the basis of their need. Bureaucracies are concerned with specifying who is to receive service and under what circumstances— hours of work, forms to fill out, location of offices, qualifications of staff, allocation of resources, and so on. Stanton's study of the Pangloss Mental Health Association illustrates this problem when it describes a Christmas party for mental hospital inmates which meets bureaucratic needs and rules much more than client needs or desires.[11] The confrontation of bureaucratic rules and professional values is also seen in several major social welfare system problems:

1. *Gaps in service.* An agency sometimes offers only part of the services needed by a client, such as a Catholic Social Service agency that refuses to provide family planning information.

2. *Dividing the client.* In this situation, an agency divides up a client's problems into specialized parts, assigning different workers to deal with each part. Dividing the client and gaps in service can both be handled by referring clients to needed resources, but this requires follow-up to make sure that the referral has been successful. This often does not happen.

3. *Competition for resources.* Each organization seeks to preserve itself, and competes with other agencies for resources. Since each organization is accountable only for its own functioning, there is little encouragement for agencies to cooperate, although outside forces may require that they do so (United Fund drives or legislation mandating such cooperation, for example).

Exhibit 3-3 provides examples of some of these problems.

EXHIBIT **3-3**

Battered Freddy

The following is a discussion of Adam Kline's "Battered Freddy's New Chance at Childhood," an article that appeared in a 1970 issue of the *Baltimore Sun Magazine*. At the end of the exhibit, there is an analysis of the bureaucratic and professional issues involved.

At 17, one year after his parents were arrested for child abuse and he had had the benefit of warm professional care, Freddy was 4 ft. 6 in. and weighed 75 pounds. One of Freddy's doctors said, "I think he can grow to about five feet now, maybe a little more. . . . But it's pretty certain he'll always be stunted."

Before his aunt swore out a warrant for the arrest of Freddy's parents on child abuse charges, Freddy's name slipped in and out of the files of three city agencies, a private organization for retarded children, and the police, all to no avail.

1. A policewoman visited the home and, noting Freddy was small for his age, referred him

From Adam Kline, "Battered Freddy's New Chance at Childhood," *Baltimore Sun Magazine*, October 11, 1970, pp. 20ff. Used by permission.

to a special school at Rosewood State Hospital. "However, there were no vacancies at the time," and contact was ended.

2. Since Freddy was first brought to public school at age 12, he was not allowed to register as a regular student, and was referred to the Department of Education's Psychological Service Division for testing and evaluation. Contact was ended when "the Psychological Services Division was completely unsuccessful in getting the parents to bring Freddy in for an evaluation. . . ."

3. The Psychological Service Division referred Freddy to a public health nurse who noted "that although he was 12 years old, he seemed no more than 5." She made several attempts to get the parents to bring Freddy

to the Health Department's diagnostic and evaluation center, which they never did. After more than a year of frustrated attempts to have the boy taken to a doctor, and after an appointment at Johns Hopkins Hospital was broken by the parents, the nurse gave up.

4. The case was referred to the Baltimore Association for Retarded Children. After futile attempts at contact, "The Association notified the Health Department . . . that no progress could be made."

5. Referral was next made to the Department of Social Services. The worker there was allowed to take Freddy to the Department of Education for comprehensive psychological and intelligence testing. They recommended he be placed in a city school for trainable retarded children, but his parents refused to grant their permission. After another broken contact initiated by the parents, the Department of Education closed their file on Freddy. The Health Department did the same since it "had not been able to obtain evidence of physical maltreatment. . . ." This was followed by similar action by the Department of Social Services.

6. The warrant for the arrest of the parents was sworn out by Freddy's aunt.

Regarding this case, the agencies said:

Health Department. "There was never any evidence of physical maltreatment that we could get a handle on. . . . If we sense a case of child neglect, we can only turn it over to Social Services; technically it would do no good to notify the school system of truancy, because he was never registered in a school to begin with. If there is any department that could have taken it to Juvenile Court then, it's Social Services, not us."

Social Services. "A charge of contributing to the delinquency of a minor would be irrelevant. They kept him out of school, sure, but what school would have taken him anyway by the time it was brought to our attention? And not only that, he was almost 16, the age when school attendance becomes optional. If the parents weren't going to cooperate at that point, we felt there was nothing we could do. Look, it seems there was so much happening to the child, but we had no evidence of that; to tell the truth, we had no real evidence of anything other than that the boy was retarded and that they weren't doing anything to help him. The only way we could have found out more is by breaking down their front door, and this isn't a police state, we don't do things like that. The papers said the neighbors seemed to know what was going on, but, damn it, they never told us a thing."

ANALYSIS

This case is an excellent example of each agency having followed the rules, but none having solved the problem. Note that each agency is right—each one did what it was structured to do. However, in terms of fulfilling professional values, each was quite ineffective, and looking at this case from a professional value perspective, it is disheartening at best. This case is also a good example of many parts of the social welfare system being brought to bear on a problem, with several social service professions becoming involved. Note the ultimate reliance on the family to mobilize the social service network in a meaningful way, and the final ability of the system to act being based on the societal mandate given to certain professional systems (in this case the police) to forcibly intervene in the family. As the social service worker says, this is a serious decision requiring a great deal of evidence because of its police-state implications, and it illustrates the delicate societal decisions often encountered in social welfare work.

A third consideration is the effects of bureaucratic functioning on the provision of adequate services. It was noted above that bureaucracies tend to develop certain characteristics, many of which can interfere with the provision of services. For example, technicism, trained incapacity and informal organization can all impede bureaucratic functioning under some circumstances. Besides these potential problems, the very structure of a bureaucracy can be a problem:

> Youths trying to get help from an agency encountered multiple barriers, intended or otherwise. Rigid eligibility requirements that involved filling out long application forms prevented many from starting the process, caused some to give up in the middle, and turned many others away who were determined to be ineligible for service. Being minors away from home prevented many from receiving medical treatment. Being drug-users prevented many from receiving help without risking arrest. Other obstacles blocking agencies' service to street people were the long waits for service, entailing waiting lists and appointments at a future date instead of the date of contact, the extensive records, including extremely personal and sometimes socially damaging information . . . and the . . . cold atmosphere and middle-class appearance of the agency setting.[12]

Structure is the very nature of bureaucratic functioning—it is what gives it its durability and organization. Yet it also gives it a certain inflexibility and creates something of a barrier between it and those who use it. Especially when dealing with certain client groups, such as the street people described above, or in certain types of emergency or sensitive situations, bureaucratic structure can effectively prevent or distort service.

FINDING WAYS TO MAKE PROFESSIONS AND BUREAUCRACIES COMPATIBLE

Having raised some of the rather serious issues of appropriateness of the bureaucratic form of organization for professional tasks and characteristics, the alternatives need to be explored. The fact that so much of the social system in which the welfare network exists is bureaucratically organized, and given the massive scale at which the social welfare system operates, strong pressures are exerted on both social welfare professions and organizations to embrace bureaucratization. But the problems social welfare bureaucracies have in specifying goals is being increasingly recognized. Without such specification, it is impossible to organize a rational bureaucratic structure. The problems inherent in bureaucracies are also being felt. The social welfare system is today faced with the challenge of finding ways to provide large-scale, complex, specialized services in a more flexible, responsive, and effective manner. Although this search is in its infancy, some exciting possibilities are emerging.

After some years of increasing centralization of planning and services, decentralization is being explored as one means of providing more accessible and less rigid and formal services. Departments of Social Services in some locations are establishing neighborhood branches to decentralize their service. In many communities, food stamps may now be sold in banks and other neighborhood locations rather than just at the Department of Social Services.

Recreation programs are dispersing throughout many cities in the attempt to bring them closer to their users. This decentralization seems to hold a great deal of promise, but it is also limited. When highly specialized services are needed—psychological consultation or specialized medical care, for example—it will probably always be necessary to refer a client to a central facility, since the costs of having all services decentralized will probably remain prohibitive. Nevertheless, for the normal kinds of daily services people need, decentralization offers much hope as a way to enable professionals to function in a system that is structured and manageable, but also flexible and accessible.

A second promising experiment is with comprehensive neighborhood service centers that are not necessarily part of a large formal structure (as are the decentralized services discussed above). The free clinic is a model of this kind of organization. Dunbar and Jackson discuss the following characteristics of such facilities:[13]

1. *Trust.* Relations between professionals and users, and between professionals themselves, are characterized by compassion and acceptance regardless of the characteristics of the individual (unkempt hair, etc.) or his problem (drug use, etc.).

2. *Friendliness.* Professionals mingle with users on an informal basis, as well as having a more formal relationship with them. Users are not pressured and are free to make their own choices.

3. *Immediate service.* There are no waiting lists or eligibility requirements, although persons can make appointments if they wish to.

4. *Records.* Records are kept to a minimum in order to avoid labeling, protect users, and to minimize time taken away from working with the individual.

5. *Hours.* Hours are set which are responsive to the needs of the users. This usually means that there are evening hours instead of or in addition to daytime hours.

There are often ties between professional staff and more formally organized agencies, for referral purposes. The comprehensive neighborhood service center usually includes a range of professionals working together to provide as comprehensive a service as possible. They attempt to deal with people's needs as they exist rather than as organizations have planned for them. This tends to maximize professional commitment and self-regulation, and minimize formal structure. It can also lead to a scarcity of resources and lack of mandate by the larger professional and societal communities.

A third attempt to deal with the problems of the professional in the bureaucracy is the use of ombudsmen and indigenous persons. As was seen above, many problems of bureaucratic functioning entail a lack of accessibility, services that are too specialized, and obstacles to professionals operationalizing their commitment to provide service. One approach to these problems is to have a mechanism for users of a service to find out about services and have an advocate when they feel that their needs have not been met. The ombudsman accomplishes this, being a person or agency that reaches out into the community to identify need and help persons effectively use community services. This allows organizations to be as specialized and formal as they need to be and still provides a way for users not to get lost or crushed within them. It does not directly help professionals except that they are reassured that their services are reaching those needing them, and that bureaucratic obstacles are not seriously interfering with service. Indigenous personnel—that is, persons who live in the community being served—operate in a manner somewhat similar to ombudsmen in a social welfare agency. By being members of the community, they have greater knowledge about and access to it than would the typical professional person.

A fourth possibility is to work from within a bureaucratic structure to try to make it more compatible with professional objectives. A recent government report included the following order of priorities in modifying bureaucratic structures to increase agency effectiveness and worker satisfaction:

> (1) Agency goals—clear, common understanding of goals and commitment to them by agency personnel; (2) agency policies—common understanding of policies by all personnel; (3) communication adequacy—procedures and practices that insure timely transmission of required information to all personnel; (4) supervisory practices—actions that enhance the autonomy, initiative, and professional commitment of agency personnel; (5) agency-imposed constraints—reduction of excessive and unnecessary administrative controls; (6) stability of work environment—avoidance of excessive turbulence within the agency through careful planning and communication of required changes in programs, policies, and personnel; and (7) structure—optimization of complexity and formalization through reduction of administrative levels and increase in supervisory span of control.[14]

There appears to be considerable management flexibility in making bureaucratic structures more responsive to the goals and needs of those who work within them. However, it is well known that large-scale organizations tend to generate their own inertia, and one of the problems facing attempts to change bureaucracies from within will be their power to resist such change.

Other strategies for making bureaucracies more responsive to professional and client needs have been proposed. Delbert Taebel has proposed the following, based on the strategy that the less dependent the client is on the bureaucrat, the more responsive the bureaucracy will be.[15]

1. *Political pressure.* Mobilizing professional and client resources to try to bring political pressure on bureaucracies to achieve change. This tactic has been used in a variety of ways, including sit-ins, nonviolent protests, lobbying, the creation of the National Welfare Rights Organization, and unionizing social welfare workers.

2. *Developing competitive structures.* To the extent that the social welfare service delivery system is a monopoly, this is a difficult strategy to pursue, although free clinics may be one possibility.

3. *Positive input.* Having professional and client groups support the useful aspects of the bureaucracy, building good will within the structure for use when there are grievances against it.

4. *Self-help programs.* A strategy for developing competitive structures as well as fostering autonomy and self-help. This is limited by lack of resources and expertise, but might be made possible by obtaining grant monies and using volunteer professional assistance.

5. *Boycotting or overloading the system.* Boycotting the service delivery system is difficult because people usually are dependent on it for their basic needs. Overloading the system—that is, having everyone eligible request everything for which they are eligible—has been used as a successful strategy to force an organization to respond to the needs of professionals and clients. These strategies are perhaps more difficult to implement than earlier ones mentioned, but are nevertheless potential tools for change.

None of the attempts to overcome the limitations of bureaucracies discussed above completely solves the problems noted. Even in using these possible strategies, however, it is wise to exercise care in mounting too great an assault against bureaucracies. In spite of the problems that have been noted, the bureaucracy gives some semblance of order and objectivity to the massive, fragmented social welfare system, and gives it some strength relative to competing societal structures. Yet at the same time it can block the humane attainment of social welfare goals and in so doing erode professional motivation and performance. This leads to what can be called the professional's dilemma.

There are some fundamental decisions the professional must make in trying to reach a personal solution to structural conflict. The first is deciding how much of one's responsibility is to the agency for which one works and how much is to the clients one serves. If the balance of one's commitment is to the agency, then there will be a tendency to follow established agency rules rather than challenging those rules when they interfere with attempts to provide service to clients. For example, once when working with an unmarried mother, it seemed appropriate to have contact with the father of the child, who had been uncooperative in all previous attempts to meet with him. Since he worked at a job where he was paid by the hour, he was understandably reluctant to come to the office during the agency's hours, since they coincided with his work hours. The impasse was finally broken by arranging an appointment after agency hours, but this was against agency policy and required some considerable negotiation and special arrangements within the agency. Such agency rule-bending naturally carries risks, since bureaucracies tend to invest considerable normative value in their rules. The risks will be worth assuming only if service to the client is the primary consideration in a particular situation.

A related decision involves the extent of one's identification with an agency's goals compared to identifying with professional goals. When agency goals are dominant, there will usually be more willingness to follow agency procedures rather than adopting a more flexible approach to problems growing out of professional values and skills. For example, when working in a Catholic agency, in which it was against agency policy to discuss birth control with clients, a social worker had to deal with a woman having personal, marital, and child-rearing problems, and who was frightened of becoming pregnant again. Professional judgment suggested that birth control was an appropriate part of the helping relationship, at least until the other problems could be resolved, but agency policy forbade it. In this situation, the woman's own ambivalence about birth control was substantial, given that fact that she was Catholic, but it appeared that she was seeking some support to confront this issue in a way that would still enable her to maintain a healthy image of herself. Ultimately a discussion about planning and developing a plan for birth control did occur, but again, there were considerable agency repercussions.

A third decision involves the willingness to inconvenience oneself if necessary to help others. A desire to keep one's professional commitment within clearly delimited boundaries tends to make the order, predictability, and limited range of activities of the bureaucracy more appealing. A final decision relates to the commitment to follow social norms versus a belief in the appropriateness of norm violation when necessary. Adherence to the established social norms tends to make it more likely that the bureaucracy's inherently conservative qualities will be accepted.

Clearly these four decisions are related, and have related consequences. The professional who generally accepts the limits defined by the bureaucracy will tend to resist any information or pressures that suggest his or her work is ineffective. To the extent that such pressures exist, the worker may be tempted to minimize professional identification; or, if the pressures are great enough, the professional may resolve the problem by retreating into apathy or simply leaving the field. Decisions made favoring professional values and commitment are likely to generate substantial frustration with bureaucratic limitations. These frustrations can lead to frequent job changes in the search for a more acceptable structure, cynical exploitation of the bureaucratic structure to attain one's professional goals, or direct confrontation with the bureaucratic structure. Such confrontation can take many forms—personal actions, such as complaints or suggestions for more appropriate bureaucratic regulations; group actions, such as strikes, petitions, or informal organizations to counteract the bureaucratic structure; or group organization, as in the mobilization of consumer power to intervene in the agency structure, in political action, or in conjunction with other professional groups.

The ways in which the professional's dilemma can be solved are many and varied. Some are consistent with professional values, while others are closer to bureaucratic rules. Some are conservative, and others are more radical. Some involve quiet, personal thoughts; others include involvement in turbulent political and organizational activities. Which are selected comes down to a very personal decision based on one's financial and personal needs. Exhibit 3–4, below, illustrates how one doctor dealt with his dilemma.

EXHIBIT **3-4**

One Man's Solution

The following story is taken from *Parade Magazine*, September 15, 1974. It illustrates how each professional must accept responsibility for his own professional dilemmas, and how the creative professional can find solutions that are professionally sound, personally satisfying, and helpful to clients.

Dr. Richard E. Palmer, chairman of the American Medical Association's board of trustees, said recently that physicians were not trying hard enough to reduce medical costs.

One physician, perhaps the most unusual in the country, whom Palmer was not referring to is Dr. Richard Grayson, an internist who practices medicine in St. Charles, Ill., a town of some 10,000 people, 35 miles west of Chicago.

Dr. Grayson tells all his patients that if they judge the bills he sends them to be out-of-line, they can reduce them as they wish.

The Grayson method is to enclose with each monthly bill a [signed] note which reads: "My fee schedule is based upon standard medical practice in this area. However, for retired persons on limited pensions, or any others whose circumstances are difficult due to extensive illness, unemployment, or for any other reasons, I will reduce my fees."

"Under these circumstances," the note continues, "I suggest a 25 percent reduction, but more or less may be appropriate to your situation. No discussion is necessary—simply write the amount

of reduction you choose on the statement with your remittance."

Dr. Grayson, 49, has been using this technique since 1969 when he read an article in *Medical Economics*. Recently he was publicized in *AMA Update*, the newsletter published by the American Medical Association, and reports, "I'm taking quite a bit of kidding from my colleagues. They're offering to send me all their poor-paying patients."

According to Grayson, "Money—or the lack of it—is the cause of emotional stress in some families these days. Emotional distress often leads to ulcers and other physical ailments. I see plenty of ulcer patients already; and I'd just as soon that my bills did not create more."

Grayson says that only 2 or 3 percent of his patients reduce the bills he sends out and that only one, a young father who had just lost his job, ever asked him to write off the bill.

Grayson modestly insists that he is neither altruist nor philanthropist. "I feel," he explains, "that arguments with patients about bills can interfere with my emotions for hours. It can stimulate all sorts of stress, and who needs that? Neither I nor the patient."

A rare physician, Dr. Richard Grayson. Are there many more like him?

From *Parade Magazine*, September 15, 1974, p. 21. Used by permission of Parade Magazine, Inc.

There are no best solutions; there are only those that each individual can devise and accept for himself. Finding acceptable solutions is difficult and their impact will only be known when actually on the job. However, early recognition of the interaction between societal, bureaucratic, and professional values will foster a mature approach to the fundamental value and organizational issues that underlie the contemporary social welfare institution in American society.

ACCOUNTABILITY
AND
EFFECTIVENESS
IN SOCIAL
WELFARE

Throughout this discussion of the organization of social welfare services has been the underlying thread of effectiveness. As the system grows in size and complexity, the need for resources also increases. Since resources always involve policy decisions based on priorities, the social welfare system is increasingly being asked to prove its effectiveness and efficiency, thereby justifying the allocation of further resources to it. As Newman and Turem note, "Efficiency involves weighing alternatives against costs."[16] However, they further explain that "efficiency . . . does not mean that what is done is done for the lowest cost but that the ends achieved cannot be brought about in another way or an even lower cost."[17] These authors go on to assert that "the current crisis in social services is a crisis of credibility based on an inadequate system of accountability. Social programs are in trouble because they focus on processes and not results."[18] This goes back to the very heart of formal organizations—they can only be effective if they can specify their goals and the means to be used to achieve these goals. One of the persisting problems of social welfare organizations, and one that is being seriously attacked today, is their inability to specify exactly what actions will yield what results.

The whole question of accountability has created anxiety and resentment among many social welfare professionals. Indeed, Rosenberg and Brody entitled an article "The Threat or Challenge of Accountability."[19] In the attempt to meet criticisms raised against the social welfare service delivery system, management by objectives has become popular (often referred to as MBO). Exhibit 3–5 looks at MBO in some detail. The fear which accountability and MBO raise in the minds of many social welfare professionals is that the search for proof of efficiency and effectiveness will yield a service delivery system that is arbitrary in its definitions of what services will be provided, and limited in its perspective on human needs. This is a realistic fear. There have already been numerous examples of programs which, in their effort to prove themselves both efficient and effective, have focused only on those users who showed the most potential for success, and focused on services that could be easily measured or counted—number who got jobs, number of housing units rehabilitated, number of children enrolled in school, and so forth. These programs may indeed have been very successful in performing such tasks, but one of the enduring problems of a social welfare system is to help those least able to understand and use services, and to deal with those complexities of human functioning and need which are not so easily measured or so rapidly accomplished—curing mental illness, improving self-acceptance and feelings of self-worth, improving child-rearing values and behaviors, coping with permanent and total disability, providing meaningful life patterns for the isolated aged, among others.

EXHIBIT 3-5

Management by Objectives

In the search for more effective and efficient ways to provide social welfare services, new approaches to management and the utilization of resources are being explored. One of the most popular has been management by objectives, which is described below. This material is taken from Jane W. Bailey, *MBO Objective Statements: What They Are, How to Write Them, How Not to Write Them* (1974).

STATING IN TERMS OF RESULTS

MBO emphasizes planning toward *RESULTS,* the *final product* one is planning to produce. The assumption behind this emphasis is that one is more likely to get where he's going if he knows where he's headed before he begins. Knowing one's precise destination enables him to better plan the means he should use to get there.

There are four levels of RESULTS-oriented statements in MBO, as practiced by the Department of Human Resources:

1. *GOAL*—Broad, general statement(s) of the overall "mission" to be accomplished on any level.

2. *OBJECTIVE*—More concise, specific, measurable, limited statement(s) under the goal statement.

3. *STRATEGY*—Statement of the "means" to accomplish the "ends"; the dated major action steps one takes to accomplish an objective.

4. *MILESTONES*—Breakdown of strategy steps into completed pieces of action, charted according to dates and numbers.

Used by permission of the North Carolina Division of Human Resources.

Each level of planning is derived from and integrated into one preceding it.

In MBO, the key RESULTS-oriented statement is the *objective.* It is really a working plan in precise statement form. When one learns the correct way to write it, he should have no difficulty in being able to write the other results-oriented statements.

A good objective is *specific, measurable, limited in time, realistic, a commitment between a supervisor and supervisee* (or worker and client; or co-workers, etc.) and *integrated into the total organization.*

CHARACTERISTICS OF WELL-WRITTEN OBJECTIVES

First, should identify what the individual must be able to *DO* or *PERFORM* when demonstrating accomplishment of the objective. This should be stated in terms that are clear, understandable, and not subject to a wide range of interpretation.

Vague examples:
to know . . . ; to understand . . . ; to appreciate . . . ; to believe . . . ; to enjoy . . . ; to enable . . . ; to serve . . . ; to accept . . . ; to realize . . . ; to develop . . . ; to sense . . . ; to be aware . . . ; to feel . . .

(*Note:* One *can* use these in objective statements provided he states what he *means* by them: the criteria for measuring their accomplishment.)

Clearer examples:

to identify . . . ; to increase . . . ; to decrease . . . ; to list . . . ; to prevent . . . ; to clarify . . . ; to decide . . . ; to interpret . . . ; to change . . . ; to complete . . . ; to begin . . . ; to refer . . . ; to accompany . . . ; to transport . . . ; to type . . . ; to purchase . . . ; to terminate . . . .

Second, should state the criteria for *HOW WELL* you want the individual (or group) to be able to perform the objective.

Examples:

1. Indicate a time limit (by June 30, 1974 . . . ; within 10 days . . . ; at 3-month intervals beginning on July 1, 1974 . . . ; 3 hours per day . . . ; 100 words per minute . . .)
2. Specify *numbers* to be achieved, affected, reached, etc. (increase from 200 to 350 . . . ; a minimum of 35 AFDC mothers . . .)

3. Indicate the *cost factor* (at a cost not to exceed $1,500 . . . ; to decrease County funding from $4,000 to $2,500 . . .)

*4. Indicate *percentage or proportion* (30 percent of new cases . . . ; 45 percent of VR clients referred . . . ; 70 percent of couples seeking counseling . . . ; 90 percent of service time . . . ; 3 percent error rate . . .)

Third, should describe any special *CONDITIONS* under which accomplishment of the objective is to occur. These usually name extenuating circumstances, particular barriers, reality factors, hardships, etc.

Caution: When using a percentage, be sure there is some way of measuring it. Don't include a percentage in a statement just to make it "look good," if there's no reliable means for calculating it. . . .

The contemporary thrust toward efficiency and effectiveness is good. If social welfare professionals seek to improve social functioning and minimize suffering, they must have some techniques to measure whether or not their actions are accomplishing these goals. If they are not, they must find new ways to try to deal with peoples' needs. With limited resources available to the social welfare system, it is a professional obligation to use these resources in the most effective manner. The accusation that there has been too much emphasis on process rather than results—that is, how many persons were counseled rather than how many persons that were counseled received some measurable benefit from such counseling—is a valid one, and will be explored in more detail later when looking at social work interventive methods. Yet the fact remains that it is very difficult to measure effectiveness in many cases, and more efficient alternatives are often unknown.

In the short run, social welfare systems must help society to understand the complexity of the human problems with which they must deal humanely and comprehensively, and resist pressures to reduce people and their problems to the most easily tabulated numbers. In the long run, the dictates of professional values as well as the very realistic pressures of funding and societal values make it imperative that social welfare professionals use all of their theoretical and research capabilities to find demonstrably more effective ways of utilizing societal resources to meet human need.

The examination of the organization of social welfare services already undertaken is one part of the search for more effective and efficient services, since the structure of services is a very important part of their success or failure. The knowledge upon which social welfare services are based, to be discussed in following chapters, is also an essential part of this effort—there simply is no place in our complex social welfare system for ignorant social welfare practitioners, no matter how sensitive and concerned they may be. But a third part of the search for greater effectiveness and efficiency is the development of meaningful criteria to use in evaluating social welfare services. How can we know if a service is meeting the needs of those it is trying to service? How can we know if all of those who need the service are receiving it? How can we know whether services are equitable? These are some of the issues involved in the evaluation of social welfare services, and to which we now turn.

THE STRUCTURE OF SOCIAL WELFARE PROGRAMS

Before being able to evaluate programs, it is necessary to understand them. There are five categories that may be used to understand the structure of social welfare services.*

Public Income-Transfer Programs. An income-transfer program is one that attempts to use money collected from one group for the benefit of another group. For example, income taxes are graduated, meaning that those with higher incomes pay a proportionately higher percentage of their taxable income than do those with lower incomes. This tax money is taken into general revenues in the United States Treasury. It is from these general revenues that the money for grant programs comes, such as AFDC and SSI, meaning that there has been a transfer of income from the wealthier to the poorer members of our society. A public program is one in which there is governmental policy-making and public funding. Exhibit 3-6 compares some of the major features of public and private programs.

Income transfers may be made in four ways: (1) through cash grants, as when tax money is paid to public assistance recipients; (2) through in-kind payments, as when public monies are used to purchase food, housing, training programs, and so on, which are then made available to client groups; (3) through tax allowances, in which money due the public treasury is purposefully not collected so that client groups may keep more of their resources (various income tax exemptions are examples of tax allowances); and (4) through social insurances, in which individuals contribute to a fund on which they will ultimately draw. Since any insurance spreads the risk, some never live to draw their contributions, while others draw more than they contribute. In this way, a social insurance may be seen as an income-transfer program. Any income-transfer program focuses on the importance of financial resources for the maintenance of an adequate life pattern. A public

*The terms public and private will be used to distinguish between those programs supported with public and voluntarily contributed funds, respectively. Some prefer to use the term voluntary programs instead of private programs. This teminology will not be used here, in order to avoid confusion with programs—whether public or private—that use volunteers as part of their staff.

income-transfer program is recognition of the society's commitment to utilize public policy and public resources to help those in need.

Public Social Service Programs. A social service is a noneconomic service which contributes to the improvement of social functioning. Public social services involve the use of governmental policy-making and public funds to establish and maintain such services. There are many kinds of public social services that are used in conjunction with public income-transfer programs, such as marital counseling, birth-control information, personal counseling, psychological testing, and others, when provided for public assistance recipients. However, public social service programs need not be tied to income-transfer programs, just as income-transfer programs do not necessarily have associated social service programs. Any social service program is recognition of the fact that many problems exist which are not created solely by a lack of financial resources.

When considering public programs, it is important to realize that there are several governmental levels at which public policy is made and public funds collected and distributed. The federal government has the most wide-ranging responsibility for policy-making and financial management. Many of the most significant public welfare programs originate and operate at this level, including Social Security, SSI, various poverty programs, and medical research programs. State governments have the next greatest impact on public policy and funding, including public assistance, education, law enforcement, and consumer protection. Local governments have smaller spheres of influence, but have important effects on some types of public welfare, including recreation facilities, law enforcement, and public transportation. The diversity and complexity of public social welfare are major causes of problems in the formulation and operation of a unified public welfare system. Such factors also make it difficult for change to occur rapidly in public programs.

EXHIBIT 3-6

Differences between Public and Private Agencies

Arthur Dunham, in *The New Community Organization* (1970), has a very helpful summary of sources of the major differences between public (governmental) and private (voluntary) agencies. This summary is reproduced on the facing page as a way of helping the reader to understand the different sanctions, functions, problems, and potential of each.

Table (opposite) from *The New Community Organization*, by Arthur Dunham. Copyright © 1970 by Thomas Y. Crowell Co., Inc. Used by permission of the publisher.

Sanctions

Governmental (Public)	Voluntary (Private)

1. Established by law:
  a. Legal authority for its activities.
  b. Must carry out provisions of the law.
  c. Cannot go beyond the law.
	1. Usually established by interested group of persons. Articles of incorporation, constitution, by-laws, or charter from national agency is usually its instrument of government.

2. Law tends to define powers and duties fairly precisely; relatively inflexible.	2. Objectives and functions may be expressed in fairly general terms; program may be potentially quite flexible.
3. Law is difficult to amend; requires legislative action.	3. Constitution and by-laws usually easy to amend. Articles of incorporation usually stated in general terms. National charter amendable only on national level.
4. Part of the larger structure of local, state, or federal government.	4. Usually more or less autonomous association, sometimes a subsidiary unit of a national agency. The agency's governing board usually determines most of the policies.
5. More tendency toward large size and bureaucratic organization.	5. Size varies, though usually not as large as major governmental agency in same size community.
6. Personnel usually employed under civil service.	6. Employment standards usually determined by agency; may be determined or influenced by national agency or United Fund.
7. Subject to outside administrative controls—chief executive (governor, mayor, etc.), personnel, budgeting, auditing, legislative committees, courts.	7. Outside administrative controls usually limited mainly to United Fund, national agency, laws regarding licensing, etc.
8. Agency is a part of a political "administration." It is related to governmental and political power structure and may be subject to partisan political pressures.	8. Agency is related to the "community power structure"—primarily the economic power structure.

Support

Governmental (Public)	Voluntary (Private)
9. Income derived primarily from tax funds, appropriated by a legislative body.	9. Income (in the past) usually derived primarily from voluntary contributions, either to the United Fund or the national agency.
10. Funds obtained through governmental budgeting and appropriation process.	10. Funds obtained usually through United Fund budgeting process or through arrangements with national agency. [May also contract with public agencies to provide specified services.]
11. Accounting and auditing procedures subject to law and governmental regulations.	11. Accounting and auditing procedures usually subject to procedures of United Fund or national agency.

Private Income-Transfer Programs. Private income-transfer programs share many characteristics with similar public programs. They involve a reallocation of resources through cash grants, through in-kind payments, and through various types of insurance. However, a private social welfare program draws upon voluntary funding, and policy is established in privately supported social welfare organizations. This distinction between public and private income-transfer programs can be exemplified by tax allowances. A tax allowance must be a public policy, since taxes are determined by appropriate governmental bodies. However, part of public policy in the United States is to allow contributions to recognized private welfare organizations to be deducted as exemptions from taxable income. Here we can see the cooperation of public and private social welfare programs, as well as the greater resource potential of public programs over their private counterparts.

Private Social Service Programs. Private social service programs are privately supported noneconomic services, very similar in nature and intent to public social service programs. The more limited resource base for the support of such programs is again an important consideration. However, it should be noted that private programs can be considerably more flexible than public programs. Without the need for public ratification of private social welfare policy, private organizations are better able to change their policy more rapidly, to focus on specialized problem groups and problem areas, and to supplement public programs. These are important advantages, and they help private programs to remain important parts of the total social welfare system in the United States. Increasingly, however, many private agencies are obtaining public funds through contracts with public agencies, and it appears that private giving to social welfare is stabilizing or even declining. These factors may ultimately reduce the potential advantage of private agencies vis-à-vis public agencies, a topic dealt with at more length later in this chapter.

Programs for Special Groups. A variety of public and private programs exists for the benefit of special groups. These may be income-transfer or social service programs, and result from public and private concern with special groups due to various social and historical circumstances. Some examples include groups affected by war (servicemen and their families, refugees, prisoners of war, and the like); groups affected by natural disasters; groups of persons suffering from chronic, disabling, or disfiguring illness; and groups for which the social structure creates extreme disadvantage. The special circumstances giving rise to such programs frequently give them characteristics quite different from other programs. In some cases, special programs duplicate already existing programs.

Many income-transfer programs may be viewed as income-maintenance programs. Income-transfer programs usually affect the income levels of recipients, increasing them in most cases. To the extent that this is true, they are income-maintenance programs. In the extreme case of the financially indigent, income maintenance is crucial to survival. However, we have seen that some income-transfer programs, such as social insurances and tax allowances, may benefit those who are not financially indigent. Income-transfer programs that involve direct cash grants, such as public assistance or the currently debated guaranteed annual income proposals, have a direct effect on income maintenance. Other programs that involve deferred or reduced contributions by participants, such as social insurances and tax allowances, have a more indirect effect on current income.

In-kind income-transfer programs, such as food stamps and public housing, also have indirect effects on income maintenance. They make it unnecessary to spend current income for the resources provided on an in-kind basis, thereby conserving income. Social services can also supply indirect income-maintenance programs to the degree that they provide free services that would otherwise have to be purchased. Free personal counseling by a family service agency may be used in lieu of costly counseling by a psychiatrist, for example. However, social services are usually more concerned with their effects on individual and community functioning than on income maintenance. The latter only becomes important if it would interfere with the use of needed social services.

Even if in-kind income-transfer programs are effective as income-maintenance devices, they raise the important issue of recipient autonomy. One of the important structural characteristics of an income-maintenance program is the degree to which the income can be spent as the recipient wishes. Food stamps do improve nutritional levels of users, but they also deprive users of the choice of purchasing nonfood items with their resources. For this reason, in-kind programs may be avoided by persons who need income support, but who find lack of choice demeaning or wasteful. Since in-kind programs also usually require a complex administrative structure for resource distribution and supervision, unrestricted cash income-maintenance programs would seem to have several structural advantages.

In-kind income maintenance raises the question of the purpose of income-transfer programs. Social service programs generally focus on the development of social skills that facilitate individual and community functioning. Income-transfer programs, however, in fulfilling their primary income-maintenance function, commonly focus on concrete resources. Concrete resources are essential to social functioning, and often problems of personal and social functioning are generated by a lack of such resources. On the other hand, the provision of concrete resources is no assurance that related social or personal problems will be helped. In-kind programs are justified on the basis that they tie needed concrete resources to the solution of a specific problem, thereby increasing their effectiveness and economy. For example, food stamps can only be used to purchase food, thereby increasing nutritional levels of users. However, such a paternalistic approach to problem-solving is a poor mechanism for the development of social skills. Is the goal simply to support income, or through income support to help an individual or community develop the strengths and skills to function autonomously and effectively? Income-transfer programs that achieve income maintenance while also being consistent with social service goals of improved individual and community functioning are the most effective manner of structuring social welfare services.

A final structural consideration is whether an income-transfer or social service program focuses on the individual or the group. Programs to aid individuals sometimes isolate recipients, meeting the needs of each but never helping them to share their resources to overcome their common problems. Welfare mothers may have their economic needs met at a minimal level through public assistance, but it took the National Welfare Rights Organization to meet their needs for recognition, hope, and participation. Focusing on groups encourages individuals to plan together and combine their resources to achieve their goals. For example, urban renewal involves income transfers, income maintenance, and social services of various kinds. Its use of these approaches may focus primarily on the provision of housing for individuals or the creation of a community. The first approach yields improved housing for the individuals helped. The second approach, however, helps participants plan how the resources and social services that are to be expended can help them collectively and individually to attain a more satisfying and effective community life, an objective far beyond improved housing alone. Obviously some needs must be met individually, but the issues involved in the structuring of income-transfer, income-maintenance, and social service programs come together when considering individual and group approaches to the solution of social welfare problems.

Returning to the structural characteristics and relationships of public and private social welfare programs, Kramer notes the following functions as the ones generally ascribed to private agencies: (1) innovative programs; (2) guarding values; (3) strengthening and expanding public services; and (4) filling service gaps.[20] Each of these functions deserves brief elaboration.

Innovative programs. The flexibility that private agencies may have because of their freedom from the legislative process has made it possible for some of them to experiment with programs for which there would not be adequate political support. Behavior modification, birth-control counseling, and halfway houses are examples. Some of these innovative programs are later taken over or supported by public agencies, confirming their value.

Guardian of values. Private agencies can be responsive to the needs of special-interest groups, and are accessible to citizen participation. Indeed, many private programs depend very heavily on volunteer participation, such as the Red Cross. In a multicultural society, having the needs of all groups expressed can be very functional.

Strengthen and expand public services. Private agencies can serve as a stimulus to public agencies to improve their services. They can help people identify and obtain services from public agencies, and they may communicate with the public agency to push for more adequate services when a need has been identified.

Filling the gaps. Because private agencies can be more flexible, they have traditionally tried to provide services that were not provided by public agencies.

Kramer summarizes his review of the traditional functions of private agencies by noting:

> Both theory and experience suggest that the discretion-potential of the [private agency] is probably its most outstanding feature . . . setting the limits of its responsibility and choosing whom it will serve, to what extent, how, where, and in what ways. . . . Once choices are made, they tend to become institutionalized, resist change, and be subject to a host of constraints and organizational commitments.[21]

In spite of their potential for innovative, flexible, specialized programs, private agencies have been criticized for several reasons:[22]

1. *Progressive detachment from the poor.* The limited resources of private agencies have combined with their emphasis on professionalism to create a network of services frequently oriented toward the sophisticated consumer rather than the most needy.

2. *Overreliance on individual treatment.* Private agencies have generally been characterized by a belief in individual counseling rather than group or community oriented intervention. This is inherently limiting, but all the more so because many of the techniques traditionally used have been seriously questioned in terms of effectiveness and efficiency.

3. *Neglect of social change.* To the extent that the focus of private agencies has been on the nonpoor, there has been much less emphasis on social change, since the nonpoor are not so likely to suffer from existing conditions.

4. *Increasing bureaucratization, unrepresentativeness, and professionalization.* As private agencies have focused on the needs of special groups, and focused on highly professionalized treatment, they have tended to become more rigid and less responsive to the range of needs that may exist in a community.

5. *Dependence on mass, impersonal fundraising.* In an attempt to maximize fundraising efficiency, and minimize antagonism created when many agencies solicit funds from the same people, cooperative community fundraising efforts, such as the United Fund, have been used. Unfortunately, the donor then has little direct contact with the agencies to which he is contributing.

In spite of their flexibility, private agencies are in trouble, as Exhibit 3–7 illustrates. Public expenditures for social welfare are far in excess of private expenditures. This reflects society's commitment to a more adequate social welfare system. But public resources are expanding while private resources are not, and the inability of private agencies to generate resources will affect a detachment from change-oriented services for the poor. This tends to make their services, tending to minimize innovative capacities while accentuating them even more responsive to the special interest groups that provide funds. Yet Kramer notes that the trend toward more public services may not be desirable because of bureaucratic problems. Practically any service can be provided under public or private auspices, but evaluating its effectiveness must examine this dimension of its structure in order to match resources, structure, and the societal mandate.

EXHIBIT 3-7

A Comparison of Public and Private Spending

Tables 1 and 2 present data on private funding. United Way campaigns are unified community voluntary fundraising efforts that benefit the major private social welfare agencies in the community. The data indicate that contributions obtained in such campaigns are growing less rapidly than in the past, and the current period of inflation will no doubt further restrict growth. Table 2 shows that voluntary giving for welfare purposes has been growing, but much less spectacularly than giving for other purposes. Table 3 presents a breakdown of government expenditures for social welfare. These expenditures are far greater than the private system could bear. The growing federal role in welfare expenditures is obvious.

TABLE 1 United Way Campaigns

	1960	1965	1970	1971
Number of Campaigns	2,148	2,232	2,255	2,241
Fund Raised (in millions)	$466	$594	$817	$840
Percent of Specified Goal	97%	100%	97%	Not available.

TABLE 2 Private Philanthropy (in millions)

	1960	1965	1969	1972[a]
Total	$8,912	$12,210	$18,557	$22,680
Source:				
Individuals	7,150	9,276	13,600	16,910
Foundations	710	1,125	1,800	2,200
Corporations	482	785	1,027	840
Bequests	570	1,024	2,130	2,730
Allocation:				
Religion	4,545	5,983	8,000	9,750
Education	1,426	2,076	3,000	3,570
Welfare	1,337	855	1,300	1,610
Health	1,070	2,076	2,950	3,680
Foundations	534	1,220	3,307	4,070

Data are from *Pocket Data Book: USA 1973* (Washington: Government Printing Office, 1973), pp. 191, 192, and 180, respectively. Table 2 is reprinted by permission of the American Association of Fund-Raising Councils, Inc.

[a]Estimated.

TABLE 3 Government Social Welfare Expenditures (includes federal, state, and local governments—in billions of dollars)

	1960	1965	1970	1972[a]		1960	1965	1970	1972[a]
Total	$ 52.3	$ 77.2	$146.0	$192.7	*Categories of expenditures:*				
Percent federal	48%	49%	53%	55%	Social Insurances	$ 19.3	$ 28.1	$ 54.8	$ 75.1
Total as percent of gross national product	11%	12%	15%	18%	Education	17.6	28.1	50.8	61.1
					Public assistance	4.1	6.3	16.5	25.6
Total as percent of all gvt. expenditures	38%	42%	48%	53%	Health	4.5	6.2	9.8	12.4
					Veterans	5.5	6.0	9.0	11.5
					Housing	0.2	0.3	0.7	1.4
Expenditures per person (1972 dollars)[b]	$379	$492	$753	$908	Other	1.1	2.1	4.4	5.7

[a]Preliminary.
[b]Based on total U.S. population, including armed forces.

EVALUATING
SOCIAL
WELFARE
PROGRAMS

Winnifred Bell has developed eight criteria helpful in evaluating the effectiveness of social welfare programs, whether public or private.[23] The greater visibility of the policy-making process in public programs makes it easier to apply Bell's criteria to such programs, but any program can be evaluated using these criteria.

Objectives. These are the purposes of the program as formally stated. A program may be successful in attaining these objectives, it may be partially successful, it may attain other objectives not planned for, or it may simply be unsuccessful. While the stated objectives guide one's evaluation of a program, the attainment of unanticipated objectives should be included in the evaluation of a program. In some cases they may be as important as the originally intended objectives.

Legislative authorization. This will normally be applicable only to public programs. Considering legislative authorization helps to relate programs to others created at the same time, as well as establishing a historical perspective for such programs. When programs fail, it is often because legislation did not build-in adequate implementation procedures. Exhibit 2-5, on the War on Poverty (in Chapter 2), is an example of this problem.

Source of funding. Funding is crucial to program implementation. In public funding, there is sometimes a distinction between legislation and the appropriation of funds to carry out the legislated program—both the authorizing legislation and the appropriations legislation are necessary for a functional program. Private funding may also have the duality of an agency recognizing a need for a program, but not having adequate resources to implement it.

Administrative structure.   We explored, earlier in this chapter, the several ways in which administrative structure can influence program effectiveness. Such structural considerations include the internal functioning of an organization (specified goals and means, structural problems such as technicism, and the like), and the relationships between several organizations which may be involved in a program (cooperation between the Department of Agriculture and local departments of social services that operate Food Stamp programs, for example). The systems nature of social welfare is also significant in administrative structure. A program can be greatly helped or seriously hindered, depending on whether its structure provides for meaningful system ties. For example, when the Office of Economic Opportunity was created, it had strong presidential backing and the authority to initiate action in many parts of the social welfare system. In its last days, it had virtually no support and little power to gain the cooperation of other parts of the system.

Eligibility requirements.   These determine who is eligible to participate in a program. If a program is institutional in scope, need is the only criterion for eligibility. The more residual a program is, the more stringent the eligibility requirements are likely to be, as was illustrated in the earlier comparison between the AFDC and SSI programs.

Coverage.   Eligibility requirements establish the boundaries of the potential client population, while coverage refers to the number of those eligible who actually participate in the program. It is a good measure of the program's effectiveness in reaching the target population, and it is frequently the case that more people are eligible for a program than actually receive benefits.

Adequacy.   Adequacy is a measure of the program's effectiveness in meeting the need of the target population. Sometimes programs are planned to meet only a percentage of the estimated total need, hoping to encourage self-help and to spread scarce resources as far as possible. However, the result is often a residue of unmet need, making the program inadequate in attaining its ultimate goal of need satisfaction. Many states, for example, pay AFDC recipients less than the budget calculated as necessary to meet minimum survival needs. Whereas some AFDC recipients are successful in finding some other source of help, many are not, with the unmet need being reflected in lead paint poisoning of desperately hungry children, and pregnant women suffering from malnutrition.

Equity.   Whereas coverage is a measure of the actual population served by a program, equity measures the degree to which a program discriminates between categories of persons who qualify for coverage. One of the accusations against Social Security is that it is not equitable in its treatment of working married women, since they cannot receive separate Social Security payments upon retirement in spite of the fact that they made separate payments during their working years. Instead, they receive a payment tied to their husband's benefits, and this is less than they would receive if they collected their benefits independently (see Exhibit 2-2, Table 4, in Chapter 2).

Exhibit 3–8 presents comparative data for Medicaid and Medicare. It is suggested that you take some time to use the above evaluative criteria to look at these two programs and try to evaluate their effectiveness. On the basis of your analysis, what changes do you think should be made? You might want to then compare your ideas with the material in Exhibit 3-9 (pp. 123–26), which presents data on cross-cultural social welfare programs. Looking at the ways in which other societies attempt to meet the needs of their citizens can be very instructive for our own society. Notice, however, that all societies face the same issue—what are the priorities in the allocation of social resources? When looking at Exhibit 3-8, you should also be alert to how it illustrates the differences between an insurance and a grant-in-aid program. Notice in particular how funding, administration, coverage, adequacy, and equity are affected.

There is one additional criterion that can be used to evaluate social welfare programs, namely the degree to which user participation is involved. Participation can occur on at least two levels. The first is participation in planning, something which is rarely done. Since bureaucracies have specialized tasks organized into a rational, hierarchical structure, it is difficult for users of the services to have input into that structure. Decision-making processes that determine what those services will be and how they will be provided are usually not directly accessible to users. Bureaucracies that operate within a market system are presumed to permit user feedback through their decisions to use or not use the service offered. However, many social welfare service areas are not provided in a market system. If a recipient of public assistance is unhappy with the amount of his benefits or the procedures governing the distribution of them, his alternative is usually no assistance rather than assistance from another source. It is for this reason that social welfare services have been called a monopoly. In Reid's words, "There is no market relationship between their producers and their primary consumers."[24]

EXHIBIT 3-8

Medicare and Medicaid Compared

The comparison of Medicare and Medicaid on the following pages is taken from the pamphlet, "Medicaid, Medicare—Which is Which?" published by the Department of Health, Education, and Welfare in July 1972.

	MEDICARE	*MEDICAID*
Objectives	Providing protection from financial need caused by medical-care costs	Providing protection from financial need caused by medical-care costs
Legislative Authorization	Social Security Act—Title 18	Social Security Act—Title 19
Funding	An insurance program: MEDICARE HOSPITAL INSURANCE is financed by a separate payroll contribution (part of the regular Social Security withholding). MEDICARE MEDICAL INSURANCE is financed by monthly premiums. The federal government pays half and the insured person pays half. These monthly premiums now are: $5.80 from the federal government for each insured person; $5.80 from each insured person. MEDICAID can pay this $5.80 for those who qualify for MEDICAID coverage.	A grant program: MEDICAID is financed by federal and state governments. The federal government contributes from 50 percent (to the richest states) to 83 percent (to the state with the lowest per-capita income) of medical care costs for needy and low-income people who are aged, blind, disabled, under 21, or members of families with dependent children. Money is obtained from federal, state, and local taxes. States pay the remainder, usually with help from local governments.
Administration	MEDICARE is run by the federal government. MEDICARE is the same all over the United States. The Bureau of Health Insurance of the Social Security Administration of the United States Department of Health, Education, and Welfare is responsible for MEDICARE.	MEDICAID is run by state governments within federal guidelines. MEDICAID varies from state to state. The Medical Services Administration of the Social and Rehabilitation Service of the United States Department of Health, Education, and Welfare is responsible for the *federal aspects* of MEDICAID.
Eligibility	MEDICARE is for people 65 or older. Almost everybody 65 or older—rich or poor—can have MEDICARE. Some people 65 or older can have both MEDICARE and MEDICAID.	MEDICAID is for *certain kinds* of needy and low-income people: • the aged (65 or older) • the blind • the disabled • the members of families with dependent children • some other children Some states also include (at state expense) other needy and low-income people.
Coverage	MEDICARE paid medical bills last year for over 10 million people. HOSPITAL INSURANCE protected 20.3 million people. 19.8 million people were signed up for MEDICAL INSURANCE. This means that almost 10 percent of all the people in the United States have the protection of MEDICARE.	MEDICAID paid medical bills last year for more than 18 million people who were aged, blind, disabled, under 21, or members of families with dependent children. In addition, some states paid medical bills for low-income people *not* aged, blind, disabled, under 21, or members of families with dependent children.

	MEDICARE	MEDICAID
Coverage (cont.)	MEDICARE is available everywhere in the United States.	
Adequacy	MEDICARE pays part—but not all—of hospital and medical costs for people who are insured. HOSPITAL INSURANCE pays inpatient hospital bills *except* for the first $68 in each benefit period. MEDICAL INSURANCE pays $4 out of each $5 of reasonable medical costs *except* for the first $50 in each calendar year—does not pay any of the first $50. MEDICARE HOSPITAL INSURANCE provides basic protection against costs of: • inpatient hospital care • post-hospital extended care • post-hospital home care • health care MEDICARE MEDICAL INSURANCE provides supplemental protection against costs of physicians' services, medical services and supplies, home health-care services, outpatient hospital services and therapy, and other services.	MEDICAID can pay what MEDICARE does not pay for people who are eligible for both programs. MEDICAID can pay the $68 MEDICARE does not pay in each benefit period for eligible people. MEDICAID can pay the first $50 per year of medical care costs and can pay what MEDICARE does not pay of the remaining reasonable charges for eligible people. MEDICAID pays for at least these services: • inpatient hospital care • outpatient hospital services • other laboratory and x-ray services • skilled nursing home services • physicians' services • screening, diagnosis, and treatment of children • home health care services In many states MEDICAID pays for such additional services as dental care, prescribed drugs, eye glasses, clinic services, intermediate care facility services, and other diagnostic, screening, preventive, and rehabilitative services.
Equity	Tied to Social Security which has not achieved universal coverage and tends to be least likely to cover the unskilled, transient worker. Is available only to those 65 or older. While hospital insurance is automatic for those covered by Social Security, medical insurance is optional and requires an additional payment.	Does not apply in two states, and benefits are not the same in all states having programs. Tied to receipt of public assistance or Supplemental Security Income —public assistance is known to have incomplete coverage within the eligible population and to discourage participation through restrictive eligibility requirements and demeaning application procedures.

In enumerating the problems that tend to result when social welfare services are provided in a monopolistic manner, Reid has pointed out the following concepts:[25]

1. Organizations not accountable to consumers often define service goals vaguely or not at all. When the goals are unclear the means to attain them cannot be precisely defined and often change.

2. Lacking accountability to consumers, organizations may allocate energy and resources in a way that is not consistent with the needs of service users. Since the organization is presumed to be worth preserving, it spends an inordinate amount of energy preserving itself rather than serving its users.

3. Clients (users) tend to be defined as irresponsible. With the emphasis of the organization so clearly internal, demands of users are seen as threats to the organization's goals, and therefore tend to be resisted. One way to do this is to rationalize user demands as irresponsible.

4. Workers get caught between their professional values, client demands, and organizational structure, becoming alienated from the agency and seen as adversaries by clients.

Reid goes on to suggest some strategies for the reform of the social welfare monopoly.[26] The first is to strengthen the influence of professionals within the organization and in service planning contexts. This runs into one of the problems with professions themselves. It was noted earlier that they are built on a specialized knowledge base, and are characterized by professional autonomy and self-regulation. This can result in professionals being detached from the people they serve, since by definition users lack the specialized knowledge with which to evaluate the service they are receiving from the professional. This potential for professional isolation from its users can serve to reinforce the monopolistic tendencies within social welfare delivery systems. A second strategy involves the development of countervailing power, that is, developing power structures that clients can use to have an impact on social welfare delivery systems. An example would be the National Welfare Rights Organization. There are obvious problems in the development of countervailing power. Users run the risk that they will be excluded from the services they may desperately need, and there is frequently inadequate educational and financial resources with which to develop viable countervailing power structures. An additional problem in the use of this strategy is the possibility that clients may use their power unwisely in terms of selecting services. However, as in all aspects of the helping situation, sometimes the right to assume responsibility for one's own life entails making mistakes as part of the growth process.[27]

The last strategy discussed by Reid is that of creating competing services, thereby allowing users to have an impact on the service delivery system by selecting the services they feel are most helpful. This would most directly strike at the monopolistic character of the social welfare delivery system.

It could be operationalized through a system of vouchers that clients could use in whatever agency they wished. Since any agency, public or private, must at some point justify its existence in order to obtain resources, lack of selection by users would presumably seriously undermine an agency's ability to justify itself. This strategy would require that there be a meaningful choice of services for each need, so that someone needing income maintenance would be able to select from two or more agencies. This could result in a proliferation of agencies, and raises interesting possibilities for the use of advertising by social welfare agencies in order to attract users. Were this to be the case, the problems an uninformed consumer has in selecting wisely among alternative and highly advertised commercial products could invade the social welfare field. Obviously any strategy to reduce the disadvantages of a monopolistic social welfare delivery system will have its own set of problems and disadvantages, but they are worth thinking about in the quest for more efficient and effective services.

Different types of strategies for increasing the input of users into the services that so greatly affect their lives may be found in practices of other societies. Perlmutter, talking about Yugoslavia, notes that "the central organizing principle of its society is one of citizen participation or self-management within a highly decentralized structure."[28] An individual lives in a commune, which is "not merely a political unit, but a social-economic political community in which the citizen is represented both as an individual and as a worker."[29] Social welfare needs are met in such communities along with a range of other daily needs. There are managing bodies in these units which are "formed to include three constituencies: (1) users of the services; (2) the organizations providing the services; and (3) work-organization representatives. . . . Accessibility and participation are the guiding principles. Therefore the size, location, and even quality of service are designed to meet these objectives, even if this brings about a less professional program."[30] Professionals have their major impact in setting program standards, but citizens at the local level decide on the actual programs.

A similar approach is used in China, where there has also been decentralization and broad planning at the level of the central government. Local communities, however, choose the specific methods for implementing these planning decisions.[31] In addition, the principles of "self-reliance, mutual help, serving the people, and learning by doing" are basic to the culture, and they encourage a wide range of citizen participation.[32] For example, in talking about medical care in China, Sidel describes the system as follows:

> Since the Cultural Revolution many paraprofessionals have been trained to help give medical care and be a bridge between the general population and the medical professions. In the rural areas "barefoot doctors" have been trained in immunization, health education, and the treatment of minor illnesses. Barefoot doctors are peasants who receive approximately three to six months formal training and then work half time as agricultural workers and half time as medical workers; they are paid as full time agricultural workers. "Red Guard doctors," usually housewives, are

the urban counterparts of the barefoot doctors, but are generally unpaid and work in neighborhood health centers under the supervision of fully trained physicians after only ten days' training. . . . The "worker-doctor" with one to three months' training works half time *as* a medical worker in his factory. Both in cities and rural areas "health workers" have been trained by and are directly responsible to barefoot doctors or Red Guard doctors. . . . All four categories of paraprofessional health personnel— barefoot doctors, Red Guard doctors, worker-doctors, and health workers —incorporate social service functions into their medical work.[33]

In such a system, there is no longer the wide gulf separating social welfare services from their users. Services are integrated into the fabric of life and are performed by many types of citizens, ranging from highly skilled professionals to minimally trained but professionally supervised paraprofessionals. The questions of social service monopolies, bureaucratic rigidities, and professional privileges fade in importance in such systems. The emphasis is on citizens helping citizens in a wide variety of ways and in a wide variety of contexts, but always so that they are meaningful to users and providers alike.

These cross-cultural examples lead into the second type of citizen participation, helping in the actual delivery of services. The Chinese approach obviously involves citizens in both the planning and delivery of services. In the United States, citizen participation in planning has been quite limited. The War on Poverty created by the Economic Opportunity Act attempted to generate "maximum feasible participation of the poor" in the planning and, to some extent, the carrying out of social welfare programs.[34] The demise of the Office of Economic Opportunity has reduced the thrust toward such participation, although there is still some level of citizen involvement in some social work programs and local educational planning. The picture is more optimistic in terms of citizen participation in the delivery of services, due to a new interest in the use of volunteers. In comparison with the kind of citizen participation existing in China, the use of volunteers in social welfare programs in this country offers rather limited opportunities, but is nevertheless an attempt to involve citizens in the social welfare system in a participatory manner.

The involvement of citizens in service delivery can have several benefits. In a large, specialized, industrialized society it is very difficult for different groups to have a realistic sense of the problems faced by members of other groups. Particularly in times of prosperity, it is difficult to understand that there may be pockets of poverty and social need. Members of majority groups may have trouble understanding that various kinds of discrimination occur, and they may only dimly perceive the effects of such practices. The sheer size and anonymity of the society make it easy to lose touch with one's fellow man, and to lose a feeling of responsibility for what happens to other members of the society. Being a volunteer can provide the direct exposure to people and their needs which makes a citizen more understanding, empathetic, and willing to help. Volunteers can also help give programs a local flavor, so that users of services face friends and neighbors rather than what are considered to be faceless bureaucrats. This can be very useful in humanizing large, sterile bureaucratic environments, making the users of services more willing to cooperate in the helping process. Finally, volunteers can help to stretch resources. The realities of contemporary American society make it unlikely that adequate resources will ever be allocated to make it possible to eliminate need. Indeed, in most programs there are barely adequate resources to attain designated assistance levels, even though these normally fall far short of providing adequate assistance. Volunteers can be a way for programs to increase the manpower available to provide service, extending the type of service available and freeing more highly skilled professionals to do what they do best.

EXHIBIT 3-9

Comparative Social Welfare Systems

Social welfare systems result from a society's assessment of its resources and priorities in their use and development. Each society establishes a system that reflects its particular history, value system, and needs, resulting in great variation among social welfare systems in different societies. In this exhibit, four rather different societies will be compared in terms of selected aspects of their social welfare structure, including some social insurance, income-transfer, and social service programs. In all cases, only public services will be discussed; in several cases, a highly developed network of private services provides strong support for the public services discussed. This exhibit simply attempts to provide an overview of the different ways different societies attempt to meet the social welfare needs of their members, and does not explore details of program structure and functioning. Such information is available in the sources of data cited elsewhere in this exhibit.

The four nations to be compared are the following: Britain, Japan, the United States, and the African nation of Zaire. To begin, brief descriptive notes on each country may be helpful.

Britain. Britain includes England, Scotland, Wales, and Northern Ireland (The Republic of Ireland has its own welfare system). Britain has an area of approximately 94,200 square miles, and a population of approximately 55 million persons (1971 census). As the earliest great industrial power, Britain has long been concerned with meeting the social welfare needs of its citizens, and this is reflected in a well-developed social welfare system. Data for Britain are taken from *Britain 1974: An Official Handbook* (London: Her Majesty's

Stationery Office, 1974), and *Social Services in Britain* (London: Her Majesty's Stationery Office, 1973).

Japan. Japan is comprised of four main islands with an area of approximately 142,700 square miles and a population of approximately 101 million persons (1968 census). Although an ancient and traditional society, Japan has recently emerged as a great industrial power. It has been strongly influenced by contemporary Western cultures, and its social welfare system reflects the society's traditional and Western influences. Data are taken from *The World Almanac* (1970, p. 534), and *Social Welfare Services in Japan, 1973* (Japan: Ministry of Health and Welfare, 1973).

United States. Composed of 50 states, the nation has a land area of approximately 3.6 million square miles and a population of just over 208 million persons (1972 data). Among the richest nations on earth, political structures and value issues have hindered the development of the kind of national, comprehensive social welfare system that might be expected on the basis of the nation's wealth. Basic data are taken from *The World Almanac* (1970, p. 659).

Zaire. Previously the Belgian Congo, this Central African nation has approximately 905,000 square miles and an estimated population of 21 million persons (1972 estimate). Zaire attained its independence in 1960, and a measure of political stability under President Mobutu's leadership in 1969. The Belgian legacy of exploitation and limited economic development has created serious obstacles to the nation's growth. Although rich in minerals and agricultural potential, basic government services and daily essentials are problematic, and most of the population lives at the subsistence level. National priorities presently stress national development instead of individual services. Data are from *National Geographic* (March 1973, p. 407), and an interview with a Zairian social worker held in Bukaru, Zaire, in July 1974.

Social Insurances

	Health	Retirement
Britain	National Insurance—financed by contributions from employer/employee/government. Provides for free hospital and physicians' services, as well as a community-based network of services focused on prevention, home care, aftercare, and education. Universal coverage. Some services require payment of a modest fee (eye glasses, for example).	National Insurance—financed by contributions from employer/employee/government. Universal coverage for retirement, disability, payment of survivors' benefits, and funeral costs.
Japan	National Insurance—financed by contributions from employer/employee/government, operationalized through several separate plans that provide free services and attain universal coverage. Like in Britain, combination of national and locally organized services.	Welfare Pension Insurance—financed by contributions from employer/employee. Almost universal coverage for retirement, disability, and payment of survivors' benefits.
U.S.	Medicare—hospital care for recipients of Social Security benefits is automatic, physician's care plan is optional at extra premium cost. Financed by contributions from employer/employee/government. Coverage limited to recipients of Social Security benefits.	Social Security—financed by employer/employee contributions. Almost universal coverage for retirement, disability, and payment of survivors' benefits.
Zaire	None	Social Security—financed by employer/employee contributions. Universal coverage for retirement benefits for those employed. Program very erratic in operation due to graft and theft by employers. Large segments of the population not covered because not employed in covered setting.

Income-Transfer Programs

	Families	*Single Adults and Aged Persons*
Britain	Family Allowances—automatic government benefits to families with children. Family Income Supplements—supplemental payments if income falls below specified level (must be at least one child in the house). War Pensions —for those disabled or bereaved by war. All programs funded by national government.	Supplementary Benefits—supplemental payments for any adult with income below specified level. War Pensions. Both programs funded by national government. Reduced fare transporation for the aged.
Japan	Daily Life Security Law—provides assistance if resources fall below specified level. National and local government funding. Child-Rearing Allowance—financial assistance to widows according to number of children. Nationally funded. Children's Allowance—automatic government benefits to families with children. National, local, employer funding.	Daily Life Security Law—provides assistance if resources fall below specified level. National and local funding. Grant of Medical Cost—payment of any medical costs not covered by insurance. National and local funding.
U.S.	Aid to Families with Dependent Children— supplemental payments if financial resources fall below a specified amount. Includes eligibility for food stamps and Medicaid, hospital and physician's services assistance. Veterans Benefits—for those disabled or bereaved by war. All programs funded by national and state-local governments (except Veterans Benefits, which is a national program).	Supplemental Security Income—supplemental payments if financial resources fall below a specified amount (aged, blind, and disabled only). Includes eligibility for Medicaid. Funded by national government (may be supplemented by state governments).
Zaire	Children's Allowance—automatic government benefits to families with children. Financial Assistance—financial aid and in-kind aid to those whose resources fall below a set standard. Both programs nationally funded, but both practically inoperable due to administrative and financial problems.	Financial Assistance—financial and in-kind aid to those whose resources fall below a set standard. Practically inoperable.

Social Services

Britain	Personal Social Services—comprehensive network of social services organized around the following: the elderly, disabled, mentally disordered, physically handicapped, homeless, young children, and deprived or delinquent children. For example, services for children include day care, institutional care, foster care, adoption, delinquent care, youth recreational services, a youth employment service, plus comprehensive health and educational services. Public housing and homemaker services are also available. Available to all members of society.
Japan	Social Welfare Services—comprehensive network of social services, including family planning, personal counseling, day care, employment training, homemaker, foster home, adoption, and

Japan (Cont.)	institutional services. Available to all members of society. Special services also available for the handicapped, retarded, and aged.
U.S.	Child Welfare—foster care, adoption, child abuse, homemaker, and institutional services. Personal and Family Social Services, including personal counseling, marriage counseling, and family planning services. Recreation Services. Public Housing on limited basis. Vocational Rehabilitation and Mental Health Services on a limited basis. Youth and Legal Aid Services. Day Care Services on a limited basis. Services for the Aged on a limited basis. Employment Services. In general, social services may be tied to income level, being intended primarily for the poor and disabled or disadvantaged.
Zaire	Women's and Men's Activities—educational programs to teach literacy, vocational, homemaker, and child-rearing skills, recreational services. Social Services—limited institutional facilities for the aged, handicapped, mentally ill, and orphans. Community Development—formation of agricultural and fishing cooperatives, teaching basic functional skills. Available to all members of society.

With all of its benefits, volunteerism as currently practiced in the United States is limited in effectiveness. It is not totally integrated into the service delivery system as is the case in China. It has not been conceptualized and organized in such a way that there is a comprehensive network of volunteers and paraprofessionals which feeds into professional helping contexts. Some agencies use volunteers more extensively and effectively than others, and there is evidence that sometimes volunteers are relatively ineffective and even manipulated by agencies for rather devious purposes.[35] In spite of these problems, volunteerism remains a viable and valuable way for citizens, users and nonusers alike, to participate in the important work of the social welfare institution. Returning to our original focus, the ability and willingness of an agency and a program to use volunteers and paraprofessionals to maximize the scope and effectiveness of its program may be considered another criterion usable in program evaluation. Exhibit 3-10 discusses the nature of the volunteer experience and tasks that volunteers can perform.

This chapter has dealt with agency and program efficiency and effectiveness. The basic value systems and societal mandates discussed in the previous chapters enter into such considerations. But ultimately those values and mandates must be made operational, and that occurs through organizations that allocate resources and structure client and worker behaviors. Each professional has the responsibility to make sure that personal professional values are respected by the organization in which she works, so that she can ultimately apply professionally sound evaluative criteria to her work. It is important to demonstrate to herself, her clients, and society that her work is as efficient and effective as our present levels of knowledge and practice wisdom make possible. This evaluation cannot be complete without input from the users of the services, and the communities that support the services. Client participation in program planning and service delivery makes this possible. Again we cannot avoid the realization that the social welfare institution is part of a total societal system. In the attempt to help people to function more effectively many people and structures get involved. The wise use of social resources involves highly skilled professional judgment, but it also involves organizational structures and the participation of user groups and community citizens. In the long run, the social welfare professional is himself a citizen, and his work must reflect the needs of his fellow citizens.

EXHIBIT 3-10

The Volunteer Experience

The following is taken from "A Guide for Friendly Visitors," a mimeographed pamphlet by the Guilford County (North Carolina) Department of Social Services. It examines the characteristics that competent volunteers should possess, discusses the kinds of tasks involved, suggests skills necessary to be developed, and describes the relationship of the volunteer to the agency. It is interesting to note the use of the term "friendly visitor" instead of volunteer, a throwback to a term used before the development of social work as a profession when well-meaning citizens of a community undertook charitable activities. It illustrates one of the functions of volunteers, that is, helping to reduce the anonymity of welfare bureaucracies for clients so that they perceive themselves as dealing with friends and neighbors rather than impersonal specialists.

We welcome you as a volunteer to aid in a Friendly Visiting Program among elderly or handicapped people. Without you this service would not be possible.

Your contribution is fourfold:

- It *enriches* the often cheerless and lonely life of an individual.
- It *supplements* the work of the professional staff.
- It is a *direct service* to your community.
- It enables *you* to grow in understanding and maturity.

What Is the Friendly Visiting Program?

The Friendly Visiting Program is an organized plan

Used by permission of Guilford County (North Carolina) Department of Social Services.

for visiting among people whose emotional and physical well-being is impaired by illness, injury, loneliness, or other misfortune.

Who Are the People Visited?

Elderly or handicapped people who live alone, in nursing or county home, or in any situation where warmth of friendliness is needed. All have one need in common—the need for someone to take a personal interest in them.

Who Are the Friendly Visitors?

Volunteers—intelligent, friendly, dependable men and women who recognize the value of this program to the persons whom they visit and as a service to the community.

How Does the Program Operate?

Your local Social Services Department staff find the need for this service among the people with whom they come in contact. If you want to volunteer you should contact the Social Services Department in your city or county.

Attendance at an orientation course is a prerequisite for each Friendly Visitor. This course, of no more than three sessions, is offered free of charge as the need arises.

The Friendly Visitor works with the agency caseworker or staff person requesting this service. The contact person provides the Friendly Visitor with further information and direction, has the story and pertinent facts about the person or persons to be visited and usually accompanies the volunteer on the first visit. Special emphasis is placed on matching interests on the basis of talents, hobbies, nationality. The Friendly Visitor reports directly to the agency contact person.

The above information pertains to Friendly Visitors volunteering as individuals or in connection with a group project.

What Do Friendly Visitors Do?

Create a warm and friendly relationship.

Chat of everyday affairs, except religion and politics.

Read aloud, write letters, play games, do puzzles.

Listen to and show respect for opinions and often-repeated stories.

Emphasize self-reliance but give assurance of help when needed.

Provide small, worthwhile jobs to do.

Assist with recreational activities.

Develop creative interests.

Admire and give importance to personal possessions.

Shop occasionally, with approval of the contact person.

Send seasonal greeting cards. Remember birthdays.

Take magazines, books, garden flowers, etc.

Cooperate with community affairs. Make posters, favors, place cards.

What Are the Duties of Friendly Visitors?

To observe the rules of the agency at all times.

To know and to keep within their privileges and limitations.

To visit regularly. If unavoidably detained, telephone. Should phoning not be possible, send an explanatory note.

To give full attention to the person visited.

To be a good listener. Consider the interests, likes and needs of each individual.

To refrain from discussion of controversial or depressing subjects.

To avoid criticism.

To guard against personal jokes and "talking down."

To respect names. It may be all there is left.

To help the older person assume responsibility for his own decisions.

To dress simply.

To keep confidential matters confidential.

To understand that all information about the residents, the staff, and the home are to be given out only by the person in charge. Publicity in any form is not the prerogative of Friendly Visitors.

What Qualifications Are Needed?

An *understanding* of and *liking* for elderly people.

A *sense of humor.*

Patience: Handicapped, confused, or senile persons are slow. Patience can go far to help a negative, irritable person to solve his own problems.

Tactfulness: To smooth over sensitive feelings.

Tolerance: To avoid unpleasant arguments.

Dependability: Disappointments are defeating.

Honesty: Admit mistakes. Don't be afraid to say you don't know.

Humility: Be willing to learn, and to accept constructive criticism with an open mind.

Generosity: Be willing for others to take the limelight.

Maturity: To communicate a sense of security and confidence. Understand that the elderly need to be useful and needed. They need to be loved and to have someone to love.

To recognize the spiritual values inherent in the warmth of friendliness.

Suggestions for Friendly Visitors

Establish a good rapport with the staff.

Check frequently with contact person to learn of developments.

Several visits may be required to gain the confidence of the persons visited.

Keep visits reasonably short. Do not stay through meal hours unless especially invited.

Be relaxed. When staying for only a few minutes do not appear hurried. Sit down in a chair where you can be easily seen. Do not sit or lean on the bed.

For the very ill, an affectionate pat may be better than a handshake.

Keep promises. Be careful what you promise.

Do not start anything that you are not prepared to carry through.

Refrain from talking in the corridors. Bits of conversation may be overheard, misinterpreted, and cause alarm.

Be a friend and companion. You are not expected to be a social worker, a pastor, a doctor, or a lawyer. Your visit means much to one who is shut away from normal family living. You may even be filling the place of the family.

Enjoy your visits. Cheeriness is contagious.

What Are the Responsibilities of the Friendly Visitors to the Agency?

To report regularly to the agency contact person. Any change in emotional, religious or physical problems should be reported immediately, and guidance and help requested.

To report to the contact person inability to accept or to continue an assignment once it has been accepted.

To recognize that Friendly Visitors supplement, not replace, the professional staff.

To avoid criticism of the policies of the agency.

To ask for a change if unhappy in the assignment.

Needs and Characteristics of the Elderly

The greatest contribution will be made by the volunteers who have a thorough understanding of the needs and characteristics of the elderly.

Some important factors are:

- Most older people are normal and have the same basic needs they have always had.
- They need to maintain their self-respect and as much independence as possible.
- Many have suffered loss of personal ties and are lonely. They feel rejected.
- They have to make adjustments continually to drastic and often tragic changes in their personal lives. These may include loss of husband, wife, or family; physical infirmities; changed economic circumstances; loss of employment and income; unfamiliar living arrangements; loss of community standing and influence. Many need reassurance. They are afraid of old age, of being alone, of illness, of not having enough money, or being pushed around. They fear death. They tend to be suspicious of anyone not connected with their own routine.

The Friendly Visitor can stimulate interest in the outside world and help renew a sense of personal dignity and worth.

Rehabilitation to self-care through personal attention, creative activity, physical exercise, and intellectual stimulation is worth all the time and effort that may be required.

Code of Volunteers

"As a Volunteer, I realize that I am subject to a code of ethics, similar to that which binds the professional. I, like them, in assuming certain responsibilities, expect to be accountable for those responsibilities. I will keep confidential matters confidential.

"As a Volunteer, I agree to serve without pay, but with the same high standard as the paid staff expect to do their work.

"I promise to take to my work an attitude of open-mindedness; to be willing to be trained for it; to bring to it interest and attention.

"I believe that my attitude toward volunteer work should be professional. I believe that I have an obligation to my work, to those for whom it is done, and to the community.

"Being eager to contribute all that I can to human betterment, I accept this code for the Volunteer as my code, to be followed carefully and cheerfully."

STUDY QUESTIONS

1. After reading the material on the characteristics of professions, are you convinced that professions are different from any other occupation? Compare a profession to a nonprofession (being a secretary, for example), and see what differences you find. On the basis of your analysis, should professions have the degree of autonomy that they claim? If professions were less autonomous, what regulatory mechanisms would you suggest?

2. Read the "165 Howell Street" case in the Appendix at the back of the book. Then consider the effect that the structure of services has on the services provided in this case. Would having less structure help, or would it create other problems? Can you think of more effective service delivery structures that would have been helpful in the Howell Street case?

3. Evaluating the effectiveness of social welfare programs is difficult. Make a list of the criteria noted in the book down one side of the page, leaving ample room between each. On the other side, briefly note why each criterion is or is not an accurate indicator of two things: (1) Is the recipient of the service actually functioning more effectively? (2) Did the professional worker do a good or bad job in helping the recipient of the service? If you find some of the criteria are not very helpful in answering these evaluative questions, what criteria seem more appropriate to you?

REFERENCES

1. In February 1971, there were 1,181,310 recipients of public assistance in New York City, according to Department of Health, Education and Welfare figures. *Public Assistance Statistics*, February 1971 (NCSS Report A-2, 2/71), p. 4.

2. Nicos Mouzelis, *Organization and Bureaucracy: An Analysis of Modern Theories* (Chicago: Aldine, 1968), p. 39.

3. Ibid.

4. Ibid., p. 99. He defines informal organization as "the structure and culture of the group, which is spontaneously formed by the interactions of individuals working together."

5. Ibid., pp. 102–103.

6. See Donald Roy, "Quota Restriction and Goldbricking in a Machine Shop," *American Journal of Sociology* 57 (1952): 427–42.

7. Richard N. Hall, "Professionalization and Bureaucratization," *American Sociological Review* 33 (February 1968): 92–104. See also Harold Wilensky and Charles Lebeaux, *Industrial Society and Social Welfare* (New York: Free Press, 1958), pp. 284–85.

8. Ellen Dunbar and Howard Jackson, "Free Clinics for Young People," *Social Work* 17 (September 1972): 34. Reprinted by permission of the National Association of Social Workers.

9. A classic example of occupational socialization is Howard S. Becker et al., *Boys in White* (Chicago: University of Chicago Press, 1961).

10. John Wax, "Developing Social Work Power in a Medical Organization," *Social Work* 13 (October 1968): 62–71.

11. See Esther Stanton, *Clients Come Last* (Beverly Hills: Sage Publishers, 1970), pp. 145–58.

12. Dunbar and Jackson, op. cit., p. 28.

13. Ibid., pp. 29–30.

14. Joseph Olmstead, "Satisfaction and Performance in Welfare and Rehabilitation Agencies," *Social and Rehabilitation Record* 1 (September 1974): 28.
15. Delbert Taebel, "Strategies for Making Bureaucrats Responsive," *Social Work* 17 (November 1972): 41–43. Paraphrased by permission of the National Association of Social Workers.
16. Edward Newman and Jerry Turem, "The Crisis of Accountability," *Social Work* 19 (January 1974): 15. Reprinted by permission of the National Association of Social Workers.
17. Ibid.
18. Ibid.
19. Marvin Rosenberg and Ralph Brody, "The Threat or Challenge of Accountability," *Social Work* 19 (May 1974): 345–50.
20. Ralph Kramer, "Future of the Voluntary Service Organization," *Social Work* 18 (November 1973): 61–62. Paraphrased by permission of the National Association of Social Workers.
21. Ibid., p. 63.
22. Ibid., p. 62.
23. Based on material in Winnifred Bell, "Obstacles to Shifting from the Descriptive to the Analytical Approach in Teaching Social Services," *Journal of Education for Social Work* 5 (Spring 1969): 5–13.
24. P. Nelson Reid, "Reforming the Social Services Monopoly," *Social Work* 17 (November 1972): 47. Reprinted by permission of the National Association of Social Workers.
25. Paraphrased from ibid., pp. 47–50, by permission of the National Association of Social Workers and the author.
26. Ibid., pp. 50–54.
27. Alan Keith-Lucas, *Giving and Taking Help* (Chapel Hill: University of North Carolina Press, 1972), pp. 60–63.
28. Felice Davidson Perlmutter, "Citizen Participation in Yugoslavia," *Social Work* 19 (March 1974): 226. Reprinted by permission of the National Association of Social Workers.
29. Ibid., p. 228.
30. Ibid., p. 229.
31. Ruth Sidel, "Social Services in China," *Social Work* 17 (November 1972): 5. Reprinted by permission of the National Association of Social Workers.
32. Ibid., p. 6.
33. Ibid., p. 10.
34. Ralph Kramer, *Participation of the Poor* (Englewood Cliffs, N.J.: Prentice-Hall, 1969).
35. Stanton, loc. cit.

SELECTED READINGS

The problems of organizing and delivering social welfare services are major ones, and of crucial importance for the future of social welfare. The following sources examine various facets of these problems.

Bucher, Rue, and Anselm Strauss. "Professions in Process," in Meyer Zald, ed., *Social Welfare Institutions.* New York: Wiley, 1965, pp. 559–53.
Edgar, Richard. *Urban Power and Social Welfare.* Beverly Hills: Sage Publishers, 1970.

Etzioni, Amitai. *Modern Organizations.* Englewood Cliffs, N.J.: Prentice-Hall, 1964.

Friedlander, Walter. *International Social Welfare.* Englewood Cliffs, N.J.: Prentice-Hall, 1974.

Galper, Jeffrey. *The Politics of Social Services.* Englewood Cliffs, N.J.: Prentice-Hall, 1975.

Gilbert, Neil, and Harry Specht. *Dimensions of Social Welfare Policy.* Englewood Cliffs, N.J.: Prentice-Hall, 1974.

Kahn, Alfred. *Social Policy and Social Services.* New York: Random House, 1973.

Morris, Peter, and Martin Rein. *Dilemmas of Social Reform.* New York: Atherton, 1967.

Shostak, Arthur. *Modern Social Reforms: Solving Today's Social Problems.* New York: Macmillan, 1974.

Stanton, Esther. *Clients Come Last.* Beverly Hills: Sage Publishers, 1970.

Steiner, Gilbert. *Social Insecurity: The Politics of Welfare.* Chicago: Rand McNally, 1966.

U.S. President's Commission on Income Maintenance Programs. *Background Papers.* Washington, D.C.: Government Printing Office, 1969.

Vinter, Robert D. "Analysis of Treatment Organizations," in Paul Weinberger, ed., *Perspectives on Social Welfare.* New York: Macmillan, 1969, pp.. 428–43.

Wilcox, Clair. *Toward Social Welfare.* Homewood, Ill.: Richard D. Irwin, 1969.

PART II

Social Science and Social Welfare: A Base for Practice

4

Psychological Bases

*I*N DISCUSSING the concept of social welfare in earlier chapters, it was defined as society's attempt to help its members function more effectively with minimal suffering. In looking at the history of attempts to more adequately and effectively operationalize this concept, and in discussing organizational factors in service delivery, it has become clear that this society still searches for better ways to structure its social welfare institution. Formulated in other terms, while we have a general objective, we are still struggling with the best means to attain that objective. The issue then becomes, How do we go about deciding what our services and service delivery structure should be?

THE RELATION OF THEORY TO PRACTICE

Leaving aside the political and economic factors involved in the decision-making process itself, there are two major ways in which we usually try to understand problems and develop solutions to them in social welfare. The first is sometimes called "practice wisdom," the accumulated experiences of social welfare professionals. Culture is cumulative, and we constantly draw upon the earlier experiences of others to help us understand our own situation. Specialized professional literature exists to enable professionals to share with each other their thinking and their experiences. If one community tries a methodone-maintenance program for drug addicts, it may report its results in journals, enabling other communities faced with the same problem to benefit from the experience of others. Practice wisdom is an empirical approach; that is, it is based on actual experience. However, it is not necessarily scientific. Decisions to act or not act are not necessarily based on theory and carried out under specified, controlled conditions. In practice wisdom, all one knows is what was done and what the results were. The theoretical foundations and implications of such behavior are not necessarily explored. Even so, practice wisdom can be important information for others considering a certain behavior.

Discussing practice wisdom raises the need for skill in evaluation of programs and behaviors. The social welfare practitioner must be able to look at the experiences of others and have some criteria for evaluating the degree to which what occurred could be expected to occur again. One can, of course, trust to intuition or faith. An alternative approach lies in the application of scientific research methodology in which mathematically based principles and analytical tools are used to evaluate the probable occurrence of events. The use of such methodology enables the practitioner to specify the probability of the events under consideration occurring again, or perhaps lead him to conclude that the information available is too uncertain to permit any assessment of future occurrence. Whenever one deals with empirical behavior, skill in research methodology is a very important tool in evaluating the utility of various interventive possibilities. Just because practice wisdom suggests that a certain approach to problem-solving works does not mean that in fact it does, or that it does under all circumstances. Research skill enables one to evaluate critically such situations, and make more informed decisions about whether or not to use a given technique. When discussing social work interventive methods in later chapters we will see once again how practice wisdom, while a significant source of potential interventive approaches, may also lead to erroneous assumptions if accepted uncritically.

The second way in which we try to understand human problems and their solution is through the study of social science theory. Theory is most simply a way to organize what is known about behavior, and is closely related to the empirical research that provides the facts upon which theory is built.[1] Theory may include general statements about relationships between types of behavior, as well as more specific statements concerning specific behaviors. For example, sociological theory in social stratification tells us that there are measurable differences between ranked groups of persons, such as differences in education, occupation, and income. These groups are called social classes, and we know that social class is specifically related to life chances (incidence of mental illness, type of treatment, and the like) as well as life styles (child-rearing patterns, leisure activities, and so on). This information is useful in structuring services and interventive strategies appropriate to people's needs and behavior patterns.

There are several social and physical sciences, each having a large body of theory. The major social sciences drawn upon by the social welfare professions in the past have been psychology and sociology, although there has been a more recent interest in political science and economics. Discipline boundaries are to some extent arbitrary, since there are many areas in which the social sciences overlap and interrelate. This and the two succeeding chapters will look at these disciplines in some detail. Before going into detail, it may be useful to get an overview of the kinds of theory that can be helpful to the social welfare professional. Helen Harris Perlman has used the term "biopsychosocial whole" to indicate the need to look at the person as a physical and psychological entity existing in a social environment.[2] Once again the concepts of system and institution recur, for Perlman's terminology is one especially descriptive way to refer to the fact that human behavior is a complex whole. To understand any part of it we must also be aware of the context in which it occurs. Using the idea of the biopsychosocial whole, we may identify three major theoretical areas of significance to the social welfare professional, and several subareas related to them.

Human Development through the Life Cycle.　Basic to an understanding of the individual and his functioning is an awareness of the interrelatedness of inherited physical capabilities and limitations, social experiences that permit or impede physical development, and the integration of social experiences and physical potential into a personality structure. The life cycle refers to the progression through socially structured experiences during which the individual draws upon her physical and social resources to solve problems and achieve gratification, becoming a functioning human being in the process. This will be discussed in more detail later in this chapter.

Personality.　Personality is the individual's distinctive and regular manner of confronting persons, problems, and situations. It results from the social shaping of individual physical and emotional needs and abilities, and it provides a framework through which the individual understands the world around him. The study of personality usually includes common personality abnormalities and their effects on behavior. This will also be discussed in more detail in this chapter.

Social Environment.　The human individual lives in groups, and these group affiliations define appropriate behavior. Each individual must adjust his personal needs to the rules and structures established by the group. There are several groups that are of particular significance.

Family.　The family is the primary group responsible for sexual reproduction, socialization of new members into society, and the transmission of resources between generations. It is a significant context for intimate, primary-group relationships between the husband, wife, and children that form the family unit.

Peers.　Peer groups provide significant socialization and social-skill learning contexts. They are also primary groups, enabling members to express themselves in intense, person-to-person relationships.

Secondary Groups.　Industrial societies are characterized by a wide variety of secondary groups, groups that focus on a specialized type of goal-oriented behavior rather than the intimate, personal relationships that exist between members of primary groups. Among the more important secondary groups are work, education, and recreation groups. The discussion of bureaucracies and professions in Chapter 3 deals with many of the issues of secondary groups.

Communities.　Social behavior takes place within a definable geographic unit. At the local level, this is the community, and the context within which patterned relationships occur and decisions are made.

Societies.　A society is also a geographic unit, one that encompasses many communities. Its effect on patterning behavior is primarily in terms of establishing a culture-based value system for its members, and creating structures for coordinating the diverse activities performed in the society. Both communities and societies are significant because they are decision-making arenas in which scarce societal resources are allocated. All of the components of the social environment are discussed in the next chapter, except for decision-making and resource allocation, which form the contents of Chapter 6. The social processes that result from attempts to structure group behavior in primary and secondary groups, communities, and societies are also discussed in the next chapter.

World Context. The sophisticated level of transportation and communication technology that characterizes the contemporary world has elevated our awareness of the fact that increasingly, events within our own society are affected by and in turn affect other societies. Such issues as birth control, food supplies, energy supplies, nuclear destruction, and space exploration cannot be resolved internally. The cross-cultural data provided in Chapter 3 gives some perspective on world relationships, but this is an area just beginning to emerge systematically in the study of social welfare, and is not dealt with further in this book.

CHOOSING THEORIES FOR PRACTICE

Perhaps it seems that the student of social welfare must know everything when looking at the above list of significant areas of theory. Obviously this is not possible. How, then, does the student and the professional decide which theoretical knowledge is most useful given the massive and sometimes competing bodies of knowledge available? There are at least four criteria that can be helpful in choosing theory which will form the foundation for action, and these are discussed below. However, every social welfare professional must have some level of mastery of all of the theory briefly mentioned above and discussed in more detail later. This is necessary because of the interrelated nature of human activity. Although one may specialize in services to victims of rape, for example, this problem is enmeshed in physical, psychological, and social events and ramifications that must be included in an effective interventive plan.

The following criteria may be helpful in selecting specific theory when attempting to develop an interventive approach.

Values. Each of us has a value stance from which we approach the search for knowledge. For some, religious beliefs form an important part of their world view and their perception of cause and effect. For others, scientific methodology and empirically verified concepts and relationships are basic to their understanding of themselves and others. Yet others may have a very existential approach to the human condition. All of these attempts to understand are appropriate, but each will suggest bodies of theory which are compatible with it.

It is important to be aware of one's own values regarding acceptable sources of knowledge. Not only does this aid us in our search for knowledge, but it makes us aware of what knowledge we reject, and why. The following excerpts from an article discussing social work with American Indians illustrates what happens when a client group uses theory that has its foundations in tradition, while the professional uses theory based on practice wisdom or social science.

> The worker must not intervene unless the people request an intervention, and he is likely to wait a long time for such a request. The credentials of his profession, his position, status, knowledge, skills, achievements, and authority, though respected by the agency, are in most cases completely without merit among the Indians. Such things belong to Anglo culture and are not readily translatable into Indian culture. His standing in the Anglo community does not give him a license to practice intervention among Indian people. . . . In every case, the people utilize the established, functional, culturally acceptable remedy within their own native system.[3]

Evidence.   A second criterion that can be used in choosing theory for practice is the evidence that supports it. Of course the whole question of what is acceptable evidence relates to values as discussed above, but however evidence is defined, that which is most strongly supported would appear to be the most promising as a basis for intervention. For example, within a scientific perspective, there is considerably more empirical evidence to demonstrate the effectiveness of behavior modification than psychotherapy. This might be one criterion to use in deciding between the two theories.

Practical Implications.   Another way to choose between theories is the practical implications of each. For example, which suggest interventive approaches that achieve results more rapidly? At lower cost? With all user groups rather than with just selected ones? When faced with racial discrimination in a school, there are at least two competing sociological theories one could use. One says that values must first be changed, which obviously is a long, slow process. The other says that changing behavior will automatically change values, something that can be done much more rapidly (as President Eisenhower proved in Little Rock). Given that the first approach will take a generation or more to yield results, while the second approach may be used immediately and potentially be effective within a matter of a few years, one might wish to select the latter approach, all other things being equal (that is, if the second approach had much less evidence to support it than the first, one might not want to use it in spite of its rapidity).

Relevance.   A final criterion usable in selecting theory is its applicability to the problem at hand. Out of the mass of existing social science data, certain segments will be most useful in dealing with a specific problem. Institutional discrimination and inequality has many causes, and many types of theory are relevant to its understanding. However, when dealing with a particular manifestation of it in a community, certain theory is more directly relevant than others. For example, when dealing with a large corporation's reluctance to hire the handicapped, focusing on corporate decision-making makes more immediate sense than giving equal weight to less directly manipulable factors such as social processes that create prejudice and discrimination toward the handicapped.

THEORY AND PROBLEM-SOLVING

Theory provides the social welfare professional with directions in her search for solutions to problems. Social welfare is essentially problem-solving behavior. It is an attempt to find the best way to identify and use resources to help people function more effectively with less suffering. As such, social welfare is a very conscious, rational endeavor, one in which all of the elements of the problem are explored, the resources identified, and the potential obstacles clarified. (Exhibit 4-1 explores the problem-solving process in some detail.) In order to explicate all of the elements of a problem and its solution, we inevitably return to a systems formulation, since problems and resources exist in persons seeking help, those attempting to provide help, those not intending or wishing to be part of the problem or helping situation, and the social structure as a whole.

Linking Theories: A Systems View. A systems approach to problem-solving requires a broad foundation of knowledge about individuals as biological and psychological beings; about the web of social relationships an individual has with significant others in his environment (such as family members, friends, and neighbors); about the individual's participation in larger group and societal structures (such as school, work, and special interest groups); and about the manner in which society is organized, which affects decision-making about resource allocation and group functioning for all members in the society. The social and biological theory upon which social welfare professional practice is based provides a range of concepts and data. The professional practitioner draws from this theory to develop a framework to understand the behavior she sees. Although theory is abstract, it is precisely this abstractness that provides general organizing relationships flexible enough to encompass the wide range of specific behaviors that practitioners see in their daily work.

Sometimes it is difficult to see beyond the immediate problem to understand the relevance of theory. The practitioner dealing with a hostile, unemployed, depressed, impoverished minority-group member is confronted with a variety of very real, specific problems needing attention. Yet the practitioner must have some guidelines for making decisions about the best way of solving each of these problems. Theory relevant to the many systems involved provides a framework to help in this task. Understanding each person's need for recognition and feeling of success, especially in a society that rewards competition and achievement, helps to understand the client's depression and hostility, given his unemployment and poverty. The relationship of poverty and unemployment in a work-oriented society can be understood within a framework of institutional inequality, which frequently discriminates against minority-group members. A helping plan for this person begins to emerge on the basis of a theoretical understanding of the causes and dimensions of the problems he faces: personal counseling to strengthen his self-image and allow him to ventilate his quite understandable, although potentially destructive, hostility; planning for job training that may be needed, as well as help in job-seeking and job-performance skills; exploration of resources in the community that may be available to help compensate for institutional deprivation (upgrading minimal reading and writing skills, for example); concern for the effects of the client's impaired functioning on family members and others within his social network; and participation in agency, community, and political efforts to eliminate institutional inequality and its effects.

EXHIBIT 4-1

Problem-Solving in Social Welfare

Social welfare basically deals with people with problems coming to skilled professionals who attempt to solve the problems in cooperation with the client. Problem-solving is not confined to social welfare, of course, and there are many approaches ranging from the most scientific to the most idiosyncratic.[a] Below is an adaptation of a problem-solving approach used in a training manual for paraprofessionals in the human services. It is a good summary of the basic principles involved, and may be used by individuals or groups.

1. Define what your problem is. What is your goal and what do you want to accomplish in relation to the situation from which one is starting? Make sure there is agreement on what the problem is before attempting to solve it.

2. Probe for what makes it a problem. Study the obstacles to the attainment of the goals by specifying the causes underlying each obstacle, and by getting all relevant facts.

3. Search for all possible solutions, even unlikely looking ones. Reserve judgment and criticism until the next step.

4. Test the potential solutions. If you understand your problem well, you can now begin to pick out the most promising solutions. Weigh them carefully in the light of the facts, not prejudices.

5. Choose the best solution. In groups, it should be an informed, democratic decision.

6. Map out a plan of action to put your solution to work. You may have to develop a comprehensive or long-range plan, with "easy stages." It should be a realistic plan with a good chance of successful execution. In groups, make use of the potential contributions of all members.

7. Take a pause for appraisal and evaluation, which may bring out new facts that alter the solution or possibly cause you to set new goals. Problem-solving is a continuous process.

From Janet Rosenberg, *Breakfast: Two Jars of Paste* (Cleveland: Case Western Reserve University, 1969), p. 28. Used by permission of Community Development Institute of Southern Illinois University.
[a]Guy Swanson, *Social Change* (Glenview, Ill.: Scott, Foresman, 1971), pp. 150–53.

Without a broad systems-focused theoretical base, it becomes very easy for the professional to fall into the trap of seeing the individual in isolation. Individual behavior fits into complex webs of social relationships that in turn shape the individual. Trying to deal only with the individual is like trying to fix a broken-down automobile engine by concentrating only on one piston. Theory, then, assists the practitioner in several ways: it helps to organize specific observed behavior; it suggests the range of factors that need to be considered in understanding and intervening in social behavior; and it is grounded in concrete data that help the practitioner make decisions about the validity of potentially relevant theoretical alternatives.

No single book can bring together all of the relevant theoretical materials the social welfare professional needs to understand to function. This chapter and the two following attempt to summarize some of the major psychological, sociological, political, and economic theory helpful to the social welfare practitioner. It is assumed that the student will have had more detailed exposure to each of these areas in other courses. The intent of these chapters is to review pertinent theory, and to help the student begin the life-long professional task of analyzing theory for its implications in practice.

HUMAN DEVELOPMENT AND THE LIFE CYCLE
A psychological perspective on behavior focuses on the internal mental development and functioning of the individual. This entails a three-pronged approach: (1) the individual organism begins with a biological inheritance, which has developmental potential and internal organization; (2) the organism is affected by its social environment; and (3) the organism perceives, organizes, and responds to its internal and external environment.

A psychological perspective can be turned either inward or outward. Looking inward, one can focus on such internal processes as cognition, perception, and reflex responses. An outward view would include personality and the environment, behavior and its social reinforcers, environmental effects on learning and perceptual organization, and so on. Since the social welfare system attempts to improve individual functioning and increase personal gratification, both psychological perspectives have great utility. However, the outward view has been the one which has had the greatest effect on interventive methods, and is the one to be discussed at some length in this chapter. So far, the inward view has been of greatest utility to psychologists, and has generated theory still to be translated into practice principles.*

One of the persistent problems faced by social welfare practitioners has been that of understanding the social-organic totality that is the human being. The social sciences are founded on the belief that human behavior is

*Internal psychological processes obviously affect behavior. However, the point being made here is that practice relies most heavily on external behavior. Theory that is useful in understanding internal processes must still be translated into its external behavioral effects, whereas theory focusing directly on external behavior avoids this two-step progression.

more or less patterned and regular, but the attempts to explain how this happens have been many and varied.[4] However, all attempts recognize that biological growth and social experiences develop together, and that they coalesce into socially defined periods commonly referred to as the life cycle. Later in this chapter, when discussing the work of Freud and Erikson, specific theoretical formulations of stages will be presented. At this point, it will be helpful simply to summarize the concept of the life cycle and its utility in social welfare professional contexts.

The life cycle extends from birth to death, including in the normal course of development: infancy, childhood, adolescence, adulthood, and old age. The life cycle is a concept that recognizes the biological fact of development and aging. As these processes occur, society establishes boundaries to mark transition points from one level of development to another. Often there are socially structured quasipublic events that signify that an individual has moved from one point in the life cycle to another. For example, entry into school is clear recognition of childhood, while graduation from the primary grades and entry into junior high school is one marker of the transition into adolescence. Marriage is a significant social event acknowledging that the individual is assuming the responsibilities of adulthood, and retirement signifies the passage into old age. Having such social events to mark one's passage through the life cycle can help the individual recognize one's developing social position as well as help others in one's life recognize changes and help the individual to deal with new situations and responsibilities. Each society has its own ways of defining important stages of the life cycle, and its distinctive ways of recognizing their occurrence.

At each major stage in the life cycle, at least three biological and social situations occur. First, individuals have different internal biological resources available for use. The infant is very limited biologically. He can only grasp, suck, thrash, and cry, with even his sight emerging only gradually. The child has considerably greater mobility, perceptual acuity, intellectualizing capacity, and affect. Adolescence and adulthood bring greater strength, intellectual organizing capacity, and mature sexual functioning among other abilities. As one moves toward old age, biological capacity begins to decline —less vigor, mobility, strength, perceptual acuity, and learning flexibility. Taking these varying developmental stages into account, society demands different skills and behaviors from individuals at different points in the life cycle. This is one of the reasons why each society attempts to define stages in the life cycle, and provides social recognition of their progressive attainment. It is only by acknowledging a given stage in the life cycle that society can reasonably impose expectations on its members. We don't expect a newborn to read; we don't expect adults to suck their thumbs.

Second, individuals have different external social resources available for use. In recognition of the individual's developing biological capacities, societal resources are structured in ways that are appropriate to the individual's needs and abilities. The newborn is surrounded by a family which cares for him and protects him from unreasonable demands by others. In the nurturing process, the emerging person is helped to understand and accept himself. As an adult, the family will make radically different demands and provide very different resources. Adults have responsibility for the financial security and interpersonal integrity of the family. Now mature persons, they share intimacies and tasks which are mutually supportive, and which help the young to develop. In old age, one becomes reliant to some extent on others again. One may need help getting on and off buses. One may need financial and social assistance. One may need homemaker services when cooking and housekeeping become too difficult. At each point in the life cycle, one is surrounded by different group and organizational contexts, each making different demands and providing different resources.

Third, individuals face different crises at different points in the life cycle. As noted earlier, the life cycle is partly biological and partly socially created. The stages defined by society impose demands and limits on individuals, and by so doing may create problems for them. At each stage in the life cycle, there are predictable crises that may occur, and, to some extent, that society attempts to anticipate. Stated in another way, the individual is "at risk" in different ways at different stages in the life cycle. For example, the infant and the child are defined as being relatively passive participants in the social spectrum. They are cared for by others, they make few concrete contributions in a complex industrialized society, and they are expected to be learning and growing up. The risk of being cared for by others is that one is dependent on others, and one can therefore be easily abused by them. Some children are physically abused, some are emotionally scarred, and some are simply ignored. All are risks of being a child or an infant in a life cycle that defines the young as relatively helpless. Adults, on the other hand, are defined as being active participants in society, the makers and the doers. The risk in adulthood is therefore different. Adults worry about being incompetent, ineffective, unnecessary. Work becomes very important—lack of job skills and unemployment are very real threats. Interpersonal relations become important—being unpopular and socially isolated is dreaded.

Much of the psychological theory in this chapter, and the sociological theory in the next chapter, can be appreciated more fully if tied to the life cycle. The social welfare professional must understand the biological and social changes that occur in the maturation and aging processes. She must also understand the structure of society, which assumes that its members have certain skills and needs at different points in their development, and which structures demands and resources accordingly. Although there are some broad uniformities in the human development of most people, each individual confronts the crises at each major stage in the life cycle with different internal and external resources. For each, the ability to surmount the crises successfully will vary. For each, the need for help from the social welfare institution will vary. Knowledge of human development and the life cycle sensitizes the social welfare professional to the changes that occur over the life span, the different crises the process of living brings, and the need to structure different services at different points in the life cycle.

PSYCHOANALYTIC PERSPECTIVES

Sigmund Freud created a theoretical framework that attempted to unify the physiological and social events of the life cycle in a theory that explained personality formation and malfunction. "As a result of the specificity and generality of psychoanalytic theory, it seems fair to say that at the present time no theory of human behavior comes closer to accomplishing the full purpose of a behavioral theory; no other theory accounts for all the data of human behavior, its development, and its pathological deviations in terms of a basic set of postulates and derivations."[5] An added attraction of Freud's work was that it was relatively scientific for its time, and capitalized on the emerging belief that human behavior could be scientifically studied.

Personality has been defined as "the sum of an individual's interrelated drives, temperament, and social roles; the unique . . . [combination] of characteristics which the individual manifests in his behavior."[6] Freud postulated that the human personality develops "through the stages of psycho-sexual development as the primary source of libidinal gratification shifts from the mouth to the anus to the genitals."[7] These stages are the oral, anal, phallic, latency, and adolescent. The major functioning personality units become differentiated as a result of stage development. These units, which Freud called "mental structures," are the id, ego, and superego. They may operate at one or more of three levels: the unconscious, the preconscious, and the conscious.[8] Since the Freudian personality is one with limited psychic resources (libidinal energy), the ego and superego grow by using energy originally utilized by the id.

Freud saw the personality developing as a result of two processes: the confrontation of the physical organism (id) with the social world, which results in the formation of the ego and superego; and passing through five stages in the course of the transformation of the physical organism into a fully socialized personality. The importance of the stages is that:

> Each stage can be thought of as confronting the child with a new problem, exposing him for the first time to a particular interpersonal relationship. . . . As a consequence of each stage, a certain amount of the individual's cathexes are fixated at that stage, and thus certain attitudes, fears, fantasies, defenses, and expectations are more or less permanently built into the personality. Major psychopathology results when excessive amounts of libido are fixated at an early developmental stage and the accompanying pattern of adjustment developed at that stage is maladapted to the demands of adult life.[9]

Consequently, we can see that the Freudian theory of personality development is a stage and conflict theory. The features of the personality develop through a series of stage transitions and grow out of the competition by each of the mental structures for its share of the existing libidinal energy. Exhibit 4-2 illustrates the major parts of the personality as described by Freud.

EXHIBIT **4-2**

The Freudian Personality at a Glance

Although an artificial construct for illustrative purposes, an effective way to see the scope of the Freudian theory of personality is in the following diagram taken from class notes of a lecture by Dr. Westman at the University of Michigan School of Social Work on October 23, 1962.[a]

The diagram schematically represents the three mental structures and the functions that each plays in the personality. The total psychic (libidinal) energy within the system is fixed and it is a closed system; therefore, if the boundaries between any structures are to be changed, it will necessarily mean a redistribution of energy (which is why it is called a "hydraulic theory"). These structures develop in the process of moving through stages. Since the hydraulic nature of the system means one structure's gain is another's loss, defense mechanisms exist for each structure's use in trying to protect itself; hence the conflict nature of the system. Note that the Id is completely unconscious, while the Ego and Superego have conscious, preconscious, and unconscious components.

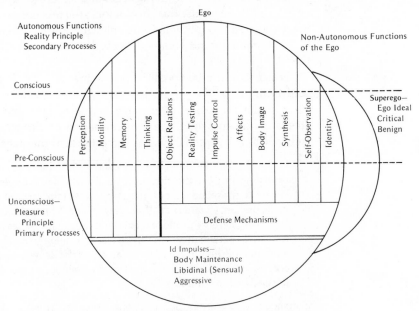

From a personal communication with Jack C. Westman, M.D., Professor of Psychiatry, University of Wisconsin. Used with permission.

[a]For an elaboration of any of the concepts used, refer to Charles Brenner, *An Elementary Textbook of Psychoanalysis* (Garden City: Doubleday, 1957).

Freudian theory generated a number of "neo-Freudians" who modified and extended Freud's work in a variety of ways. For example, Otto Rank emphasized separation trauma as a motivating personality force,[10] and C. G. Jung developed his analytical psychology.[11] Two of the neo-Freudians who have had considerable contemporary influence on the adaptation of Freud's ideas to social welfare contexts have been Erik Erikson and Carl Rogers.

Erikson's work is in part an attempt to elaborate the stages beyond adolescence, the last discussed by Freud. David Elkind says of Erikson,

> His descriptions of the stages of the life cycle, for example, have advanced psychoanalytic theory to the point where it can now describe the development of the healthy personality on its own terms and not merely as the opposite of a sick one. Likewise, Erikson's emphasis upon the problems unique to adolescents and adults living in today's society has helped to rectify the one-sided emphasis on childhood as the beginning and end of personality development.[12]

Erikson begins with "an epigenetic principle of maturation,"[13] which postulates that each individual has a physical timetable governing her maturation. This timetable determines when libidinal energy will be shifted from one part of the body to another.

> This means that stages of development do not grow out of each other. For example, the stage when anal-type functioning is dominant does not result from the child-environment interaction necessary to successful passage through the oral stage. . . . The primary condition (for the oral to anal transition) is his maturational code, which determines when the locus of instinctual investment will be shifted from the oral to the anal zone. . . . But continuity between stages is also implied by the epigenetic principle insofar as each organ must already be a potential part of the ground plan in order for it to grow out of it and mature at the proper time.[14]

Erikson, then, is giving a different kind of emphasis to the biological component of personality from that assigned it by Freud. Whereas Freud saw the personality being shaped by a confrontation of internal biological and external social forces, Erikson says biological forces set a timetable to which social forces must adapt if the personality is to be a healthy one. Once a given biological stage is passed, the individual must move on, whether he has achieved a successful social adaptation to the earlier stage or not.

The combination of a genetic time clock and the fact that biological changes occur throughout the life cycle made it natural for Erikson to extend Freud's stages beyond adolescence. Erikson's eight stages are:[15]

1. *Oral stage.* Crisis of trust in the person on whom one is most dependent for one's sustenance.

2. *Anal stage.* Crisis of whether one will develop feelings of autonomy or shame and doubt about oneself, one's actions, and one's ability to be autonomous.

3. *Phallic stage.* Crisis of acquiring a sense of moral responsibility result-

ing from the initiative and consequent guilt in the resolution of the Oedipal problem.

4. *Latency stage*. Crisis of industriousness versus feelings of inferiority and overconformity.
5. *Adolescent stage*. Crisis of identity adoption versus identity diffusion.
6. *Genital stage*. Crisis of gratification from intimacy and solidarity versus isolation and withdrawal from relationships.
7. *Adulthood*. Crisis of caring for others and being a contributor versus self-absorption, stagnation, and interpersonal impoverishment.
8. *Senescence*. Crisis of ego integration versus despair.

Elkind summarizes the significance of Erikson's eight stages as follows:

> Their presentation . . . frees the clinician to treat adult emotional problems as failures (in part at least) to solve genuinely adult personality crises and not, as heretofore, as mere residuals of infantile frustrations and conflicts. This view of personality growth . . . takes some of the onus off parents and takes account of the role which society and the person himself play in the formation of the individual personality. Finally, Erikson has offered hope for us all by demonstrating that each phase of growth has its strengths as well as its weaknesses and that failures at one stage of development can be rectified by successes at later stages.[16]

Exhibit 4-3 (see pp. 150-51) summarizes the major components of the stage theories discussed above.

The work of Carl Rogers is not concerned with stages of development. Instead, it focuses on the person's perception of himself and his situation, sharing with Erikson's work more of a focus on current functioning than on the early childhood foundations of behavior. Rogers uses the terms nondirective and client-centered to describe the relationship the professional has with the person being helped. In his words, "it is the counselor's aim to perceive as sensitively and accurately as possible all of the perceptual field as it is being experienced by the client, with the same figure and ground relationships, to the full degree the client is willing to communicate that perceptual field . . .".[17] He adds that "the fact that I enter with deep understanding into the desperate feelings that exist but do not attempt to take over responsibility, is a most meaningful expression of basic confidence in the forward-moving tendencies in the human organism."[18] Exhibit 4-4 (pp. 152-53) provides more detail about the propositions underlying his client-centered theory of personality. It is sufficient for our purposes in this chapter to note that Rogers, like Erikson, has taken a basic psychological approach to human functioning, but adapted it to encompass the totality of the life cycle and to focus on conscious intervention in areas of problematic personality functioning.

Although the work of neo-Freudians like Erikson and Rogers has helped to increase the scope and flexibility of a psychoanalytic approach to personality development and functioning, psychoanalytic theory has some basic assumptions and characteristics that can be problematic for the social welfare practitioner. On the other hand, psychoanalytic theory also has some distinct advantages. Both the advantages and disadvantages need to be appreciated by the social welfare practitioner if maximum effective use of the theory is to be achieved in her work, and if it is to be most effectively compared with other possible theoretical approaches.

Classical psychoanalytic theory is historical in nature, emphasizing early childhood experiences. It asserts that there are universal life stages that everyone must traverse due to physiological needs and an epigenetic maturational plan. There is said to be a normal progression through the stages, with given physical and social skills developing in each. The mental structures assumed to be developing concurrently with the stage progression cannot be seen or directly measured. They must be inferred from behavior that is considered symptomatic. However, since the personality system is closed with respect to psychic energy available, changing symptoms may only produce another symptom rather than achieving a change in the underlying mental structures. The focus in using the theory is on identifying and ultimately overcoming those stage fixations that have prevented subsequent personality growth according to the ideal model. In other words, the view tends to be backward and inward rather than present or future and outward.

There are several problems with psychoanalytic theory, which have important effects on attempts to translate the theory into social welfare practice principles. The first is the problem of empirical validity: "The primary findings obtained by the therapeutic method are rich verbal characterizations of the individual's uniqueness. Nevertheless, one is struck by how little such data have seemed either to test the validity of psychoanalytic assertions or to lead to revision of the theory as to the nature of psychosexual, psychosocial, and ego development."[19] Stated in another way, "the basic criticism to be made of psychoanalytic theory is that it focuses upon thoughts and feelings as the real data and these are relatively inaccessible."[20]

A second problem is that of objectivity: "The data are uniquely confounded with the therapist's interpretation, and therapists tend to interpret the same observations differently, that is, in accordance with different theoretical assumptions. Thus, not only are the data not reliable, but it is also not always certain which theoretical assertions they are relevant to."[21] The third problem is the inferential nature of the theory with respect to normal behavior: "Little is done to examine average or normally expectable psychological development directly. Rather, the initial and fundamental conceptualization of normal behavior is based upon extrapolations from abnormal behavior."[22] Fourth, the theory does not clearly specify the natures of the id, ego, and superego at each stage of development: "It is therefore not clear what characteristic functional differences and causal or interactive functional relationships exist between the personality structures and psychosexual, psychosocial, perceptual, coping, and intellectual activity at each stage."[23] Finally, not all aspects of the theory have been equally developed, detracting from its logical consistency and explanatory power.[24]

EXHIBIT 4-3

Stages at a Glance

This chart is taken from notes from a lecture given by Dr. Mary Burns at the University of Michigan School of Social Work. It is an excellent summary of major stage theories, showing the relationship between physical and social development.

PSYCHOBIOLOGICAL DEVELOPMENT

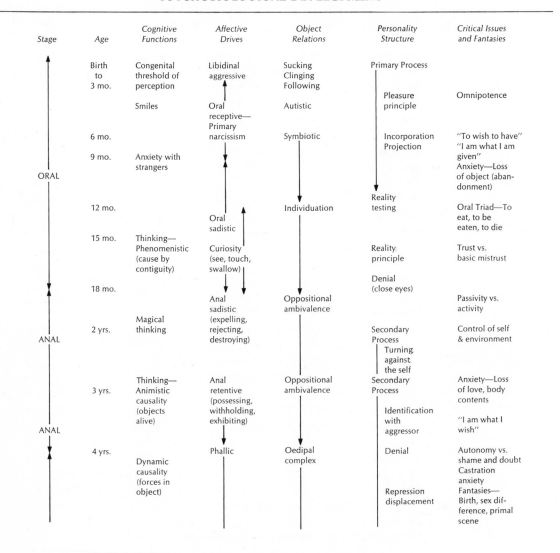

Stage	Age	Cognitive Functions	Affective Drives	Object Relations	Personality Structure	Critical Issues and Fantasies
ORAL	Birth to 3 mo.	Congenital threshold of perception	Libidinal aggressive	Sucking Clinging Following	Primary Process	
		Smiles	Oral receptive— Primary narcissism	Autistic	Pleasure principle	Omnipotence
	6 mo.			Symbiotic	Incorporation Projection	"To wish to have" "I am what I am given" Anxiety—Loss of object (abandonment)
	9 mo.	Anxiety with strangers				
	12 mo.		Oral sadistic	Individuation	Reality testing	Oral Triad—To eat, to be eaten, to die
	15 mo.	Thinking— Phenomenistic (cause by contiguity)	Curiosity (see, touch, swallow)		Reality principle	Trust vs. basic mistrust
	18 mo.		Anal sadistic (expelling, rejecting, destroying)	Oppositional ambivalence	Denial (close eyes)	Passivity vs. activity
ANAL	2 yrs.	Magical thinking			Secondary Process Turning against the self	Control of self & environment
ANAL	3 yrs.	Thinking— Animistic causality (objects alive)	Anal retentive (possessing, withholding, exhibiting)	Oppositional ambivalence	Secondary Process Identification with aggressor	Anxiety—Loss of love, body contents "I am what I wish"
	4 yrs.	Dynamic causality (forces in object)	Phallic	Oedipal complex	Denial Repression displacement	Autonomy vs. shame and doubt Castration anxiety Fantasies— Birth, sex difference, primal scene

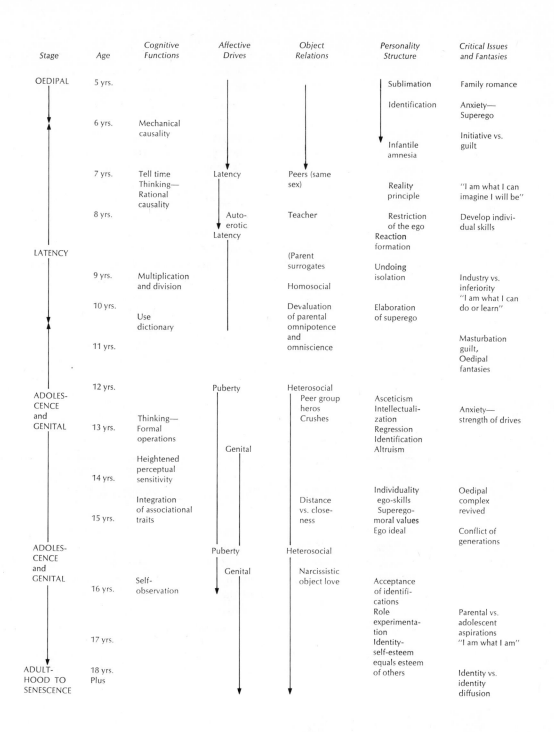

Stage	Age	Cognitive Functions	Affective Drives	Object Relations	Personality Structure	Critical Issues and Fantasies
OEDIPAL	5 yrs.				Sublimation	Family romance
	6 yrs.	Mechanical causality			Identification / Infantile amnesia	Anxiety—Superego / Initiative vs. guilt
	7 yrs.	Tell time Thinking—Rational causality	Latency	Peers (same sex)	Reality principle	"I am what I can imagine I will be"
	8 yrs.		Auto-erotic Latency	Teacher	Restriction of the ego / Reaction formation	Develop individual skills
LATENCY				(Parent surrogates		
	9 yrs.	Multiplication and division		Homosocial	Undoing isolation	Industry vs. inferiority "I am what I can do or learn"
	10 yrs.	Use dictionary		Devaluation of parental omnipotence and omniscience	Elaboration of superego	
	11 yrs.					Masturbation guilt, Oedipal fantasies
ADOLESCENCE and GENITAL	12 yrs.		Puberty	Heterosocial Peer group heros Crushes	Asceticism Intellectualization Regression Identification Altruism	Anxiety—strength of drives
	13 yrs.	Thinking—Formal operations	Genital			
	14 yrs.	Heightened perceptual sensitivity			Individuality ego-skills Superego-moral values Ego ideal	Oedipal complex revived
	15 yrs.	Integration of associational traits		Distance vs. closeness		Conflict of generations
ADOLESCENCE and GENITAL			Puberty Genital	Heterosocial Narcissistic object love		
	16 yrs.	Self-observation			Acceptance of identifications Role experimentation Identity-self-esteem equals esteem of others	Parental vs. adolescent aspirations "I am what I am"
	17 yrs.					
ADULTHOOD TO SENESCENCE	18 yrs. Plus					Identity vs. identity diffusion

On the basis of the above analysis, several practical problems emerge when attempting to use a psychoanalytic approach in the average social welfare setting. The first is the caution that must be used with a theory which has resisted empirical validation for as long as psychoanalytic theory has. The social sciences are not presently at a stage in their development that enables a practitioner to expect definitive empirical proof before using a potentially relevant social science theory. However, without such proof professional ethics require that a theory be used carefully and under controlled conditions. A second problem is that psychoanalytically based practice requires three scarce resources: (1) practitioners skilled in its considerable complexities; (2) ample time to explore the client's early life history; and (3) a verbal client. Until the amount of training necessary to become a certified competent psychoanalyst is lessened, it seems unrealistic to anticipate large numbers of them, thereby limiting the social welfare contexts in which psychotherapy can be used. As will be seen below, social welfare practitioners may make use of psychoanalytic theory in a variety of ways. However, they should not be thought of as junior psychotherapists since they do not have the knowledge base to control all of the processes involved (transference and counter-transference, for example). The historical nature of psychoanalytic theory always exerts a push toward lengthy analysis, and this is impossible in many social welfare contexts (public assistance agencies with large caseloads, medical settings where contact with clients is often limited, police work, and the like).

EXHIBIT 4-4

The Basic Propositions of Rogers's Client-Centered Approach

Carl Rogers has outlined nineteen propositions that underlie his client-centered theory of personality, and upon which Rogerian therapy is based. In looking at these propositions, it will be a useful exercise to think about the points at which they are similar to Freudian psychoanalytic theory, points at which they expand Freudian theory, and points at which they contradict psychoanalytic theory as Freud expressed it. On the basis of your analysis, do you find Rogers's approach to be more or less useful? Why?

1. Every individual exists in a continually changing world of experience of which he is the center.

2. The organism reacts to the field as it is experienced and perceived. This perceptual field is, for the individual, "reality."

3. The organism reacts as an organized whole to this phenomenal field—alteration of any part will affect other parts.

4. The organism has one basic tendency and

striving—to actualize, maintain, and enhance the experiencing organism.

5. Behavior is basically the goal-directed attempt of the organism to satisfy its needs as experienced, in the field as perceived.

6. Emotion accompanies and in general facilitates such goal-directed behavior, the kind of emotion being related to the seeking versus the consummatory aspects of behavior, and the intensity of the emotion being related to the perceived significance of the behavior for the maintenance and enhancement of the organism.

7. The best vantage point for understanding behavior is from the internal frame of reference of the individual himself.

8. A portion of the total perceptual field gradually becomes differentiated as the self.

9. As a result of interaction with the environment, and particularly as a result of evaluational interaction with others, the structure of self is formed—an organized field, but consistent conceptual patterns of perceptions of characteristics and relationships of the "I" or the "me," together with values attached to these concepts.

10. The values attached to experiences, and the values which are a part of the self-structure, in some instances are values experienced directly by the organism, and in some instances are values introjected or taken over from others, but perceived in distorted fashion, as if they had been experienced directly.

11. As experiences occur in the life of the individual, they are either (a) symbolized, perceived, and organized into some relationship to the self; (b) ignored because there is no perceived relationship to the self-structure; (c) denied symbolization or given a distorted symbolization because the experience is inconsistent with the structure of the self.

12. Most of the ways of behaving which are adopted by the organism are those which are consistent with the concept of self.

13. Behavior may, in some instances, be brought about by organic experiences and needs which have not been symbolized. Such behavior may be inconsistent with the structure of the self, but in such instances the behavior is not "owned" by the individual.

14. Psychological maladjustment exists when the organism denies to awareness significant sensory and visceral experiences, which consequently are not symbolized and organized into the gestalt of the self-structure. When this situation exists, there is a basic or potential psychological tension.

15. Psychological adjustment exists when the concept of self is such that all the sensory and visceral experiences of the organism are, or may be, assimilated on a symbolic level into a consistent relationship with the concept of self.

16. Any experience which is inconsistent with the organization or structure of self may be perceived as a threat, and the more of these perceptions there are, the more rigidly the self-structure is organized to maintain itself.

17. Under certain conditions, involving primarily complete absence of any threat to the self-structure, experiences which are inconsistent with it may be perceived, and examined, and the structure of self revised to assimilate and include such experiences.

18. When the individual perceives and accepts into one consistent and integrated system all his sensory and visceral experiences, then he is necessarily more understanding of others and is more accepting of others as separate individuals.

19. As the individual perceives and accepts into his self-structure more of his organic experiences, he finds that he is replacing his present value system—based so largely upon introjections which have been distortedly symbolized—with a continuing organismic valuing process.

The verbal nature of psychoanalytic theory raises two issues: many client groups are simply not verbally oriented, and many problems are concrete rather than attitudinal or emotional. There is evidence to indicate that some client groups, such as lower-class clients, are not accustomed to verbalizing, do not do so easily, and do not believe that talking about a problem solves it.[25] To some extent, clients skeptical of talking about problems are correct; poverty may be related to early childhood experiences, but talking about poverty or its origins early in life is not likely to solve the poverty problem. Hence, the verbal orientation of psychoanalytic theory runs the risk of elevating concrete problems to verbal abstractions, thereby rendering the professional-client relationship sterile.[26]

There have been on-going attempts to overcome the problems of highly specialized training, lengthy treatment, and a reliance on verbal communication. For example, Phillips and Weiner talk of short-term psychotherapy; this includes several possible techniques (including some nonverbal ones), but requires a firm therapeutic structure to use in changing behavior as directly and efficiently as possible.[27] They also see a role for the psychotherapist as "directing the work of others who will help in accomplishing change and [not being limited to] the practice of psychotherapy in the consulting room."[28] Other attempts to reduce the time spent in psychotherapeutic methods have included focusing on specific problems or personality components,[29] and focusing therapy around crisis situations.[30] The ego psychologist's concern with rational processes and potential for coping with present problems has also tended to reduce the time spent in treatment.[31] There have also been attempts to develop psychoanalytically based nonverbal treatment approaches, many of them using artistic media such as painting or dance.[32] As noted above, Erikson and Rogers have also achieved some success in reorienting the focus of psychoanalysts to permit a more current, reality-based approach to treatment. While none of these attempts to overcome the problems of highly specialized training, lengthy treatment, and a reliance on verbal communication has been completely successful in resolving these problems inherent in a psychoanalytic approach, they have broadened the contexts in which this approach can be used.

Further problems can result from a theory that is based on developmental stages. A stage theory posits a set developmental progression for everyone. This tends to minimize the focus on individual differences. It encourages the selective picking out of data indicating that a given stage was encountered and completed, or that there was an encounter and subsequent fixation. Since stage theories are sensitive to the unique experiences of each individual as these affect stage developments, a minimizing of differences need not occur. However, it becomes very easy to almost unknowingly select information that allows a tidy diagnosis rather than grappling with complexities that could otherwise resist therapeutic organization. The haste often created by too-large caseloads, and the somewhat inbred nature of professions, also tend to foster a reliance on formulas rather than an open appraisal of each unique situation.

If one attempts to resolve the problem objectively, the nonempirical nature of the psychoanalytic system makes it difficult to "prove" the stages. On one hand there has been cross-cultural evidence to show that culturally determined child-rearing patterns tend to produce distinctive patterns of child development. This suggests that a formulation of universal stages may be at least partially inadequate. On the other hand it is clear that the child goes through a genetically patterned physical maturational sequence, and since the stages are related to physical development, there is some support for stage theories. The alert social welfare practitioner needs to be wary of premature categorization, and until the controversy is settled on the basis of empirical data, erring on the side of individual uniqueness minimizes chances of harming a client.

A final problem to consider with psychoanalytic theory is its nonbehavioral nature. Given that its constructs are basically historical and nonvisible, the social welfare professional is in a difficult interventive position. Untrained for in-depth psychoanalysis, and lacking adequate time, the historical nature of the system tends to exclude his participation. Having to deal with internal personality constructs whose existence is inferred creates other barriers. Ego psychology's stress on ego strengths is probably the best solution to these problems. They provide a point from which to progressively test the individual's capacity to cope with present reality, using the internal and historical constructs as potentially useful tools to understand the individual's relevant life history.

In spite of the problems the psychoanalytic approach has for use in a variety of social welfare contexts, it does have real utility. As noted earlier, it is a total system to explain personality development, a crucial area of knowledge for the social welfare professional. We need only think how heavily we rely on such ideas as the influence of the social environment on an infant, the significance of parents and peers in human development, and the potential conflicts between physiological needs and wants and social norms and structures, to realize how much of what we know about human development comes from a psychoanalytic perspective. Furthermore, although one may be primarily concerned with present functioning, few things and no people spring full-blown into the world: current levels of functioning must be at least partially understood with reference to past experiences. This time-experience continuum becomes especially important in future planning, where the social welfare practitioner attempts to find a social environment that will be related to past and present experiences in certain defined ways.

A related utility of the psychoanalytic system revolves around the concept of diagnosis. A person with a problem needs some help in understanding what the problem is, how it occurred, and what the possible solutions are. The psychoanalytic approach can be helpful in understanding those problems that are strongly related to personal feelings and personality characteristics, and may be especially helpful in trying to understand how the problem occurred. This process of understanding the problem and its causes is called diagnosis. Treatment usually refers to the planning for and carrying through of solutions to the problem.[33] The totality of the psychoanalytic system has also had the beneficial effect of balancing the view of the human personality as both a physical and social entity. Psychoanalytic theory is built on both physical and social maturation, and this rounded perspective can serve as a welcome antidote to more narrowly conceived attempts to understand and change human behavior.[34]

Having briefly reviewed psychoanalytic theory and its implications for use in social welfare contexts, perhaps the best conclusion would be that it has its advantages and disadvantages.[35] Yet its development has stagnated because it is subject to many interpretations that are not easy to verify empirically. This has stimulated a search for other psychological theories that avoid some of the problems of psychoanalytic theory. Behavioristic psychological theories are successful in doing this. Because these theories are primarily concerned with individual behavior rather than internal states of the organism, they suggest a very different approach to behavior modification than does psychoanalytic theory.

BEHAVIORAL
PERSPECTIVES

The social welfare practitioner wants to be able to modify given behavior according to the problem-solving plan worked out with the client. In order to do so, she must have some theoretical conception of how behavior is learned and maintained. Psychoanalytically oriented and behavioristically oriented practitioners are working toward the same goal of behavior modification, but have different theoretical conceptions of how behavior is learned and maintained. The psychoanalytically oriented practitioner focuses on the individual's early biological, psychological, and social experiences. The logical intervention point, then, is internal. The practitioner attempts to modify behavior by modifying the internal personality structure which is the source of behavior. As will be shown, the behaviorally oriented practitioner proceeds quite differently and from a rather different conception of personality structure and functioning.

Behavioristic theory asserts that behavior is learned in separate units (acts); that the units (acts) are related to each other; and that the units (acts) become established in the individual's behavior repertoire by means of external reinforcement.

> Central to the [behavioristic] conception of growth is the *environmentalistic* assumption that the source of all psychological phenomena is stimulation from the outside world . . . [and] psychological phenomena, like all other natural occurrences, are really physical in quality, or, at least, reducible to characterization in *physicalistic* terms.[36]

In a behavioristic perspective, acts are stimulated by the environment, and are associated with each other into habits (learned behavioral patterns). Since acts are associational, behavior already learned does affect future behavior. "Stored associations influence the child's responses to environmental stimulation. The major [behavioristic] developmental hypothesis is therefore that early conditioned associations affect the child's behavior later in life."[37] While the ideas of environmental influence on behavior, and early behavior affecting later behavior, are not incongruent with a psychoanalytic approach, the fact that no internal personality structure is specified is quite different from psychoanalytic theory. The focus on individual acts implies that they can be modified without a major realignment of the personality structure, a belief that is also quite divergent from psychoanalytic postulates.[38]

There are three ways in which behavioral theorists assert that behavior may be learned: classical (or respondent) conditioning; operant (or instrumental) conditioning; and imitation. Conditioning is most simply defined as the association of stimuli with responses. Classical (or respondent) conditioning is built on the principles of the unconditioned reflex and contiguity. An unconditioned reflex is an "innate response to stimuli,"[39] while the contiguity principle specifies that "the contiguity of two stimuli tends to give one of them the ability to elicit responses previously made to the other."[40] Classical conditioning, then, involves stimulus substitution. An unconditioned stimulus (one that evokes an unconditioned reflex) is paired with a conditioned stimulus (one that would not normally evoke the unconditioned reflex). Eventually the conditioned stimulus evokes the behavior previously evoked by the unconditioned stimulus. The famous Pavlov experiment illustrates classical conditioning.

EXHIBIT 4-5

Classical Conditioning Illustrated: Pavlov's Dog

This excerpt is from Alfred Baldwin's *Theories of Child Development*. For more detail, an original source is suggested: I. P. Pavlov, *Experimental Psychology and Other Essays* (New York: Philosophical Library, 1957).

In his original experiments, Pavlov conditioned the salivary response in the dog. The dog was operated on, so that the secretion of the salivary gland could be measured accurately, ordinarily in drops of saliva. The dog salivated whenever a food powder was introduced into his mouth. This salivary response to the food powder occurred on the first trial, so the salivation is called the *unconditioned*

response, and the food powder the *unconditioned stimulus.* The conditioning process consists of pairing some other stimulus with the unconditioned stimulus. In one of the famous Pavlovian experiments, a bell was rung slightly before the food stimulus was presented. After this combination of bell and food had been repeated a number of times, the dog began to salivate whenever the bell was rung, even if on that particular trial no food was given. So the bell is called the *conditioned stimulus* or *conditioning stimulus,* and the salivation to the bell the *conditioned response.*

Notice that there is a built-in limitation to the learning that may occur in classical conditioning. Since this type of conditioning depends on the existence of an unconditioned stimulus and response, only responses that already exist can be tied to different stimuli. Although classical conditioning is usable in social welfare contexts, a more flexible learning mechanism would clearly have greater utility.

Operant (or instrumental) conditioning is just such a tool. In operant conditioning, an individual's behavior is reacted to in some way by the environment (the individual can in some respects be his own environment). Behavior that is responded to in a reinforcing way has the probability of its repetition increased. If the behavior continues to be reinforced it can be established as a habit. Operant conditioning may occur for randomly performed behaviors, or it may be shaped. Shaping starts with randomly performed behavior, successively reinforcing it and eliminating it as new behaviors closer to the ultimately desired behavior occur and are in turn reinforced and eliminated. Shaping is discussed in more detail later in this chapter.

> There is one major difference between classical and instrumental (operant) conditioning. In classical conditioning, an action that is already a response to a stimulus can be put under the control of a stimulus by contiguity of the two stimuli. In instrumental conditioning, an action that is not tied to any specific stimulus can be put under the control of a stimulus by rewarding the action consistently when it is performed in the presence of the stimulus. Thus, randomly occurring actions can be made into reliable, controllable responses or regularly recurring actions.[41]

Two of the major issues to be faced in operant conditioning are the nature of the reinforcements and the schedule (frequency) of reinforcements. It is believed that individuals are ready to respond to stimuli in different ways at different times (called the drive state), and that different drive states have different drive stimuli. Therefore, there is not a general uniformity of conditioning states; what will be reinforcing will vary between individuals and by drive state of any given individual. While candy may be a generally effective reinforcer for the average child, it will not be for certain children, and will be less effective for any given child at some times than at others. Clearly the individual's past reinforcement history will be important in understanding the crucial question of what is reinforcing for that individual, and this in turn is tied to cultural values and behavior patterns. Without such knowledge, the practitioner's ability to control behavior in an operant context is limited. A further complication is that the frequency of reinforcement also affects the learning that occurs. It has been experimentally shown that the frequency and patterning of reinforcements produces different learning patterns, again suggesting that the operant conditioning context is more complicated than might at first be assumed.[42]

A third behavioristic learning device is observational learning, or, specifically, imitation. Observational learning "describes the fact that people can learn behavior patterns merely by watching other people perform them, that their own acts can be reinforced or inhibited by observing reinforcements and punishments to other people, and that they can acquire conditioned emotional responses to stimuli which accompany a painful stimulus to another person."[43] Whether observational learning occurs through imitation is affected by the individual's history of reward for imitation, her history of reward deprivation, her level of self-esteem and general dependency, and her drive state. Observational learning may occur in primary or secondary contexts (that is, direct viewing or via a mechanical medium such as television).

Bandura and Walters suggest four major behavior modification techniques based on behavioral principles.[44] Most directly related to conditioning as a learning process is positive reinforcement—the teaching of behavior through the manipulation of positive reinforcements (rewards). The environment commonly dispenses rewards that enable social learning to occur in many societal contexts. Social welfare practitioners may manipulate rewards in purposeful ways to strengthen existing behaviors that are rarely or randomly performed. For example, a common problem of many marginally employable persons is their lack of skill in job-interview situations. In such a case, the helping person could use positive reinforcements to strengthen those behaviors appropriate to the job-interview context, such as punctuality, style of dress, and so on.

Shaping is a particularly potent adjunct of positive reinforcement as a behavior-changing technique because of its use in teaching behaviors that do not exist in the client's behavioral repertoire (in conjunction with extinction, discussed below). Social welfare practitioners are often in the situation of teaching new behaviors that are more socially acceptable ways to achieve client goals. A behavior modification technique that can capitalize on existing adaptive behavior and also teach new behavior is highly desirable. Positive reinforcement and shaping are especially desirable because they accentuate the positive. The positive reinforcement process is one which achieves change in a way that is likely to be acceptable to the client and that does not require that he recognize his problems. The recognition by a client of problems in his functioning is often productive and important, but there are times when such recognition is itself part of the problem, and when the emphasis on problems can be destructive to the client's self-esteem.

The question of problem awareness raises ethical issues in the use of behavior modification techniques. In a psychoanalytic approach, the talking through of the individual's problems and social history presumably insures at least a minimal recognition and acceptance of the behavior-change process by the client. In the behavioristic approach, since behavior modification occurs through the manipulation of stimuli, reinforcements, and models, it is entirely possible for an individual's behavior to be modified without him knowing it (see Exhibit 4-6).

Some have questioned the desirability of behavior modification techniques because of their obvious subversive potential. However, the resolution of the problem of misuse of a therapeutic tool does not lie in its abandonment. Doctors are known occasionally to misuse their techniques, but few would seriously propose that the techniques therefore be abandoned. The resolution of the issue in medicine lies in the strength of the profession to regulate member behavior, and this must be the solution in those professions using any form of behavior modification techniques. Ethical behavior is a professional responsibility, and has its foundation in effective professional socialization and sanctioning.

EXHIBIT 4-6

The Student's Revenge: Reinforcing the Instructor

The following incident is said to have happened at a large state university. It is an excellent example of positive reinforcement working without the knowledge of the person being reinforced; student readers may also gain other satisfactions from this account.

In a course dealing with principles of behavioral modification, the students decided to band together to control the behavior of the instructor in the classroom. When the instructor lectured from one corner of the room, the students showed interest and enthusiasm; when he was in the other corner, they showed apathy and boredom. Soon they had the instructor confined to the corner in which he was rewarded by the students' interest. In this example, one notes that the instructor was responsive to student reaction, and found student interest rewarding. There may be instances, of course, where an instructor is unaware of student reaction and interest, in which case the students would have to find other rewards to manipulate.

A common goal of social welfare professionals is to achieve behavior change. Such change may result from therapeutic intervention with individuals or groups, or from social structural change that alters the environment in which individuals live, thereby facilitating individual and group behavior change. The social welfare practitioner cannot avoid the considerable responsibility entailed in behavior change. He or she must first be certain that efforts toward change, including methods and objectives, are acceptable to the people who will be affected by them. Having assured oneself of this, one is committed to the appropriate use of the most relevant and effective skill and knowledge at one's disposal in planning and executing change.

Psychoanalytic and behavioral techniques are two possible approaches to achieving behavior change. In trying to decide which approach to use in any given problem situation, the practitioner will want to consider the empirical evidence relating to demonstrated effectiveness, and considerably more evidence exists for behaviorally based techniques than for psychoanalytically based ones. Such evidence must then be weighed in terms of the appropriateness of a behavioral approach, given the conditions under which the practitioner and client must work, and the acceptability of such an approach to the client. Ultimately it always comes down to a matter of individual judgment and conscience,[45] but these decisions should always rest on the evaluation of the behavior change desired by the practitioner and the client as well as a consideration of the demonstrated effectiveness and appropriateness of alternative behavior-change techniques.

Whereas positive reinforcement was shown to be a powerful tool in strengthening and maintaining behavior, extinction is a tool usable in weakening and eliminating behavior.[46] Thomas defines the use of extinction as "withholding the reinforcer when a response, previously reinforced by that reinforcer, is emitted."[47] In many respects, extinction is the reverse side of positive reinforcement, and is based on the same principle that behavior will be performed when it results in gratification for the actor. Extinction is a planned process of making sure that the reinforcement that previously occurred (thereby maintaining the behavior) no longer occurs. Under such conditions, the basis for the future performance of the behavior will be eliminated and the probability of its future occurrence reduced until it is eliminated altogether.

EXHIBIT 4-7

An Example of Extinction

. . . A twenty-one-month-old boy . . . engaged in tyrannical tantrum behavior. The child would scream and fuss when put to bed and his parents couldn't leave the bedroom until he was asleep. The parents generally spent one-half to two hours simply waiting in the room until the boy went to sleep.

After it was determined that the tantrum behavior was sustained by the attention provided by the parents at bedtime, it was decided to institute a

From Edwin Thomas, ed., *The Socio-Behavioral Approach and Applications to Social Work* (New York: Council on Social Work Education, 1967), pp. 3–4. Reprinted by permission of the Council on Social Work Education.

regimen of extinction. The treatment program was based upon research indicating that by steadfastly withholding reinforcers that sustain the behavior, there will eventually be a diminution of the behavior in question. It was decided to put the child to bed in a leisurely and relaxed fashion. Then, following the usual pleasantries, the parent was to leave and the door to be left closed. On the first night, the child screamed for forty-five minutes; on the second, he did not fuss at all; on the third, he screamed for ten minutes; on the fourth, for six; on the fifth for three, on the sixth, for two; and, finally, after seven sessions, there was no screaming at all. In a follow-up, there were no side- or after-effects, and the child was found to be friendly, expressive, and outgoing.

Related to extinction, but distinct from it, is punishment. Thomas sees punishment as "being a consequence of responding that reduces the future rate of that response."[48] He goes on to say that "there are two operations following an operant response that may have this effect. One is the presentation of a stimulus that is usually 'aversive' [unpleasant], and the other is the removal of a positive reinforcing condition. . . ."[49] The removal of a positive reinforcement is closely related to extinction, which entails withholding such a reinforcement. However, the distinction between removing and withholding produces rather different results. Punishment as a technique has some potential side effects that can limit its effectiveness, while extinction does not. Before considering the use of punishment in behavior modification, the practitioner should consider the costs, alternatives, conditions for its use, and possible side effects (such as avoidance, aggression, or loss of control).[50]

A third behavioral technique is counter-conditioning, sometimes called reciprocal inhibition. "The fundamental principle in using counter-conditioning therapeutically, is to establish a response which is incompatible with a maladaptive response so the latter is eliminated."[51] Counter-conditioning is a tool usable in eliminating undesirable behavior. It is based on the obvious fact that one cannot do two incompatible things at once. Rewards are provided to strengthen the desired behavior, which are more attractive than the rewards maintaining the undesired behavior. Counter-conditioning frequently includes desensitization, which involves the purposeful manipulation of the stimulus evoking the undesired behavor. It is first presented in mild forms so that the resulting undesired responses are relatively weak and thus readily extinguishable.[52] As the desired behavior is progressively more strongly established, the stimulus evoking the undesired behavior may be presented in its normal form. The undesired response will now be more weakly reinforced than the desired response and will therefore be extinguished.[53]

EXHIBIT 4-8

An Example of Counter-Conditioning

A now classic example is the treatment of fear of rabbits, rats, and other furry objects, in a three-year-old child named Peter. . . . Feeding was used as an incompatible response, but if Peter was given sweets with a rabbit near him, his fear was so

From Derek Jehu, *Learning Theory and Social Work* (London: Routledge & Kegan Paul; New York: Humanities Press Inc., 1967), p. 84.

strong that he ignored them in favor of escaping from the animal. To overcome this difficulty, while Peter ate, a caged rabbit was first introduced into the far corner of the room, and then gradually over a number of sessions, it was released from the cage and brought nearer to him, until finally he quite happily held the animal on his lap and allowed it to nibble his fingers.

Most often one's goal is not simply to eliminate an undesired behavior. Techniques for eliminating an undesirable behavior are commonly used along with techniques to establish or maintain a desired behavior. In some cases an individual knows an appropriate behavior, but is being rewarded for performing an inappropriate behavior rather than the appropriate one. In such cases, the undesired behavior may be eliminated and the desired behavior strengthened, through, for example, the simultaneous use of extinction and positive reinforcement. In other cases an individual may not know an appropriate behavior, so elimination of the undesired behavior could create a behavioral void. In such cases a technique to establish a new behavior is required. Two such techniques will be presented below.

One technique used in establishing a new behavior is "shaping." It begins with a spontaneously emitted behavior and then uses differential reinforcement of selected responses to achieve closer approximations of the desired behavior.[54] However, shaping can be a long, complex procedure. It is best suited to teaching relatively simple behaviors when an approximation of that behavior is already spontaneously performed. As Bandura has said,

> Differential reinforcement alone can be employed to evoke new patterns of behavior under conditions where responses are composed of readily available elements, stimuli exist that are capable of arousing actions that resemble the desired pattern, erroneous responsiveness does not produce injurious consequences, and the learning agent possesses sufficient endurance.[55]

Shaping, then, is based on reinforcement and can be used to teach new behavior, but it is somewhat limited in the range of behaviors easily taught in this manner.

Modeling, on the other hand, offers a more flexible teaching technique. Modeling—observational learning—results in new behavior when an observer faithfully reproduces a model's behavior that was not previously in the observer's behavioral repertoire. Observing a model can also serve to inhibit or disinhibit an observer's behavior, depending on the consequences to the model of his behavior. Inhibition, disinhibition, and response facilitation are not mechanisms for learning new behaviors. These involve already existing behaviors being performed more or less frequently as a result of exposure to a model.[56] Modeling may occur when the model is physically present or when the model is presented vicariously, and characteristics of the model will affect the amount of modeling that takes place (the model's prestige and power, age, consequences to the model of his behavior, and so on).

Having briefly reviewed some major behavioral concepts, and having seen some of the specific behavior-modification techniques resulting from such theory, we can now examine some of the general considerations in the use of these techniques in social welfare settings. One is struck by the everyday nature of many of these techniques. Social welfare personnel frequently reward clients for desired behavior, as when a worker nods and smiles when a client tells him significant information. Similarly, rewards are commonly withheld in personal and professional settings when someone has not acted properly. This realization of the common usage of behavioral techniques reveals their strength in being usable in almost any situation. It also suggests that social welfare personnel must have a high level of self-awareness to use these common techniques in a planned way rather than inadvertently reinforcing or extinguishing behavior. For example, a doctor can easily extinguish preventative visits by patients if she fails to keep appointments, has unpleasant auxiliary staff, or has unreasonably high fees, even though she may actually want to encourage preventative medical practice. It is also evident that practitioners subscribing to nonbehavioral treatment approaches are, whether they realize it or like it, practicing behavioral modification techniques.[57]

A second implication of this approach is that behavior change must be carefully planned. A variety of techniques is available, selected according to the problem at hand. Each technique has its distinctive application requirements, and must be specifically applied in any given situation. As just one example, it has been noted that there is no such thing as a uniform reward; what is rewarding will vary from person to person and situation to situation. Once rewards have been selected, the schedule of their presentation must be determined as well as the specific behaviors to which they will be related. This approach is clearly contradictory to psychoanalytic approaches, which assume that any problem may be solved using one basic technique. The resolution of this confrontation between approaches is an individual decision, but it appears that the weight of empirical evidence is on the side of behavioral approaches.

A third issue in behavioral techniques is the control needed for effective use. Since reinforcers and stimuli must be manipulated, behavioral techniques can be most effectively used in settings allowing complete control of the client and his environment. Although this is possible in some social welfare settings, such as prisons and mental hospitals, many settings permit variable, partial control. Some behavior modification can occur under such conditions, and may then be generalized to situations not directly under the practitioner's control, as, for example, when a social worker positively reinforces promptness in keeping appointments. However, in many cases the lack of the practitioner's ability to control all the significant rewards or stimuli can seriously interfere in the behavior-modification process. Lack of access to all controlling variables may also make it difficult to determine what the meaningful rewards and stimuli are, especially when there are socioeconomic and cultural differences between practitioner and client.

A fourth point to consider about the utility of behavioral techniques is their close relationship to the social environment. Since behavior is seen as supported by rewards that are most often external to the individual, a behavioristic approach is quite social. This suggests that such techniques are very accessible to practitioners (with the limitations noted in the preceding paragraph). Behavior can be seen and directly manipulated, while internal processes can only be dealt with indirectly. On the other hand, it is obvious that social processes maintaining behavior may be very difficult to change, and, if individual change depends on social change, the prognosis for both may be poor. This serves to emphasize the important point that social welfare practitioners must function at both the individual and community levels to have maximum impact on the ability of individuals to function effectively in society.

CONCLUSION This chapter has attempted to introduce the value of theory for practitioners, as well as reviewing some especially useful psychological theories. Any theory helps the practitioner to organize her knowledge and concrete observations. It provides leads in the search for meaning when trying to understand behavior, and suggests relationships between seemingly discrete events. A basic area of understanding for the social welfare professional is the way in which the individual grows, both physically and emotionally, in the course of encountering social experiences. Freud, Erikson, and Rogers, all working within a psychoanalytic perspective, provide distinctive insights into the process of personality development and functioning. The behaviorists take a rather different approach in trying to explain this same process.

The well-informed social welfare professional must understand both these approaches, and have thought through the implications for explaining and changing behavior derivable from these theories. All of the theories reviewed in this chapter help to understand the structure and functioning of the social system and its members, and are therefore essential ingredients of the social welfare institution. However, any psychological perspective on social behavior concentrates on individual functioning rather than on other levels of functioning. In the next chapter selected sociological perspectives important to an understanding of the social welfare institution will be discussed.

STUDY QUESTIONS
1. Stop and think about the way you attempt to solve a problem facing you. To what extent do you draw upon previous experience of your own? On general principles you know are applicable to the problem? On data you seek from others, from books, or from your own observations? How can these thoughts help you to better understand how someone seeking help might behave, and also how a helping person could be expected to behave? Would you expect similar or different behaviors? Why?

2. What limitations, if any, do you find in psychological approaches to understanding problems? Are there certain kinds of problems for which a psychological perspective is not very helpful? Does a psychological approach tend to narrow the behaviors at which one looks when analyzing problematic behavior? Is it possible to understand behavior without reference to psychological concepts? Be specific and refer to concrete examples in your thinking about these questions.

3. Make a chart for yourself that compares and contrasts psychoanalytic and

behavioral approaches to personality development. Include such items as: internal personality structures postulated; the effect of external social events; the sequence of the development of personality structures and behavioral characteristics; and points of intervention for changing the personality. On the basis of your chart, try to work out ways in which the two approaches could be made compatible with each other.

REFERENCES

1. Robert Merton, *Social Theory and Social Structure* (rev. ed.; New York: Free Press, 1957), pp. 85–117.
2. Helen Harris Perlman, *Social Casework: A Problem-Solving Process* (Chicago: University of Chicago Press, 1957), pp. 6–7.
3. Jimm Good Tracks, "Native American Non-Interference," *Social Work* 18 (November 1973): 33. Reprinted by permission of the National Association of Social Workers.
4. An overview of the different social science perspectives on human behavior may be found in Edward Norbeck et al., *The Study of Personality: An Interdisciplinary Appraisal* (New York: Holt, Rinehart and Winston, 1968), pp. 88–100.
5. Alfred Baldwin, *Theories of Child Development* (New York: John Wiley, 1968), p. 375.
6. Arnold Rose, *Sociology: The Study of Human Relations* (2nd rev. ed.; New York: Alfred A. Knopf, 1967), p. 729.
7. Baldwin, op. cit., p. 350.
8. For brief summaries of the Freudian system, the following can be recommended: developmental stages, Baldwin, op. cit., pp. 351–73, and Charles Brenner, *An Elementary Textbook of Psychoanalysis* (Garden City: Anchor, 1957), pp. 16–32; levels of consciousness, ibid., pp. 35–37; mental structures, ibid., pp. 37–140.
9. Baldwin, op. cit., p. 351.
10. A representative work is Otto Rank, *Will Therapy*, trans. Jessie Taft (New York: Alfred A. Knopf, 1968).
11. A representative work is C. G. Jung, *Analytical Psychology: Its Theory and Practice* (New York: Pantheon, 1968).
12. David Elkind, "Erik Erikson's Eight Ages of Man," in Annual Editions, *Readings in Sociology, 74–75* (Guilford, Connecticut: Dushkin, 1974), p. 14.
13. Jonas Langer, *Theories of Development* (New York: Holt, Rinehart and Winston, 1969), p. 33.
14. Ibid., p. 34.
15. Ibid., pp. 36–46.
16. Elkind, op. cit., p. 22.
17. Carl Rogers, *Client-Centered Therapy* (Boston: Houghton-Mifflin, © 1951), p. 34.
18. Ibid., pp. 35–36.
19. Ibid., p. 49. See also Alfred Baldwin, op. cit., 374–84.
20. Baldwin, op. cit., p. 384.
21. Langer, op. cit., p. 49.
22. Ibid.
23. Ibid., p. 50.

24. Baldwin, loc. cit.
25. The problems of using verbal techniques with certain socioeconomic groups is well illustrated in August Hollingshead and Frederick Redlich, *Social Class and Mental Illness* (New York: John Wiley, 1958).
26. A good example of this is in E. Larkin Phillips and Daniel N. Wiener, *Short-Term Psychotherapy and Structured Behavior Change* (New York: McGraw-Hill, 1966), pp. 159–85.
27. Phillips and Wiener, op. cit., pp. 1–10, esp. p. 9.
28. Ibid., p. 9.
29. Leonard Small, *The Briefer Psychotherapies* (New York: Brunner/Mazel, 1971).
30. Howard Parad, ed., *Crisis Intervention: Selected Readings* (New York: Family Service Association of America, 1965).
31. See Robert Roberts and Robert Nee, eds., *Theories of Social Casework* (Chicago: University of Chicago Press, 1970), pp. 129–79 and 265–311.
32. For example, see Edith Kramer, *Art as Therapy with Children* (New York: Schocken, 1971).
33. A thoughtful discussion of diagnosis as a concept and its utility in social welfare contexts may be found in Carol Meyer, *Social Work Practice* (New York: Free Press, 1970), pp. 110–15.
34. See Don Gibbons, *Society, Crime, and Criminal Careers* (Englewood Cliffs, N.J.: Prentice-Hall, 1968), pp. 139–70; and George Vold, *Theoretical Criminology* (New York: Oxford University Press, 1958), pp. 28–40.
35. Another perspective on the advantages and disadvantages of a psychoanalytic approach to the solution of the problems commonly encountered in social welfare contexts is in James Whittaker, *Social Treatment* (Chicago: Aldine, 1974), pp. 103–109.
36. Langer, op. cit., p. 52.
37. Ibid, p. 55.
38. An interesting attempt to relate psychoanalytic and behavioral approaches may be found in V. Meyer and Edward Chesser, *Behavior Therapy in Clinical Psychiatry* (New York: Science House, 1970).
39. Langer, op. cit., p. 56.
40. Baldwin, op. cit., p. 397.
41. Ibid., p. 398.
42. Albert Bandura and Richard Walters, *Social Learning and Personality Development* (New York: Holt, Rinehart and Winston, 1963), pp. 4–7.
43. Baldwin, op. cit., p. 428.
44. Bandura and Walters, op. cit., pp. 224–46; for applications of their theory, see Edwin Thomas, ed., *The Socio-Behavioral Approach and Applications to Social Work* (New York: Council on Social Work Education, 1967).
45. Albert Bandura, *Principles of Behavior Modification* (New York: Holt, Rinehart and Winston, 1969), pp. 70–112.
46. Edwin Thomas asserts that the objectives of sociobehavioral intervention are the acquisition, strengthening, maintenance, weakening, or elimination of behavior. See p. 12 of his "Selected Sociobehavioral Techniques and Principles: An Approach to Interpersonal Helping," *Social Work* 13 (January 1968): 12–26.
47. Ibid., p. 18.

48. Ibid., p. 23.
49. Ibid.
50. Ibid., pp. 23–24.
51. Derek Jehu, *Learning Theory and Social Work* (New York: Humanities Press, 1967), p. 84.
52. Ibid., p. 430.
53. Ibid., pp. 424–554.
54. Thomas, "Selected Sociobehavioral Techniques . . . ," op. cit., p. 21.
55. Bandura, op. cit., p. 144.
56. Ibid., p. 120.
57. Ibid., pp. 52–112.

SELECTED READINGS

In reviewing major psychological theories, the Baldwin, Langer, and Lidz books are helpful in providing a comprehensive comparative approach. Bandura, Walters, and Brenner are excellent summaries of specific theoretical approaches. Thomas's work focuses on problems of application.

Baldwin, Alfred. *Theories of Child Development.* New York: John Wiley, 1968.

Bandura, Albert. *Principles of Behavior Modification.* New York: Holt, Rinehart and Winston, 1969.

Bandura, Albert, and Richard Walters. *Social Learning and Personality Development.* New York: Holt, Rinehart and Winston, 1963.

Brenner, Charles. *An Elementary Textbook of Psychoanalysis.* Garden City: Doubleday, 1957.

Franks, Cyril, ed. *Behavior Therapy: Appraisal and Status.* New York: McGraw-Hill, 1969.

Langer, Jonas. *Theories of Development.* New York: Holt, Rinehart and Winston, 1969.

Lidz, Theodore. *The Person: His Development Throughout the Life Cycle.* New York: Basic Books, 1968.

Thomas, Edwin, ed. *The Socio-Behavioral Approach and Applications to Social Work.* New York: Council on Social Work Education, 1967.

5

Sociological Bases

THE CUMULATIVE IMPACT of World War I and the Great Depression was a major stimulus to sociology taking its rightful place alongside psychological theory in understanding social welfare issues.[1] Sociology as a scientific discipline began to develop in a systematic way in the mid-1800s.[2] However, it took the major social upheavals of the period from 1915 to 1935 to make the sociological perspective seem appropriate in analyzing the social changes that had begun in the Industrial Revolution.[3]

The sociological perspective focuses on the major group contexts of human behavior. Freud rightly questioned the advantages and disadvantages of group life,[4] but the size, complexity, and productivity of contemporary social life would be impossible without the functional advantages of groups.[5] The group has its own structural needs, and each group member must learn the culture of the group to which he belongs in order to function effectively.[6] Such learning is the process of socialization,[7] in which the rules (called norms) of the group are taught as well as the consequences of not obeying the group's rules.* Socialization is necessary to develop the human being's social and biological potential, and it does so in a way specifically adapted to the groups in which the individual will be living.

Normative behavior helps to introduce stability into social life. Ideally each individual knows the behavior expected of him and others, and the group can plan its structure knowing what kinds of member behavior may be expected. Such social stability leads to the social psychological processes of identity and self-concept formation, in which the individual comes to perceive herself through interaction with others in socially defined contexts.[8] In reality, socialization is made difficult by the fact that in a large, complex society, we are all members of many groups. Appropriate behaviors must be learned for each, creating a complicated learning network, made even more so when rules of two or more groups conflict, or when group memberships are changed. The sociological perspective, then, sees the environment as the stimulus and context for individual behavior. Although this view focuses on group structures, rather than starting with the individual as the psychological

---

*Norms are rules for behavior defined by the group. The consequences of deviation from norms are called sanctions, which may be positive (rewarding normative behavior) or negative (punishing deviant behavior). The exercise of sanctions is the process of social control.

perspective does, the sociological and psychological perspectives are closely related and complementary.

Sociological theory is particularly useful for understanding the structure and interaction of the major components of the social system. This perspective involves considerably more variables affecting behavior than was true when reviewing psychological perspectives, and as a result some of the theory lacks precision and specific practice applications. However, the lack of theoretical sophistication of much sociological knowledge in no way reduces the importance of the social behavior studied by it. It simply magnifies the need for further theoretical development and its translation into practice principles.

ROLE THEORY Role theory is the study of how tasks are organized and distributed in society.[9] Societies have tasks that must be performed in socially approved (normative) ways. These tasks are grouped into positions, which are named collections of persons performing similar functional behaviors. Examples of positions would be mother, social worker, physical therapist, and the like. For each position, there are appropriate behaviors that occupants of a position are expected to perform; these expected behaviors constitute the role behavior associated with a position. In the position of doctor, for example, each occupant is expected to treat patients, prescribe drugs, use medical instruments, keep abreast of new medical technology, and so on. A role, then, is made up of norms clustered around a certain position, and positions and roles together enable society to perform needed functional behaviors in normative ways.

Since positions and roles exist so that society can perform its functions in an effective and orderly fashion, they must be flexible. As society's needs change, the structure to meet these needs must also change. For example, modern technology has created a whole new range of automated mechanical and electronic equipment, which has created new positions (computer programmer, for example) and virtually eliminated others (such as steam engine fireman).[10] Just as importantly, roles associated with positions may also change. For a variety of reasons women are becoming more and more active in the work force. As this has occurred, traditional role expectations associated with the positions of woman, mother, and wife have changed dramatically, with inevitable effects on related positions—such as husband, son, or daughter.

This kind of structural flexibility is one of the most basic characteristics of human societies. Societies, and the cultures on which they are based, are made by people and are thus changeable. As new needs emerge, and as new ways of meeting old needs are found, societies can elect to change their norms, roles, and positions. It is this flexibility that enables human groups to adapt and survive. However, this flexibility can also be the source of deeply felt individual and social problems. Socialization teaches people certain ways of doing things. When these ways are changed by society, new generations learn the new ways, but those who learned the old ways often find it difficult to change and adapt.[11] These changes in norms, positions, and roles can lead to several potential problems. All of them share an important characteristic. These problems are socially created, yet they are manifested by individuals. A basic assertion of sociology is that individuals are strongly affected by society and the specific groups to which they belong in society. Individual behavior is a reflection of group memberships, and is generally reinforced by the groups to which one belongs. Indeed, one of the most serious problems in a large, complex, industrial society like the United States is how to deal with people who have become lost in the social structure and have no meaningful group ties.[12]

Yet social ties can themselves be the source of individual problems. As members of groups, we learn appropriate behavior and attempt to act accordingly. Usually we are rewarded by other members of our group. As society changes, our group may be threatened, and the behaviors it teaches and practices may be suddenly challenged.[13] In a very basic sense the individual is not at fault—often his or her behavior has not changed. It is the social environment that has changed, and by changing, has made the individual's behavior problematical or deviant. There are countless examples with which social welfare professionals are familiar: a woman suddenly unsure of her female role; a worker suddenly displaced by economic or technological changes; a retired person suddenly excluded from his life's work; a minority-group member arbitrarily excluded from opportunities for a secure existence. Individuals carry these role-related problems, but their source is in a dynamic society that finds ever new ways of structuring its business. Exhibit 5-1 illustrates how role behavior is learned and how it then affects behavior.

These socially created role problems can be formalized sociologically into several categories. One is when vestiges of old role behaviors that are no longer appropriate in new role contexts persist. A second type of problem results from the lag in the societal definition of an appropriate role constellation for new positions. A contemporary example is the position of dissenting priests. A third category of role problem is role ambiguity, in which the role definition is unclear. Ambiguity may result from lack of clarity in the societal definition of the role, as with adolescence in the United States. It may also result from inadequate socialization, as when the lower-class child is unsure of how to behave in the middle-class school. A fourth type of role problem—role conflict—results when there are conflicting expectations existing in one or more positions at the same time. Role conflict is caused by the complexity of the role structure. We occupy many positions at the same time, and society has few methods of avoiding conflicting expectations between all possible roles associated with these positions. Role conflict may occur within one position, as when a college professor is expected to be an objective evaluator of students and at the same time their counselor and friend. It may also occur between two or more positions, as when the demands of being an adequate mother conflict with the expectation to remain a physically attractive and sexually vital wife.

Two techniques society uses to minimize role conflicts are: (1) role sets, where complementary roles are defined in relationship to each other; and (2) definitions specifying when given roles are manifest (to be acted upon) and when they are latent (not to be acted upon). However, such attempts are rarely completely successful, with the individual being left to try to solve his own particular problems. This he may do in the short run, such as compromising conflicting expectations, or in the long run by changing the role definitions or leaving the roles.[14] Another way in which role problems are resolved is through the welfare system, which may be seen as an institutionalized way to cope with role problems when they occur. For example, various social welfare structures are concerned with strengthening and supplementing socialization contexts to try to minimize problems resulting from inadequate socialization.

EXHIBIT **5-1**

Where Does It Start?

The following is an excerpt from Oscar Lewis's *La Vida*. It expresses well the unequal conditions under which the achievement struggle occurs, and gives one pause when thinking about the magnitude of social change that would be needed to alter the conditions under which families such as this live in the future.

When I was a child my stepmother told me my *mamá* was a prostitute but I didn't believe her. I said I wanted to see my *mamá*, to know her and my stepmother would say that there was no reason for me to see that bitch because she was no mother, the way she treated us. She said that my *mamá* didn't want to cook for us and that she went out with men, carrying on and drinking and leaving us dirty and alone at all hours of the night.

I didn't care what my stepmother said. I was

From Oscar Lewis, *La Vida* (New York: Random House, 1966), p. 299. Used by permission.

sad because my *mamá* and *papá* were living apart and the only thing I wished was that they'd get together again so they could be a good example to us.

My stepmother mistreated us kids and didn't want to cook for us or send us to school. According to my grandmother, Hortensia would throw our bread and food to us on the floor. She didn't want to buy us clothes, and would beat us if we sat down in the living room. Once Crucita was crying, and Hortensia went and grabbed her and threw her to the floor and that's why she is lame. But my stepmother says it was meningitis that made Cruz a cripple.

To summarize, role theory emphasizes the importance to society of a structure in which important social functions are performed according to existing norms. This is accomplished by having individuals participate in groups of similarly acting individuals (positions). As society changes, appropriate position and role behavior changes, creating potential problems in role definitions and relationships. As society becomes increasingly complex, each individual occupies increasing numbers of positions, and this can create conflicts between the role expectations of the various positions. Throughout, the individual generally acts in good faith, attempting to act out the social script learned during socialization. Once learned, the script is hard to forget, leading to many problems expressed in an individual-by-individual way, but with roots deep in the social system. (This thread will be followed throughout this chapter and elaborated later in the book.) The effective social welfare practitioner must do more than deal with individual problems, since such problems may depend on social changes for their solution.

SOCIAL
STRATIFICATION
THEORY

A basic concern in a social structure is the distribution of social positions, since power and influence are vested in positions. The mechanisms society uses to define and allocate positions become extremely important in determining which groups will have access to which social rewards. Definitions of desirable social rewards and their accessibility to societal members is an ideological function in society,[15] and as such affects the actual distribution of positions. However, Marx noted long ago that the reverse is also true, since those having power will create social structures to maintain their privilege.[16]

Allocation of positions may be made on either of two bases: ascription, where positions are assigned without consideration of an individual's abilities; or achievement, where positions are assigned on the basis of demonstrated ability.[17] Ascription characterizes caste societies, although every society uses ascription to the extent that positions are distributed according to age, sex, physical appearance, and so on. When ascription is the dominant allocation mechanism, one's life chances are determined from birth, and social welfare structures would seek to change behavior only within limits appropriate to one's caste position. In the United States, positions are said to be allocated on the basis of achievement, so that changes in positions and life patterns are possible. Achievement places a far greater emphasis on individual effort and responsibility. Lack of success or change can thereby easily be attributed to individual failure even if in fact caused by social conditions. For example, Exhibit 5-2 illustrates the fact that even in a society that values achievement, ascriptive criteria are still used—age, race, sex, and so on.

However positions are assigned, every society has a ranking system that defines some as being more desirable than others.[18] This indicates that a competition is established in society to obtain socially defined rewards, whether they be money, cows, or wives. Such competition is said by some to be functional for the society, in that it motivates persons to seek difficult positions that offer great rewards.[19] Others point out that a conflict system is created, which may have its own functions,[20] but which may also be disruptive to the social order.[21]

Regardless of societal functions, such competition practically guarantees that there will be losers, since individuals enter the competition with differing amounts of physiological and social resources. Parts of the professional social welfare role can be seen as attempts to equalize the competitive positions of all members of society as far as possible, as well as providing concrete and emotional help to those who are losers in the competition.

EXHIBIT 5-2

Sex, Physical Appearance, and Ascription

The following letter written to Ann Landers is a pathetic reminder of how sex and physical appearance continue to be used as a basis for ascription in the United States.

Dear Ann Landers:

I could never talk to anyone about this problem and I must tell it to somebody. It is getting me down.

My husband and I have been married 10 years. Our son, who is now 8, is a very handsome boy. He has my husband's eyes and smile, my nose, a great shaped head and strong jaw-line. Everyone remarks on his good looks.

Our daughter is 2 years old, and I am sorry to say she is the homeliest child I have ever seen. Nature really played a dirty trick on us. It would

From Ann Landers, in the *Washington Post*, April 15, 1971. Used by permission of Field Newspaper Syndicate.

have been much better if the boy had been homely and the girl had been good looking. A girl needs beauty—a boy doesn't.

Our daughter inherited the worst features of both my husband and me. When people see her they don't know what to say. Occasionally someone will ask, "Is that your child, or is she adopted?" I know what they are driving at.

When our daughter is older we can have her protruding ears fixed, her chin built up and her nose remolded. Hopefully she will have a good figure. If she doesn't, there are several things a girl can do. But the growing up years are going to be very hard on this pathetic child. Please tell me how to face the future cheerfully. If you could name some movie stars who were homely youngsters, it would help a lot.—Star Crossed

---

A stratification system obviously creates and perpetuates inequality, and institutionalizes its desirability in a society. There are haves and have-nots, with the latter category clearly and systematically disadvantaged in its attempts to wrest power from the former group. To the extent that societal members are free to compete for societal positions, the successful can attribute their privileged social position to their own efforts and abilities and thereby justify their position regardless of the many problems it creates for the less successful. However, when ascription is built into the process by which positions are allocated in a systematic but unacknowledged way, the assertion that everyone can succeed if she tries is simply untenable. It is clear that race, sex, and socioeconomic background are commonly used in an ascriptive manner, so that many kinds of opportunity are quite unequally distributed. Under such conditions, competition creates frustration rather than incentive.[22]

When inequality exists in one part of the social system, it has repercussions throughout the system, and creates a system of institutional inequality. The fact that some children are born and raised in poor families becomes a lifelong problem. Poor childhood nutrition may stunt growth and physical and intellectual development; school performance is impaired, often leading the child to try to escape from a learning environment that is frustrating and demeaning; teachers may react by stereotyping a student as "unmotivated," and ignore or punish the child; poor or incomplete schooling puts the developing adult at a severe disadvantage in an increasingly credentials-oriented employment market; unskilled, low-paying, uncertain employment generates low income; and the cycle has come full circle. This brief account even understates the problems caused by inequality, since the individual may develop a damaged self-image which can lead to borderline mental functioning, as well as deviant or destructive behavior.

There are several major sources of ascription that lead to institutionalized inequality. These are often spoken of as the "isms": racism, sexism, and ageism. In addition, there is ethnicity and poverty. Each of these factors creates automatic barriers within the major institutions of society so that individual ability is often left undeveloped or ignored. When an individual belongs to a group discriminated against on ascriptive criteria, the major social institutions tend to block rather than facilitate behavior. The family teaches values that discourage achievement—for example, "a woman's place is in the home." The school develops tracks so that the "unmotivated" black child does not interfere with "motivated" white counterparts. The employment market has no place for older persons. The political system has to run a "popular" candidate—not a Chicano or a welfare mother. Life patterns become increasingly restricted—middle class suburban housewives turn to drink; racial and ethnic minorities suffer high rates of mental and physical illness; old people sink into despair and isolation.

Obviously it is not the intent of the social system to reduce a significant proportion of its population to hopelessness, but it happens. One reason is that a more open system based on achievement threatens existing power structures, and one function of institutionalized inequality is to allow the privileged to pass their advantage on to their offspring, a very natural desire. Another reason lies in the distinction Jones makes between individual and institutional racism (it applies to any type of discrimination): "A landlord who refuses to rent a house to a black person is practicing individual racism. A city or court that fails to ameliorate the black man's grievances is practicing institutional racism."[23] While it is perhaps understandable that an individual may wish to preserve his privilege, the values existing in America require the society to protect the person being discriminated against. When this is not done, the system becomes dysfunctional for many of its members.

Social welfare as an institution must insure that it is not being used to perpetuate such inequality.[24] In many respects, social welfare values conflict with societal values which support inequality of opportunity and inequality of life chances. Being committed to helping all persons achieve their highest potential and a satisfying life, social welfare values cannot accept the inevitability of a competitive system which by its nature generates disadvantaged persons. This is not to suggest that everyone must be equal. Persons have widely differing potential, and the magnitude of their achievement must recognize such differences. Nevertheless, social welfare is committed to achieving a social system that gives everyone an equal opportunity to attain her potential, as well as developing a service structure providing needed services in an adequate and equal manner.[25] An achievement orientation in society has many advantages, but if they are to be realized, then the struggle for achievement must be under rules that do not automatically handicap certain groups.

One of the problems encountered in dealing with institutional inequality is difficulty in finding a way to break into the circle. There have been at least three strategies developed to try to deal with institutional inequality, two of which directly involve the social welfare institution. To begin with the one that does not utilize social welfare structures directly, one strategy to overcome the effects of institutional inequality is to give preferential treatment to members of groups that have been discriminated against. For example, many colleges and universities are now actively recruiting members of "ism" and ethnic groups, attempting to achieve a balanced student population that includes members from all major groups in society. This strategy is also frequently used in hiring practices.

There is an obvious—and ironic—problem with this strategy. In the attempt to compensate for the earlier use of ascriptive criteria and to give more emphasis to achievement, a new ascriptive system is established. The fact that an individual is a member of an "ism" group continues to be important. The difference is that such group membership can now be an advantage instead of a disadvantage. This may be necessary in the short run, but the other strategies to be discussed appear to have fewer undesirable side-effects. A further potential problem with this strategy is that bringing a person into a position that assumes a level of prior training or experience which that individual does not in fact have because of inequality in other parts of the institutional structure is likely to guarantee failure and frustration.

A second strategy involves providing compensatory services to overcome disadvantages caused by inequality. Programs such as Head Start, Job Corps, and remedial resources in schools are examples of such an approach. This particular strategy would appear to be a feasible short-run solution to the effects of inequality. However, it cannot be a substitute for a revamping of society's major institutions to insure that the American society of the future does not, in its normal functioning, systematically generate need and inequality.

The third strategy moves in this direction. It is the provision of adequate resources to all members of society so that no group is systematically disadvantaged. Institutionalized services like public education and public employment counseling are examples. Current legislative activity that may yield national health insurance and guaranteed annual income plans would be further steps in the direction of making American society one that facilitates goal attainment for all its members. These concrete actions will have to be accompanied by value changes that reject discrimination on any ascriptive criteria. Although economic recessions and depressions are far from desirable, one of their side-effects appears to be helping people to realize that being a helpless victim of society is humiliating.[26]

To summarize, social stratification theory in sociology raises many issues as it documents the existence of inequality and attempts to understand its causes. Like role theory, it suggests that many individual problems are socially generated and must be dealt with in the social system. It further develops the concept of social systems discussed in earlier chapters. Finally, it raises important issues about the place of the social welfare institution in the social structure, including the caution that social welfare services themselves may be manipulated by those in power to preserve inequality. To conclude this section of sociological theory, Exhibit 5-3 takes an in-depth look at a group struggling with its ascribed status—the aged.

EXHIBIT 5-3

Problems and Prospects of the Aged

The following analysis examines in some detail the plight of the elderly in contemporary American society. It illustrates how prejudicial attitudes, which often have no basis in fact, conspire to lump older people together into a group that is defined as peripheral to the significant work of society. The effects are devastating. Some alternatives to the waste of old age are also discussed. This exhibit is taken from Ronald C. Federico, *Sociology* (1975).

Once old people played a central role in the family and in society. Today the elderly are more often tolerated, patronized, or ignored than respected.

From Ronald C. Federico, *Sociology* (Reading, Mass., 1975). Reprinted by permission of Addison-Wesley Publishing Co., Inc.

Like other minority groups, the aged are segregated, discriminated against, and, in a great many ways, misunderstood. More than other minorities, they are isolated and lonely. Only recently has the American public become aware of the shameful plight of old people in society. Sociologists have played a central role in this enlightenment—by gathering data, studying what it means—physically and psychologically—to be old; and suggesting alternatives to an old age of poverty, social isolation, and helplessness.

WHO ARE THE AGED?

There seems to be some truth in the popular saying, "You're as young as you feel." In a survey of working- and upper-middle-class men, Bernice Neugarten (1968) found that unskilled laborers feel that a man reaches maturity at the age of 25 or 30, when he takes on the responsibilities of a job, marriage, and a family; that 40 marks the beginning of middle age; that by 60, a man is old. In contrast, business executives and professionals see 30 as the time to settle into a career, 40 as "the prime of life," 50 as the beginning of middle age, and old age as a condition that sets in at about age 70. Perhaps the best subjective definition of old age is the point at which a person begins thinking in terms of the years he has left rather than in terms of the years he has ahead. Objectively, we can define old age as 65 and beyond—65 being the age at which most people retire.

How Many Are There? In 1880, 3.4 percent of this country's population was 65 and older. Today the proportion is closer to 10 percent—that is, 20 million senior citizens—and the percentage is growing. There are two main reasons for this change. First, people are having fewer children today than they did in the past so that the proportion of young people in the country is declining. (In 1880, 38.1 percent of Americans were 15 or younger; in 1970, 27.3 percent.) Second, people live longer today than they did at the turn of the century. Improved health care and nutrition have raised the average life-span of American women to 81 years, that of American men to 78 years. Unfortunately, more often than not, these "extra" years are spent in loneliness and poverty. Only four out of ten elderly people live with members of their families (their spouses or other relatives). Approximately 44 percent of the women 65 to 74 years old and 71 percent of the women 75 and older are widows. In contrast, only 12 percent of the men between 65 and 74 and 34 percent 75 and older are widowers (Rosenberg, 1970, pp. 172–73). Relatively few find old age to be their "golden years."

The Poorest of the Poor. The aged are truly the poorest of the poor in America. In 1960, approximately half of this nation's old people were living in poverty. The average annual income for households headed by persons 65 and older was $1,200—less than the average income for blacks, for Spanish-Americans, or for Indians (U.S. Department of Health, Education, and Welfare, 1966). About 30 percent of these households depended on welfare to meet day-to-day expenses. Fully 70 percent of Americans 65 and over are unemployed—some voluntarily, but many not.

THE OLDER WORKER: FIRST TO BE LAID OFF, LAST TO BE HIRED

According to a government study completed in 1965 (Grunewald, 1972, pp. 2–3), 3.5 million people aged 45 and over lost their jobs in 1964 alone. The cost of unemployment insurance for these workers that year reached $1 billion because few were able to find new jobs. A survey of private employers indicated that half of all job openings were categorically closed to workers 55 and over; one-quarter were closed even to middle-aged workers—45 and over. Employers simply refused to consider "mature" applicants. Moreover, many companies were committed to a seniority system that forced them to promote insiders rather than hire outsiders. The Age Discrimination Act, passed in 1967, makes it illegal for employers to discriminate because of age in advertising job openings, hiring, job retention, or salary. However, in many instances it is difficult to prove that a person was fired or an applicant turned down because of age. Why do employers discriminate against the older worker?

Can They Compete? Government researchers found that many employers believe efficiency and productivity decline with age. The older a person gets, the slower he works; 50- and 60-year-old workers are more likely to call in sick than younger employees. To an extent, this is true; approximately half of the workers who retire each year do so because of failing health (Maddox, 1966). However, there is no evidence that healthy older workers are any less competent or productive than 25- and 35-year-olds. In fact, some companies found that the reverse is true. Nevertheless, myths about the effects of age on the body, mind, and personality continue to force significant numbers of older workers into unemployment.

Education and Skills. A second difficulty for the older worker is training. Typically, he has less formal education than his young competitors. This is particularly true in fields that require technical know-how and specialized skills. Many more people are completing high school and attending college or professional schools today than was true twenty or thirty years ago. Why should an employer hire a 45-year-old man with a high school diploma when he can hire a younger man with an M.A. in marketing? Employers tend to believe that education makes an individual efficient, whereas on-the-job experience makes a person inflexible, or set in his ways. In addition, older workers lose jobs because their skills have become obsolete. Antidiscrimination laws do not protect the clerk who is replaced by a computer. Nor do they protect the woman who leaves the job market to raise a family, thereby losing ten or fifteen years' experience. And although the government funds numerous job-training programs for high school dropouts and other young people, there is little interest in retraining the unemployed middle-aged person.

Mandatory Retirement. Finally, many workers are forced to retire at age 65—whether or not they have demonstrated their competence and desire to continue working. Companies that automatically "terminate" an employee at 65 are acting within the law. In fact, mandatory retirement is often written into labor contracts. Social pressure forces others to retire—the idea being that a person who continues working even though he is eligible for retirement benefits is keeping a younger worker, who may have children to support, out of a job. Contrary to what younger workers who are unhappy with the nine-to-five routine believe, retirement is not an extended vacation.

The Retired Worker: How Does He Live? Nearly always, retirement means a drastic reduction in one's standard of living. Retired workers live on a fixed income—that is, they receive the same amount month after month, regardless of changes in the cost of living. Inflation can and does reduce what seemed like a comfortable pension or a secure nest egg into pauper's wages. This fact was brought home in the spring of 1973 when supermarket managers in Miami, a retirement city, reported an increase in shop-lifting (*New York Times*, Jan. 10, 1972). What does the retired worker live on?

Social Security and Pensions. Social Security payments depend on the number of years a person worked and the salary he earned during those years. In 1970, the average monthly Social Security check was $117 a month—a 20 percent increase over the average payment in 1967 (Chen, 1971, p. 31). By law, if a person between the ages of 62 and 72 who draws Social Security earns between $140 and $240 a month, the government deducts $1 for every $2 he earns from his Social Security check; if he earns more than $240 a month, his check is reduced dollar for dollar. The retired worker may also receive pension benefits. However, a survey conducted in 1968–69 indicated that less than half of the retired men and a fifth of the retired women who had worked in private industry were receiving pension benefits (Heidbreder, 1972, p. 53). The median payment in 1967 was $75 a month (Chen, 1971, p. 36). Workers are not insured against failures in private pension plans because of fraud, bankruptcy, and the like. Changing jobs or unions, early retirement, even early retirement because of disabilities, may make a worker ineligible for pension checks. Nader and Blackwell (1973) estimated that half of the people who are enrolled in pension plans in private industry never receive a penny. Elderly people who are not eligible for either Social Security or pensions may seek support from the government's Old-Age and Survivors Insurance and Old-Age Assistance programs.

THE PHYSIOLOGY OF AGING

What does it mean to grow old? Because few Americans live with their grandparents or great-grandparents, most of us have little first-hand knowledge of the aging process. In this section we look at the biological facts.

Bodily Changes.[a] Graying hair, baldness, wrinkles, and circles under the eyes mark the onset of middle age. Skin texture and facial appearance begin to change. As Vincent expressed it, "Until we are 35

[a]This section and the next are based on Bischof, 1969, chap. 4.

or 40, our faces are those God gave us; after that they are the faces which we make for ourselves" (in Bischof, 1969, p. 211). Some people develop "laugh lines" around their eyes; others, "worry lines" on their forehead. These changes do not affect the individual's health, only his vanity. This is particularly true in a youth-oriented society such as our own. Middle-aged people also tend to put on weight, especially around the middle. Overweight may affect health as well as vanity.

Strength and Stamina. With regard to strength, most people reach their peak between 25 and 30. An active person may continue to build up muscles until about 50, when those in the back, legs, and arms begin to atrophy. There is less flexibility; postures harden. Starting at about age 45, the bones begin to lose density and strength and to decline in size. Breaks are more common in the 70- or 80-year-old; often they do not heal. Old people "breathe harder and with less satisfaction" than younger people. Also an older person's heart takes longer to recover after strenuous exercise. Birren pointed out that numerous factors contribute to heart failure, which is more common among inactive men:

> The high mortality from cardiovascular disease results from a confluence of many factors, diet, urbanization, occupational strain, body type, heredity, and others. . . . Masculinity, high activity or drive, productivity, and responsibility appear positively related to the development of cardiac disease [Bischof, 1969, p. 202].

Changes in heart strength and metabolic rate affect endurance.

To some extent, the senses "wear out" in old age. The elderly are less sensitive to taste, smell, and touch than younger people. Eyesight declines rapidly after the age of 40: most old people wear glasses. Hearing, too, gets worse. But although many people lose the ability to hear high pitches, most do not become totally deaf.

Sexual Changes. Sexual changes also take place in middle and old age. Between 40 and 50, women gradually cease ovulation (menopause)—a transition most people associate with agitation, insomnia, depression, and general emotional instability. However, current research indicates that these emotional upsets are a psychological reaction

to "the change," not a biological reaction. Somewhat later and more gradually, men also cease to be fertile (climacterium). These changes do not affect the individual's desire for or ability to enjoy sex. However, social pressure—ridicule directed at the "dirty old man" and the "shameless old lady" —may cause old people to hide their feelings (see de Beauvoir, 1972).

Finally, the older a person is, the longer it takes him to recover from illness or disability. However, as Bischof (1969) suggested, adjusting to physical changes is often more of a problem for the old person than ill health itself.

Mental Changes. Does aging affect a person's ability to remember, to learn, to think and reason? There is no easy answer to this question. We know that the size of the brain decreases after age 30 (in fact, no new cells are added to the brain after birth), but what does this mean? Comparing old and young people's scores on intelligence tests is problematic. As Bischof wrote:

> It is just as fair to give an adult a child-oriented intelligence test as it would be to give a child an adult-oriented intelligence test that concerned itself with income-tax filing . . . driving an automobile, and all of the things an adult must do in using his mental ability to exist in this world [Bischof, 1969, p. 215].

On the other hand, studies based on tests and retests of the same individuals are rare and incomplete. What information exists suggests the following.

Slowing down. First, there seems to be a general slowing down. Older subjects generally do better on tests of vocabulary, information, and verbal comprehension than on object assembly and block design tests, which require speed. In part, this is because their reaction time is slower.

Memory loss. Second, there seems to be a decrease in short-term memory and in ability to learn. Elderly people seem to have difficulty on tests of newly acquired material. Whether this is because their brains are "filled to capacity" (to simplify the issue), or because their ability to retrieve information is impaired, is difficult to say. However, it seems old people remember things they learned in the past better than things they learned recently.

Inflexibility. Finally, the elderly are usually less flexible than young people. For example, old people can repeat a series of numbers (a digit span) about as well as young people, but they have difficulty repeating a digit span backwards. In part, this is because they are more conservative in their answers. Old people take fewer risks and make fewer guesses than young people. Summarizing these findings, Bischof wrote:

> We come to the general conclusion the old dog can learn new tricks but the answer is not a direct and simple one. It appears that the old dog is reluctant to learn new tricks. He is less likely to gamble on the results, particularly when he is not convinced that the new trick is any better than the old tricks, which served him so well in the past. He may not learn the new trick as rapidly as he did in the past, but learn it he does. Further, the best evidence seems to indicate that if he starts out as a clever young pup, he is very likely to end up a wise old hound [Bischof, 1969, p. 224].

THE SOCIOLOGY OF AGING

In every culture there is a time to play, a time to learn, a time to marry, a time to raise a family, and a time to retire—what Bernice Neugarten (1968) called the "social clock." People are expected to act in a way that is appropriate to their age and sex. We treat children, students, young parents, middle-aged people, and old men and women differently—according to our age and sex in relation to theirs (Neugarten, 1968, p. 143). The sociology of aging is concerned with the ways in which people adjust to declining health and to their social roles as old men and women.

Social Isolation and Disengagement. For men (and to some extent for their wives), "retirement is a rite of passage . . . between productive maturity and nonproductive old age" (Maddox, 1966, p. 119).[b] In our society, an individual's occupation in large part determines his status. A man is a construction worker, a teacher, or an executive to his friends

[b]For nonworking housewives, the marriage or departure of the last child is also a "rite of passage"—from being primarily a mother to being primarily a wife again.

and neighbors; a breadwinner to his family. Retired people find this "social anchorage" cut. The ex-cabdriver no longer has the pocket money to buy rounds of drinks for his friends; the retired board chairman has little influence or company gossip to exchange with his cohorts; fathers find themselves turning to sons for financial aid. Added to these concrete changes in status is the sense of *personal* obsolescence. The Puritan ethic holds that a man is worth what he does. But what is a man with nothing to do worth?

Often retirement leads to social isolation. Today relatively few old people live with their children or grandchildren. Most do not want to burden their children; many even regard giving advice as meddling. As a result, the old person's family life—particularly if his or (more likely) her spouse has died—is limited to visits and phone calls. Old people are excluded from many social events. For example, a young couple may invite the young couple next door to a party, but it is unlikely they will invite the old woman two doors away. Physical disabilities which make traveling difficult and dangerous isolate the elderly even further.

Time to Kill. Time becomes a new kind of problem for the aged. Compare Neugarten's description of the ideal 50-year-old executive with May's interview with an old man:

> A business executive . . . makes a thousand decisions a day. . . . He manages his time, buffers himself from certain stimuli, makes elaborate plans and schedules, sheds some of his "load" by delegating some tasks to other people over whom he has certain forms of control, accepts other tasks as being singularly appropriate to his own competencies and responsibilities, and, in the same 24-hour period, succeeds in satisfying his emotional and sexual and aesthetic needs [Neugarten, 1968, p. 140].

For an old man, time is another kind of problem.

Q. What did you do after supper?
A. I filled out my diary and my mail book. . . .
Q. What mail book?
A. Oh, I notice generally the mail I get and send.
Q. And you keep track of it in a book?

A. Everything. . . .

Q. And that's what you did after supper?

A. Yes. It only takes a little while. And then I rest a while again, with the window open to get some wind and look at the trees, and I'm glad that I can look at them.

Q. How long did you look at the trees?

A. Oh, I can't tell you. Then I look at the television program . . . at 10:00 generally I retire to bed with a whole lot of books.

Q. Did anybody come to the door?

A. No [May, 1965, p. 104].

The loss of an occupational identity, economic problems, cultural prohibitions against too much involvement in their children's lives, age segregation, physical disabilities, and aimlessness all contribute to disengagement from the world outside. Many old people withdraw from their social environments, both physically and psychologically.

Self-image. Whereas young and middle-aged people usually see the world around them as something to conquer and assimilate, old people tend to "perceive the world as complex and dangerous, no longer to be reformed in line with one's wishes, and the individual as conforming and accommodating to outer-world demands" (Neugarten, 1968, p. 140). Some become preoccupied with their own needs. For example, Hochschild (1973) found that in one old-age community status depended on having one's health, on one's loved ones being still alive, and on one's closeness to children. People who had these things tended to gloat over the "poor dears" who did not.

How does the approach of death affect old people? Neugarten suggested that the consciousness of mortality creates a desire to review and evaluate one's life, to take a final self-inventory. Introspection leads to reminiscence: the old person daydreams about his past much as the adolescent daydreams about his future—to make peace with himself. These changes from an active to a passive approach to the world, from involvement with others to egocentricity, from outer- to inner-world orientation and reminiscence represent "a new and final restructuring" of personality. Thus, old people often seem disoriented, perhaps childlike.

FULFILLING THE PROMISE OF OLD AGE

What are the alternatives to an old age of poverty and isolation? It is doubtful that Americans could return to the extended family even if they wanted to—and most do not (Hochschild, 1973, p. 57). Efforts to find new solutions to the problems of the aged have focused on Social Security reform, the creation of livable retirement communities, and building bridges between the older and younger generations.

Economic Support. In its 1970 report, the President's Task Force on Aging recommended five basic changes in Social Security and related programs. First, the Task Force argued that all benefits to the aged should be keyed to the cost of living rather than fixed. Second, it recommended abolishing the "income test" whereby old people who work lose all or part of their benefits. Next, the Task Force pointed out that households where husband and wife contributed equally to the family income are receiving less than households that depended on the husband's income, so that in effect working wives are penalized for their initiative. This, the Task Force argued, should be changed. The fourth proposal is the establishment of a guaranteed annual income of $1,700 for single old people and $2,100 for elderly couples (with automatic adjustments for rises in the cost of living). Finally, the Task Force noted that many old people are reluctant to accept any sort of assistance: steps should be taken to remove the stigma from old-age benefits.

Old-age Communities. What about isolation and disengagement? Although there is some disagreement on the subject (see Poorkaj, 1972), studies indicate that retirement communities can prevent the kinds of loneliness and aimlessness we described above. Merrill Court—an apartment complex housing 43 elderly people (37 of them widows) with moderate to low incomes—is an example. Hochschild (1973) found that residents of Merrill Court are intimately involved in one another's lives. They exchange gossip, baked goods, plants, and services. They know one another's schedules well enough to know if something is wrong; they care for the sick and bedridden among them. In addition, through their service club, they make cakes and pies for a nursing home, rag dolls for an orphanage, and so on. Unlike the old people living in institutions, who are unable to reciprocate for services rendered by nurses and attendants, residents of Merrill Court build their own system of mutual obligations. They create and enjoy responsibilities. Hochschild suggested that age-segregated communities provide the elderly with a kind of autonomy and freedom they could not find elsewhere. For example, they can joke, dance, and flirt openly—behavior young people might consider inappropriate; they can talk frankly about death with one another.

> The sisterhood at Merrill Court is no substitute for love or children and contact with them; but it offers a full, meaningful life *independent* of them [Hochschild, 1973, p. 57, italics added].

Merrill Court people are neither isolated, as are the aged who live alone, nor dependent, as are the elderly who live with their children or in institutions. They take care of themselves. In a very real sense, Merrill Court is a commune.

Bringing the Old Back Home: Foster Grandparents. Society as a whole loses something by leaving old people to themselves. One of the more interesting ideas in recent years is the Foster Grandparent program initiated by Taves, Kent, and Tibbitts, and financed by the Department of Health, Education and Welfare. In this program, people 60 and over are paid a minimum of $1.25 an hour to spend 4 hours a day, 5 days a week, in orphanages and other children's institutions. Their job? To give small children the love, warmth, and attention these youngsters need so badly. Their reward? The knowledge that they are needed and loved, that they are playing a useful role in the community. The Foster Grandparent program is a very positive solution to the problem of disengagement—for the institutionalized children as well as for the old. As of October 1968, 20,000 children in 40 states had a foster grandparent (Streib, 1971, p. 25).

Personal Development and Self-expression. The study of old people in America has given sociologists new and pertinent insights into society as a whole. As Maddox pointed out in "Retirement as a Social Event in the United States" (1966), the problem of alienation—of disengagement, boredom, and time to kill—is not confined to the aged. In the years to come, work will probably occupy less and less of the average American's time. Up until the present, we have spent most of our energy working. We have focused on giving every individual the opportunity to accumulate things. As a nation, we lack "a strong cultural tradition of leisure," a tradition of using free time for self-fulfilling and self-expressing activities.

> In a world in which the ratio of hours spent in the nonwork and work roles is changing dramatically in the direction of nonwork, the necessity of having the educational system address itself to the development of personal and social skills which are relevant for living as well as for making a living is increasingly clear [Maddox, 1966, p. 365].

After all, old age is one minority that most of us expect to join some day.

SMALL-GROUP THEORY
People live in groups of various sizes, ranging from the largest societal contexts to the small groups in which everyday tasks are commonly performed. Group dynamics refers to behavior in small-group contexts. Such behavior must be understood by any social welfare practitioner if she is to have a conceptual and practical base for intervention in the many kinds of groups she is likely to confront. The family will be the first small group analyzed, since it occupies an important mediating function between large societal groups and smaller group contexts.

It has been seen that socialization is an essential part of the humanizing process, serving to liberate the potential of the human animal and establish social control boundaries that allow people to live together in relative harmony and productive order. At the same time, socialization can stifle human growth and lead to ethnocentrism, the culture blindness that tends to restrict our ability to openly accept other cultures and persons. The socialization process, in its good and bad aspects, is entrusted by society to a variety of small-group contexts, of which the family is the earliest and in some ways the most important. The family as a social institution is clearly undergoing change, and in that sense is a dynamic, flexible group structure not easily described. However, some major functions of the family in American society may still be noted.[27] (1) The family is the approved social context for reproduction and sexual behavior. To the extent that homosexual behavior is accepted, and as reproduction is shifted toward a zero-population-growth concept, this function of the family may be modified in the future. (2) The family serves as a mechanism for the transmission of family name and resources. This makes the family one of the very important institutional supports for a system of social stratification, since regardless of equality of opportunity, family inheritance gives persons differential starting points in life. (3) The family is a major context of primary-group satisfaction, whereby its members can interact as total human beings rather than as role performers acting in socially circumscribed ways. As society becomes increasingly complex and secondary relationships predominate, this function of the family assumes increasing importance in the maintenance of stable individual personalities.

The fourth and fifth major functions of the family, education and economic functioning, have been profoundly affected by changes in the societal structure. (4) As specialized educational structures have grown, they have taken over many educational functions previously performed in the family. This progressive differentiation of function has been accelerated by the society's emphasis on formal certification of competence (such as test scores and academic degrees) and the proliferation of the knowledge base to the point that the family cannot hope to encompass extant knowledge. Nevertheless, the family still serves as an education context, especially in such areas as learning appropriate sex roles and informal skills, although the progressive reduction of the educational function has no doubt contributed to the decreasing authority of adults in the family context. (5) The economic function has shifted from a primarily productive function to a consumption function. The family rarely produces its own basic needs, but does serve as an important context in which consumption decisions are made. The family is still productive in that the adults in the family typically work for wages that then make consumption possible.

The family exemplifies several characteristics of small groups. It has a substantial impact on its members through the socialization process and primary-type interaction patterns. It includes task-oriented behavior (such as work, shopping, and child-rearing) as well as socioemotional behavior (such as kissing, joking, chatting, or advice-giving). It has an identifiable structure, with norms, roles, and positions being organized in relationship to each other. There are power relationships, leadership patterns, and periods of cooperation, conflict, consensus, and exchange. Generally speaking, the family and any small group is a microcosm of general societal group processes, and much social science research has been done on small groups in the hopes of more clearly understanding such processes.[28]

Robert Bales, in attempting to conceptualize small-group structure and dynamics, proposes four main problems confronting a small group: adaptation to outside forces that affect the group; instrumental control over the performance of group tasks; the expression and management of the feelings of group members; and group integration.[29] Bales's conceptualization is useful because it highlights several significant factors in small-group structure and behavior, especially the social context of the group, the group's purpose, and leadership in the group. Like any other facet of social life, a group exists in a larger social system and is affected by its social environment, making knowledge of the relevant environment essential. In cases where the environment is hostile to the group, the hostility can help the group to achieve cohesion with which to preserve itself. It is also possible for such hostility ultimately to destroy the group.

Group purpose may be seen in several ways, but perhaps the most generally usable perspective is to draw a distinction between task-oriented and process-oriented groups. In the former, the main focus of the group is on the achievement of a task, such as fundraising. In the latter, the primary emphasis is on the pleasure derivable from the interaction of group members, as in various kinds of social groups. In social welfare one often hears the term *therapeutic group*, which is generally task-focused in attempting to achieve a specified therapeutic goal, but which may also try to maximize member interaction as part of the therapeutic environment. The conditions under which interaction occurs in task-oriented groups are also significant. Conditions in which cooperation is possible and encouraged tend to lessen hostility and dissatisfaction with the group, although task performance is not necessarily maximized. Competitive conditions in which one member's goal attainment will hinder the goal attainment of others tend to have opposite effects.[30]

A consideration of group purpose leads naturally into the issue of leadership in small groups, since the consensus of relevant research is that most groups have at least two leaders. The task leader is effective primarily in helping the group to achieve its goals, especially when the group is task-oriented. The socioemotional leader promotes group interaction and helps to maintain a cohesive interpersonal network within the group. Therefore, the typical task leader is respected, while the socioemotional leader is more personally popular.[31] Leadership is a complex issue, especially as it relates to task performance or group process. In particular, it has been found that authoritarian leadership maximizes task achievement but minimizes member satisfaction, that laissez-faire leadership leads to both low task attainment and low member satisfaction, and democratic leadership has limited task attainment but high member satisfaction.[32] Clearly the most desirable type of leadership depends on group purpose, which in turn can have value-based foundations.

The ways in which leadership can be attained is another important aspect of small-group leadership, and relates to the bases of power in a group. Power may be defined as the ability of one person to influence others regardless of the wishes of the persons being influenced.[33] Five bases of power have been formulated, and are very relevant to task and socioemotional leadership. Reward is the ability of the influencer to control items desirable to the influencee. Reward as a basis of power may be used by a task leader because task attainment is commonly perceived as rewarding. A socioemotional leader can use reward to the extent that pleasant interpersonal relations are rewarding. Punishment is the ability of the influencer to prevent goal attainment of the influencee, a basis of power typically more feasible for a task leader. Reward and punishment are directly related to the behavioral theory discussed in the previous chapter. Consistent with that theory, both reward and punishment tend to operate only as long as control is maintained, although reward tends to generalize to identification (discussed below), while punishment tends to generate evasion, resentment, and resistence.

A third basis of power is legitimacy, the ability of the influencer to claim the right to influence others and have the influencee agree. This base of power tends to be restricted to specified areas of legitimacy and may be hampered by conflicting definitions of legitimacy. Expertise as a basis of power refers to the ability of the influencer to influence others because of her recognized superior knowledge. There are also limits to the areas of one's claimed expertise, and it is a power base more feasible for a task leader than a socioemotional leader. Finally, identification is the ability of the influencer to win the affection of the influencee, a basis of power slow to develop but very durable once achieved. Identification frequently leads to modeling behavior, and is most usable by a socioemotional leader in his facilitation of interpersonal contacts and member satisfaction within the group. The bases of power are not conceptually clear in some areas, and will be very dependent on the group and external environments. Even so, they are suggestive of some of the ways in which group leadership occurs and is maintained.

A knowledge of small-group functioning enables the social welfare professional to understand the effect of group dynamics on behavior, and to use the group to attain social welfare goals. Since most behavior occurs in ongoing groups, the worker must be able to understand the dynamics of individual personality functioning as they interact with the dynamics of a group's structure. When the professional believes that modification of a group's structure would help to attain goals for one or more group members, he must have an adequate understanding of group principles to attain the desired changes. In some cases, new groups may need to be formed to attain specific objectives, in which case the worker would have to understand the possible group structures for the purpose desired, and then how to build such structures. In conclusion, the sociological perspective emphasizes the effect of group structures on human behavior, and such structures range from large-scale organizations discussed in Chapter 3 to smaller group contexts discussed here.

COMMUNITY
THEORY

Dentler notes that "the main feature in the setting of a community is this: It is of a size and design that allows a great range of functions to be carried out within its boundaries . . . ; a community supplies a geographical and psychological focus for institutional arrangements. A community is a place within which one finds all or most of the economic, political, religious, and familial institutions around which people group to cooperate, compete, or conflict."[34] In other words, communities have the important characteristics of spatial boundaries within which there is social interdependence. The concept of community, then, is a study in ecology, the way in which the physical environment affects human behavior and organization. In our world of resource pollution, resource destruction, and overcrowding, ecology is a vital area of study for all Americans, not just social welfare professionals and social scientists.

Communities have traditionally been conceptualized as urban or rural. Urban communities have recently received major attention to the neglect of rural communities, since urban communities have been rapidly developing at the expense of their rural counterparts:

> The result of a great cityward migration from Europe, from the American Deep South, and from the rural hinterland, and a great suburban dispersion that has occurred at the same time, is the formation of the metropolitan-area community. The Census Bureau of the United States calls these standard metropolitan areas. As of 1960, there were 212 such areas. Each contained one or more cities of fifty thousand or more residents plus surrounding localities. The areas accounted for 70 percent of the national population but less than 10 percent of the nation's land area. Within each metropolitan area, there exist satellite cities and suburbs and a kind of rural residue, or urban fringe residents.[35]

Given the tremendous surge in urbanization, it is natural for urban communities to be the focus of most study. But there is also recent recognition that rural communities have problems, which, though perhaps different from those of urban communities, are no less difficult to solve. Exhibit 5-4 illustrates both the magnitude of contemporary urban problems and the magnitude of the social welfare task in trying to solve these problems.

A major problem in the concept of community has traditionally been the diversity of social units encompassed by it. Not only are rural and urban communities quite different from each other, but so are such communities as metropolitan areas, neighborhoods, regions, and megalopolises. Each of these units has spatial boundaries, interdependence within the boundaries, and some degree of autonomy; yet each is also quite different. Traditionally, major attention was paid to what can be called center cities, the major downtown areas. Louis Wirth, for example, cited large size, high population density, and population heterogeneity as characteristic of such communities, and noted how they led to social problems.[36] However, Wirth could not foresee the growth of suburbs as a way to mitigate these problems, nor did he emphasize the effect of urban neighborhoods in providing smaller community units within larger ones.[37] To further complicate community theory, Gans asserts that urban slums may be quite cohesive and village-like,[38] while Dobriner[39] notes that suburbs are not nearly as homogeneous and personal as had been assumed by such writers as Whyte.[40]

EXHIBIT 5-4

Public Assistance in the United States: Some Illustrative Data

The societal demographic shift of population from rural to urban areas has created many social problems—unemployment, overcrowding, inadequate housing and public services, emotional tension and breakdown. These societal processes, when centered in urban areas, create a need for appropriate welfare services. The data presented in the table indicate the magnitude of the problems in selected United States cities and the magnitude of the task for the welfare system.

Recipients of Public Assistance Money Payments[a] by Selected Cities (February 1971)

City	Number	% Increase from 1/70	% of City's Population
New York	1,181,310	12.6	15.0
Philadelphia	288,297	29.8	14.8
Baltimore	137,793	20.1	15.2
District of Columbia	79,412	58.6	10.5
San Francisco	101,710	23.1	14.2
St. Louis	91,665	20.6	14.7
New Orleans	88,018	19.2	14.8
Denver	51,825	23.1	10.1

[a]Includes old-age assistance, aid to the blind, aid to the permanently and totally disabled, aid to families with dependent children, and general assistance.

Source: *Public Assistance Statistics, February 1971* (NCSS Report A-2 [2/71]), U.S. Department of Health, Education, and Welfare, Social and Rehabilitation Service, Program Statistics and Data Systems, National Center for Social Statistics, p. 4.

Warren has made an attempt to organize the tremendous diversity of phenomena subsumed under the concept of community by noting four ways in which communities differ from each other.[41] The first is the degree of autonomy in the performance of what he considers to be the five main functions of a community: production-distribution-consumption, socialization, social control, social participation, and mutual support. Obviously a metropolitan region would be quite different from a neighborhood in autonomy, with the former having greater autonomy in production-distribution-consumption, but the latter more autonomous with respect to the other functions. A second difference is the extent to which service areas in local units coincide and form a cohesive whole. Third, there are differences in the extent of psychological identification with a common locality. The last difference is in the community's horizontal pattern, or the structural and functional relation of the various units to each other. Communities, then, will vary in their size, degree of internal interdependence, and their autonomy, and these differences will be significant in understanding and ultimately intervening in community life.

As a context for social behavior, a community is very complex; to paraphrase Dobriner, the community is a microcosm of larger societal processes.[42] As such, to understand a community one must understand several levels of social functioning, brought together in a geographical area that has its own distinctive social organization. Naturally a community must first reflect its environment—other communities, larger political entities (such as counties and states), and societal values and structures. Warren states "that many of the problems which are confronted on the community level simply are not solvable on that level at all, but are *problems of the larger society of which the community is a part.*"[43] Within the community, there is a multitude of groups, organizations, and subcommunities that must be understood, and whose interaction is essential to the functioning of the community being studied. An understanding of small-group processes, formal organizational principles, and basic processes of social organization (social integration, conflict, deviance, and the like) is essential to an understanding of the structure, functioning, and change of a community. Once again the value of a systems approach is supported.[44]

Urban communities have been the geographical units developing most rapidly as contexts for human activity, and have been subject to tremendous stress. A brief look at some of the major contemporary urban community problems can therefore provide an additional community perspective. As Wirth noted years ago, a major problem is size and density, or what Dentler calls "problems of scale": "A major source of urban community problems is rapid escalation—that is, swift increases in environmental range, population, and technology—rather than population massing or some less precise process called urbanization."[45] An increase in scale creates problems because of the changes required to adapt to the changed scale, "all of them involving an increased scale of population, organization, service requirements, and institutional complexity."[46] A second problem, related to Wirth's hetero-geneity, is the residential segregation of ethnic and racial groups in the typical urban community.[47] This creates a condition of different cultural groups existing in close geographical proximity but with little cooperative interaction. Such conditions foster the development of prejudicial attitudes, discriminatory behavior, and intergroup conflict.[48]

A third problem area revolves around the maintenance of boundaries and internal power structures. The definition of a community is often vague enough to create ambiguity about the geographical area involved, and yet extensive enough to encompass a variety of quasi-autonomous political and social units. With unclear boundaries, it is difficult to identify important community resources, and the uncertainty may create chronic conflict. These difficulties exacerbate the problem of uniting diverse community elements into a coherent, democratic-community power structure that minimizes discrimination and political disenfranchisement for any group in the community. A fourth and related problem is community autonomy, or what Dentler calls "growth in *vertical aspects* of social structure: . . . the ever-elaborating ties between local agencies, institutions and services, and their counterpart units in society."[49] Here one sees that any community is deeply tied to its larger social environment, making community autonomy more difficult to achieve. The community must have its own decision-making structures and service outlets, yet it must also relate to those extra-community forces that ultimately affect its ability to exist as a political and functional entity.

Many of the major social changes of our time (industrialization, urbani-zation, migration, and so on) have had their major impact on individuals through communities, and many major social welfare programs are organized for delivery at the community level. Yet many of our communi-ties, and especially our urban communities, are in trouble. As large numbers of rural migrants move into the center city, they bring with them few resources and many needs for services. At the same time, the more affluent move to suburban communities, depriving the center cities of badly needed tax income to support the increased need for services. Population changes such as this lead to upheavals in power structures and limit the availability of skilled administrators. As cities grow, the problems of man-agement increase as more services for more people are needed. What the solutions to many urban problems are remain to be seen, but an urban society must make its urban communities viable contexts for human behavior.

Exhibit 5-5, which appears on the following pages (192 through 196), provides the reader with a more detailed examination of the most pressing issues that are involved in attempting to solve the complicated and perplexing problems of urban communities. Note that the exhibit also illustrates some of the points made in the earlier section on social stratification theory (pages 174 through 184, above).

EXHIBIT 5-5

The Challenge of Urban Communities

This exhibit is taken from Marion Robinson, "Humanizing the City" (1968), and looks at some of the realities of urban life for many urban dwellers, and also examines some of the points made earlier in the text. The figures in this exhibit are dated and not accurate for the present day, but the story that they tell in terms of relative deprivation and the magnitude of urban problems remains as true today as when the data were gathered. Written for a general audience, these excerpts lack specific citations, but they are stimulating even so.

The American Way ... Yesterday. In the United States, beginning in the mid-nineteenth century, great waves of immigrants from, in turn, Ireland, Germany, the Scandinavian countries, and the Southern and Eastern European countries found their first American homes in the city's least desirable residential areas. Unskilled labor was badly needed; the country was busily building railroads, factories, cities. Eventually the newcomers found a niche in the economy and status in the social order, moving into middle- and upper-class neighborhoods and positions of respect and power in business, industry, civil service, and politics.

Each group encountered the same experiences on the way up the ladder. As one professor of sociology ruefully puts it, "Segregated residence in slum areas, work with the lowest pay, hostility, prejudice, and discriminatory practices have never been reserved for any one newcomer or minority group. They have been democratically available to all newcomers without regard to race, religion, or origin. This has been the American Way."

... and Today. Today's ethnic newcomers to urban U.S.A.—American Negroes, Puerto Ricans, and Mexicans—share the slums with the aged poor. But the background of the Negroes who constitute the majority of today's slum residents is

From Marion Robinson, *Humanizing the City* (New York, Public Affairs Pamphlet No. 417), pp. 7–17. Copyright © 1968 by Public Affairs Committee, Inc. Used by permission.

markedly different from the immigrants of the past. Their ancestors were brought to this country as slaves and all have faced discrimination because of the color of their skins. Most of today's slum dwellers, unskilled and uneducated, have migrated from the South. Yesterday's need for unskilled labor has all but disappeared. A high school diploma and some technical training are minimum qualifications for most jobs, however menial and low paid. Segregation and discrimination based on prejudice against skin color, which dies infinitely harder than prejudice against foreign national origin or religion, continually frustrate the efforts of slum dwellers to follow their predecessors up the ladder of success.

"The plight of our minority populations is worse, not better," declares Mr. [Whitney] Young. "Since 1954, Negro unemployment has doubled. Today it is two-and-a-half times the rate of unemployment of white citizens, and among teenagers in the ghetto, it is a disastrous 27 percent. The gap between Negro and white median income has broadened. It is clear that prejudice and discrimination are national, not regional, disorders.

"A great part of the hard core of the unemployed are youth. Their enforced leisure comes at the time when all youth are restless, searching for life's meaning. They strike out against all of society's pressuring forces, and in striking out, they don't care whom they hurt—least of all themselves."

About 10 percent of our population are people over 65 years of age. In 1960, one-third of them lived in four states (New York, California, Pennsylvania, and Illinois) that are 80 percent urban. Of all public assistance recipients, the elderly account for 35 percent. In other words, among the 22 million persons now living in slums, several million are citizens who, at a time of waning physical energy and ability to cope with day-to-day living, are existing on the edge of poverty in an unfavorable, often dangerous, environment. In a predominantly young, materialistic society, they, like the ethnic populations, constitute a minority, whose potential contribution to society remains unknown. Among them, the Negro aged live in a condition of what has been called "double jeopardy," since they belong to minority groups in two ways.

The City's Change of Function. Originally, cities were built by people banding together for survival, for mutual protection against a hostile outside world. Modern cities, says a sociologist, are "made up of groups of people in competition with each other for jobs, homes, education, and other resources."

The losers in that competition have been accumulating for some time in our city slums. They suffer from two kinds of poverty. Besides financial poverty, there is, say social workers, "a poverty of culture, which develops out of generations of neglect, of being beaten down and denied access to knowledge of how to change things, how to exercise influence on communal affairs. People become apathetic, overwhelmed with their own powerlessness to affect the course of their own lives."

A settlement house worker in San Antonio observes, "The needs and demands of the hard-core poor have been ignored or neglected for decades. Where earnest work is now going on with them, it can be thought of as a sort of limited revolution. Criticism for this work can be expected because the very work points up the community's neglect."

Attitudes Based on Misconceptions. In the time of the earlier immigrants, it was assumed by the more established population that slum dwellers were morally degenerate and inferior. Even today, after America has witnessed the rise of four or five generations from slum living to positions of independence and respect—indeed, many have become prominent and beloved citizens—there is a tendency to assume that those deteriorated buildings somehow reflect the hopeless quality of the human beings who live in them. Perhaps it is easier to believe that than to face citizen responsibility.

Misconceptions and half-truths about the slum poor are commonly used as an excuse for lack of interest in their plight. It is well known that rates of delinquency and crime are higher in slum areas than in other parts of the city. But consider this report from a criminologist: "The fraud, consumer cheating, and embezzlement committed by our most 'respectable' people cost the nation almost three times as much as the more common crimes of the ghetto, such as robbery and theft. . . . A survey of 1,700 middle-class adults showed that 91 percent admitted acts for which they could have received jail sentences."

Perhaps the most prevalent misconception is that "slums are full of people on welfare who won't work." At latest report, there were 7.3 million persons receiving public assistance. Of these, 2.1 million were 65 years of age or over; 700,000 were blind or otherwise severely handicapped; 3.5 million were children; 900,000 were mothers of dependent children; 150,000 were fathers, two-thirds of whom were incapacitated. Of the entire 7.3 million persons, less than 1 percent were capable of acquiring job skills so as to become self-sufficient.

"Winner Take All." The truth is that our society operates on a "winner take all" basis. Consider the fact that our population is constantly on the move, geographically speaking. People who move because they are entering or transferring to a job in the armed forces, government, industry, or business are helped with moving expenses, often welcomed into the new community by special arrangement; wherever they go, they retain fringe benefits such as employer payments for health or life insurance, and the like. Built into the job of personnel departments is responsibility to counsel employees and refer them to community resources. All this is a matter of right, not as a favor.

When poor, unemployed people move to a new location, they encounter [many obstacles when seeking] . . . financial and other assistance. . . . Fringe benefits are not available to them. The services they need may not even exist; if they do, they may be substandard. Many of them can be obtained only after what one social worker has termed a "degradation ceremony." Applicants for help must first prove themselves to be utterly without resource. Help is given as a favor, not as a right.

SEEING BENEATH THE SURFACE

Most of us have some capacity for human understanding—the ability to comprehend the meaning of experiences and emotions which all human beings have in common. This is a beginning essential for the practitioner in the human services, but only a beginning. The United States population has converged from every corner of the earth and among our people hundreds of cultures are represented. Part of his training, then, is to understand the character of a group of people—what it is, how it has been shaped by history—and to become aware of cultural differences among people. Attitudes toward the family, the self, achievement, gratification, work, saving—all these and many more add up to a way of life, or, as some term it, a life style.

Obviously the practitioner can be of little help to people if, when he meets a life style different from his own, he assumes his job is to bring it into conformity with his own. On the contrary, his job is to suspend judgment, to see beneath the surface, to distinguish between what would be forcing an alien idea upon a person and what he can do to help the person change enough to increase his chances for survival in our society.

Culture patterns, or life styles, are not alone based on national or religious heritage. Today, our practitioners and students of the social sciences are sharply aware of differences between middle-class values and attitudes and those of the lower socioeconomic groups. Because the middle class predominates in our society, its members sometimes assume their values are "right," others "wrong." In times past, assumptions of this sort led to such patronizing phrases as "the deserving (or undeserving) poor."

Recently, a social work administrator of a large-scale social rehabilitation program in the slums of an eastern city, addressing a group of his peers about neighborhood services, protested that antipoverty programs were trying to push the chronic poor into acquiring skills and attitudes associated with middle-class living.

"Don't mistake me," he went on. "I am not knocking the obvious strengths and virtues of middle-class society. Nor am I suggesting the romantic notion that the underclass dweller should remain with the rats and garbage to escape the rigors of the suburban swimming pool and cocktail circuit."

Understanding Differences. Instead, he would have us understand these differences: "In the adult upper- and middle-classes, the life of the mind predominates, expression of instincts is suppressed or repressed, and emerges in its own grotesque character. Amongst the underclass, violence, sexuality, love, and the world of the senses predominate." Only the poets, writers, artists, and philosophers that have originated in this class—and there are many today among the so-called elite—have found a way to express this way of life and still be at home in our complex urban environment.

From another social worker, reporting on a project of assistance to a group of hard-core poor people, we get further insight: "Middle-class ideas such as postponement of immediate satisfaction for long-range goals, controls of physical aggression, rationality of decision-making, respect for property and privacy were unfamiliar to these people. Moreover, such ideas were in total opposition [to] their life experience."

A settlement-house worker describes chronically poor families of a neighborhood in which he works:

They are inconsistent copers, isolated from the agencies that could help them. They are in an unequal position to solve problems that continually affect their lives. Because they do not participate in community activities, their interests are ignored or delegated to groups who inadequately represent their interests. . . . They have definite ideas of what is right or wrong but these differ drastically from those of the more affluent. They think all politicians are crooks and it does absolutely no good to fight City Hall. They do not understand bureaucratic behavior and often have a "conspiracy theory" which further isolates them from the benefits of education, medicine, and consumer information.

In one city, inspectors were checking neighborhood houses to see if safety codes were being followed. Red tags left on some houses indicated need for follow-up inspection. Rumor got around that the red tag meant the house was condemned, and a panic started brewing. Considerable fast footwork on the part of neighborhood social workers replaced the rumor with the true information.

In order to "reach" these families, a neighborhood worker must become a sort of mediator ("almost like the old ward heelers," says one), a person to be trusted to act as a bridge between the family and the neighborhood service which they have not trusted or understood. Often the worker is accepted only when he has been able to help in a crisis—an unwed teenage daughter becomes pregnant, a drug addict runs afoul of the law, a marijuana party ends in a car crash. Reassured by his nonjudgmental help, people come to him with other problems and eventually may accept referrals for medical and social services.

Would that we all could learn, as these professionals must, not to lump together a large group of people under one stereotype. There are many kinds of people among the poor, among the Negroes, just as there are many kinds of people in any group.

In New York City, hundreds of "slum hotels" —single-room occupancy buildings—constitute the only shelter available to many of the city's losers: alcoholics, addicts, aged, crippled, chronically ill, jobless migrants from rural areas. Not sick enough or socially disturbed enough to be in institutions, they are nevertheless unable to cope with life in urban society. In recent years, several social welfare agencies have worked with the people in these derelict buildings. The Community Psychiatry Division of St. Luke's Hospital reported on such a project.

A Social Worker's Report. In a "rotting six-story building," the social worker found what seemed to her to resemble "a closely-knit, isolated, poverty-stricken village." Most residents were 40 or older. The ratio of men to women was two-to-one. Seventy-five percent had major chronic diseases or disabilities. Well over half were alcoholics. There was a mixture of whites, Negroes, Puerto Ricans;

the majority were Negroes from the rural South. Some were sporadically employed. The majority were welfare recipients.

These residents stayed within a two-block radius of the building, did not know how to use the bus or subway, felt incapable of traveling alone to other parts of the city. (Later, when the social worker was able to persuade some of the sick people to attend a clinic, the journey was "a major, anxiety-provoking event.") Most did not vote, attend church or clubs, or keep in touch with their families, chiefly because experience had taught them to expect negative, if not hostile, attitudes, beginning with their own neighborhood.

"We think of single, unattached individuals as being reclusive," reports this social worker, "but I found an unexpectedly strong social structure. The lives of all but a few were actively intertwined, as a matriarchal, quasi-family. The dominant women residents fed, protected, punished, and set norms for the group. There was an informal system of self-help. For example, one older woman had the self-assigned task of caring for bedridden residents, the only compensation for which was status in the building. A young man who had access to supplies of tranquilizers but did not use them himself, dispensed them one by one to people in trouble who came to talk with him. An ex-boxer was always sent for when a fight broke out."

After a few weeks of "developing sufficient trust to work together," the worker and the residents together built a program "in which the existing system of mutual aid was shifted and expanded to include recreation, control of antisocial behavior, and encouragement to seek medical and social service." At the time of her report she could note as plus factors: reduction of antisocial behavior, higher morale, ability of some to follow through on referral for help with medical, psychiatric, and social problems. On the minus side, there was no real success with alcoholics, although some drank less.

Of particular significance to the many people who begin to see great possibilities for the development of indigenous leadership among disadvantaged people is the fact that three of the natural leaders among the tenants of this building showed such skill in group management and learned enough about community resources that they were eventually employed as paid staff workers in similar buildings.

Social workers have learned the hard way not to expect miracles, even from the most devoted, consistent efforts. Instead, as the phrase goes, they "aim for limited goals."

"Society destroys people systematically and thoroughly over a long and painful period of time," says the director of a Midwest youth center. "We must face this fact and deal with it. Most people in the service professions know they can only buy a day of happiness, a brief period of coping with reality with these worst-off folks." Less experienced workers suffer from a "missionary syndrome"— expecting real and permanent change from a few months' helpful experience for people who have suffered from 30 years or more of negative, poor, unhappy, insecure, lonely, and meaningless existence. "The arithmetic points to a fallacy and our heads tell our hearts to beware."

But the heart must have its say. The social worker on the slum hotel project felt as if she were applying "a bandaid on a massive sore," because "the human suffering and neglect which is encapsulated in these buildings is so gross as to be incredible, overwhelming, and painful to accept as a social reality in the United States in the 1960s." Here under one roof were people who reflected our society's failures: inadequate medical and psychiatric care and knowledge, antiquated housing regulations, punitive welfare legislation, depersonalization and rejection by society of its least adequate members. But it was also "a laboratory where we renew our faith and optimism about the related, loving, and helping qualities inherent in deprived and damaged human beings."

CAN WE AFFORD IT?

To replan and rebuild our cities, truly come to grips with the problem of poverty, and demonstrate that we have, indeed, an open society, calls for a concerted, coordinated attack on many fronts at once. It will cost more money than government alone can afford. Can the country—all of us—afford it?

By now it is no secret that we can, if we will. But it will involve hard decisions, and possibly real sacrifices, if we are really to overcome today's urban problems.

SOCIAL-CHANGE THEORY

There are few phenomena of greater interest to social welfare personnel than social change, and yet few areas of theory are less helpful in understanding actual behavior. One reason for the discrepancy between theory and reality is the traditional concentration in sociological theory on macrosociological change.[50] Social welfare practitioners are typically more directly concerned with microsociological change, especially at the individual, organizational, and community levels. Yet the social system is so interlocking that macro and micro phenomena are related, and theories at each level should have some applicability at the other. In this section a brief review of theory at both levels will be undertaken, and then some ideas on their interrelationship will be presented.

An immediate problem arises in the definition of social change. Nisbet's definition as "change within a persisting identity" seems to be a simple, usable one if it is modified slightly.[51] Nisbet's definition affirms the basic point that change is most commonly measured with respect to a given function. For example, the political structure of a society may change from democratic to autocratic, but one is still talking about a political structure, and the change is described with reference to the performance of political activities. However, on some occasions one may also wish to speak of change as occurring in the elimination of a function or the creation of a new one. For example, some occupations have disappeared, while new ones have appeared, and it is questionable whether there are persisting identities in these cases. Here one is directly into the macro-micro issue, since perhaps on the macrosociological level the disappearance of an occupation may simply be a change in the overall productive function of society, while at the micro level within the given occupation there is no persisting identity. Although seemingly a semantic problem, it is this basic lack of clarity in social-change theory that underlies many problems in attempts to identify change and its causes.

Moore suggests that there are several things one needs to know in order to talk about change: the structure that is changing, the source of the change, the direction of change, and the time period in which the change occurs.[52] While it would seem relatively easy to identify the characteristics of change, it is frustratingly difficult. For example, Moore asserts that change is occurring constantly,[53] while Nisbet and Swanson suggest that persistence is the rule rather than the exception.[54] The fact that social structures are so closely interwoven creates difficulties in identifying the sources and targets of change—if one wanted to assert that the hippie phenomenon was a change, what structure or structures would one identify? The point is, then, that social science theories of social change are still evolving and need to be approached with some care.

Out of the many conflicting theories, the following seems to be a useful perspective on change. Change may be stimulated by external or internal forces. However, persistence is more likely than change, simply because any social structure is a complex system that generates vested interests in terms of psychological security and concrete advantages. Change will occur when the structure involved reaches a point of crisis, which Nisbet defines as a point at which the traditional solutions to problems are no longer effective.[55] Alternatives are needed, and they may be of several kinds. Among the internal sources of alternatives are what Moore calls flexibilities built into a social system, including variability in socialization, deviance caused by the imperfect operation of social control mechanisms, and the variability in individual role performance. Moore also sees the aggregate of small-scale changes and the inconsistency between societal values and concrete reality as additional internal sources of change.[56] Note that in some cases change is being used to explain change; nevertheless, Moore's ideas are useful.

A second source of innovation is external sources of change. These include, according to Moore, borrowing from other cultures (diffusion) and environmental changes, which stimulate social adaptation.[57] Extending Moore's ideas, Lenski suggests that further sources of internal innovation are inventions (useful combinations of already existing information) and discoveries (innovations providing completely new information).[58] Moore notes that whether or not the potential sources of internal and external change actually do generate innovative ideas will depend on five factors:

(1) the size of the culture base, which is the number of ideas existing in the social system that can be combined in new ways to generate new ideas; (2) the number of people looking for a solution, which is normally related to the population size; (3) the extent of contact with other cultures from which ideas may be borrowed; (4) environmental stability, which allows the search for innovations to proceed; and (5) the degree to which the values of the social system encourage innovation.[59]

In addition to a crisis and available alternatives, social change seems to require a change agent or advocate who will push for the selection and adoption of one of the alternatives. The characteristics of a change agent are not well understood, although charisma is commonly thought to be one of them.[60] The general framework of change presented above seems applicable to either the macro or micro level, although the focus has been mainly macro-sociological. The compatibility of this framework at the micro level can be seen by looking at Swanson's discussion of routinized change in organizations.[61] He says that the organization must first have a "generalized objective" against which all changes will be planned and evaluated—here one sees the similarity with a need or desire for innovations. Then there must be standards to select innovations, which he feels must include continuous evaluation of the operation of the organization. Innovations should be evaluated heuristically, with alternatives being selected when they are satisfactory rather than necessarily perfect (called "satisficing"). In Swanson's analysis of organizational change, then, he is basically concerned with the perceived need for change, the availability of alternatives, and, elsewhere in his analysis, the institutionalization of the change in the organization.[62]

CONCLUSION

Social welfare personnel are by definition agents of social change, whether it is by changing individual behavior or by affecting social policy. Sociological social-change theory addresses itself to changes in social structures, which then can have relevance to individual change; psychological theories of personality change are more directly focused on individual change. While the psychological view focuses on the individual's growth and functioning, the sociological view looks at the social structure within which individuals exist. Both views are necessary in social welfare. Services are most often provided to individuals, and the sources of their behavior must be understood. The ways in which social structures impinge on individual growth and functioning must also be understood. And throughout, a systems approach reminds us that human behavior is a complex network of interdependent actions. In the next chapter, theories helping the social welfare professional to understand the economic and political institutions are examined. The contemporary social welfare professional must understand the political and economic world which so strongly affects his work, but he should also recognize that economic and political behavior comprise sub-parts of the general principles of individual and social behavior discussed here.

STUDY QUESTIONS

1. What limitations, if any, do you find in sociological approaches to understanding problems? Are there certain kinds of problems for which a sociological perspective is not very helpful? Does a sociological approach tend to narrow the behaviors at which one looks when analyzing problematic behavior? Is it possible to understand behavior without reference to sociological concepts? Be specific and refer to concrete examples in your thinking about these questions.

2. What is institutional racism? Identify as many fields as you can of sociological theory (social stratification, role theory, and so on) that help to understand the causes, functions, and dysfunctions of institutional racism. Show what contribution each field you have identified makes to an understanding of institutional racism.

3. How might a sociologist analyze the functions and dysfunctions of the American social welfare system? What groups benefit from it, and what groups are disadvantaged by it? How does social welfare relate to other major social institutions? How are decisions made in social welfare, and who participates in decision-making? How could a sociologist summarize the effect of the social welfare institution on the societal structure? (Remember that as a social scientist the sociologist would attempt to state his conclusions in value-free terms.)

REFERENCES

1. Robert Nisbet, *The Social Bond* (New York: Alfred A. Knopf, 1950), pp. 5–20.
2. Ibid., pp. 21–42.
3. An excellent summary of history, characteristics, and effects of the industrialization process may be found in William Faunce, *Problems of an Industrial Society* (New York: McGraw-Hill, 1968).
4. Sigmund Freud, *Civilization and Its Discontents* (New York: Norton, 1961).
5. A classic work addressing this question is Emile Durkheim, *The Division of Labor in Society* (New York: Free Press, 1964).
6. See Talcott Parsons, *The Social System* (New York: Free Press, 1964), pp. 26–36.
7. An excellent account of socialization and institutionalization is in Peter Berger and Thomas Luckmann, *The Social Construction of Reality* (Garden City: Anchor, 1967).
8. See ibid.; and Tamotsu Shibutani, *Society and Personality* (Englewood Cliffs, N.J.: Prentice-Hall, 1961), pp. 491–594. See also Anselm Strauss, ed., *George Herbert Mead: On Social Psychology* (Chicago: Phoenix, 1965), pp. 19–42.
9. A good summary of role theory and its applications may be found in Edwin Thomas, ed., *Behavioral Science for Social Workers* (New York: Free Press, 1967), pp. 15–50 and 59–77.
10. An interesting discussion of this general point is by Russell Smith and John Hester, "Social Services in a Technological Society," *Journal of Education for Social Work* 10 (Winter 1974): 81–89.
11. An interesting example is described in W. F. Cottrell, "Death by Dieselization," in Ronald Freedman et al., *Principles of Sociology* (New York: Henry Holt, 1956), pp. 220–29.

12. See Carol H. Meyer, *Social Work Practice* (New York: Free Press, 1970), pp. 54–104.

13. An interesting example is Herbert Gans, *The Urban Villagers* (New York: Free Press, 1962), especially the Epilogue.

14. Ibid.

15. See Berger and Luckmann, op. cit.; and Kenneth Dolbeare and Patricia Dolbeare, *American Ideologies* (Chicago: Markham, 1971), pp. 1–21.

16. Karl Marx and Friedrich Engels, *Basic Writings on Politics and Philosophy*, ed. Lewis Feuer (Garden City: Anchor, 1959), pp. 26–30, 263–66.

17. John L. Roach et al., *Social Stratification in the United States* (Englewood Cliffs, N.J.: Prentice-Hall, 1969), pp. 20ff., 225–33, 537–52.

18. Ibid., pp. 11ff., 32–33, 596–97.

19. Ibid., pp. 13–20, 32–44.

20. See Lewis Coser, *The Functions of Social Conflict* (New York: Free Press, 1956).

21. Roach et al., op. cit., pp. 54–60.

22. For example, see Elliot Liebow, *Talley's Corner* (Boston: Little, Brown, 1967); Oscar Lewis, *La Vida* (New York: Random House, 1966); and Robin Morgan, ed., *Sisterhood is Powerful* (New York: Vintage, 1970).

23. Terry Jones, "Institutional Racism in the United States," *Social Work* 19 (March 1974): 224. Reprinted by permission of the National Association of Social Workers.

24. Martin Rein, *Social Policy: Issues of Choice and Change* (New York: Random House, 1970), pp. 26–27, 249–70, 353–73.

25. A useful compendium of such techniques is Si Kahn, *How People Get Power* (New York: McGraw-Hill, 1970).

26. An interesting example is in Gary Evans, "Layoffs Bring New Breed of Food Stamp Applicants," *Greensboro Daily News*, January 8, 1975, p. B1. In the article it is noted that "the new applicants are not used to asking for a dole and 'they're harder to deal with'...they are also more impatient with bureaucratic red tape."

27. See Bernard Berelson and Gary Steiner, *Human Behavior: An Inventory of Scientific Findings* (New York: Harcourt, Brace, and World, 1964), pp. 297–323.

28. See Dorwin Cartwright and Alvin Zander, *Group Dynamics: Research and Theory* (Evanston: Row, Peterson, 1960).

29. Clovis Shepherd, *Small Groups: Some Sociological Perspectives* (San Francisco: Chandler, 1964), p. 28.

30. Ibid., pp. 58–99. This chapter summarizes some of the enormous literature related to the issues involved in task and process groups, as well as presenting a useful selected bibliography.

31. An excellent example of the factors involved in task and socioemotional leadership and their interplay is William F. Whyte's classic *Street Corner Society* (Chicago: University of Chicago Press, 1943).

32. Cartwright and Zander, op. cit., pp. 512–19, 586–605.

33. John French, Jr., and Bertram Raven, "The Bases of Social Power," in Cartwright and Zander, op. cit., pp. 607–22.

34. Robert Dentler, *American Community Problems* (New York: McGraw-Hill, 1968), p. 16.

35. Ibid., pp. 24–25.

36. See Louis Wirth, *On Cities and Social Life* (Chicago: University of Chicago Press, 1964), pp. 165–78, 229–70.

37. See Suzanne Keller, *The Urban Neighborhood: A Sociological Perspective* (New York: Random House, 1968).

38. Gans, op. cit.

39. William Dobriner, *Class in Suburbia* (Englewood Cliffs, N.J.: Prentice-Hall, 1963), pp. 85–126.

40. William H. Whyte, Jr., *The Organization Man* (Garden City: Anchor, 1956), pp. 295–434.

41. Roland Warren, "A Community Model," in Ralph Kramer and Harry Specht, eds., *Readings in Community Organization Practice* (Englewood Cliffs, N.J.: Prentice-Hall, 1969), pp. 43–44.

42. William Dobriner, *Social Structures and Systems* (Pacific Palisades: Goodyear, 1969), pp. 206–10.

43. Warren, op. cit., p. 45.

44. Thomas Holland, "The Community: Organism or Arena?" *Social Work* 19 (January 1974): 73–80, presents an interesting analysis of communities using a systems theoretical approach.

45. Dentler, op. cit., p. 33.

46. Ibid., p. 37.

47. Ibid., pp. 37–38.

48. Raymond Mack, "The Components of Social Conflict," in Kramer and Specht, op. cit., pp. 327–37.

49. Dentler, op. cit., pp. 41–54.

50. A concise review of sociological theories of change may be found in Richard Applebaum, *Theories of Social Change* (Chicago: Markham, 1970).

51. See Robert Nisbet, *Social Change and History* (New York: Oxford University Press, 1969), p. 168.

51. Wilbert Moore, *Social Change* (Englewood Cliffs, N.J.: Prentice-Hall, 1963), pp. 52–68.

53. Ibid., pp. 1–21.

54. Guy Swanson, *Social Change* (Glenview: Scott, Foresman, 1971).

55. Nisbet, op. cit., pp. 282–83.

56. Moore, op. cit., pp. 45–68.

57. Ibid., pp. 77–80, 85–88.

58. Gerhard Lenski, *Human Societies* (New York: McGraw-Hill, 1970), pp. 48–94.

59. Moore, op. cit., pp. 27–44.

60. Swanson, op. cit., pp. 140–41; and Everett E. Hagen, *On the Theory of Social Change* (Homewood: Dorsey, 1962), pp. 55–182.

61. Swanson, op. cit., pp. 148–70.

62. Ibid., pp. 112–35.

SELECTED READINGS The diversity of sociological theories pertinent to social welfare creates an enormous body of potentially relevant theory. The following are of interest in and of themselves, but also have excellent bibliographies for those wishing to pursue any given area in greater depth.

Birnbaum, Norman. *The Crisis of Industrial Society.* London: Oxford University Press, 1969.

Bredemeier, Harry, and Jackson Toby. *Social Problems in America.* 2nd ed. New York: John Wiley, 1972.

Dentler, Robert. *American Community Problems.* New York: McGraw-Hill, 1968.

Downs, Anthony. *Urban Problems and Prospects.* Chicago: Markham, 1970.

Jencks, Christopher, et al. *Inequality.* New York: Basic Books, 1972.

Knowles, Lewis, and Kenneth Prewitt. *Institutional Racism in America.* Englewood Cliffs, N.J.: Prentice-Hall (Spectrum), 1969.

Lewis, Oscar. *La Vida.* New York: Random House, 1965.

Liebow, Elliot. *Talley's Corner.* Boston: Little, Brown, 1967.

Shepherd, Clovis. *Small Groups: Some Sociological Perspectives.* San Francisco: Chandler, 1964.

Spiegel, John. *Transactions: The Interplay between Individual, Family, and Society.* New York: Science House, 1971.

Thomas, Edwin. *Behavioral Science for Social Workers.* New York: Free Press, 1967.

Turner, Jonathan. *Patterns of Social Organization.* New York: McGraw-Hill, 1972.

6

Political and Economic Bases

*T*HE POINT has been made repeatedly that the social welfare institution depends upon a societal mandate to function. It must be supported by a value system that views seeking to help others as proper, and by economic resources that make such help possible. Political and economic decision-making are major sources of policy supporting or destroying social welfare activities, and consequently are of enormous significance to those seeking to understand or affect the social welfare institution.

Any society has a limited supply of those resources and social relationships considered significant and desirable. Society is the result of collective decisions that can be changed, but the decisions existing at any given time serve to structure social behavior. The political and economic institutions have a major impact on decisions creating desirable resources and social relationships, and the way in which they will be distributed among members in the society.[1] These decisions structure the daily life of society's members. As long as political power is vested in a small group of persons who are to represent the rest of the citizens, Americans will run for office and seek to influence their representatives—mostly legally, but occasionally illegally. Similarly, as long as money provides access to resources defined as highly desirable or even necessary—automobiles, adequate housing and nutrition, education, and the like—people will compete for money and seek to preserve their accumulated financial resources. Consequently, the social welfare institution is closely tied to the political and economic institutions in a society.

Involvement of social welfare professionals in the political and economic institutions has led increasingly to a greater emphasis on social policy involvement as a part of the professional role. The theoretical and practice expertise that the helping professional possesses should be an important part of societal decision-making about the structuring of social relationships. The values that provide the foundation of social welfare must also find expression in a technological society that increasingly finds it easy to lose the individual in a flurry of efficiency and cost accounting. As Kahn has said, "During the next decades, the most pressing task confronting American social work will be the defeat of personal and social isolation."[2] This chapter will first look at some of the basic characteristics of the political and economic institutions, including an examination of the effects of these structures on social welfare needs. This background will then be used as a context for an expanded discussion of social policy, and what the professional's role in the policy process is.

THE POLITICAL
BASES OF
SOCIAL
WELFARE

The American political system is structured to provide for the separation of powers. This occurs in four major ways. First is separation of powers within the federal government, which is divided into three branches.[3]

1. The executive branch, of which the presidency is the major component, although supporting offices include the vice-presidency and the cabinet. The executive branch provides overall national leadership in domestic and international relations, providing information about and initiating action to meet national needs. The executive branch also has the power to veto actions of Congress.

2. The legislative branch. The Congress is composed of two bodies, the House of Representatives and the Senate. The legislative branch has the responsibility for enacting legislation, which it can initiate, or which may be initiated by the executive branch. It also has the power to override presidential vetos.

3. The judicial branch. The courts exist as a forum within which to interpret law and individual behavior in relation to the law. It serves as a check for both the executive and legislative branches by its power to strike down legislation and actions it considers unconstitutional or illegal.

The Constitution of the United States was written in an attempt to create a federal government in which no branch would be able to gain excessive power over the others. Since members of the executive and legislative branches are the elected representatives of the people, a system was created that would minimize opportunities to seize personal power and create a totalitarian state.

The second major foundation to separation of power is a federal-state sharing of powers. Although a federal government was created to provide for general societal leadership and to meet the needs of all citizens, the several states were given the power to establish their own governing structures, and to enact legislation and formulate policies governing the daily lives of their citizens. Federal power over states is limited, and states have representation at the federal level through their elected representatives and senators. The federal-state sharing of powers rests on the assumption that there are certain needs which states cannot meet themselves, and which are best met for all of the states together at the federal level. However, it is also assumed that state government is more accessible to the people, who have the right to determine the majority of their own goals and appropriate means to attain them.

The third power base is the political parties. There are two main political parties, the Democratic and Republican. Other parties exist, but their significance in the political process has varied from election to election. Political parties serve as a means of involving people in the political process. They also express differing points of view, thereby giving citizens a choice of candidates representing alternative points of view in elections. Traditionally, the Democratic party has represented the views of those with more liberal social and fiscal beliefs, while the Republican party has tended to be more conservative. These traditional distinctions are increasingly difficult to make, however.

The fourth factor is the electoral process itself. The key persons in federal and state government are elected, in theory representing the views of the major groups in society. The major groups are assumed to have the opportunity, through political parties, to work for the nomination of persons representing their views. The fact that there are many groups seeking representation can lead to two results: a proliferation of political parties, each representing an interest and putting forth its own candidates for election, or coalitions between major groups. For a variety of financial and social reasons, the latter approach has generally been taken in America. The differing objectives of the Democratic and Republican parties have been thought to provide for the expression of different views by major groups in society.

The preceding has obviously been a theoretical view of the American political system. In practice, there are many issues that arise from such a structure. One is that whatever the considerable virtues of a system built on the separation of powers, such a system tends to generate conflict. Since access to political power is important, there is considerable temptation to use whatever means available—legal or illegal—to gain access. For example, many persons who are elected to office at either the state or federal level have the power to appoint people to other positions, such as the president's power to appoint Supreme Court judges (if there is a vacancy). These appointments may be used to solidify one's own power and value system rather than to find the best person for the position. It is one of several ways that persons already occupying political office have an advantage in keeping it. The American political system attempts to use the conflict generated by the separation of powers very explicitly as a way to encourage pluralism. In this way it seeks to use conflict primarily as a positive force in society.

Pluralism is based on three major societal values: (1) sociocultural diversity; (2) freedom of expression; and (3) the melting-pot nature of the society. It creates a system in which the many groups comprising society can freely compete in the political process. It is assumed that coalitions will be formed, creating a majority, enabling elections to occur and legislation to be enacted. In this way the majority opinion has presumably found expression, and the defeated minority accepts this opinion until the next voting opportunity when it may again have a chance to enact its wishes. Our political system, then, is a competitive one, but one that provides a structured opportunity for all groups to fight for their own particular interests.

Exhibit 6-1 (p. 208) summarizes the legislative process at the federal level. Most states have a similar process for the passage of legislation at the state level. Let's look at how the separation of powers and pluralism work in Congress. A piece of legislation has first to be introduced, which means that it has to be written in an acceptable form and it has to have a legislator who will sponsor it. Any group can decide that certain legislation is needed to help it function more effectively. For example, at present many professional groups are trying to enact legislation to license titles and practice so that they can have greater control over the quality of professional practice. These concerns must be formulated in a written piece of proposed legislation. This normally requires conferences with legislators, their aides, and lawyers. In this process, groups that are likely to object to the legislation are identified, and the group seeking the legislation must decide how it will deal with such opposition. Will it try to modify its proposed legislation? Try to win the other groups over to its way of thinking? Decide to fight the opposition by generating more political support? The decision made will obviously reflect the group's objectives and a hard-headed evaluation of who has how much power. Here we can see that, with the political process barely off the ground, a host of people and skills have been brought into play.

Once a piece of legislation has been introduced, it is referred to committee. Here it is studied intensively, and hearings are usually held during which various groups interested in the legislation can have input—pro or con. Other legislators may testify before the committee, explaining how the proposed legislation will affect their constituents. Individuals and groups may likewise explain to the committee how they will be affected by the bill. Many groups hire professional lobbyists whose job it is to contact key people to try to gain their support. They may also testify in committee hearings and present data to support the interests of the group they are hired to represent. The committee will ultimately make either a decision that the bill needs further work, in which case it will not be passed on, or that the bill is ready to be considered by the houses of Congress. The committee normally makes a recommendation supporting or not supporting the bill when it sends it on to the floor of each house of Congress. The committee, then, is a second point at which intervention is extremely important, and the point at which many people are likely to get involved in the passage of a bill.

It becomes increasingly obvious that the competition generated by a political system attempting to allow all groups in a pluralistic society to express their views turns out to be an unequal struggle. Earlier we saw that one inequality is political patronage, the ability of elected officials to appoint persons to certain offices, which helps to solidify the strength of those already in power. Access to lobbyists who can support a bill through a network of informal personal contacts and access to data is a second inequality. The National Association of Social Workers, for example, employs no more than two full-time lobbyists in Washington—and sometimes less than that. Such minimal representation is a distinct disadvantage compared to the massive lobbies employed by groups like labor unions and many manufacturing groups.

EXHIBIT 6-1

The Legislative Process—Learning to Participate

Although virtually all of us learned it in high school, can you recount the process involved in a bill becoming law? Do you know who your elected representatives are? Do you know how to write effectively to them to express your wishes? The answer to the second question can be found in a publication such as the Congressional Quarterly's *Guide to Current American Government* (issued twice yearly at $4.00 an issue, available from the Congressional Quarterly, 1735 K St., N.W., Washington, D.C. 20006, and full of much more valuable information about our government). Summary answers to the first and third questions are given in the illustration shown at the top of the opposite page, and in the tips, below. These are taken from pp. 89 and 99 of the Spring 1971 *Guide*, respectively. Another valuable reference for understanding the political system is Donald Herzberg and J. W. Peltason, *A Student Guide to Campaign Politics* (New York: McGraw-Hill, 1970).

WRITING TO YOUR GOVERNMENT: TIPS

1. Write to your own Senators or Representatives. Letters sent to other Congressmen will end up on the desk of Congressmen from your state.

2. Write at the proper time, when a bill is being discussed in committee or on the floor.

3. Use your own words and your own stationery. Avoid signing and sending a form or mimeographed letter.

4. Don't be a pen pal. Don't try to instruct the Representative or Senator on every issue that comes up.

5. Don't demand a commitment before all the facts are in. Bills rarely become law in the same form as introduced.

6. Whenever possible, identify all bills by their number.

7. If possible, include pertinent editorials from local papers.

8. Be constructive. If a bill deals with a problem you admit exists but you believe the bill is the wrong approach, tell what you think the right approach is.

9. If you have expert knowledge or wide experience in particular areas, share it with the Congressman. But don't pretend to wield vast political influence.

10. Write to the Congressman when he does something you approve of. A note of appreciation will make him remember you more favorably next time.

11. Feel free to write when you have a question or problem dealing with procedures of government departments.

12. Be brief, write legibly, and be sure to use the proper form of address.

A 15-word telegram called a Public-Opinion Message (POM) can be sent to the President, Vice President or a member of Congress from anywhere in the United States for $1. Name and address are not counted as part of the message unless there are additional signers.

HOW A BILL BECOMES LAW

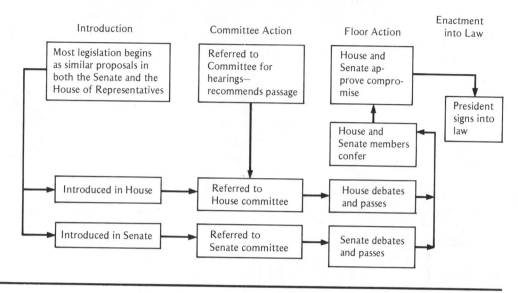

A third inequity is the complexity of the political system. It is so complex that one has to have some sophistication to be able to understand its operation. To work within it, one must progress up through the political ranks, a process that frequently requires money or obligations to those who can provide the money. Such an apprenticeship commonly leads to a changing frame of reference as one works through the system. When a position of some power is reached, the politician may be quite detached from the powerless people of her constituency. The average citizen in turn has little opportunity to learn about the political system in any practical way, and may be either frightened or cynical when considering an attempt to express himself politically—"You can't fight city hall." Exposure to the issues themselves is likely to be very limited, so that the average citizen may be unaware of proposed legislation of vital importance to her interests. If aware, knowledge about the details of the legislative process may be so meager that effective political debate with major political figures is unrealistic. Even if one is aware and knowledgeable, access to the major centers of government can be a problem. Certainly at the national level Washington, D.C. is quite remote from the majority of the country. Some states are geographically so large that it is prohibitively expensive for concerned citizens to appear personally at the state capitol to support their cause. It is simply unrealistic to think that Spanish-speaking welfare mothers in New York City are going to have the knowledge and the resources to go to Albany to fight for badly needed welfare reforms at the state level. Exhibit 6-2 illustrates the complexity of most social welfare legislation.

EXHIBIT 6-2

The Social Services Amendments of 1974

The 93rd Congress passed a bill introduced by Senator Mondale, S 4082, amending the Social Security Act to make social services available to more people. The legislation itself is many pages long, but a summary is presented below. Even this summary is long and complex, illustrating the knowledge needed and the patience required to study and understand important social welfare legislation.

SUMMARY OF SOCIAL SERVICES ACT

I. Eligibility and Priority for Federally Reimburseable Social Services. The bill provides special priority for recipients of AFDC and SSI and Medicaid by requiring that 50 percent of the federal social services funds used in a state be for services to such individuals and families.

The bill proposes that federal limitations on states in establishing those in a state eligible for federally assisted social services relate to the income of the individual or family, and would remove the requirement that recipients be classified as "former or potential welfare recipients." Federal matching for free services is available for people with incomes up to 80 percent of the median family income in a state (or the full national median, now $12,041, if less) adjusted for family size, and services at some fee up to 115 percent of the median income of a state. The $2.5 billion limit on federal payments will continue to apply.

II. Defining Social Services. The goals of the program are established as:

1. Achieving or maintaining economic self-support to prevent, reduce, or eliminate dependency.

2. Achieving or maintaining self-sufficiency, including reduction or prevention of dependency.

3. Preventing or remedying neglect, abuse, or exploitation of children and adults unable to protect their own interests, or preserving, rehabilitating, or reuniting families.

4. Preventing or reducing inappropriate institutional care by providing for community-based care, home-based care, or other forms of less intensive care, or

5. Securing referral or admission for institutional care when other forms of care are not appropriate, or providing services to individuals in institutions.

Social services would be defined by the state, required to be directed at the social services goals with parameters for such definitions established by: prohibition against funding certain activities; prohibitions against reimbursing certain medical institutions for social services provided to those living in them (but other entities could provide social services to such individuals in such facilities); and, prohibitions against funding child day care not meeting standards. The draft bill also specifically names certain services as examples of social services but it is not intended to be an all inclusive list.

III. Social Services Program Planning, Reporting, Evaluation, and Auditing. Establishes new requirements for a state to conduct a program planning process to determine the services to be provided and who is to receive such services with primary emphasis on involvement by the citizens of a state. The Governor or such other officials as

From *The Congressional Record*, Vol. 120, No. 149, October 3, 1974.

the laws of the state provide is responsible for publishing the services plan for comment and approving the final services plan for the program year. The state is also required to conduct evaluations and provide required reports to HEW and the public.

Ninety days after the end of the services program year an "annual social services program report" is approved by the Governor or other official designated under state law describing the services provided during the past year.

IV. "State Plan" Subject to Prior Approval by HEW.
The state would submit for HEW approval prior to the beginning of the services program year a document which is still called a "State Plan." It would deal with state assurances regarding: fair hearings, confidentiality of information; designation of a single agency other than the Governor to supervise the administration of the state's social services program; no durational residency or citizenship requirement; and designation of state authorities for establishing and maintaining standards.

V. Maintenance of Effort and Matching Provisions.
The bill establishes a maintenance of effort requirement for states which requires that the nonfederal share of its aggregate expenditures for the provisions of services during each services program year are not less than the aggregate expenditures for the provisions of those services during fiscal year 1973 or 1974 (whichever is less) with respect to which payment was made under the Social Security Act. The Governor is also to provide to the citizens of the state comparison of nonfederal expenditures between services program years.

Percentage of matching is not changed from present law, i.e.: 75 percent for all services except 90 percent for family planning services; 75 percent for training and retraining.

State matching may be in cash or in-kind by the state including provisions to the state by its political subdivisions. Private funds donated to the state are allowed to be utilized for nonfederal match but with certain restrictions.

VI. Federal Evaluation, Research and Demonstrations, Program Assistance and HEW Reports to Congress.
HEW is authorized to grant waivers under the proposed new title XX for Social Services to any state now under the various titles of the Social Security Act and provide reports to Congress on the results of such research and demonstration programs.

[HEW] is also to provide to Congress prior to July 1, 1977 a report on the effectiveness of the social services program along with recommendations for improvements.

VII. Effective Date of Regulations Published by the Secretary of HEW.
No final federal regulations for the program would be effective in a services program year for a state if the regulations are published within 60 days of the beginning of the state's services program year.

VIII. Continuation of Moratorium on New Regulations until Proposed Effective New Legislations.
Currently the law prohibits HEW from changing social services regulations until after December 31, 1974. The draft bill would have an effective date as to the payments of social services of July 1, 1975. The bill would also continue the moratorium on HEW implementing new regulations until July 1, 1975.

HEW NEWS

HEW Secretary Casper W. Weinberger announced his full support for the social services bill introduced today by Senator Walter F. Mondale (Minn.), together with Senators Bob Packwood (Ore), Lloyd H. Bentsen (Tex.), and Jacob K. Javits (N.Y.) The bill was developed jointly by the Congress and HEW and has the support of numerous interested groups including the National Governors' Conference.

"We wholeheartedly endorse this bill," the Secretary said. "It is the result of six months of cooperative effort and consideration on the part of the Congress, the Department, the National Governors' Conference, and many others, as well as key organizations concerned with services for children, families, the aged, and the disabled.

"All who have worked on the amendments believe their enactment would make possible a positive new federal-state relationship within which states could more effectively target their social services resources to meet the needs of their own people.

"The proposed amendments make the state social services program answerable primarily to the state's citizens, within broad federal guidelines. I am convinced that this new approach can free us all to concentrate on getting services to people.

"At present a congressional moratorium on implementation of 1973 regulations is due to expire on January 1, 1975. The amendments would extend this moratorium until July 1, the effective date of the proposed changes. This is important so that states can plan their programs effectively, and is one reason we hope for speedy enactment."

Major changes affect state program eligibility, services planning, and accountability, but not federal funding.

Federal funding would remain unchanged, with a total of $2.5 billion authorized for allocation among the states on the basis of their population. The federal share of a state's social services expenditures would continue to be 75 percent, except for family planning services for which the federal share would continue to be 90 percent.

Eligibility for services would be based on income rather than on welfare-relatedness (qualifying as a "former" or "potential" recipient), but approximately 50 percent of federal funds must be spent for people eligible for AFDC (Aid to Families with Dependent Children), SSI (Supplemental Security Income), and/or Medicaid.

Social services goals are specified in the amendments; self-support; self-sufficiency; protection for children and for adults unable to protect themselves; de-institutionalization when appropriate; and institutional placement and services within some institutions when necessary.

An annual comprehensive services plan specifying one or more services to be offered to meet each of the established goals and specifying who is to be eligible to receive services would be developed in each state by means of an open planning process with emphasis on citizen involvement. The state planning process must meet HEW requirements, but prior HEW approval is not required for the program priorities and resource allocations expressed in the comprehensive services plan.

Prior HEW approval would be required for state plans in regard to: fair hearings; state-wide applicability; merit system; confidentiality; designation of a single individual or agency to supervise program administration; designation of state standard-setting and enforcement authorities for facilities offering day or residential care; and absence of any eligibility requirement based on duration of state or local residency or of U.S. citizenship.

Public accountability to citizens of the state is insured by means of the federally required open planning process; regular reporting; independent audits; and evaluation.

1968 federal interagency day care requirements would remain in effect (at least until 1977) with one addition: for children under three there must be one adult for every two children.

Federal evaluation and program assistance to states would be mandated, as would a July 1977 report to Congress on program effectiveness.

Other major changes include (but are not limited to):

Prohibition of federal matching under the program for certain clearly specified expenditures, such as facilities construction and services that fall under other federal programs;

State-option income-related fees for services furnished to persons not eligible for cash assistance;

Fiscal sanctions for noncompliance with certain federal requirements;

A delayed effective date for any federal regulation promulgated less than 60 days before the beginning of a state's program year;

And maintenance of state fiscal effort in regard to social services.

The government often operates very slowly, creating a fourth inequity. The process by which a bill becomes law is a long and tedious one, made more so by the fact that, for a variety of reasons, most bills never complete the process. Understanding the reasons for the slow progress and being able to maintain the necessary persistence are formidable problems that greatly weight the struggle on the side of the knowledgeable, powerful, and wealthy. A final problem lies in the weaknesses of minorities. The system assumes that minority groups will ultimately form coalitions to pool whatever knowledge and power each group possesses. However, these minority groups may be characterized by different racial and ethnic backgrounds, different norms and languages, and different income and educational levels. Therefore, the basis for coalitions may be submerged under a variety of seemingly insurmountable differences. Experience has shown that the ability to form coalitions is itself a skill that is learned.[4] It requires a level of sophistication in the political process learned slowly and painfully by many minority groups.[5]

Having noted the several problems in the operation of America's pluralistic, competitive political system, the relatively new ombudsman concept must be mentioned as a way to overcome some of these problems.[6] American society today is so complex that many persons are unaware of services available, the structure of services, the political process, their rights as citizens, and so on. In the attempt to provide a link between the individual, with all of his lack of knowledge, fears, and prejudices, and the political and service structures that exist to serve him, the ombudsman concept was developed. The ombudsman is a person or group whose presence is made popularly known and whose purpose is to provide the information to help individuals find what they seek. Ideally, the ombudsman also seeks out problems in the provision of services or the involvement of citizens in the political process. Whether or not new problems are identified, the ombudsman helps the citizen obtain what he wishes in a system that is meant to serve him but which by its very scope may dwarf him instead.

Another method of overcoming some of these problems lies in the development of countervailing power: groups that can mobilize power to resist the power of others. Advocacy groups, such as Common Cause, can be effective lobbies on behalf of citizens who would have little power if they were not organized into groups. Consumer groups operate in a similar way, organizing consumers into structures that allow them to express and fight for their needs. Ralph Nader's work on behalf of consumers is a case in point. These kinds of groups have helped persons who have traditionally had little political and economic power to organize effectively on their own behalf.

It is always easiest to talk about the federal government because there is only one. When trying to talk about state and local governments the picture gets more complicated because so many differences exist. Yet, as already noted, the work of social welfare is carried on in large part at these levels, and the political processes operating at these levels are important determinants of that work. The kind of factors already discussed at the federal level tend also to work at the state level, although the professional helping person has much greater access to the political process at the state level. She is likely to be involved in state professional organizations that are active in working with politicians and other groups to attain welfare objectives in their state. The representatives and senators serving in the state house are local people, and much more readily accessible to all a state's citizens than are the state's representatives to the federal Congress.

At the community level the political process is even more accessible. Local politicians are both more easily accessible and more dependent on each voter's support. Therefore, it is easier for the social welfare worker to contact his local representative and find ways to work with her in gaining support for social welfare objectives. On the other hand, "politics" in the worst sense is likely to be more rampant at the local level so that formal and informal procedures may exist to systematically exclude segments of the community from political participation.[7] It is sometimes felt that the "real" decision-making occurs at the state or national level, and that it isn't worth getting involved in local politics. This is a very narrow view. Not only are there important decisions made at the local level (police services, for example), but the local level of government is easily accessible and may serve as an entrance into state and even national political participation. The social welfare professional must be knowledgeable about and, hopefully, involved in the political process at all levels. Exhibit 6-3 (pp. 216–17) illustrates the structure of local government.

Unfortunately, many social welfare professionals are poorly equipped to participate in the political process. Some fear that their jobs will be jeopardized if they participate, a fear that in some cases is very realistic. However, the alternative of having decisions made for the profession, which then may seriously weaken its ability to provide services, is not very attractive either. Even given the perceived desirability of participating, the problems the average citizen faces also confront the typical social welfare professional. Social welfare education has rarely included political action, and although this gap is being somewhat lessened today, the political action that is undertaken tends to be at the local level. Although very important, it must also be bolstered by national political action. A third factor is the current complexity of the welfare structure even for the professional welfare practitioner. The typical worker has limited tasks to perform, and rarely has the opportunity to study the total welfare picture. Yet when welfare-reform legislation is proposed, it is comprehensive and complex, leaving the practitioner uninformed about many details easily overlooked but of great significance. The fact that welfare professionals are often unable to see beyond their specialized interest to combine into a unified, more powerful social welfare lobby accentuates the problems the professions have in being active, effective political forces.

A final problem in the way of welfare professionals being politically active is again related to political sophistication. It is the lack of tenacity required to see legislation enacted and then implemented. Wilbur Cohen has well expressed the false optimism that can develop when working for legislation, and the crushing disappointment when one's efforts fail. He also realistically discusses the need to accept such defeats and continue to work for change.[8] Even beyond the tenacity to get legislation passed, however, is the sophistication to know that legislation is only as good as the provisions for its enforcement. Wilcox repeatedly makes the point that so much good legislation has been relatively ineffective because of inadequate implementation provisions—lack of funds, lack of structures for enforcement and supervision, lack of legal support to untangle legal problems, and so on.[9] This helps to explain why, in spite of so much legislation in areas such as school desegregation, inequities still exist. Obviously, then, political tenacity has to go much further than simply the enactment of legislation, as difficult as that may be to achieve successfully.

THE ECONOMIC BASES OF SOCIAL WELFARE

Economics is the study of the production, distribution, and consumption of scarce, socially desirable resources. No society, not even one as rich as the United States, can have all of everything its members want. The economic institution is the mechanism a society uses to ensure the production of desired resources, their distribution within the society, and their consumption by citizens. In this section, the relevance of economics to social welfare will be discussed within this same framework: production, distribution, and consumption.

The American economic system operates through a market that relates consumer demand to producer supply. The current market operates in a modified laissez-faire manner, meaning that governmental interference in the supply and demand equation exists, but in a limited amount. The legacy of earlier periods of less government intervention is the general belief that supply and demand will tend to balance each other out. Consumers will have their demands met in the most efficient manner as this occurs. While government interference does take place, it is believed that it should occur as little as possible because it tends to make the productive process less efficient. In order for there to be demand, consumers must have purchasing power—that is, money to pay for the items they want. Purchasing power in turn depends on at least two major factors: employment and the use of government fiscal policy.[10]

One of the lasting effects of the Industrial Revolution was to make people dependent on wages. The tie to the land was broken, and self-sufficiency, at least for the bare necessities, was no longer feasible. In industrial societies a wage is received in return for work performed—the workers essentially sell their labor in the marketplace in return for wages that give them access to socially desirable resources. This reliance on a wage sets up a potentially problematic situation. Supply is based on demand, but demand is to some extent based on supply—that is, if there is no production, there is no need for workers, and hence there is no wage. If there is no wage, there

EXHIBIT 6-3

The Structure of Greensboro City Government

Greensboro, North Carolina is a city of over 150,000 people. Its city government is reasonably representative of the governmental process at the local level, although naturally there is considerable variation in the governing structures of different cities. Very large urban areas in particular may have considerably more complex structures. Even in the most complex, however, representation comes down to the neighborhood level, and is considerably more accessible than the state and federal levels of government. In many areas, county government is also very important, especially in rural areas.

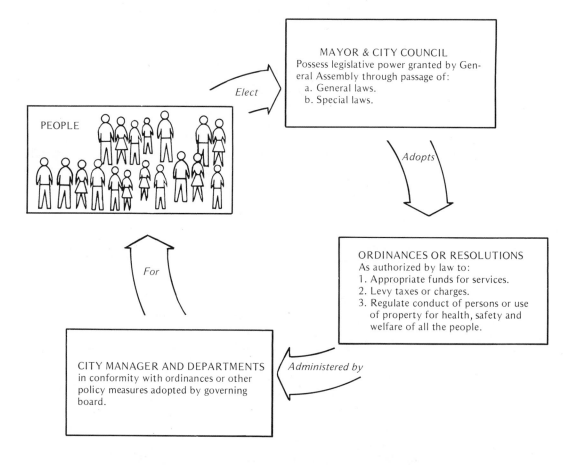

From pages 12–13 of "A Look at Greensboro's City Government," published by the City Manager's Office in Greensboro in 1974. Used by permission.

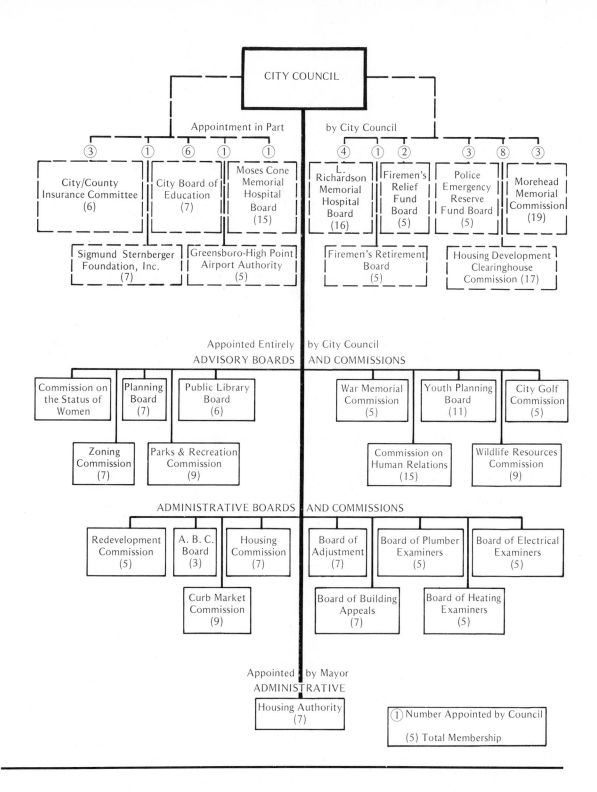

CITY COUNCIL

Appointment in Part by City Council

③ ① ⑥ ① ①   ④ ① ② ③ ⑧ ③

City/County
Insurance Committee
(6)

City Board of
Education
(7)

Moses Cone
Memorial
Hospital
Board
(15)

L.
Richardson
Memorial
Hospital
Board
(16)

Firemen's
Relief
Fund
Board
(5)

Police
Emergency
Reserve
Fund Board
(5)

Morehead
Memorial
Commission
(19)

Sigmund Sternberger
Foundation, Inc.
(7)

Greensboro-High Point
Airport Authority
(5)

Firemen's Retirement
Board
(5)

Housing Development
Clearinghouse
Commission (17)

Appointed Entirely by City Council
ADVISORY BOARDS AND COMMISSIONS

Commission on
the Status of
Women

Planning
Board
(7)

Public Library
Board
(6)

War Memorial
Commission
(5)

Youth Planning
Board
(11)

City Golf
Commission
(5)

Zoning
Commission
(7)

Parks & Recreation
Commission
(9)

Commission on
Human Relations
(15)

Wildlife Resources
Commission
(9)

ADMINISTRATIVE BOARDS AND COMMISSIONS

Redevelopment
Commission
(5)

A. B. C.
Board
(3)

Housing
Commission
(7)

Board of
Adjustment
(7)

Board of Plumber
Examiners
(5)

Board of Electrical
Examiners
(5)

Curb Market
Commission
(9)

Board of Building
Appeals
(7)

Board of Heating
Examiners
(5)

Appointed by Mayor
ADMINISTRATIVE

Housing Authority
(7)

① Number Appointed by Council

(5) Total Membership

can be no demand, unless there is some outside influence to provide consumers with money, which then reestablishes the demand-supply-demand cycle. This outside influence is usually the exercise of government fiscal policy, primarily in terms of government spending, taxation, and manipulation of interest rates. The recession of the early and mid-seventies is an example. With declining demand, there was an excess of supply, which then resulted in widespread layoffs of workers throughout the economy, especially in the automobile, textile, and service industries. With large numbers of people out of work, demand declined further. The government then stepped in: an income tax rebate (which would immediately increase the individual's disposable income, that is, the amount of money available to be spent); a lowering of interest rates for loans, making more loan money available (also aimed at increasing spending by making it easier and less costly to purchase major items); and increasing government spending through the provision of public service jobs. These actions served to stimulate demand, which then helped reestablish the demand-supply cycle.

In addition to supply and demand, production is affected by other forces as well. The costs of production is one such force. As noted above, demand is to some extent a function of supply. Producers can create demand by a variety of means, including the introduction of new products, advertising, and the like. They can also affect demand by manipulating the price of products, since in general the lower the price the greater the demand (this is especially true for products whose demand is elastic, meaning that demand will increase if price decreases, and vice versa; if the demand is inelastic, price tends to have less effect on demand). Therefore, if production costs can be lowered, price can be lowered (or profit raised), and demand may be stimulated. The costs of production are themselves somewhat variable. They depend partly on the raw materials required for production, such as steel needed for automobile production. They also depend on the costs of technology (the machines needed for production) and labor. With the advent of labor unions, collective bargaining is commonly used to determine the price of labor. Producers and union representatives attempt to obtain as great a share of the production profits as possible through contract negotiations. With unions as powerful bargaining agents, one strategy producers use is to replace as many people as possible with machines—they don't have bargaining agents.

Another source of production costs are those imposed by government intervention. Legislation that sets minimum wage standards, industrial safety regulations, quality controls, and antitrust provisions, to name a few, invariably raise the costs of production. Here, as in so much governmental intervention in the economic system, it is believed that short-run financial costs may be justified by long-range social benefits (greater product safety, worker health, and so on). Another variable cost of production that is governmentally determined is taxes. All businesses and individuals are subject to taxation, and for a business, taxes are a cost of doing that business. Taxes happen to provide an excellent example of how the theoretical considerations being discussed are always subject to influences of reality. As illustrated in Exhibit 6-4, government attempts to tax large corporations are sometimes ineffective because the complex tax structure often provides loopholes that corporations assiduously seek out and take advantage of.

EXHIBIT 6-4

Corporate Cop-Out

The following data and analysis are taken from *New Times* (January 10, 1975), and are illustrative of some of the ways that producers circumvent government policies in the unceasing attempt to minimize their costs of production.

Even on the income that they do report, major companies are as successful as the super-rich in avoiding U.S. taxation. The statutory corporate income tax rate is 48 percent, but last year the actual rate paid was 35.6 percent, thanks to an armed guard of investment credits, depletion allowances, kickbacks for export sales and other special deductions standing between company coffers and the revenue agents.

Most impregnable are the vaults of the nation's 12 leading commercial banks, which last year paid an average of *3.6 percent* of their income to the U.S. government. This wrist-tapping tithe results from the fact that banks can take advantage both of tax exempt municipal bond interest and the foreign tax credit, which permits U.S. firms to subtract income tax paid overseas directly from their U.S. tax bill, instead of treating it as a deductible business expense.

The foreign tax provision also comes in handy to the American oil companies, which years ago had their foreign royalties redefined as "taxes." Last year the top six companies paid a crushing 6.3 percent of their worldwide income in U.S. taxes.

From *New Times*, Vol. 3, No. 1 (January 10, 1975). Reprinted by permission of New Times Communication Corporation and Tax Analysts and Advocates.

No one knows what percentage of their U.S. income is paid to the U.S. Treasury because exactly where they earn their money is one of the tightest-held secrets of all multinational firms.

Obviously, the multinationals pay lower U.S. taxes than American corporations in general, but according to Harvard economist Otto Eckstein, an increasing array of congressionally approved tax shelters is making it easier for all U.S. companies to dodge the IRS. His calculations show that back in 1961 corporations were paying an effective tax rate of 43.3 percent, versus the 35.6 percent in 1973. This year, largely because so many companies understated profits, the percentage of corporate income paid out in taxes probably fell to the lowest level in at least 20 years.

The result of all this is that you and I are being asked to bear a rapidly growing share of the burden. Work of the Washington-based Tax Reform Research Group, for example, shows that corporate taxes, as a percentage of federal receipts, fell from 33 percent to 14 percent between 1944 and 1974, although before-tax profits, as a percentage of gross corporate product, remained fairly constant. During the same period, individual income and payroll taxes rose from 48 percent to 73 percent of total federal tax receipts. In 1973, while industry struggled under such tax rates as 11.5 percent (oil companies excluding the top six), 17.3 percent (metals and mining), 22.1 percent (drug companies), and 28.4 percent (food processors), a family of four in the $20,000 bracket was paying 15 percent of its income in federal taxes. At the $30,000 level, the rate rose to 20 percent (for 1971, the last year for which figures are available).

Below is a list of the top 15 corporations in the country, as ranked by *Fortune* and their tax loads for 1973:

	Chrysler	Ford	G.E.	GM	IBM	ITT	U.S. Steel	Western Electric	Westing-house	Exxon	Gulf	Mobil	Std. Oil Calif.	Std. Oil Ind.	Texaco
U.S. Tax Rate on Worldwide Income	3.1	16.8	32.3	40.2	22.5	2.8	28.9	39.5	12.2	3.7	1.6	3.2	8.7	19.8	0.9
Share to Foreign Govt.	16.0	15.9	7.1	6.2	24.0	32.5	11.7	—	10.4	53.8	61.4	55.2	37.4	11.2	31.5
Worldwide Rate on Worldwide Income[a]	19.1	32.7	39.4	46.4	46.5	35.3	40.6	39.5	22.6	57.5	63.0	58.4	46.1	31.0	32.4

[a]All figures are percentages of 1973 pre-tax financial income.
Source: Tax Analysts and Advocates, based on material filed with the SEC.

Three other factors may affect production. Competition between producers is one, and has traditionally been assumed to stimulate the search for the most effective production techniques. Competition may come from other domestic producers, or from foreign producers who ship their products to the United States (foreign automobiles, for example). Competition can have the effect of driving out the least efficient producers, but that in itself is not necessarily desirable. As smaller, less efficient producers are driven out of the market, power may become concentrated in a few massive producers who then can use their monopolistic power to raise prices. Producers can also circumvent legislation that seeks to prevent collusion, the second factor which may affect production. Collusion may occur through price-fixing, or through the formation of interlocking directorates, the practice of having the same group of people as the directors of several companies. Third, production can be affected by the interdependence that exists between producers in a complex industrial society. For example, one reason why a strike can be such an effective bargaining tool is that closing down one business (such as a railroad) will have an impact on many other businesses (such as steel mills that ship on the railroad, automobile manufacturers that use the mills' steel, automobile dealers that cannot obtain a supply of cars). To some extent, then, the costs of production may not be altogether under the control of the producers themselves.

Moving from production to distribution, we must first look at the effect of the existing production system on the market in which the products are to be distributed. A striking fact of this market in contemporary America is that it is characterized by wide disparities. Some persons are rich, and have access to virtually unlimited products. Their demand is strong and constant. For others, the market is almost entirely out of their reach. They are poor, and have access to very few products the market has to offer. Exhibit 6-5 illustrates the extent of maldistribution of resources in the United States.

Poverty is a painful subject for Americans, and one that is difficult to pin down. It is painful to realize that there are large numbers of poor people in the "richest country in the world." This creates some tendency to hide the poor, to let them live their lives forgotten in the back corners of rural counties, Appalachian hills, Indian reservations, and urban ghettos. It also makes it difficult to decide what the society means by poor. On one hand, an arbitrary figure can be used—below it people live in poverty and above it they do not. The figure often used is the money needed by an urban family of four to survive, set in 1974 at $4,200. The limitations of this approach are obvious—is bare survival the goal of our society when we assess human need? Can poverty be so arbitrarily defined? Isn't it more likely that, while families living on less than $4,200 exist in abject poverty, families living on $5,200 exist in poverty, although at a level less severe than their even poorer counterparts? Another approach is to look at relative poverty. It looks at how resources are distributed among all members of society, defining the group having access to the least resources as the poor.[11] This is a more realistic approach to the problem, because part of being poor is feeling poor, knowing that you are deprived of resources that others take for granted. Poverty is both objective and subjective. It is the objective reality that life lacks basic necessities—adequate food, shelter, social participation. It is also the subjective reality that one lives on the fringes of society, at the bottom of the social heap.

EXHIBIT 6-5

Economic Reality in the United States

The following 1973 NASW data showing family income for selected years from 1947 to 1970 demonstrate several facts. While there has been a decline in the number of families at the lowest income levels, there are still large numbers of families that live in poverty. Also illustrated is the fact that race continues to be an important factor in the incidence of poverty. Finally, it is evident that there is widespread difference in the distribution of resources in this country.

Total Money Income (1970 Dollars)	1947	1950	1960	1969	1970
Total Families (thousands)	37,237	39,929	45,456	51,237	51,948
Percentage Under $3,000	22.5%	22.8%	15.6%	8.6%	8.9%
$3,000–4,999	24.2	22.1	14.1	9.9	10.4
$5,000–6,999	22.7	23.7	16.7	11.3	11.8
$7,000–9,999	17.0	18.3	24.7	20.2	19.9
$10,000–14,999	{ 13.5	{ 13.2	19.3	27.8	26.8
$15,000 and over			9.5	22.2	22.3
Median Income	$ 5,259	$ 5,385	$ 7,376	$ 9,990	$ 9,867
Index (1947 = 100)	100	102	140	190	188
White Families (thousands)	34,120	NAa	41,123	46,022	46,535
Percentage Under $3,000	19.5%	20.3%	13.4%	7.3%	7.5%
$3,000–4,999	24.0	21.4	13.3	9.0	9.5
$5,000–6,999	23.9	24.6	16.8	10.7	11.3
$7,000–9,999	18.1	19.5	25.7	20.3	20.1
$10,000–14,999	{ 14.5	{ 14.1	20.7	28.9	27.9
$15,000 and over			10.2	23.6	23.7
Median Income	$ 5,478	$ 5,601	$ 7,664	$10,362	$10,236
Index (1947 = 100)	100	102	140	189	187
Nonwhite Families (thousands)	3,117	NAa	4,333	5,215	5,413
Percentage Under $3,000	53.6%	49.7%	36.4%	18.9%	20.1%
$3,000–4,999	23.4	28.8	21.8	18.3	17.0
$5,000–6,999	10.5	13.7	15.8	16.3	16.4
$7,000–9,999	6.6	4.6	15.3	19.5	18.2
$10,000–14,999	{ 3.9	{ 3.1	8.0	17.4	17.3
$15,000 and over			2.8	9.9	10.9
Median Income	$ 2,807	$ 3,014	$ 4,236	$ 6,568	$ 6,516
Index (1947 = 100)	100	107	151	234	232

Source: "Consumer Income," *Current Population Reports*, Series P-60, No. 80 (October 1971), Table 9.
aNot available.

Reprinted with permission of the National Association of Social Workers, from "Demographic and Social Welfare Trends," *Encyclopedia of Social Work*, Vol. 16 (3rd printing; Washington, D.C., 1974), p. 1579.

Regardless of how it is defined, poverty is considerably more than just an academic issue. The maldistribution of economic resources is important because it affects how people live, and because it creates a host of personal, family, and social problems. The poor are less able to care for themselves and their children, to function effectively, to enjoy their lives, and to participate in society. As is demonstrated by Exhibit 6-6 (page 224), the poor are disadvantaged on every criterion society uses to measure social and personal adequacy.

The reasons underlying the existing maldistribution of economic resources are many and complex. Discrimination is one, including racial, sexual, and age barriers that prevent individuals from participating freely in the marketplace. The ability of producers to manipulate demand is another, since the poor are usually more easily manipulated and are most severely affected by such practices. For example, through advertising, the poor are encouraged to purchase unnecessary or inferior products that they can ill afford. Price-fixing takes its greatest toll on the poor since they have the scarcest resources to work with. Unscrupulous credit practices inflate the prices of items purchased by the poor, and may also make the poor more vulnerable to repossession if they default on a payment. Government practices can also inadvertently hurt the poor. For example, regressive taxes (that is, those taxes that take a higher proportion from the poor than the rich) further reduce the meager resources the poor have available. Social Security is an example of a regressive tax. Social Security is withheld from salaries only up to a certain maximum ($14,200 in 1975). A person earning $6,000 a year has Social Security withheld from all of her income, whereas someone earning $25,000 has the tax withheld from only the first $14,200 of that amount. Proportionately, then, the poor pay more. There are many other factors that enter into the maldistribution of economic resources—lack of transportation, lack of consumer education, lack of choice in places to shop, and so forth. In many ways, the poor pay more.[12]

One of the functions of the social welfare institution is to help counteract the maldistribution existing in the economic institution. By supplementing the income of the poor, social welfare increases their access to desirable social resources. By educating the poor to more effective consumer practices, child-rearing methods, and homemaker techniques, social welfare helps the poor to use their money more wisely. By providing educational opportunities, by fighting discrimination in jobs and housing, and by stabilizing families in trouble, social welfare increases the opportunities for the poor to participate in the economic system. Social welfare strengthens the ability of the poor to function as both consumer and producer—knowing how to spend, and having valuable skills to sell in return for a living wage. Even so, there are problems that develop from attempts by social welfare to find a more equitable solution to problems of maldistribution. One of the most important of these is a result of the attempt to provide social welfare services in a market system.

EXHIBIT 6-6

The Problems of Poverty

The relationships between poverty and an assortment of other problems and disadvantages is made clear below. When looking at the problems of being poor, it becomes easier to see why they are so difficult to solve. The poor suffer from so many problems, and have so few resources to work with, that it is difficult to find a place to intervene effectively.

Selected Characteristic	Number of Families (millions)		Percent of Total	
	All Families	Poor Families	All Families	Poor Families
Total	47.0	9.3	100%	100%
Age of Head:				
14–24 years	2.5	0.8	5	8
25–54 years	30.4	3.9	65	42
55–64 years	7.3	1.4	16	15
65 years and over	6.8	3.2	14	34
Education of Head:				
8 years or less	16.3	6.0	35	61
9–11 years	8.6	1.7	19	17
12 years	12.2	1.5	26	15
More than 12 years	9.3	0.7	20	7
Sex of Head:				
Male	42.3	7.0	90	75
Female	4.7	2.3	10	25
Labor Force Status of Head:				
Not in Civilian Labor Force	8.4	4.1	18	44
Employed	36.9	4.6	78	49
Unemployed	1.7	0.6	4	6
Color of Family:				
White	42.4	7.3	90	78
Nonwhite	4.6	2.0	10	22
Residence of Family:				
Rural Farm	3.3	1.5	7	16
Rural Nonfarm	9.9	2.7	22	30
Urban	31.9	5.0	71	54

From Stephen M. Rose, *The Betrayal of the Poor* (1972). Used by permission of Schenkman Publishing Co., Cambridge, Mass.

Note: Data relate to families and exclude unrelated individuals. Poor families are defined as all families with total money income less than $3,000.

A public welfare system interferes with the operation of the market, and as such is counter to society's modified free-enterprise economic values. This leads to attempts to minimize the disruption of the market by welfare, thereby preserving the market as far as possible, and presumably minimizing resentment against welfare recipients. Such attempts include making welfare services either combinations of public and private services, publicly subsidizing private services, or specifically designing services so that they minimize interference with the market's operation. Health care for the aged is an excellent example of a welfare service provided partly publicly (Veterans Administration hospitals and other public hospitals), and partly privately (such as doctor's care, clinics in private hospitals, nursing homes). It also includes public subsidy for privately provided services, such as Medicare payments to doctors and hospitals, public-assistance vendor payments to nursing homes, and so on. The market is by definition not set up to protect those in need. It is a mockery of societal values to continue to believe that those who need extensive welfare assistance are able to be self-reliant, informed consumers in a free enterprise system.

The clash of free market and social welfare values inevitably creates resentment and discrimination against welfare recipients. Public monies spent on welfare must necessarily reduce the amount of such monies available for other purposes. The market model suggests that the same criteria used to evaluate private programs can and should be used to evaluate public programs. In one sense this is perfectly logical, since the public does have the right to get value for money spent. However, the difficulty of measuring human needs and appropriate services creates a tendency to concentrate on those services and persons most easily proved successful, a practice called "creaming."[13] Furthermore, the pursuit of efficiency tends to reduce complex problem clusters to simplified problems whose "solution" lies in a combination of money and chasing those needy persons alleged to be shiftless welfare exploiters from the rolls.[14] This is accentuated by societal values that stress individual achievement. They make it easy to believe that those who are in need have not tried hard enough, and need a combination of opportunity and incentive. It becomes difficult to popularize the fact that data show the great majority of welfare recipients to be multiproblem persons with enormous disadvantages and obstacles to self-sufficiency.[15]

Inevitably, perhaps, this discussion has led into the third part of the economic system, consumption. Already referred to is what can now be made explicit, the distinction between personal consumption and social effects. For example, the maldistribution of income makes it possible for the wealthy to purchase products in the marketplace at will. However, the consequences are twofold. One, already discussed, is that the poor have very little power in the marketplace unless their resources are supplemented by the social welfare system. The other is the cost of such supplementation. Poverty leads to a range of problems. As long as society has a commitment to solve these problems, it must commit some of its resources to accomplish this goal. In other words, by allowing the wealthy to accumulate economic

EXHIBIT 6-7

The Advocate and Social Policy Formation

Harry Specht talks of the formulation of social policy as one part of the social worker-advocate's task. He summarizes his discussion in the chart reproduced here, which shows how the advocate role can proceed from a perceived need to an institutional solution, and how this role relates to professional roles, tasks, and institutional resources.

Stages of Policy Formulation

Policy Stage	Tasks	Institutional Resources	Professional Roles
1. Identification of problem	1. Case-finding, recording, discovery of gaps in service	1. Agency	1. Practitioner
2. Analysis	2. Data-gathering, analysis	2. Research organization	2. Researcher
3. Informing the public	3. Dramatization, public relations, communications (writing, speaking)	3. Public relations unit, communications media, voluntary organization	3. Muckraker, community organizer, public relations man
4. Development of policy goals (involvement of other agencies)	4. Creating strategy, program analysis	4. Planning bodies, voluntary associations	4. Planner, community organizer, administrator
5. Building public support	5. Developing leadership, achieving consensus	5. Voluntary associations, political parties, legislative and agency committees	5. Lobbyist, community organizer, public relations man
6. Legislation	6. Drafting legislation, program design	6. Legislative bodies, agency boards	6. Legislative analyst, planner
7. Implementation	7. Programs-organizing, administration	7. Courts, agencies	7. Administrator, practitioner, lawyer
8. Evaluation, assessment	8. Case-finding, recording, discovery of gaps in service, gathering data	8. Agency, research organization	8. Practitioner

Reprinted by permission of the National Association of Social Workers, from Harry Specht, "Casework Practice and Social Policy Formulation," *Social Work* 13 (January 1968): 44.

resources as they wish, society incurs the social costs of the waste of human ability, the loss of participation in the social system by part of the population, and the maintenance of that part of the social welfare system needed to deal with economic maldistribution. An underlying lesson of economics is that priorities must be established—society cannot have everything it wants. One of these priorities must be the balance between individual consumption and the social costs of that consumption.

The question of the costs of individual consumption takes on even greater significance in a world whose resources are increasingly being threatened with extinction. Overpopulation is a real threat, with starvation already a way of death in some societies. Energy stores are also limited, and their availability controlled by a handful of fortunate nations. More and more animal, bird, and fish species are nearing extinction. The effects of technology on the environment are increasingly understood—polluted rivers, fouled air, and poisoned soil. These effects are to a large extent the result of individual and corporate consumption decisions. The costs have so far been borne mostly by society. However, the costs are growing to the point that society itself cannot bear them—they are becoming world problems and world costs. These economic realities may ultimately extend the concept of social welfare beyond national boundaries, and make the world community aware of its responsibility to all of its members.

SOCIAL POLICY: POLITICS AND ECONOMICS AT WORK

"It has become clear that, in seeking to solve its social problems and to achieve urban amenity, racial equality, communal integration, social justice, and an end to poverty, the United States will rely heavily upon social services as a prime instrument."[16] In this statement, Kahn provides the bridge between politics and economics and social policy. Policy is the decision-making that utilizes the political process to identify and plan economic objectives. Again in Kahn's words, policy is "the explicit or implicit core of principles, or the continuing line of decisions and constraints, behind specific programs, legislation, administrative practices, or priorities."[17] Since social policy lays the foundation for the services that will be provided and the manner in which they will be provided, it is a vital concern to all social welfare professionals. There can be no separation between direct practice with people seeking help and the formulation of policy, since one affects the other. The social welfare professional who avoids the thorny problems and the sometimes heated conflicts of the policy-making process leaves the decisions about his work and the fate of those seeking help in the hands of others— many times in the hands of those ill-prepared to make such decisions. Some of the possible professional roles involved in social policy are presented in Exhibit 6-7.

Probably the greatest problem encountered in the policy-making process is grappling with the difficult issue of priorities. There are many worthwhile and important social tasks that need to be accomplished, of which social welfare is only one. When there are limited societal resources, how will the decisions be made as to the most necessary and the most efficient? Even within social welfare itself, establishing priorities is not easy. Should services for children have greater priority than services for the aged? Is the social return greater from income-maintenance services than from social services? Would a new hospital solve more problems than a new prison? There is no formula for answering these questions. The competitive nature of the American political system, and the fact that resources are limited, mean that there will be controversy and attempts to "prove" greater need by each group seeking those resources. But a great deal of "proof" is dependent on a value system that considers some things more worthwhile than others. One can demonstrate that millions of persons live in poverty, but if the societal value system places space exploration above the solution of poverty, or if it considers poverty a personal rather than a social responsibility, the "proof," however well supported by data, will make little difference in policy decisions.

Social policy-making begins, then, with an existing value framework. It takes place within a competitive structure, each social need competing with the others for attention and the allocation of resources. Taking these factors into account, Kahn identifies several essential social policy dimensions.

The basic objective of the policy.   Programs may seek primarily to help the disadvantaged, or they may attempt to distribute resources more equally among all groups. "In general, a program that is sharply selective, focused on a deprived group . . . or available on a means-test basis, will have considerable redistributional impact. . . . A universal program, whatever its other merits, may or may not be redistributional, depending on its attractiveness to poorer members of the community . . . and on the system of information and access that affects the actual pattern of utilization."[18] There is some tendency to think primarily in terms of social welfare as helping the needy, and it does do this to some extent. However, programs to meet the needs of all persons in society, and to achieve a more equitable distribution of resources throughout the society, are also important if the long-run results of social policy are to include an institutionalized social welfare system and a more just society. For example, the Supplemental Security Income program is very selective in addressing problems of the elderly, helping only the destitute aged. Social Security offers the elderly a much more comprehensive program that seeks to meet the retirement needs of all members of the society.

Sharply selective services tend to be less expensive in that a much smaller number of people will receive them. On the other hand, they can have substantial related costs. A selective program frequently has a cumbersome and expensive eligibility system included so that only members of the intended group participate in the program. This is true of a program like Aid to Families with Dependent Children, for example. Selective programs also tend to have more hidden social costs attached. Any program that differentiates between some groups as needy and others as not needy tends to stigmatize the former groups. This leads to the kind of humiliation food stamp users experience in supermarkets when check-out personnel create a scene out of ignorance or in the attempt to make sure only food items are purchased (no soap, paper products, or other nonfood items). It may also lead to societal reaction against the groups receiving special services, and consequent attempts to reduce or eliminate such programs. The fact that departments of social services find it necessary to publish pamphlets exploding "welfare myths" is an indication of their concern that AFDC recipients are being stigmatized and that their benefits may ultimately be threatened (see Exhibit 2-4).

Deciding between consumption and investment. Policy is almost always caught up in the argument as to whether it is more efficient to meet immediate need or to invest in long-range programs that will ultimately reduce or eliminate need. It is very difficult to ignore immediate need—when people are starving, it seems heartless to give them seeds that will meet all their food needs in a year. On the other hand, immediate need is often so great that using resources to meet it would leave nothing for investment so that future need can be prevented. The material presented in Exhibit 3-9, which deals with the structure of services in a nation like Zaire, is a case in point. Current levels of need are very high, and resources are very limited. Meeting current need would easily exhaust the country's resources, and future need would remain unmet. The nation's decision to concentrate its resources on economic and social development is probably a wise one in the long run. Yet the daily encounter with abject poverty and illness is hard to live with.

Frequently the distinction between meeting immediate need and planning for the future is not so clearcut, and both can be worked on simultaneously. Many of the Office of Economic Opportunity programs attempted to do both. Head Start, for example, met immediate needs for day care and educational enrichment, while also improving the child's chances of successfully completing later schooling. Similarly, many community-development programs provide needed community resources while also helping the community to organize itself and have a structure it can use to achieve future goals. On the other hand, a program may get bogged down in meeting one objective and never accomplish the other. AFDC meets immediate need, but it was hoped that it would also help recipients develop the resources and skills to become independent. In many cases this never happened because of the inadequate level at which help was provided and the punitive restrictions built into the program.

Social utilities compared with individual services. Social utilities are basic services needed to function effectively in society. For example, physical protection, transportation, and education are all social utilities. These services cost money for society as well as for the individual users, but they are usually heavily subsidized out of general funds. Everyone is supporting them whether they wish to or not. Social utilities take a collective approach to meeting human needs in recognition of the fact that group life depends on interdependence and cooperation. Individual services, on the other hand, are oriented toward the specific needs of individuals and are provided on an individual basis. Individualizing services tends to be expensive in comparison to collectively provided services. One way to meet this cost is to have individual services available on a fee basis. However, this discriminates against lower-income persons who then cannot afford the services. Individual services also tend to discriminate against the less-educated or socially involved who often do not know that services are available, or in some cases may not even be able to identify what their needs are. A social utilities approach is very compatible with an institutionalized social welfare system and an investment approach to the provision of services. To some extent, social utilities must be provided in order to maintain the kind of complex society in which we live. The level of such services beyond those absolutely necessary is more debatable.

The manner in which services are delivered. Throughout earlier chapters of this book the point has been made that services can be provided in many different ways. Direct grants, in-kind payments, social insurances, personal counseling, and the structure of services have all been discussed. Deciding between the various ways in which services can be provided involves two kinds of question. First there is the question of which kind of service will meet the need identified—are cash grants and social insurances equally able to solve the poverty problem? Yet there remains the question of efficiency—which of the alternatives solves the problem most efficiently, however efficiency is being measured (least financial cost, least user stigma, most user involvement, and so on). These two questions require somewhat different approaches.

Looking at services that will solve a problem can be a reasonably objective effort. If people are given money directly, will they in fact spend it on necessities, or will they spend it on luxuries or to support debilitating habits such as drugs and alcohol? It is possible to conduct research projects to answer such questions, and to use the data obtained to select between various program types. Generally a given problem can be solved in more than one way, so after identifying those programs that do in fact solve the problem, it is then necessary to select the most efficient program. Here data may be of less use. A direct grant program may solve a problem along with an in-kind program, for example. The direct grant program is somewhat less efficient financially in that some of the money is spent on luxuries, while the in-kind program is efficient financially but somewhat less efficient socially because recipients of the service are deprived of a certain amount of autonomy and personal responsibility. Which program is most efficient? Obviously the answer to the question will depend on value judgments—is money more important than personal growth, for example—and upon the reality of the resources available. If the crucially scarce resource is money, it may be worthwhile paying the social costs and selecting the in-kind program. Determining the manner in which services are delivered becomes considerably more complicated than simple questions of fiscal efficiency.

Centralization of services and user participation. Related to many of the value issues raised above is the question of who makes social policy decisions. Obviously there are certain groups to whom society has given this responsibility—legislators and directors of agencies, for example. It has been suggested that all social welfare professionals, including direct service practitioners, should also be involved. When looking at the political process, it was seen that many other kinds of persons might get involved in the legislative process, which is so often an integral part of social policy-making. The segment not so often discussed is user or consumer groups, made up of those who will actually be affected by the policy decision. When looking at the complexities of the political process, some of the reasons for the lack of involvement of user groups were noted—lack of resources, lack of education, lack of transportation, and the like.

Another reality of user participation, or lack of it, resides in the helping system itself. For one thing, concentrating on individual services and problems is not likely to encourage an approach that attempts to involve clients in larger social groups and processes through which they can have an impact on policy. For another, agencies sometimes find it easier not to involve users in policy-making. Organizations, in the attempt to preserve themselves with minimal problems and maximum efficiency, may try to keep everyone in neat categories. Direct service workers may feel too harassed to take the time to teach user groups policy skills, to work with them in the exercise of those skills, and to risk organizational displeasure if the consumer groups should come up with objectives opposed to those of the agency. Once again the point must be made that policy is grappling with priorities. How important is fiscal efficiency? How much influence should the values of societal and organizational decision-makers have? How much risk can a worker or an agency afford to take? How important is the development of social awareness, personal growth, and the development of policy skills in user groups? Few professionals would deny that consumer groups ought to have some input into the policy-making that affects them, but there would no doubt be considerable differences in the priority assigned to that objective.

Accountability. Throughout this discussion, and at other points in the book, the issue of accountability has been raised. Obviously policy-making depends on it, since intelligent decisions must take into account the results of prior attempts to deal with problems. Accountability may take many forms—cost-benefit studies, operations research, performance contracts, and so forth. Such data are essential to knowing what is happening in the social welfare system, and knowing where intervention is necessary to better achieve the system's goals. But there is no substitute for knowing what those goals are, and the data collected cannot help do this. Goals are related to data in that they are formulated partially on the basis of all existing information. However, they are also formulated on the basis of social values. Once the goals have developed from existing data and social values, accountability becomes meaningful in determining to what extent the goals have been attained. But accountability can never be a substitute for clearly formulated goals.

CONCLUSION It is apparent that an understanding of the economic and political processes are essential to an understanding of the nature of the social order and avenues of change. Competition is a basic part of the American system. Nevertheless, the economic and political systems must be modified so that all citizens can find their satisfactions. The best way in which the total system can be modified has not yet been found, and the needy continue to suffer as a result. As social welfare personnel gain greater expertise in economic and political participation, and assuming that American society continues to claim a respect for the rights of the needy, the economic and political systems will ultimately help the welfare structure function more effectively.

The eclectic scope of social welfare concerns has created a vast body of knowledge with which the social welfare professional should be familiar. The preceding three-chapter overview of selected social science knowledge, specifically relevant to a more adequate understanding of the social welfare institution, indicates this is true. Rarely can all of the relevant knowledge pertaining to a specific social welfare area be mastered by a practitioner. Yet a conception of the richness of material available can help the practitioner to satisfy his interests and practice needs in an intelligent and productive way. The next two chapters deal specifically with practice principles and the nature of social welfare work.

STUDY QUESTIONS
1. Is it inevitable that in any social welfare system some groups will have to be at least partially disadvantaged in order to redistribute societal resources? Discuss your feelings about your answer—should some people be disadvantaged? Does social welfare destroy incentive by trying to redistribute resources?

2. The political system is a way to allocate social power. Once allocated, access to power tends to be self-perpetuating. What are the advantages and disadvantages of such self-perpetuating power? What opportunities exist for the social welfare system to secure some of this power? To what degree could one support the argument that so much power is already vested in the social welfare institution that we live in a "welfare state"?

3. How does participation in social policy relate to social welfare professional roles as you understand them? Are professionals obligated to participate in social policy, and if so, how can they do this in their work and in other ways? Does the professional's role in social policy include any obligation to involve users of social welfare services in the policy process? If so, what problems can you see in trying to do so?

REFERENCES
1. Examples of the changing legal rights of many groups, including juveniles, are increasingly evident. For two recent examples, see Joseph Senna, "Changes in Due Process of Law," *Social Work* 19 (May 1974): 319–24; and Warren Weaver, Jr., "Court, 5–4, Backs Pupils On Rights in Suspensions," *New York Times,* January 23, 1975, pp. 1ff.

2. Alfred J. Kahn, *Shaping the New Social Work* (New York: Columbia University Press, 1973), p. 66.

3. Congressional Quarterly, *Guide to Current American Government* (Fall 1970) (Washington, D.C.: Congressional Quarterly, 1970).

4. Charles Prigmore, "Use of the Coalition in Legislative Action," *Social Work* 19 (January 1974): 96–103.

5. Excellent examples are provided in Ralph Kramer, *Participation of the Poor* (Englewood Cliffs, N.J.: Prentice-Hall, 1969).

6. "An Educational Ombudsman for New York City," *School and Society* 99 (March 1971): 168–70.

7. See Si Kahn, *How People Get Power* (New York: McGraw-Hill, 1970), pp. 89–103.

8. Wilbur Cohen, "What Every Social Worker Should Know about Political Action," in Robert Klenk and Robert Ryan, eds., *The Practice of Social Work* (Belmont, Cal.: Wadsworth, 1970), pp. 334–46.

9. Clair Wilcox, *Toward Social Welfare* (Homewood, Ill.: Richard D. Irwin, 1969), esp. pp. 159–208. He notes the distinction between legislation and its implementation in looking at the difference between de jure and de facto segregation.

10. A few of these ideas were stimulated by Murray Tucker, "Interfacing Economics with Social Work Education," *Journal of Education for Social Work* 10 (Winter 1974): 96–104.

11. Donald Brieland, Lela Costin, and Charles Atherton, eds., *Contemporary Social Work* (New York: McGraw-Hill, 1975), p. 90.

12. See David Caplovitz, *The Poor Pay More* (New York: Free Press, 1967); and W. Ron Jones et al., *Finding Community* (Palo Alto, Cal.: James Freel, 1970), pp. 3–37.

13. Martin Rein, *Social Policy: Issues of Choice and Change* (New York: Random House, 1970), pp. 53–67.

14. Excellent discussions of moral perspectives used in evaluating the worth of recipients of public assistance may be found in John Romanyshyn, *Social Welfare: From Charity to Justice* (New York: Random House, 1971), pp. 41–46; and Gilbert Y. Steiner, *Social Insecurity: The Politics of Welfare* (Chicago: Rand McNally, 1966), pp. 108–40.

15. A good survey of some of the major contemporary problems in welfare is "The Welfare Industrial Complex," *The Nation*, June 28, 1971, pp. 808–11. See also President's Commission on Income Maintenance Programs, *Poverty Amid Plenty* (Washington, D.C.: Government Printing Office, 1969), pp. 13–41.

16. Alfred J. Kahn, *Social Policy and Social Services* (New York: Random House, 1973), p. 74.

17. Ibid., p. 8.

18. Ibid., p. 93.

SELECTED READINGS

The political and economic realities of social welfare in American society have been among the most ignored aspects of social welfare as a social institution. The readings suggested here attempt to persuade you of the need for greater political and economic awareness, and suggest some of the changes that may be necessary to strengthen the social welfare system.

Alinsky, Saul. *Reveille for Radicals*. Chicago: University of Chicago Press, 1946.

Caplovitz, David. *The Poor Pay More*. New York: Free Press, 1967.

Cohen, Wilbur. "What Every Social Worker Should Know about Political Action," in Robert Klenk and Robert Ryan, eds., *The Practice of Social Work*. Belmont, Cal.: Wadsworth, 1970, pp. 334–46.

Congressional Quarterly. *Guide to Current American Government*. Issued twice yearly. Weekly guide of current legislation may be obtained from Congressional Quarterly, 1735 K Street, N.W., Washington, D.C. 20006.

Galper, Jeffry. *The Politics of Social Services*. Englewood Cliffs, N.J.: Prentice-Hall, 1975.

Herzberg, Donald, and J. W. Peltason. *A Student Guide to Campaign Politics*. New York: McGraw-Hill, 1970.

Kahn, Si. *How People Get Power*. New York: McGraw-Hill, 1970.

Theobold, Robert. *Free Men and Free Markets*. Garden City: Anchor, 1965.

Titmuss, Richard. *Commitment to Welfare*. New York: Pantheon, 1968.

Tussing, A. Dale. *Poverty in a Dual Economy*. New York: St. Martin's Press, 1975.

PART **III**

Interventive Methods

7

Social Welfare Interventive Methods

*T*HE WAYS in which social welfare professionals go about intervening in individual, group, community, and societal processes with the goal of improving social functioning will be examined in this chapter. Each of the previous chapters has laid some part of the groundwork for understanding this kind of professional intervention. Helping people and groups to function more effectively is possible because of values and knowledge that support the desirability of such behavior. Appropriate ways of intervening in social behavior are also defined by societal values and knowledge. Existing helping structures affect the helping process through their organization of human, social, and financial resources. This organization reflects past experience and present social, political, and economic reality, and may sometimes be a barrier to effective intervention. The helping professional must function within this reality, although one of his goals may be to change that reality. After having read this chapter through once, it might be helpful to turn to the Appendix, which has two cases illustrative of the major points made in this chapter. These cases may then stimulate further thought about interventive methods, and encourage a rereading of the material in the chapter.

THE NATURE OF HELPING Before looking at specific interventive approaches, there are several elements that enter into any professional intervention. Social welfare intervention is an attempt by a professional to help others solve problems within a social-system context. As in all human behavior, communication is an essential part of the exchange between the persons involved in the helping process. Therefore, before looking at some of the specific interventive methods used in social welfare contexts, it is necessary to examine these three elements common to all interventive methods: (1) the nature of helping relationships; (2) communication and the problem-solving process; and (3) the importance of systems in helping situations.

Combs et al. note that helping involves three factors: persons, goals, and barriers.[1] The persons involved include the person seeking help, the person offering help, and significant other persons who may be involved in the helping process in some way—family members, employers, friends, other professionals, landlords, and the like. The heart of the helping relationship is the one between the helping person and the person seeking help, with others becoming more (or perhaps less) involved as this relationship develops. Sometimes others can be a factor in preventing the helping relationship from developing in a positive way. For example, a parent who refuses to cooperate with a school social worker seeing a child who has school problems related to family functioning may make it very difficult for the social worker to establish a meaningful helping relationship with the child. The effects of others on the helping relationship will be discussed in more detail later when talking about systems in helping relationships. For now, we will focus on the helping person and the person seeking help.

Keith-Lucas points out that there are three major characteristics of helping: reality, empathy, and support.[2] Helping involves the confrontation with reality, dealing with the problems—real or imagined—that are perceived. Being evicted is a reality, as is suffering a broken leg in an automobile accident. Feeling unloved is also a reality for the person having those feelings, whether or not other people in fact have loving or hostile feelings toward that person. Each of these realities creates problems, although the differing nature of these problems may suggest somewhat different barriers to be overcome and resources available to be used. Helping must deal with whatever the reality is. Avoiding reality may be tempting to the person seeking help and occasionally even the helping person, since much reality is very unpleasant and complex. Sometimes the avoidance of reality may even be unrecognized when it occurs. A basic reality may be denied by concentrating on related but less significant behaviors, for example. Succumbing to the temptation to avoid reality by either the person seeking help or the helper almost always guarantees failure, since it usually circumvents the behaviors that are the problem or support the problem.

Because reality can be so unpleasant, threatening, and complex, its confrontation in the helping situation must be tempered with empathy and support. Empathy is the ability to comprehend another's subjective reality and feelings from that person's point of view. Empathy is more objective than sympathy because it does not include sharing feelings with the other person—it is instead sharing an understanding of what the feelings are and their importance. This enables the helping person to understand without being overwhelmed by what may be very upsetting and immobilizing feelings. Empathy and support are necessary to enable the person who needs assistance to utilize resources—both personal and outside resources—to develop and implement a solution to the problematic reality. The helping relationship does not entail a professional helping person assuming the problems of the person he seeks to help. "In the helper-helpee relationship, it is the *helpee* who knows and the *helper* who does not; the *client* has the crucial information and he must do the changing."[3] The helping person is an enabler, enabling the person seeking help to understand and confront reality, and utilize all available resources to formulate and attain goals, taking reality into account. In order to do this, the helping person must understand the reality of the situation, both objectively and in terms of its meaning for the person seeking help. She then supports the person seeking help as he explores, selects, and uses resources (of which the helping person is one).

Keith-Lucas has written that "the helping relationship is . . . only the medium in which help is offered. It is not help itself."[4] He sees eight characteristics of the helping relationship.

A mutual relationship: As was suggested above, the helping person does not change the person she is helping. She provides the knowledge, interest, sensitive perception and communication, and support that makes it possible for the person being helped to confront and deal appropriately with his own reality. Each person, the helper and the helped, has an important part to play in the helping process. Each shares with the other, responding to feelings and communication. When a relationship loses this mutual quality, it becomes control, and control generally destroys growth, the assumption of self-responsibility, and self-expression and acceptance.

Elements of unpleasantness and hostility: Reality can be very unpleasant. Struggling with problems and reality can temporarily overwhelm persons seeking help so that they strike out in fear and frustration. Learning to accept responsibility for oneself, and to accept oneself in the process, can be frightening. The helping person may react to hostility expressed towards him by a client with emotional reactions of his own. In many ways, the helping relationship may entail strong feelings and negative situations. It is through the confrontation of these situations that reality is more fully understood and progress made. Trying to artificially smooth over real and appropriate feelings, however unpleasant, impedes progress.

Feeling as well as knowledge: A significant feature of human beings is that they learn to interpret events, and to integrate them into a value system that assigns feelings to them. These feelings are significant aspects of behavior, and enable or prevent people from accepting events and themselves as worthwhile. Concentrating on the objective characteristics of events and behaviors without understanding the feelings involved can lead to serious misinterpretation and block communication and empathy.

A single purpose. Helping relationships involve problem-solving behavior (discussed in more detail below). Problem-solving is an orderly examination of the perceived problem, causes of the problem, obstacles to problem-solving, and goals. Lack of focus on a single purpose at each point in the helping relationship leads to confusion of goals and means, and can shift the helping relationship away from reality.

Occurs in the here and now. As each purpose is formulated and then pursued within a reality framework, the helping relationship deals with the present—in time and in place. Jumping ahead to future steps in the problem-solving process, or shifting to behavior appropriate to a different time and place, may make the confrontation with reality less painful by partially avoiding it. However, it is likely to do very little to advance the helping relationship. Planning in the present depends on appropriate information about the past that is relevant to the current situation.

Offers something new. As much as the person seeking help may have struggled with the problems in his reality, he is often unable to see aspects of his situation or understand some of those of which he is aware. This frequently includes his inability to understand his own feelings about himself and his situation. Furthermore, he may have little idea of how to go about planning to solve his problems, or the resources available to him while doing this. The professional helping person offers help in seeing the previously unseen, and understanding that which has been perplexing. Empathy allows the helping person to understand and interpret feeling and behavior. Her knowledge helps her to perceive relationships and identify resources. By being outside of the problems which the person seeking help faces, yet deeply interested and highly skilled as a professional helping person, the professional illuminates facets of reality and resources that assist the person seeking help to find solutions to his problems.

Choice is a meaningful alternative. Most simply stated, this means that the person being helped ultimately makes his own choices, even if the helping person disagrees with those choices. When the helping person's professional judgment suggests that the choices being made by the person seeking help will lead to failure or further problems, it is painful to allow those choices to be made. While the professional person may use all of his skill to help the other person understand why he disagrees with the choices being made, he must stop short of taking over responsibility for those choices. Choice, to be meaningful, must include the right of selecting any of the possible alternatives, even those that may lead to further difficulty. Otherwise it is control rather than choice. It is through the person assuming responsibility for her own decisions that growth occurs. The successes of the future sometimes depend on learning that results from the mistakes of the present.

Helping must be nonjudgmental. This does not mean that the helping person has no opinion about what is happening in the helping relationship. Quite the contrary, the empathy involved means that one is very deeply involved. What it does mean is that the person seeking help is accepted as a worthwhile human being regardless of his or her problems, mistakes, or choices. There is a separation of person from behavior. Although people often act in deviant or destructive ways, they are still worthwhile, autonomous human beings. The helping person may disapprove of their behavior, and try to help them change that behavior. But one has an abiding respect for the person as a human being with unlimited capacity for growth and change. This respect underlies every aspect of social welfare. Without it, control and manipulation cannot be avoided, and basic human values are easily trampled.

The helping process, then, is a complex interaction of two people (or several people when the "person" seeking help is instead a group). The professional person utilizes the knowledge of human behavior and social systems, skill at communicating and empathizing, and values which respect the person or persons with whom he is working. The person seeking help brings perceptions about himself and his situation, feelings about what he believes is happening to him, and motivation to help himself. Together these two (or more) people communicate and share, exchanging concern and information, giving trust in return for information and support. But always there is a limit. The helping person's information and empathy are made available to the person seeking help, never thrust upon the client in such a way as to deprive the person of basic human rights, including the right to try and fail, and to refuse and reject.

As is obvious by now, helping is difficult, delicate, and sometimes exhausting. What kind of a person can engage in this activity? There is, of course, no simple answer to such a question. There are many types of persons that make effective helpers. Keith-Lucas suggests the following:

> Courage, humility, and concern may then give us some characterization of the helping person. Other qualities such as dependability, patience, integrity, or a sense of humor are of course also desirable, or perhaps simply facets of these. Intelligence and imagination can be of help. But the helping person is an essentially human being, with many of the faults that all of us share. There is nothing ascetic or infallible about him or about his knowledge. He is disciplined but no automaton, sensitive but no seer, knowledgeable but not necessarily intellectual, unselfish but not self-denying, long suffering but no martyr. When we meet him we will probably like him but not, perhaps, be too impressed.[5]

Whatever her individual characteristics, the professional helping person must possess self-awareness, and be aware of any particular strengths and weaknesses, skills and deficiencies, preferences and pet peeves. As Keith-Lucas notes, all of us have faults and weaknesses, and helping professionals are no exception. They must recognize theirs so that as they work these faults will not interfere with the helping process.

PROBLEM-SOLVING IN A SYSTEMS CONTEXT

As has been noted, the helping relationship involves problem-solving within a systems framework. In Chapter 1 Pincus and Minahan's discussion of systems involved in helping situations was summarized. To review briefly, they see four systems:

1. *The change agent system.* This includes the helping person and the organization for which she works or, if a private practitioner, with whom she works.

2. *The client system.* These are the people who seek help from the professional helping person, and may be an individual, a group, a community, or an organization.

3. *The target system.* These are the people the change agent needs to change or influence in order to accomplish his goals.

4. *The action system.* These are the people with whom the helping person works in attempting to accomplish the tasks and achieve the goals of the change effort.

Although the helping relationship concentrates on the interaction between the helping person and the person or group seeking help, any attempt at problem definition and solution must take into account a far broader range of participants.

Each individual exists in a social network of other individuals, groups, and organizations. A married man has a wife, children perhaps, a boss, work partners, bowling friends, and many other persons in his life that tie him to a variety of groups—a family, a place of work, a friendship group. In trying to disentangle the causes, meanings, and solutions of a problem, all of these persons and groups must be taken into account. Otherwise the helping person runs the risk of missing an important part of the problem puzzle. The process gets complicated by the fact that one type of interaction (marital friction) may have its roots elsewhere (work dissatisfaction), and its solution even elsewhere (job retraining). While helping is a person-to-person endeavor, even in a group setting, the resources and knowledge needed to understand and solve a problem may exist completely outside the individual, or in the interaction of an individual with others. An often over-looked fact, which Pincus and Minahan's formulation helps us to recognize, is that sometimes the helping person himself or the context in which he works (that is, the change-agent system) may be part of the problem. For example, the burdensome application procedures used by an agency may discourage those in need from seeking help.

Problem-solving in helping situations involves several elements. The first is listening to the problem as it is expressed by the person seeking help. Often a problem is expressed in such a way that it masks a more basic under-lying problem. Knowledge of the fact that the individual or group may not recognize or cannot accept the more basic problem is an important first step in understanding the total problem context. Again it is important to empha-size that feeling is as important as objective reality. It may take some time to discover exactly what the problem is, as the person seeking help shifts among several potential problem situations. It takes considerable skill in communication and interpretation to disentangle the many strands that may relate to, yet also hide, a problem. This is especially the case when dealing with community problems, where there may be several conflicting defini-tions among different groups in the community. In addition, the helping person's perception of a situation may reveal yet different problems from those perceived by individuals or community members. For example, a couple may come in to discuss a marital problem, completely neglecting the fact that their children are paying a heavy price for the conflict in the house and are in need of physical and emotional help.

As a problem is presented and clarified, the feelings attached to the problem are usually expressed. These feelings are important, for they begin to suggest the resources that are available to solve the problem, and the motivation that exists to sustain the individual or group through the problem-solving process. Feelings, and the values they represent, are an im-portant part of the problem-solving process. Religious values that rule out birth control may be a significant factor when developing a plan to try to solve a marital problem, or help a woman more effectively deal with house-keeping and child-rearing problems. Working within the emerging limits imposed by values and feelings, the range of resources within the client and action systems must be identified. The assessment of resources must include personal and social resources. These include such factors as the ability of the individual to understand a problem, the availability of financial resources, cooperation from significant others, the availability of services (health care, vocational rehabilitation, schooling, etc.), and physical resources (housing, proper physical development and functioning in an individual, recreation, etc.). The helping person, and hopefully the whole change-agent system, will also be part of this assessment. When it appears that a given helping person or social organization cannot help a person or group seeking assistance, it is professionally responsible to make a referral to a more appropriate change-agent system. A referral is only complete when a client has been connected to a resource that is ready to help him.

Problem-solving must also include an assessment of barriers to success. The client system and the target system are the most likely sources of barriers. The person or group seeking help may be unable to accept reality, or may lack the skills and resources to attain goals that have been identified. It is frequently the case that a meaningful solution to the client system's problem lies elsewhere, in other systems. Social Security levels may be too low to live on, for example—a problem depending on congressional action for its solution. The common discrimination by employers against ex-convicts makes it very difficult for such persons to develop a plan for financial self-sufficiency. Economic inflation, which erodes the resources of older persons living on fixed incomes, is well beyond the control of that particular client system. The awareness that some of the most serious barriers to effective problem-solving lie outside client systems is essential to professional understanding of the range of interventive skills a helping person must have. A single-minded devotion to the client system as the source of problems and their solutions is frequently counterproductive.

Once the problem, resources, and barriers have been identified, it is possible to consider alternative solutions. Usually there will be several approaches to solving a problem. Each of them will have certain costs— emotional, relational, and financial. In assessing these costs, a systems approach again provides a useful framework for identifying those persons and groups that will be affected and involved. Deteriorated housing may lead to health problems for an aged person, yet movement to a different neighborhood may break meaningful social ties for a person whose mobility is limited. A recreation center used by both teens and senior citizen groups may be a financially attractive way for a community to meet its citizens' recreational needs, but the activities of the two groups may be incompatible. An agency's move to a new modern facility may improve the morale of its workers, and the quality of its services, but be inaccessible to those who use it. There is no easy solution to the problem of selecting among the various alternative solutions possible. Priorities have to be established, and solutions selected according to the dominant priorities. Sometimes professional priorities differ from client priorities, in which case the right of persons seeking help to self-determination must be respected. One of the hardest lessons for a technologically sophisticated society to learn is that the "best" solution to a problem is not necessarily the most efficient one from a financial or technological point of view. It is difficult to do, but human costs and human priorities must enter into the efficiency equation, and into the development of priorities.

Helper-helpee contracts are increasingly used to insure that the goals of the helping relationship are explicit and that they include the objectives of both parties. A contract, often in written form, is developed at the beginning of the problem-solving process. It specifies the objectives of the helping process, and details who will be responsible for the activities to attain each objective. For example, the helping person will agree to consult with a state legislator about the appropriate form of proposed legislation to protect the elderly. The residents of a public housing project for the elderly (the group seeking help) will get signatures on a petition supporting such legislation. The contract usually also specifies a time frame within which the contract itself will be reassessed and changed if necessary.

Contracts have several advantages. They enable all persons involved in the helping relationship to express their goals. The contract then is built around them, or if that is not possible, everyone involved knows from the beginning what to expect and can choose accordingly. The contract aids the helper and helpee to know what they are expected to do, and how their behaviors fit together to attain specified objectives. The objectives themselves can be readily evaluated at specified time periods, so it is easier to determine whether or not the helping process is successful. If not, the helper and helpee are encouraged either to reassess their plans or to decide to terminate the relationship. If the process is successful, all persons involved have the satisfaction of seeing success and being motivated to continue working toward whatever objectives may remain. Most importantly, perhaps, contracts maximize choice. Persons seeking help have input into the setting of objectives, and at all times are able to judge whether the objectives are being met. Helping persons are also assisted to develop a specific, realistic interventive plan, and to evaluate it in very concrete terms. After all, if the helping process isn't helping, there is little point to continue it. Contracts make it easier to make this assessment.

When a solution has been selected, it must be implemented. If the resources available and the potential barriers have been carefully evaluated and incorporated, implementation should be possible. When client systems insist on making decisions that professional helping persons know are unworkable, attempting to implement the decision may lead to failure. However, it is through this kind of failure that growth may occur—again, priorities must be established. Through failure, a given objective has not been attained, but if self-awareness, maturity, and problem-solving skills are increased, the failure may be the best possible outcome.

INTERVIEWING At various points in this discussion of helping and problem-solving, communication skill has been mentioned. It is one of the most basic skills a professional helping person must possess. Human beings draw upon an enormously complex and rich culture that is generally transmitted through symbols—words, numbers, physical expressions, and visual images of many kinds. Human behavior is made up of both action and feelings, as has already been discussed. Communication patterns reflect this, with certain types of communication best suited to the expression of concrete events and behaviors (words and numbers, for example), and other types being best suited to the expression of feelings ("body language" is a good example). The helping professional must master a wide range of communication techniques, and be skilled in interaction in many kinds of communication contexts—on the street, in structured interviews, in board meetings, and so on. Most often, the helping professional is using communication for specific purposes—to find out information, to discover feelings, to verify hunches. Such purposeful communication is known as interviewing, and is a basic interventive tool.

De Schweinitz distinguishes two types of interviews: objective, which are goal and task oriented (as when interviewing to determine eligibility for receipt of services); and therapeutic, which are more subjective and introspective (as when allowing a client to express his feelings).[6] Most interviews have elements of each, but to maintain an interview's focus it is often helpful to keep the distinction in mind.

Three major parts of the interviewing process may be identified: (1) conditions of good interviewing; (2) the interview itself, including the beginning, the main part of the interview, and the end; and (3) post-interview activity.[7] There are at least four conditions maximizing the chances for a successful interview. First, there is the physical setting for the interview. This pertains to the actual place where the person is interviewed, including comfortable seating arrangements, privacy, visual attractiveness, and comfort items such as a coat rack, ashtrays, and so on. The physical setting also includes the convenience of the location for the client, whether there is a long wait before the interview, degrading reception procedures, and the presence of a place for children to stay during the interview. It is remarkable how common it is for clients to have to travel some distance, often by public transportation with children, wait if the worker is busy, be gruffly received by a receptionist who obviously feels her position is degraded by dealing with clients, and then sit in a large, bare waiting room in full view of everyone. When the interview finally begins, it should be no surprise if the client is tired, nervous, and sullen. Frequently a practitioner plans interviews in the client's home or other community setting. In such instances, interviewing conditions may be less than ideal and not easily manipulated by the practitioner, but using the client's natural environment can be a convenience for him that results in greater cooperation. Interviewing in the home or community can also be an aid in understanding the client's social environment.

A second element of the physical setting is confidentiality. People are often quite upset by their problems, and sensitive about discussing them. They rarely appreciate having to discuss problems where others can overhear, and commonly interpret privacy as an indication of a worker's respect. Third, the worker has a professional obligation to have obtained as much background information as possible. This includes studying any case records that are available from previous contacts, and includes basic knowledge of community and agency resources. Having this information at hand enables the worker to avoid repetition in the interview, which most clients appreciate. It also makes maximum use of available time, and draws upon other community resources as appropriate. It is sound practice to refer a client to another agency if it is likely to be better able to work with her and her particular problem. Fourth, note-taking, for the purpose of recording the content of the interview, must be planned. Too much note-taking can distract a client and impede communication. On the other hand, it has to be adequate to record significant facts. A workable compromise is to take notes on factual information, with minimal notes on other content. Mechanical recording devices can sometimes be used, but the client's permission must always be sought first, and such equipment should be as unobtrusive as possible.

Beginning the interview has at least five relevant factors. First, the client has a right to know the realities of the interviewing context, such as the time period likely to be involved, costs involved if any, limits to confidentiality, the client's responsibilities, psychological investment, and the like.[8] Second, one should be particularly aware of the physical conditions at the beginning of the interview to establish an obstacle-free context as quickly as possible. A third concern is to try to make one's genuine interest in the client as explicit as possible by paying complete attention to what the client has to say. Fourth, it is important to begin where the client wishes. The worker may have his own ideas about the problems involved, and may want to begin exploring those areas right away. The client, however, must have the freedom to tell his story in his own way, talking about the things he is feeling and thinking, and having a chance to find a comfortable method of expressing himself to the worker. The worker can always channel the interview at a later time, but at the beginning one does not want to risk stopping communication. Finally, it is important to be especially sensitive to clues the client gives that indicate areas of special meaning and feeling at the beginning of the interview. These clues guide a worker in his further approach to the individual, and suggest areas for further exploration.

The main body of the interview uses five rather specific techniques: listening, observation, questioning, responding, and guiding. Information will be obtained by listening and observing, and these are crucial to the flow of communication. Listening must be done with understanding, accepting silences naturally and allowing the client to find his own means of expression. There are few better ways to stifle communication than breaking in prematurely, keeping up a constant chatter that makes it impossible for anyone to collect his thoughts, or only half-listening, indicating to the speaker that her conversation is not really of interest. Observation is another form of listening, since everyone also speaks nonverbally through his actions.[9] Nonverbal communication often indicates the feeling behind the words, one of the many ways it can supplement verbal communication. Nonverbal communication can be especially valuable in indicating the client's feelings about the interview context itself, as when someone is excessively tense or refuses all offers of hospitality.

A third technique is concerned with questioning. The worker may need to obtain information not spontaneously offered, clarify a point, or probe beyond the point at which the client stopped talking. Questioning should be done sensitively and questions formulated carefully, since harsh questioning into overly sensitive areas can either stop communication or evoke information neither desired nor easily handled. Responding is a way to maintain communication, to put the client at ease, and, where appropriate, to begin to move toward behavior modification. Everyone wants some assurance that her communication has been received, so some small sign indicating that the worker is following what the client is saying is appropriate: perhaps a nod, a word or two, or a request for clarification. In this regard, the worker must be aware of his own nonverbal communication, since wandering eyes, doodling, and yawning are responses the client is likely to understand all too well.

The client may ask personal questions about the worker, quite natural behavior given the importance the worker may assume in his life. Such questions should be answered simply and honestly, but at the same time the focus should be redirected back to the client.

Responding establishes the give and take through which the client gets the benefit of the worker's skill and professional experience. The worker expresses her feelings, provides information, gives advice, and provides a behavioral model. Responses, however, should not be too quick or too autocratic. The worker must be cautious and flexible in interpreting interview content, careful not to make promises that are unrealistic, and watchful not to eliminate the client's participation.

The last technique, guiding the interview, grows out of the previous four. On the basis of information already given, the worker's interpretation of it, and the need for further information, the interview should remain focused on the problems at hand as seen by the worker and the client. Here one must remember the dual components of feeling and objective content, since "facts" should not dominate the feelings that give the facts meaning. Often, for example, a client seems to return again and again to the same point or recount the same story. This makes the maintenance of focus difficult, but it also indicates an area of great importance to the client.

In ending the interview, there are several points to keep in mind. Usually time is limited, and the interview must be ended when the time is up. At the same time, one should try to find a natural stopping point rather than abruptly terminating the interview. It is usually helpful to summarize the progress made in the interview so that the client feels some satisfaction that progress is being made, and gets some indication of the worker's interpretation of the content discussed. So far as possible, the worker should try to insure that the client leaves composed and in good spirits, with some guidelines for handling himself in difficult situations that may arise before the next interview. And finally, the arrangements for the next interview should be clarified, with due care for the convenience of the client (i.e., conditions of good interviewing), assuming that there will be further interviews.

EXHIBIT 7-1

An Outline of the Interviewing Process

Below is an outline of the interviewing process used in the Social Worker Technician program of the U.S. Army Medical Field Service School at Ft. Sam Houston, San Antonio, Texas. Although it differs in a few details from the above discussion, it is an excellent summary of the major components of interviewing.

A. *Interviewing Concepts*
  1. *Beginning of interview*
     a. Begin where the patient is
     b. Attempt to set patient at ease
     c. Attention to patient's comforts
     d. Efforts to establish rapport

  2. *Interest in patient*
     a. Courtesy
     b. Treating the patient with dignity
     c. Individualize patient
     d. Warmth
     e. Tone of voice
     f. Demonstrated sincerity of involvement
     g. Attentiveness and eye contact
     h. Remaining patient-centered, not note-centered

  3. *Drawing out affect*
     Encourage patient to express feelings, i.e., anger, sadness, warmth, joy, despair, hostility, and others

  4. *Skill in responding to patient's behavior*
     a. Recognition and appropriate use of verbal communication
     b. Recognition and appropriate use of non-verbal behavior

  5. *Clarification and consistency of role*
     a. Self-control of stress, prejudice, and judgmental feelings
     b. Appropriate appearance
     c. Conveying one's purpose in the interview

  6. *Questioning technique*
     a. Proper balance between general and specific questions
     b. Questions which guide the patient in telling story in his own words
     c. Transitions

  7. *Listening techniques*
     Proper use of silence which encourages the patient

  8. *Ending*
     a. Brief summarization of interview content
     b. Opportunity for patient feedback on interview
     c. Proper explanation of future plan/view in regard to the patient

After the interview, the worker should elaborate on any notes taken, making them complete enough to enable him to record accurately the interview's content at the appropriate time. He may also want to fill in some of his own reactions and thoughts by taking a moment after the interview to review it, thinking about meaning and interviewing technique. Diagnosis is the process of interpreting information and developing tentative approaches to solutions. This important step in problem-solving can best be done when the relevant material is fresh in one's mind.

Exhibits 7-1 and 7-2 summarize the major points of interviewing. When working with human beings, there is no substitute for effective communication. Helping can only occur when problems are explored by a helping person and someone seeking help, taking the many persons and groups that affect the problem into account. Effective communication makes such exploration possible. It is these fundamentals—helping, problem-solving, systems, and communication—that form the core of the specific interventive methods to be discussed in the rest of this chapter.

EXHIBIT 7-2

Some Do's and Don't's of Effective Interviewing

This list of elements that facilitate and hinder effective interviewing is taken from a summary of do's and don't's of interviewing as compiled and edited by Wallace Phillips and Alexander B. Pierce, Jr. at the University of North Carolina in Greensboro, and used with their permission. It is based on material in Alfred Benjamin, *The Helping Interview* (Boston: Houghton-Mifflin, 1969).

DO be cordial and receptive.

DO create a setting conducive to establishing a good relationship. Chairs that face each other convey a feeling of openness and equality. A desk can become a barrier to communication.

DO be aware of body language. Neatness of dress, posture, and facial expressions all send messages concerning what you and the interviewee really think and feel about the situation.

DO employ open-ended lead-in questions as a means of allowing the interviewee to begin at her own starting point. Take your cues from that point.

DO be empathetic. Be natural. Be yourself.

DO move into the interviewee's internal frame of reference so that she may tell you how she genuinely feels about the situation.

DO use silence when appropriate. In effect you will be saying, "I am waiting and giving you time to develop your ideas more clearly."

DO ask direct questions in order to obtain specific information about the situation.

DO repeat some of the interviewee's phrases exactly in order to explore more fully thoughts or feelings that the interviewee had begun to express.

DO be supportive. Reinforce the interviewee by letting her know that her thoughts, feelings and opinions are important.

DO make the tasks to be accomplished a joint effort.

DO demonstrate that you believe in the interviewee's capacity to use her own resources.

DO return to the central theme or presenting problem of the interview. This can be done by the use of an open-ended restatement. "You mentioned that Jimmy doesn't like his class. . ."

DO refer to other resources when appropriate.

DO be honest. Do not be afraid of admitting that you do not know.

DO assume an appropriate share of the responsibility in carrying out agreed-upon goals.

DO summarize the highlights of the interview with emphasis on the explicit action each will take in meeting the mutually agreed-upon goals. Preferably, the interviewee states her part in the action and the interviewer states her part. This confirms with clarity the contract between them.

DO make a definite statement of the plans for your next meeting.

DO be sincerely interested. Every word, gesture and mannerism sends the message.

DON'T be unfriendly or indifferent. The setting for the interview should be conducive to the creation of a warm and friendly atmosphere.

DON'T ask a question beginning with "why." This puts the interviewee on the defensive.

DON'T interrupt. Not only does this cut off the interviewee's thoughts, it is just plain rude.

DON'T intimidate or threaten. This confirms the lack of respect for the interviewee and is telling him that you see yourself as the authority.

DON'T ridicule or be sarcastic. This hardly enables the interviewee to be anything but angry with you, and justifiably so.

DON'T use cliches. They don't usually effectively convey sincerity.

DON'T show disbelief. You are questioning the validity of the interviewee's statement.

DON'T use leading questions. Try to use indirect questions which avoid putting the interviewee on the defensive or putting words in her mouth.

DON'T ask two questions at once. How is the interviewee to know which one to answer?

DON'T convey the idea that the interviewee's ideas and thoughts are unimportant by rejecting them.

DON'T use a double question. "Now, is there something else, or can we discuss the rest in the group meeting?" This places the interviewee in an "either-or" position, a bind which leaves no real alternative.

DON'T avoid the reality of the situation as the interviewee sees it. That is why she came to you in the first place.

DON'T scold.

DON'T allow other things to seem more important than the interview that you are engaged in at the moment. If you do you are telling the interviewee that you are not really interested in her.

DON'T tell the interviewee what to do. Instead help her to arrive at her own decision.

THE SEARCH FOR EFFECTIVE INTERVENTIVE METHODS
We live in a time when traditional ways of intervening to help people solve their problems are being reexamined. Although this may be upsetting to professionals trying to decide on their own interventive approaches, the history of social welfare interventive methods has been characterized by a continuing search for more effective helping techniques. We have already seen that helping has been a part of social life from the earliest records of human existence. However, when talking about interventive methods, we begin at the time when helping became a codified, professional activity rather than one left to the charitable impulses of friendly visitors.

Our earlier discussion of the charity organization societies noted that they served as a catalyst for the development of professional social work through their emphasis on individual case study and supervision.[10] The many changes the Industrial Revolution was creating stimulated the development of many kinds of helping—especially in the treatment of the physically and mentally ill. In these professions, the scientific base was obvious. This base was not so obvious in social work and other more relationship-oriented helping professions. As Lubove points out,

> A major source of irritation to social workers anxious to elevate their professional status consisted of those "many popular misunderstandings of social work, which identify it with nursing, with mental testing, with occupational therapy, with neighborliness." Psychiatry in the early twentieth century played a significant role in strengthening the social worker's conviction that she offered a distinct and valuable service which required specialized skill and training.[11]

This, combined with the charity organization society emphasis on case study, led to the dominance of casework (individual counseling) as an interventive method and a strong alliance between casework and psychiatry, especially Freudian psychoanalysis.

Other effects of the Industrial Revolution, including rapid urbanization, the rise of factories, and the shift from extended to nuclear family structures, created problems of illness, poverty, exploitation, mobility, and isolation that were obviously beyond the control of individuals or families. These problems were especially noticeable in the large numbers of immigrants that arrived on America's shores full of hope but often sick, homeless, and ignorant of the language and customs of their new country. In Jane Addams's words, "The Settlement (settlement houses, a type of community center), then, is an experimental effort to aid in the solution of the social and industrial problems which are engendered by the modern conditions of life in a great city. . . . It is an attempt to relieve, at the same time, the over-accumulation at one end of society and the destitution at the other. . . ."[12] Addams is asserting that another important focus of social welfare is to intervene in the social processes that create problems for individuals, rather than concentrating only on the individuals. Her statement also lays the foundation for social action as she talks about the need for a more equitable distribution of resources between the rich and the poor.

The social welfare professions, and social work in particular, began with two thrusts, the individual and the social. The attractiveness of the idea of scientifically based solutions to problems, plus the obvious complexity and political and economic risks of community development and social action, gradually led to a period in which casework dominated approaches to problem intervention. Nevertheless, the limitations of focusing primarily on a one-to-one interventive approach became obvious, and the community and social action heritage of social work were never completely lost. Gradually the need for a broader view of problem causation and solution led to the development of a group approach to problem-solving, called group work, and the latent community and social action heritage found new expression in community organization. As social welfare professionalism increased, the need for administrative skills and research data also became evident, and they joined the ranks of important interventive methods. As we turn to an overview of each of these interventive approaches, notice that they are methods-focused. That is, a method is developed which problems are then fit into. For example, a social worker utilizing the casework method would deal with a range of problems—marital problems, foster home placement, school truancy, and mental illness, for example—by applying casework skills to these problems. We will see later that some persons are now suggesting that adapting problems to a method may be less effective than adapting a method to a problem.

CASEWORK   There are many definitions of casework, reflecting the diversity of approaches possible. The Council on Social Work Education's definition is a concise summary of the basic approach: "a method of social work which intervenes in the psychosocial aspects of a person's life to improve, restore, maintain, or enhance his social functioning by improving his role performance."[13] Florence Hollis has said, "Central to casework is the notion of the person in his situation,"[14] while Helen Harris Perlman talks of a "biopsychosocial whole"[15] providing the focus in casework. Perlman further explains that casework involves a person with a problem coming to a place where a professional uses a method to help him.[16] Thus it can be seen that casework embodies the goal of improving social functioning, which characterizes social welfare as a whole. It does so by concentrating on one person in some depth, looking at her biological-psychological-social behavior, and looking at the individual in her social context. This is consistent with a systems approach as already discussed.

Before delving into some of the specific parts of the casework method, a look at the pre-casework process, explicated by David Landy, is important.[17] Landy noted that while caseworkers (and social welfare practitioners in general) are intent on the perfection of their practice techniques, they neglect the factors impinging on the client that influence whether or not he will ever get to the agency, and in what state he will arrive, when and if he does. Landy points out that the process of seeking help is often difficult and complex. It begins with a recognition that something is wrong, but such recognition is hampered by the common tendency to deny failing in some aspect of our lives. This is encouraged by a societal value system that preaches self-reliance and the belief that individuals can and should solve their own problems. Under these circumstances, it is not surprising that people often seek help only when they are desperate, and when the problems are so complex that they are very difficult to solve. Seeking help is admitting that one has "failed" in coping with her problems, a situation others may also become aware of. The stigma attached to seeking help is one reason why people tend to turn first to those in their indigenous environment for help: family, friends, or clergy. Here, problems can be discussed informally. Entry into the professional social service network implies that the problem is serious.

Landy also notes that the act of seeking help places the applicant in a dependent position and requires that he relinquish some autonomy (answering endless questions, having to travel to an inconvenient agency location, keeping appointments, and the like). The role of the helped is often an uncomfortable one, involving the confrontation with painful memories, unpleasant insights into oneself and others, and emotional stress. A person with problems may not be at all eager to temporarily endure more stress in order to achieve ultimate solutions. Talcott Parsons, a sociologist, has analyzed the role of those having a physical illness. It seems very relevant in understanding the problem of the person seeking help in our culture, emphasizing the rights and obligations incurred in the process.[18] Landy's point, then, is to remind the social welfare practitioner that asking for help is a major step, and one that is likely to be stressful for a client. He suggests that the casework process ought to include the pre-casework experience in a planned way.

Casework, like most of the methods to be discussed, makes conscious use of helping, problem-solving, and communication. It does so primarily on a one-to-one basis, concentrating on individualizing the situation of the person seeking help.[19] That is, the caseworker seeks to understand the specific biopsychosocial situation of the person with whom she is working. This includes the individual's personality structure and functioning, personal and social resources, typical behavior patterns in interaction with others, and real or potential problem areas. In doing this, the caseworker first seeks to obtain information through the skillful use of interviewing techniques. This information is called the social history. Although most characteristic of the beginning phase of the casework process, obtaining information continues to some extent throughout the relationship. This information is then interpreted, which is the process of diagnosis. In interpreting information, the caseworker begins with the information as presented by the client, including evidence of the meaning of the information for that person. Gradually the professional person places this information into a professional context, attempting to identify causes, effects, relationships, and possible solutions. Diagnosis is also something that continues throughout the casework relationship. As additional information is obtained it may affect interpretations tentatively made on the basis of earlier incomplete information.

Part of diagnosis is an assessment of the individual's situation. Whether there are any immediate crises that must be resolved, significant persons in the individual's life and environment, and available resources are explored. As situational assessment begins, the helping relationship begins to deepen, since the person seeking help must now take an active role in developing solutions to his problems. As planning for problem solution is begun, the caseworker provides empathy, support, and information as appropriate. As a caseworker, one consciously uses a planned professional technique so that one can be of maximum help with as few of one's own problems as possible blocking communication and planning. As the person being helped selects solutions, the caseworker helps that person to implement the chosen plan.

After a problem-solving plan is developed and implemented, the casework relationship is reassessed. If the implemented plan is successful in solving the problem for which it was developed, the caseworker may explore whether there are other problems the person seeking help wishes to solve. If the plan turns out to be unsuccessful, the reasons for this failure need to be explored, and a new plan developed—even if it is referral to a potentially more effective helping environment. Whenever it is decided that the relationship is to be terminated, the caseworker plans for this event, being sure that there is agreement on the desirability of termination and being equally sure that the person being helped is ready to function without the support of the helping relationship. Since persons being helped can become dependent on caseworkers, and also become personally attached to them, it is important that the helping person work throughout the relationship to minimize these effects so that termination is neither resisted nor traumatic.

The therapeutic component of casework has focused on the behavior change that would eliminate a problem, as well as the counseling to help a client adapt to his problem if it could not be solved.[20] Some have criticized casework for helping people to adapt to problems,[21] yet it seems realistic to see some problems as essentially unsolvable. A crippled person cannot regain her original capacities, and this kind of problem must be accepted. Casework would include getting such a person to realistically accept her limitations as well as positive efforts to minimize the range of such limitations through physical therapy and vocational rehabilitation. Casework should reach for as many problem solutions as possible, but there will always be persons who, unfortunately, have no choice but to accept certain problem conditions.

Recognizing the caseworker's responsibilities for achieving behavior change as far as possible, the social broker and advocacy functions have been increasingly stressed. Social brokerage entails serving as an intermediary between the client and existing services he needs; Meyer feels this will be the major function of the caseworker of the future.[22] Brokerage facilitates change by maximizing the resources the client has available for use, and implicitly recognizes the dependence of the individual on his social environment. A mother whose children manifest behavior problems may be faced with inadequate housing, no husband and father, lack of protection from criminal influences in the neighborhood, and so on. In such a situation, the caseworker may wish to review the mother's personality resources and child-rearing techniques. However, she would also want to explore more adequate housing resources, such as public housing; possible resources to provide a male influence for the children, such as Big Brothers or the Police Athletic League; recreational facilities to offer the children a wholesome play environment, such as the "Y" or a settlement house. Here the caseworker is attacking a problem by tying the client into the full range of resources available to help solve her problem.

In cases where adequate resources simply do not exist, the caseworker may need to assume an advocacy role. As an advocate, one is concerned with "uncovering both incipient and unmet needs and blazing a trail of advocacy toward new methods of meeting those needs."[23] The advocacy role acknowledges that each individual is dependent on his social environment even more than the broker role does. The advocate believes that some individual change can only be accomplished by changing the environment that is creating the problems or inhibiting constructive change. For example, when unemployment rates are high, and when a society has moved beyond the need for extensive unskilled labor, the two forces combine to push a large number of unskilled persons into involuntary unemployment and poverty. The solutions lie in changes in societal values regarding work, in alleviating those conditions that create unskilled persons, and in a public assistance system whose level of payments keeps people from living in poverty. These are changes that cannot be accomplished by talking to those with the problems. They must be solved by an advocate willing to work in the appropriate economic and political systems. (See Exhibit 6-7.)

GROUP WORK "When one gets down to the central core of what really happens that makes the group experience so meaningful and so useful, one discovers the simple truth that people with similar interests, similar concerns, or similar problems can help each other in ways that are significantly different from the ways in which a worker can help them in a one-to-one relationship. This is not to say that the group method is better—simply that it is different."[24] Put another way, "the group is the mediator between the individual and society. . . . Man can join with others in an effort to control what is happening to him."[25] The differences between casework and group work begin to emerge: (1) casework is usually a one-to-one relationship, while group work involves a worker and a small group of clients; (2) the worker-client relationship is the important process in casework, while in group work the group itself is the context and the process through which change occurs; and (3) casework and group work are methods with different requirements, and are most effective in the solution of different types of problems.

Group work builds on casework in that the group worker uses casework skills in relating to individual group members. It goes beyond casework when such relationships are supplemented by the interaction between group members, and as the structure of group activity generates social resources much greater than those available in a two-person group. Casework is more suited to problems involving extensive data-gathering, the discussion of strongly held feelings, and individual resource utilization. Group work is particularly effective in teaching interaction skills, achieving group goals, and providing recreation opportunities.

The American Association of Group Workers defines group work as follows:

The group worker enables various groups to function in such a way that both group interaction and program activities contribute to the growth of the individual and the achievement of desirable social goals.[26]

The basic professional goal of group work is helping people function, and many aspects of the group process may be used to attain this goal. Wilson draws a distinction between groups with two distinct purposes:

> In [the task-oriented group], the group-enabler's primary responsibility is to support the group to accomplish its task; in [the growth-oriented group], the enabler's primary responsibility is to help members to use the group experience to resolve problems which are interfering with their personal growth and their social adjustment.[27]

Groups may exist, then, to accomplish group goal attainment or the social enjoyment and enrichment of its members. Wilson's emphasis on primary function suggests that one function may be dominant at any given time. However, she also implicitly recognizes that there are elements of both goals in all groups, as one would expect from the small-group literature reviewed earlier. Wilson also speaks of the professional person as an enabler in the group process. This concept is of great importance in interventive methods, and grows out of the professional value of client self-determination. Rather than imposing personal judgments on the clients, either individual or group, the worker helps the clients identify and develop knowledge and skills appropriate for the attainment of their goals.

Elaborating somewhat on Wilson, groups may be seen as focusing around member enjoyment (interest), the attainment of a specific goal through concerted group organization (concerns), or the use of the group as a therapeutic milieu (problems). As would be expected on the basis of small-group theory, different kinds of groups will have different structural characteristics. Vinter suggests that one needs to examine the following structural properties of a group to be aware of its purpose and potential: the social organization of the group patterns, roles, and statuses; activities, tasks, and operative processes; group culture, norms, and values; and the group's relationship to its external environment.[28] An example of the utility of this kind of analysis is Rapoport's identification of the following structural characteristics of therapeutic (problem-oriented) groups: democratization of decision-making; permissiveness in the discussion of behavioral problems; communalistic, tight-knit, intimate relationships; and confrontation, the use of the group as social reality.[29]

Such a structural analysis helps to understand how the group affects individual behavior, and helps identify goals consistent with the group's structure. In both Vinter and Rapoport the importance of external reality for the group is emphasized. No matter how significant the group may become for its members, they ultimately must transfer their new-found skills to the larger social world beyond the group. Even the group itself is affected by the environment in which it exists. For example, there may be organizational restraints in therapeutic groups, limited recreational facilities for pleasure groups, and a lack of appropriate community structures for groups seeking to achieve goals.[30]

Tropp attempts to integrate these elements of group structure and functioning into an analytical framework that focuses on group purpose ("why it is formed"), group function ("what the group members are supposed to do to carry out the purpose"), and group structure (how the group will do what it is supposed to be doing).[31] He proposes that purpose, function, and structure be used as tools with which to evaluate interventive approaches in group work. The approaches that Tropp considers the most common in contemporary practice are: group education, including orientation and information programs aimed at a group of people with a common interest (such as informing parents about adolescent drug use); group counseling, where a group discusses a problem common to all its members (as when parents of retarded children meet to discuss ways of coping with their special child-rearing problems); group psychotherapy, which is "a group method for the treatment of individuals with psychiatric disorders, and . . . aims at achieving basic personality change, which none of the other group approaches attempts"[32] (a very specialized therapeutic approach); group recreation, where group members enjoy informal, play-oriented interaction; and social group work, defined as "the process known as group-goal achieving . . . , [which] aims at the full utilization of forces in group life to bring about social growth in individual members."[33] Tropp concludes with the following: "The group work method thus includes, in addition to goal-achieving by the group, the dimensions of group recreation, group education, and group counseling, but any of these methods can be used separately."[34] In concluding this brief discussion of group work, the range of goals this method may be used to attain is worthy of emphasis, as is the relationship of group work to many of the skills discussed under casework. However, in addition to casework skills, the group worker must deal with the many social processes involved in group structure and interaction.[35]

COMMUNITY ORGANIZATION

Since communities are types of groups, community organization may be seen as an expanded form of group work. The latter typically deals with groups of fifteen and under, and the former with larger groups functioning in community contexts. This size distinction has inevitable implications: therapeutic goals are more difficult to attain, while task-oriented goals are more feasible. However, the attainment of goals assumes that a structure exists through which such goals may be sought, and this may not be the case in many communities. This gives rise to two major thrusts in community organization: (1) a task focus, in which the attainment of a community need is emphasized (a new playground, more social service agencies, political redistricting, and the like); and (2) a process focus, where the emphasis is on the building of viable, effective community structures in which people can work to accomplish their goals.[36] This latter focus is sometimes called "community development," in an effort to distinguish between the two major parts of community organization.[37] Actually the task and process distinctions that tend to surface in community organization underlie all social welfare practice. Any interventive method attempts to solve specific problems while also trying to make it possible for the individual or individuals involved to be better able to solve the problems of the future.

Murray Ross's definition can be used to summarize community organization. He sees it as "a process by which a community identifies its needs or objectives, orders (or ranks) these needs or objectives, develops the confidence and will to work at these needs or objectives, finds the resources (internal and/or external) to deal with these needs or objectives, takes action in respect to them, and in so doing extends and develops cooperative and collaborative attitudes and practices in the community."[38] In discussing the nature of communities in an earlier chapter, it was seen that community organization actually involves working with shifting population groups. Their basis of organization may be of many kinds, or nonexistent, and they may be strongly influenced by forces outside the community. These factors intimate that the tranquility of Ross's definition of community organization may be unrealistic, although the general goals of identifying problems and resources for purposes of community action are sound.

There are many ways to approach the process of community organization; the following is comprehensive enough to encompass most others. First, the community must be identified. Drawing on earlier content, this must include geographical as well as functional dimensions. Second, community resources need to be identified; they may be of many kinds.[39] The groups within the community have their own social, physical, and organizational resources, which may be of potential use to the community at large. The geographical characteristics of the community create certain kinds of potential for recreation, industry, services, and so on. The physical organization is also crucial for the juxtaposition of various kinds of resources with the needs that may exist in the community. The community power structure can be a functional resource usable by social welfare practitioners, although the relationship of social welfare agencies to the community structure is an important intervening consideration.[40] The question of types of community power structures is a hotly debated one in the social science literature, but whatever the structure in a given community, those individuals who have leadership positions or potential can be of great utility to the community organizer.[41]

A third step in the community organization process is identifying the problems that exist and for which there is a realistic chance of solution using community organization principles. Given that communities are commonly diverse in social composition, the various community components are likely to have their own definitions of existing problems, as well as their own order of priority for problem solution. In assessing stated problems, one wants to be sure to give all community groups a chance to express their views. The extent to which there is uniformity or competing views on significant problems (and the order of priority in their solution) can then be assessed. After having done this, the practitioner will want to: (1) examine the extent to which there may be unexpressed problems that must be confronted before the expressed problems can be solved; and (2) the possible existence of problems ignored by the community. The question of problems ignored by the community can be a delicate one, since the worker should not try to force his views on a community. However, he may also recognize the potential impact of existing behavior and organization more fully than community members, he is less bound by community and subgroup values that may block community recognition of certain problems, and he is more likely to be concerned with the effects of community functioning on individuals and groups with no avenue of self-expression. The degree to which the worker chooses to introduce his perception of existing problems is part of his strategy (discussed below), although he can always try to get the community to recognize a previously unrecognized problem, without his direct intervention.

Having studied the community, the worker begins the actual organization process. It is common to begin with a clearly specified task that has a high probability of successful accomplishment. This helps establish the belief that change is possible, and draws people into a "winning team."[42] In some respects this can be seen as a community-level expression of the value "start where the client is." Then one must begin with a workable group, those who are willing to participate and who have relevance to the tasks at hand. It is important not to alienate those not participating at the outset. The initial organization should be as nonantagonistic as possible, and leave the way open for the participation of others at a later time as that becomes feasible and desirable. With a task set and a working group organized, the strategy for attainment of the established goal becomes crucial. For some time community organizers automatically tended to think in terms of cooperative and conciliatory strategies that were clearly within the established community power structures. Rocking the boat was to be avoided for several reasons: fear that insurgent groups did not have the power to force the power structure to change; fear that the social welfare agencies involved in power tactics would be punished through withdrawal of community sanction and funds; and an ingrained respect for due process of law.

Several significant events changed these perceptions, and helped to make Ross's view of community organization as a tranquil, orderly process somewhat limited. First, as Michael Harrington and others pointed out, after decades of sporadic social reform, major social problems remained. Second, the black revolution made it abundantly clear that aggressive community organization brought results that more passive, agreeable methods did not. Third, the black experience also stimulated more direct federal involvement in what were essentially community organization activities, so that the participants would be given some protection from retribution from the local community power structure. Fourth, the swelling magnitude of need threatened to topple many existing programs unless newer programs, more efficient and more acceptable to the recipients, were developed. Finally, the social welfare professions recognized that human need transcended job security, so that the risk of retribution against agencies and practitioners had to be run if programs consonant with professional values were to be obtained.[43]

Community organization thus rapidly expanded its range of possible strategies to adapt to a variety of new community conditions and needs.

Ralph Kramer, in his *Participation of the Poor*, examines the experiences of several San Francisco Bay area communities in promoting maximum feasible participation of the poor in community action.[44] Out of these experiences, he develops three strategies: collaboration, campaign, and contest,[45] which Specht extends to include violence.[46] (1) Collaboration is rational and democratic, with an attempt made to get the facts and reconcile viewpoints. Common interests are assumed, and a problem-solving model is appropriate. This strategy clearly falls within Ross's definition, and is usable in many

EXHIBIT 7-3

Strategies and Tactics

Specht presents the following chart in his article on "Disruptive Tactics." It relates strategies (each of which he calls a "mode of intervention") with specific behavioral tactics. It gives a concrete idea of the actual practitioner behaviors one could use.

Mode of Intervention	Tactics	Mode of Intervention	Tactics
1. Collaborative	a. joint action b. cooperation c. education	3. Contest or Disruption	a. clash of position within accepted norms b. violation of normative behavior (manners) c. violation of legal norms
2. Campaign	a. compromise b. arbitration c. negotiation d. bargaining e. mild coercion	4. Violence	a. deliberate attempts to harm b. guerilla warfare c. deliberate attempts to take over government by force

Reprinted by permission of the National Association of Social Workers, from Harry Specht, "Disruptive Tactics," *Social Work* 14 (April 1969): 9.

instances where it is simply a matter of getting a community to make choices about common goals and means. (2) A campaign is a planned effort to overcome apathy and moderate opposition when there is a difference of opinion on issues. It is assumed that agreement is possible, but that its attainment will involve an exchange of valued resources in return for concessions, rather than just calling for discussion. (3) The contest involves the temporary abandonment of the quest for consensus in order to further one's own side of an issue, despite opposition of other groups. This is accomplished by coercive threats of disruption, and the pressure of public support and attention. It is used when there is dissent (no congruence on values or interests), and agreement is not expected. (4) Specht sees violence as a relevant strategy when there is a need for the reconstruction of the entire system. Exhibit 7-3 summarizes Specht's analysis of strategies and tactics.

Important parts of the strategy decision concern the worker's role and the social welfare agency's organizational goals. Rein and Morris look at the latter,[47] while Grosser examines the former.[48] Grosser sees four possible worker roles: enabler, broker, advocate, and activist. The enabler role is "the traditional stance of the community organizer,"[49] recognizing that the community organization practitioner avoids imposing his ideas on the community. Self-help is emphasized instead. As a role it is limited in its activism, and seems to be most compatible with a collaborative strategy. The broker role sees the worker as an intermediary between service structures and their users. In community organization contexts, the community is both service structure and user, with brokerage also needed between the community and external structures. The advocate role is described as "a partisan in a social conflict, and his expertise is available exclusively to serve client interests. The impartiality of the enabler and the functionalism of the broker are absent here."[50] The broker and advocate roles seem most compatible with a campaign strategy. The activist encourages client groups to take direct action to attain their goals, and is most compatible with a contest strategy. For agencies, workers, and communities, then, appropriate roles and strategies must reflect community organization goals.[51]

The fifth and final community organization technique is to follow through to make sure that the community neither becomes too easily satisfied nor prematurely discouraged. When some goals have been attained, there is a tendency to relax and feel that the battle has been won. Lack of goal attainment may lead to discouragement and lack of interest. In both cases momentum is lost, and the community organization enterprise put in jeopardy. Once momentum is lost, it may be doubly hard to regain in the future, so the practitioner needs to be especially sensitive to premature cessation of effort and momentum. Rosenberg has noted at least eleven barriers to success of which the community organization worker must be aware.[52]

1. Passivity, whereby the brains, decisions, or influence of others are relied on.

2. Apathy, when people feel that they do not belong and nobody cares about them.

3. Prestige-seekers, where self-glorification is more important than the end result.

4. Superiority complex, in which groups refuse to cooperate with others said to be inferior in some way.

5. Vested interests, when change is resisted because it might be personally disadvantageous.

6. Intense specialization, leading to fragmented tasks, specialists, and overadministration.

7. Time shortage, in which responsibility is avoided due to other commitments.

8. Autocratic approach, where democracy is spoken but not enacted.

9. Inferiority complexes, lack of confidence by an individual or a community.

10. No skills, so basic information is lacking.

11. Dreamless peace, the obstacle of no vision of a better community.

Hopefully at this point several ways of avoiding these problems occur to the reader on the basis of previously discussed theory and interventive methods.

ADMINISTRATION,
MANAGEMENT,
AND RESEARCH

In addition to casework, group work, and community organization, administration is often considered an important social work interventive method. As social welfare programs have become more and more complex, administration has become increasingly essential for the effective use of resources and for effective planning. However, administration has typically referred to a hierarchical kind of supervision which, although important, only deals with part of what is a larger need for the effective management of resources. Therefore, the term management will be used rather than administration in this discussion so that a broader range of management skills may be examined.

When discussing formal organizations and their effect on the structure of social welfare services in Chapter 3, it was noted that such organizations require careful planning so that means and goals relate to each other. We also saw that such organizations are characterized by hierarchical organization in which authority and responsibility generally flow from higher positions to those lower down in the organizational chart. This model is applicable to the majority of social welfare organizations.[53] The typical department of social services has a director, other administrative personnel, supervisors, workers, and support staff such as secretaries. The ultimate responsibility for organizing these people, and the resources they need for performing their tasks, is vested in the director. She must also work with specified planning groups at the community, county, state, and national levels when formulating agency policy and securing resources.

The kinds of administrative tasks just discussed are essential if the resources—human and financial—which society makes available for the performance of large-scale, complex social welfare services are to be properly managed. However, the management of resources takes place at practically all other levels of the organization, an idea which the professional model helps to make explicit. In a profession, there is considerable autonomy and internal control by the professional group itself. One of the implications of this is that each professional has considerable responsibility for effectively managing her own work load and resources. For example, a social worker is assigned a caseload and a supervisor. The worker must then decide such questions as how to allocate her time between cases, how often to confer with the supervisor and for what purposes, how many appointments to make out of the office, and how much time to spend in a given interview. In a sense, then, each professional person is an administrator, making decisions about policy and resource utilization within his own sphere.[54]

Any management attempt must be bolstered by data that measures the results of a given action or policy. Just as an agency must know how much it costs to provide services for how many persons, so an individual worker must know how much time is being spent filling out forms rather than interviewing clients. Data collection and analysis, the process of research, is generally thought of as highly formal. Much of it is, as when a sociologist like Jacqueline Wiseman does a study of skid-row alcoholics (see Exhibit 1-3). Individual workers, however, are constantly collecting data as they interview clients, talk with other professionals, and process forms. Throughout all of these tasks, they are exposed to data which are relevant to the question of how effective their activity is and what tasks remain to be done (either by themselves, by their agency, by some other agency, or by society). The problem generally arises because the worker never takes the time to systematically organize the data and analyze it. Although the data concerning the use of time during the working day may be part of a worker's calendar, the data may never be analyzed to discover that more time is being spent filling out forms than providing services to clients.

Management and research are skills that pervade the helping effort. Agency administration and planning by specialized administrators will always be important to the development and carrying out of an effective social welfare structure. However, developing management and research skills by all professionals is also important if the day-to-day, increasingly complex activities they perform are to be effectively organized. In talking about accountability in Chapter 3, the importance of being able to demonstrate effectiveness was discussed. Research is a major way in which this is done, but it in turn is only as effective as the planning that makes data available. Professional helping persons need to be much more aware of the need for data. They must also accept responsibility for managing their resources —knowledge, time, skill, and all the rest—so the resulting data demonstrate that social welfare makes a significant difference in helping people to function more effectively.

Teare and McPheeters,[55] and Bisno,[56] have cogently discussed the problems of the traditional approach to interventive methods. They note that focusing on methods encourages a restricted view of problems and solutions, and tends to lead the worker to be more concerned with his own methodological and bureaucratic problems than with the needs of the people he is trying to help. Bisno emphasizes these problems in the traditional approach by quoting Kaplan on the "law of the instrument":

> I call it *the law of the instrument,* and it may be formulated as follows: Give a small boy a hammer, and he will find that everything he encounters needs pounding. It comes as no particular surprise to discover that a scientist formulates problems in a way which requires for their solution just those techniques in which he himself is especially skilled.[57]

Bisno, in suggesting that the "law of the instrument" is applicable to social welfare practice, is saying that a worker's identification with one interventive method tends to limit her view of appropriate intervention techniques to that method. He believes that it would be more productive to begin with an analysis of the problem, and include all the possible ways to solve such a problem. Aside from the practical limitations of the "law of the instrument," Bisno also provides a thoughtful analysis of some of the theoretical problems growing out of the traditional approach.[58]

In developing a new perspective on interventive methods, Teare and McPheeters begin with the problem rather than the job. Once the problems have been defined and categorized, they focus on the tasks that could help to solve these problems. Then a rational way to group the designated tasks is developed.[59] This approach focuses on client needs, and allows the professional to distinguish clearly between the needs of the client, the professional, and the organization, all of which are important in the interventive process. The difference in approach, then, between the methods approach and the newer problem approach to interventive methods lies in the fact that the former often forces a problem into the method, while the latter tries to shape a method to solve a given problem.

Traditional marital counseling, for example, is commonly done by psychiatrically oriented professionals who talk to the couple and possibly their children in an office setting. The problem approach might try to identify the components of the marital problem and use a range of interventive approaches. These could include psychiatric counseling, reaching out into the community to find or develop recreational outlets for the children, helping the husband find job training or better employment to ease financial burdens, and mobilizing the couple and their neighbors to improve housing, since these issues can all be components of what is termed a marital problem. This comparison does not imply that the methods approach has been ineffective, but it does suggest that in many cases new perspectives can approach intervention in a more task-focused, flexible, creative manner than traditional approaches.

In attempting to identify the major problem areas requiring social welfare intervention, Teare and McPheeters list the following: health, education, employment, integrity of the family, money and financial resources, and integrity of the neighborhood and community.[60] The obstacles creating problems in these areas can be any of the following: deficiencies within individuals ("lack of education or training, inappropriate values, personal instability, poor physical health"); environmental deficiencies ("lack of resources or lack of access to them"); rigid or inequitable laws, regulations, policies, and practices (discriminatory practices, restrictive eligibility requirements, fraudulent contracts); and results of catastrophes.[61] Given these major problem areas and obstacles, four general functions of social welfare for meeting the identified needs are suggested by Teare and McPheeters: (1) promoting positive social functioning (promoting self-actualization); (2) preventing problems from occurring (providing accessible resources and developing skills in using these resources); (3) providing treatment (helping persons solve their problems); and (4) providing maintenance support for those unable to solve their problems.[62]

With the major problem areas, obstacles, and general goals of intervention specified, Teare and McPheeters develop nine "major objectives to social welfare activity," which can in turn be translated into specific tasks and ultimately clusters of tasks.[63]

1. *Detection*—"to identify the individuals or groups who are experiencing difficulty [at crisis] or who are in danger of becoming vulnerable [at risk] ... [and] to detect and identify conditions in the environment that are contributing to the problems or are raising the level of risk."[64]

2. *Linkage or Connection*—"to steer people toward the existing services which can be of benefit to them. ... A further objective is to link elements of the service system with one another."[65]

3. *Advocacy*—"to fight for the rights and dignity of people in need of help ... [including] fighting for services on behalf of a single client, and ... fighting for changes in laws, regulations, etc. on behalf of a whole class of persons or segment of the society. Therefore, advocacy aims at removing the obstacles or barriers that prevent people from exercising their rights or receiving the benefits and using the resources they need."[66]

4. *Mobilization*—"to assemble and energize existing groups, resources, organizations, and structures, or to create new groups, organizations or resources and bring them to bear to deal with problems that exist, or to prevent problems from developing."[67]

5. *Instruction-Education*—"to convey and impart information and knowledge and to develop various kinds of skills."[68]

6. *Behavior Change and Modification*—"to bring about change in the behavior patterns, habits and perceptions of individuals or groups."[69]

7. *Information Processing*—"the collection, classification, and analysis of data generated within the social welfare environment."[70]

8. *Administration*—"the management of a facility, an organization, a program, or a service unit."[71]

9. *Continuing Care*—"to provide for persons who need on-going support or care on an extended and continuing basis ... in an institutional setting or on an out-patient basis."[72]

In looking at the problem areas of concern to social welfare practitioners, and some of the obstacles commonly encountered in dealing with them, Teare and McPheeters set the parameters within which interventive methods must be effective. They then go on to discuss general functions of social welfare within these parameters, and finally the specific objectives of interventive methods. It should be clear that they have not yet spoken of actual methods to be used in achieving the objectives, although by looking at the objectives one can see that a social welfare practitioner's tools must include the following skills: (1) to identify needs in the community; (2) to link those in need with services available; (3) to insure that services are accessible to those in need; (4) to utilize all possible community resources; (5) to participate in the development of new services; (6) to administer and monitor services; and (7) to change or support behavior as appropriate. Since these objectives are not mutually exclusive (for example, a social welfare practitioner may change behavior by helping a client find and use available services), the specific methods used to achieve these objectives may be grouped into varying combinations, depending on the objectives being sought. This introduces the need not only to specify the methods necessary to attain professional objectives, but also the need to consider ways in which objectives and methods may be grouped into clusters.

Teare and McPheeters identify twelve "roles," tasks which the professional helping person may perform as she develops an interventive strategy to work with the person seeking help to solve a problem.[73]

Outreach worker. Reaching out into the community to identify need and to make sure referrals to other appropriate agencies are followed through. It is known that many people need and are eligible for services, but either do not know about them or are blocked from reaching them, such as old people who have no transportation, minority-group members who fear harassment, and people of many kinds who believe there is a stigma attached to accepting help. The outreach worker attempts to identify persons in need, and then help them to identify and reach social welfare services that can meet their need.

Broker. Knowing what services are available and making sure those in need reach the appropriate services. One of the results of the increased scope, complexity, and bureaucratization of social welfare services has been increased confusion and frustration experienced by users. The family doctor and house calls are things of the past. Large numbers of specialists now provide more expert but more impersonal treatment than did the general family practitioner. When emergencies arise, it is necessary to go to the emergency room of the nearest hospital, where treatment first depends on filling out certain required forms. Indeed, in many communities it is difficult to find a doctor who will accept new patients, so the person seeking medical attention may not know where to turn for help. The broker helps to deal with these problems, directing persons in need to available and appropriate services, explaining procedures, and providing assistance and support when procedures are lengthy and complicated.

Advocate. Helping clients obtain services when they might otherwise be rejected, and helping to expand services to cover more needy persons. The history of some social services, such as Aid to Families with Dependent Children, has been fraught with attempts to deprive potential recipients of their rights to the service for a host of usually moralistic excuses. The advocate works with such persons to insure that they receive the services to which they are entitled when they apply. Advocates also seek to expand services to meet the needs of groups whose needs are not being met with existing programs.

Evaluation. Evaluating needs and resources, generating alternative ways of meeting needs, and making choices among alternatives. There is an on-going need for professionally trained persons to monitor the effects of existing programs, and to develop more effective ways to meet needs. The project undertaken by the League of Women Voters to monitor the effectiveness of revenue sharing in improving social welfare services, reported in Chapter 2 (footnote 61), is an example of the need to evaluate the effectiveness of a program.

Teacher. Teaching facts and skills. When discussing the helping relationship earlier in this chapter, it was seen that the helping person provides empathy and support to the person seeking help. Part of the support commonly offered is information needed to make a decision, and the development of skills to use in problem-solving—greater insight into one's own behavior, appropriate behavior and dress when having a job interview, child-rearing and homemaker skills, and so forth.

Mobilizer. Helping to utilize existing services most effectively. Many persons and groups have potential resources that can be coordinated to develop more effective social welfare services. The mobilizer helps such persons and groups to accomplish this. For example, residents of a public housing project may feel that the project manager is providing inadequate janitorial and security services. If the manager refuses to provide more adequate services required by the residents, they may not know other techniques to get the manager to act. A mobilizer can help the project residents to understand the power they have in numbers, and the various strategies available to them to encourage positive action by the manager—such as rent strikes, sit-ins in his office, contacting other city officials, and picketing, to name a few possibilities.

Behavior-changer. Changing specific parts of a client's behavior. This is perhaps the closest role to traditional methods approaches, and would be exemplified by a psychologist who used a behavior modification program to end a child's bed-wetting.

Care-giver. Providing supportive services to those who cannot fully solve their problems and meet their own needs. Sometimes helping people to function more effectively must of necessity mean helping them simply to be more physically comfortable or to adjust to a permanently impaired level of functioning. For example, helping professionals who work with the aged in nursing homes generally have goals that focus on maintaining some level of physical comfort and social interaction in the face of physical and mental deterioration.

Consultant. Working with other professionals to help them be more effective in providing services. Here again the professional's responsibility to the profession is raised, with each professional utilizing his knowledge and skills for the benefit of other professionals as well as assisting persons and groups seeking help.

Community planner. Helping community groups to plan effectively for the community's social welfare needs. The professional's specialized knowledge base combines with her daily experience to make such persons among the most informed and concerned about a wide range of community structures, community needs, and community resources. Professional social welfare persons have a responsibility to participate in community planning and decision-making structures so that their expertise will help the clients they represent have their needs met.

Data manager. Collection and analysis of data for decision-making purposes. The massive scope and complexity of the contemporary social welfare system makes sophisticated data collection a necessity if the system is to be properly evaluated. Rational decision-making is based on such data, as, for example, Social Security benefit levels are raised to keep pace with increases in the cost of living.

Administrator. The activities necessary to plan and implement a program of services. This may occur at the agency, community, state, and national levels and should be based on information provided by data managers and consultants. The scope and complexity of the contemporary social welfare system makes rational, carefully planned and structured administration a necessity. It is also well to reemphasize at this point the relationship of administration to management as discussed elsewhere in this chapter.

Having developed the above roles, Teare and McPheeters do not suggest clusters of roles to achieve any of their earlier noted objectives. They do note that in general a practitioner would use several of these roles (a generalist) rather than specializing in only one (a specialist).[74] They apparently intend that their role clusters remain flexible, consistent with their assertion that an interventive plan must be built around the desired objectives. In their words, "the rationale for grouping roles into single jobs will depend to some degree on client needs and to some degree on agency goals."[75]

As much as Teare and McPheeters's roles should remain closely related to objectives, there is both theoretical and practical justification for looking at some of the role clusters that could be expected to occur with some frequency. From a theoretical perspective, the roles clearly grow out of the objectives sought, so any time a specified type of objective is sought, the roles appropriate to that objective will be used. For example, the use of the behavior-changer role will normally be used to alter self-destructive behavior of many types (i.e., a behavior-changer role to achieve a behavior-change objective). Practically speaking, bureaucratically organized welfare structures require some consistency in objectives and methods for purposes of program planning, recruitment, resource utilization, and so forth. In practice, then, any given service structure is likely to deal with a limited range of problems, objectives, and methods, with somewhat standard role clusters resulting. For purposes of rethinking the whole purpose and nature of therapeutic intervention in social welfare, the work of Teare and McPheeters is extremely important. However, its implementation requires attempts to organize their ideas into patterns that have theoretical and practical utility.[76] Two men have recently attempted to do this.

Ralph Dolgoff has built on the work of Teare and McPheeters in his discussion of "modes of strategic intervention."[77] He develops seven social welfare practice objectives, and then relates specific method clusters to them as follows:

Objectives	*Role Clusters*
1. Facilitating linkages and communication	Mediator, conciliator, broker
2. Rehabilitative and developmental	Enabler, helper, therapist, mobilizer
3. Supportive	Provider, care-giver
4. Instructional	Teacher, guide, expert
5. Detection and problem-finding	Initiator and outreach
6. Confrontation and social action	Advocate, adversary, activist, organizer
7. Research and disseminator of information	None specified

Although different in some details, Dolgoff's objectives and roles are quite closely related to those of Teare and McPheeters. For example, Dolgoff talks of an instructional objective and teacher, guide, and expert roles, while Teare and McPheeters think in terms of an instruction-education objective with, presumably, their roles of teacher, consultant, administrator, and community planner being appropriate. Dolgoff, then, suggests some appropriate role clusters for given service objectives.

Dolgoff states that an appropriate definition of the problem(s) is basic to the selection of objectives and modes of intervention. Once objectives have been defined, and a mode of intervention selected, the worker can choose the helping roles that are most appropriate. Thus, the skills of information-gathering, analysis, assessment, problem definition, strategy and role selec-

EXHIBIT 7-4

Bisno's Theoretical Framework

Problem	Role	Techniques
1. Actual or potential conflict of interest or purpose	Adversary	Negotiation, bargaining, conflict generation through articulation and advocacy of competing interests
2. Lessen or eliminate conflict or competition	Conciliatory	Compromise, maximize similarities and minimize differences, accept a subordinate position, clarify misinterpretation
3. Lack of resources or the desire to mobilize those that exist or are potentially usable	Developmental	Role-playing, coordination and establishment of new power centers in the community
4. Transmit professional skill and knowledge to others	Facilitative-Interactional	Advice-giving, lectures, staging, role-playing, serving as role model, giving performance evaluation
5. Lack of professional knowledge and need for evaluation	Knowledge Development & Testing	Theory-building and research skills
6. Restore a given level of social functioning	Restorative	Counseling, sensitivity training, provision of material resources
7. Need for regulation of behavior	Regulatory	Conditioning techniques, analysis, provision of information
8. Implementation of laws, policies, programs, procedures	Rule-Implementing	Administration, policy interpretation, translation of policy into programs
9. Formulate new rules, policies, laws	Rule-making	Legislative lobbying, debates, policy briefs, public statements

Based on material in Herbert Bisno, "A Theoretical Framework for Teaching Social Work Methods and Skills, with Particular Reference to Undergraduate Social Welfare Education," in Frank Loewenberg and Ralph Dolgoff, eds., *Teaching of Practice Skills in Undergraduate Programs in Social Welfare and Other Helping Services* (New York: Council on Social Work Education, 1971), pp. 78–82.

tion are all part of the problem-solving process. Dolgoff emphasizes the importance of problem definition and stresses the variety of potential strategies from which social workers can choose. The enactment of roles within various interventive approaches is the means by which persons, groups, families, and communities are to be helped. Dolgoff also suggests that most social workers need greater expertise at problem definition and need to be sensitized to the possibility of many different kinds of interventions. The more strategies and roles available (including the knowledge and values which underlie them), the more the worker can help people in problem situations.

Herbert Bisno has attempted to develop a unified framework that relates objectives, roles, and skills.[78] His framework begins with a problem, which is quite similar to the objective of Teare and McPheeters. He then proceeds to look at the role best suited to the solution of the problem, as well as some of the specific interventive techniques of which the role is comprised. A summary of Bisno's theoretical framework is illustrated in Exhibit 7-4.

There is a basic similarity between Teare and McPheeters, Dolgoff, and Bisno in their assessment of the significant elements of social welfare intervention. Exhibit 7-5 may help to make this clear. They all take a task approach, whereby the role is selected on the basis of the task to be performed, rather than starting with a method and fitting the task into it. Second, they suggest that specific roles must and should be combined, as necessary, to deal with the dimensions of the task at hand. Third, one can deduce from the first two points that social welfare training in the area of intervention skills should be generic. Every social welfare practitioner should have basic competence in these roles, rather than being trained only in one role or cluster.

The basic idea of generic training is not new in social welfare education. Traditional interventive methods have been taught so that every student had basic exposure to casework, group work, and community organization. However, each student also chose her specialization, and developed her professional identity as a specialized practitioner. The new perspectives summarized in Exhibit 7-5 do not solve this problem, since it is not at all certain how these roles can all be taught and how much expertise is needed in each. Yet it is clear that a great deal of methodological flexibility will be required in a practice environment in which methods adapt to problems. Even considering that agencies tend to specialize in certain problems or problem groups (unwed mothers, marital problems, crime, and so on), problems often come in multiproblem clusters, and workers do move to different agencies. Because the problem approach in intervention is relatively new, details need to be worked out; however, the concepts underlying this approach are important.

CONCLUSION   The work of Teare and McPheeters, Dolgoff, and Bisno suggests a general overview of the interventive process. First, problems must be identified, requiring one to reach out into communities to find the problems with which people are struggling, individually and collectively. This can be accomplished

EXHIBIT 7-5

A Comparison of Teare and McPheeters, Dolgoff, and Bisno: Their Frameworks for Analyzing Intervention in Social Welfare

OBJECTIVES-PROBLEMS			ROLES			TECHNIQUES
Teare-McPheeters	Dolgoff	Bisno	Teare-McPheeters	Dolgoff	Bisno	Bisno
Detection	Detection and Problem finding	None specified	Outreach	Initiator-Outreach	None specified	None specified
Linkage or Connection	Facilitating linkages and communication	Eliminate conflict	Broker-Outreach	Mediator-Conciliator, Broker	Concilitory	Compromise, clarification, minimize differences, be subordinate
Advocacy	Confrontation and social action	Potential conflict, new policy	Advocate, Community planner	Advocate-Adversary-Activist-Organizer	Adversary, Rule-making	Negotiation, bargaining, conflict generation, lobbying, debates
Mobilization	None specified	Lack of resources, use of those existing	Mobilizer-Broker	None specified	Developmental	Role-playing, co-ordinate and establish new power centers
Instruction-Education	Instructional	Transmit knowledge and skills	Teacher-Consultant, Community planner	Teacher-Guide-Expert	Facilitative-Interactional	Role-playing, lectures, role-modeling, advice, performance evaluation
Behavior change	Rehabilitative and Developmental	Restore given level of functioning, regulative behavior	Behavior-changer	Enabler-Helper-Therapist-Mobilizer	Restorative, Regulatory	Counseling, conditioning, material resource use, provision of information, sensitivity use, analysis
Information processing	Research and Dissemination of information	Need for knowledge, evaluation	Evaluator-Data manager	None specified	Knowledge development and testing	Theory-building and research skills
Administration		Implementing policy	Administrator-Consultant	None specified	Rule implementing	Administration, policy-planning and interpretation
Continuing care	Supportive	None specified	Care-giver	Provider-Care-giver	None specified	None specified

by actually seeking out people in their environment, or by using the power of statistical fact to document need. Second, an evaluation of resources at all levels—individual, community, social welfare agencies, and society as a whole—must be accomplished to understand when needs can be met with existing resources and when new resources are necessary. This requires a diagnostic ability to understand individuals and groups, a sound knowledge of the social welfare service structure, and a grasp of the effects of societal values and structures on various types of problems. After evaluating resources and needs, the third and fourth steps are the joining of those in need with those who can meet the need, and then working to establish ways in which the unmet needs of the present can be met in the future.

A fifth step entails working with an individual or group to locate the best resource once the problem is identified. This may involve considerable behavior change, or it may be a long-term dependency on the resource. In either case it requires that the practitioner has considerable knowledge of psychological, biological, and personality variables and processes. A sixth and final part of the interventive process is the recognition that every practitioner has the responsibility for generating support for new and better resources, sharing his skills with others, cooperating with other professionals and nonprofessionals, and enhancing his own personal self-awareness and growth. The great value of the new perspectives on interventive methods discussed in this chapter is not only the explication of these basic interventive procedures in some detail, but also the assertion that every professional is involved to some extent in all of them.

Some mention should be made of the relationship between intervention as it is practiced in a methods approach and as it is practiced in a problem approach. The basic interventive skills involved are not really that different, although the manner in which they are selected and organized can be quite different. For example, many of the techniques developed by Bisno and presented in Exhibit 7-4 are ones used in casework, group work, and community organization—role-playing, theory-building, research, administration, counseling, conditioning, and policy-planning can specifically be mentioned. Bisno does suggest that their traditionally fragmented, ideological organization minimizes their effectiveness in many cases, but he does not suggest that they are inappropriate or useless. However, the skills used in the traditional methods focused approach are broadened as well, especially in terms of conflict, legislative involvement, outreach, and brokerage.

Even though there is a tradition of social action in social welfare work, for decades methods have been intellectualized and rather detached from legislative and conflict contexts. There has also been some middle-class withdrawal from the horrible conditions under which many needy persons live their lives. Bisno and others are again supporting the use of conflict, when necessary, to insure the rights of the needy; they are reaffirming the need to organize, and to make the legislative process as responsive to the needs of those who have *not* as well as those who *have;* and they are reaffirming the

EXHIBIT 7-6

An Approach to Problem-Focused Interventive Methods

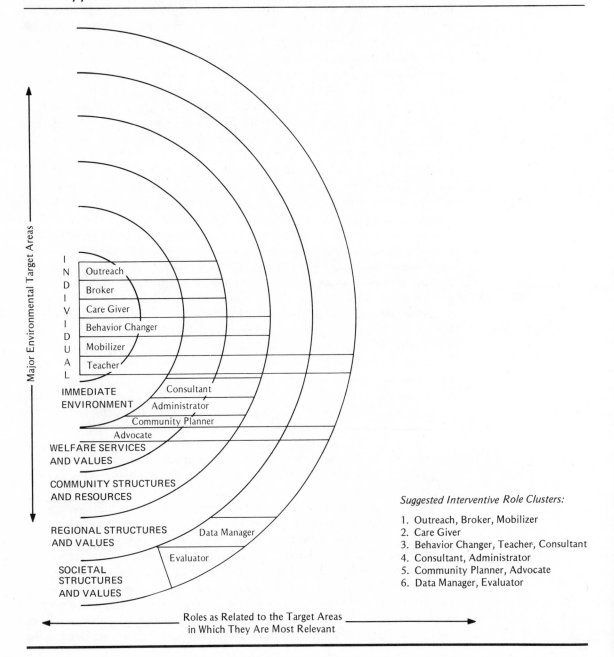

Major Environmental Target Areas

INDIVIDUAL

- Outreach
- Broker
- Care Giver
- Behavior Changer
- Mobilizer
- Teacher

IMMEDIATE
ENVIRONMENT

- Consultant
- Administrator
- Community Planner
- Advocate

WELFARE SERVICES
AND VALUES

COMMUNITY STRUCTURES
AND RESOURCES

REGIONAL STRUCTURES
AND VALUES

- Data Manager
- Evaluator

SOCIETAL
STRUCTURES
AND VALUES

Roles as Related to the Target Areas
in Which They Are Most Relevant

Suggested Interventive Role Clusters:

1. Outreach, Broker, Mobilizer
2. Care Giver
3. Behavior Changer, Teacher, Consultant
4. Consultant, Administrator
5. Community Planner, Advocate
6. Data Manager, Evaluator

basic humanity of all. The social welfare practitioner struggles with the needs of anyone who has need, rather than moving away from the unpleasant, the different, and the seemingly hopeless.

This chapter, then, must end where it began, with the on-going search for more effective interventive techniques to use in helping people solve their problems. Each professional helping person constantly struggles with this search. As a concluding example, Exhibit 7-6 presents logical clusters of roles as suggested by Teare and McPheeters. It represents this author's attempt to grapple with the search for better tools for helping.[79]

STUDY QUESTIONS

1. How would you define the ideal helping person? Include personal characteristics, knowledge possessed, and skills available to be used. If you aspire to be a social welfare professional, how do you rate yourself at present in terms of this ideal?

2. Go to a public place, such as a bus station, airport, or large post office, and observe the people you see. What kinds of different behaviors do you observe between those providing and receiving help? Select one person and try to observe as many things about him or her as you can. After doing so, try to construct a portrait of that person's life—where does he live? Is she married? What kind of work does she do? Is he happy or sad? How could you go about getting additional information about this person if you had to? (Be sure to consider the range of human and nonhuman resources you could use.)

3. What relationships can you see between the methods and problem-focused approaches to intervention? Do they involve different helping skills? Do they require different kinds of agency structures? Do they require professional persons with different kinds of training? Are they usable in similar situations, or is one more suited to certain kinds of problems and the other to different kinds? Which approach do you prefer? Why?

REFERENCES

1. Arthur Combs, Donald Avila, and William Purkey, *Helping Relationships: Basic Concepts for the Helping Professions* (Boston: Allyn and Bacon, 1971), p. 170.

2. Alan Keith-Lucas, *Giving and Taking Help* (Chapel Hill: University of North Carolina Press, 1972), p. 71. For his elaboration of these factors, see pp. 77–88.

3. Combs et al., op. cit., p. 170.

4. Keith-Lucas, op. cit., p. 65. The eight characteristics of helping relations are discussed in detail on pp. 47–65.

5. Ibid., p. 108.

6. Basic references for interviewing in social welfare are Annette Garrett, *Interviewing: Its Principles and Methods* (New York: Family Service Association of America, 1942); and Elizabeth and Karl de Schweinitz, *Interviewing in the Social Services* (London: National Institute for Social Work Training, 1962), pp. 9–11.

7. This discussion of interviewing principles draws heavily on ideas in Garrett, op. cit.

8. See Lydia Rapoport, "Crisis-Oriented Short-Term Casework," in Klenk and Ryan, eds., *The Practice of Social Work* (Belmont, Cal.: Wadsworth, 1970), p. 108.

9. A good reference for nonverbal communication is Edward T. Hall, *The Silent Language* (Garden City: Doubleday, 1959).

10. Roy Lubove, *The Professional Altruist* (Cambridge, Mass.: Harvard University Press, 1965), esp. pp. 1–54.

11. Ibid., p. 55.

12. Jane Addams, *Twenty Years at Hull House* (New York: New American Library, 1960), p. 98. See also pp. 90–100.

13. Russell Smith and Dorothy Zeitz, *American Social Welfare Institutions* (New York: John Wiley, 1970), p. 249.

14. Ibid.

15. Helen Harris Perlman, *Social Casework: A Problem-Solving Process* (Chicago: University of Chicago Press, 1957), pp. 6–7.

16. Ibid.

17. David Landy, "Problems of the Person Seeking Help in our Culture," in Mayer Zald, ed., *Social Welfare Institutions* (New York: John Wiley, 1965).

18. Talcott Parsons, *The Social System* (New York: Free Press, 1951), pp. 285–91, 476.

19. There are many good, standard books that describe casework. The Perlman text already mentioned is one. Two well-known books are Florence Hollis, *Casework: A Psychosocial Therapy* (2nd ed.; New York: Random House, 1972), and Carol Meyer, *Social Work Practice* (New York: Free Press, 1970). A concise discussion of the major casework concepts may be found in Jonathan Moffett, *Concepts in Casework Treatment* (New York: Humanities Press, 1968).

20. The concepts of therapeutic casework, and social broker and advocacy functions in casework, are based on Scott Briar's discussion in "The Current Crisis in Social Work," in Klenk and Ryan, op. cit., pp. 91–97.

21. Ibid., p. 91.

22. Meyer, op. cit., pp. 83–104.

23. Harry Specht, "Casework Practice and Social Policy Formulation," in Klenk and Ryan, op. cit., p. 131.

24. Emanuel Tropp, "The Group: In Life and in Social Work," in Klenk and Ryan, op. cit., pp. 176–77.

25. Janet Rosenberg, *Breakfast: Two Jars of Paste* (Cleveland: Case-Western Reserve University, 1969), p. 93.

26. Reproduced in Gisela Konopka, *Social Group Work: A Helping Process* (Englewood Cliffs, N.J.: Prentice-Hall, 1963), p. 14.

27. Gertrude Wilson, "Social Group Work: Trends and Developments," in Klenk and Ryan, op. cit., p. 170.

28. Smith and Zeitz, op. cit., pp. 253–54.

29. Ibid., p. 255.

30. The effect of the group's environment on its functioning is discussed in Lawrence Shulman, *A Casebook of Social Work with Groups: The Mediating Model* (New York: Council on Social Work Education, 1968), esp. pp. 23–30.

31. Emanuel Tropp, "The Group: In Life and in Social Work," in Klenk and Ryan, op. cit., p. 179.

32. Ibid., p. 182.

33. Ibid., p. 183. This total discussion is based on pp. 180–83.

34. Ibid., p. 183.

35. See Robert Vinter, "The Essential Components of Group Work Practice," in Paul Weinberger, ed., *Perspectives on Social Welfare: An Introductory Anthology* (New York: Macmillan, 1969).

36. See Arthur Dunham, *The New Community Organization* (New York: Thomas Y. Crowell, 1970), pp. 4, 86. His relationship goals would be included under process goals in the framework being used here.

37. For a more detailed discussion of the distinction between community organization and community development, see ibid., pp. 175–79.

38. Murray Ross, *Community Organization: Theory and Principles* (New York: Harper & Row, 1955), p. 39.

39. An excellent discussion of practical approaches to identifying community resources appears in Sy Kahn, *How People Get Power* (New York: McGraw-Hill, 1970), pp. 11–20.

40. See Mayer Zald, "Organizations as Politics: An Analysis of Community Organization Agencies," in Ralph Kramer and Harry Specht, eds., *Readings in Community Organization Practice* (Englewood Cliffs, N.J.: Prentice-Hall, 1969), pp. 143–54.

41. Kahn, op. cit., pp. 21–38. See also Richard Edgar, *Urban Power and Social Welfare* (Beverly Hills: Sage, 1970).

42. Ibid., pp. 57–67, esp. p. 62.

43. See Irwin Saunders, "Professional Roles in Planned Change," in Kramer and Specht, op. cit., pp. 269–84, esp. p. 277.

44. Ralph Kramer, *Participation of the Poor* (Englewood Cliffs, N.J.: Prentice-Hall, 1969), pp. 182–86.

45. Ibid., p. 184.

46. Harry Specht, "Disruptive Tactics," in Kramer and Specht, op. cit., pp. 372–86.

47. Martin Rein and Robert Morris, "Goals, Structures, and Strategies for Community Change," in Kramer and Specht, op. cit., pp. 188–200.

48. Charles Grosser, "Community Development Programs Serving the Urban Poor," in Klenk and Ryan, op. cit., pp. 266–75.

49. Ibid., p. 269.

50. Ibid., p. 271.

51. For further elaboration, see Kahn, op. cit., pp. 69–113.

52. Rosenberg, op. cit., pp. 115–16.

53. See Harry Schatz, ed., *Social Work Administration: A Resource Book* (New York: Council on Social Work Education, 1970).

54. Focusing on the teaching of management skills at all levels in professional functioning is relatively new. One resource for further study includes Southern Regional Education Board, *Administration and Management Curriculum Development for Undergraduate Social Welfare Workers: Sourcebook I* (Atlanta: the Board, 1974).

55. Robert Teare and Harold McPheeters, *Manpower Utilization in Social Welfare* (Atlanta: Southern Regional Education Board, 1970), pp. 4–8.

56. Herbert Bisno, "A Theoretical Framework for Teaching Social Work Methods and Skills, with Particular Reference to Undergraduate Social Welfare Education," in Frank Loewenberg and Ralph Dolgoff, eds., *Teaching of Practice Skills in Undergraduate Programs in Social Welfare and other Helping*

Services (New York: Council on Social Work Education, 1971), pp. 72–78, 84–85.

57. Ibid., p. 84.
58. Ibid., pp. 75–77.
59. Teare and McPheeters, op. cit., pp. 7–8.
60. Ibid., pp. 11, 66–70.
61. Ibid., p. 12.
62. Ibid., pp. 17–18.
63. Ibid., pp. 19–21.
64. Ibid., p. 20.
65. Ibid.
66. Ibid.
67. Ibid.
68. Ibid.
69. Ibid., pp. 20–21.
70. Ibid., p. 21.
71. Ibid.
72. Ibid.
73. Ibid., pp. 34–35.
74. Ibid., p. 37.
75. Ibid., p. 36.
76. Teare and McPheeters are emphatic in noting that their work is just a beginning, which will ultimately be developed in theory-building and practice contexts.
77. Ralph Dolgoff, "Basic Skills for Practice in the Human Services: A Curriculum Guide," in Loewenberg and Dolgoff, op. cit., p. 25. Reprinted by permission of the Council on Social Work Education.
78. Bisno, op. cit., pp. 78–82. Reprinted by permission of the Council on Social Work Education.
79. These ideas grew out of discussions with Winifred Thomet and a workshop operated by the Southern Regional Education Board (SREB), for whose help I am deeply grateful. Exhibit 7-6 was originally done in a slightly modified form for a paper entitled "Theoretical Bases for Interventive Methods," written as part of the SREB workshop mentioned above.

SELECTED READINGS

There is a huge body of literature on interventive methods. Much of it is vague and ideological, but much of the new material is stimulating and creative. These are among the clearest and most seminal.

Compton, Beulah, and Burt Galaway. *Social Work Processes.* Homewood, Ill.: Dorsey, 1975.

Frank, Jerome. *Persuasion and Healing.* Baltimore: Johns Hopkins Press, 1961.

Garrett, Annette. *Interviewing: Its Principles and Methods.* New York: Family Service Association of America, 1942.

Glasser, Paul, with Rosemary Sarri and Robert Vinter, eds. *Individual Change through Groups.* New York: Free Press, 1974.

Hollis, Florence. *Casework: A Psychosocial Therapy.* 2nd ed. New York: Random House, 1972.

Keith-Lucas, Alan. *Giving and Taking Help.* Chapel Hill: University of North Carolina Press, 1972.

Klenk, Robert, and Robert Ryan, eds. *The Practice of Social Work.* 2nd ed. Belmont, Cal.: Wadsworth, 1974.

Kramer, Ralph, and Harry Specht, eds. *Readings in Community Organization Practice.* Englewood Cliffs, N.J.: Prentice-Hall, 1969.

Landy, David. "Problems of the Person Seeking Help in Our Culture," in Meyer Zald, ed., *Social Welfare Institutions.* New York: Wiley, 1965.

Levin, Lester, ed. *Teaching Social Welfare.* 3 vols. Atlanta: Southern Regional Education Board, 1971.

Loewenberg, Frank, and Ralph Dolgoff. *Teaching of Practice Skills in Undergraduate Programs in Social Welfare and Other Helping Services.* New York: Council on Social Work Education, 1971.

Meyer, Carol. *Social Work Practice.* New York: Free Press, 1970.

Pincus, Allen, and Anne Minahan. *Social Work Practice: Model and Method.* Itasca, Ill.: Peacock, 1973.

Schatz, Harry, ed. *Social Work Administration: A Resource Book.* New York: Council on Social Work Education, 1970.

Schulman, Eveline. *Intervention in Human Services.* St. Louis: C. V. Mosby, 1974.

Smalley, Ruth. *Theory for Social Work Practice.* New York: Columbia University Press, 1967.

Teare, Robert, and Harold McPheeters. *Manpower Utilization in Social Welfare.* Atlanta: Southern Regional Education Board, 1970.

8

Occupational Contexts

*I*N STUDYING the social welfare institution, we have been moving gradually from the general and theoretical to the specific and practical. We have looked at the values underlying social welfare, the knowledge that social welfare practitioners must have, and the skills that enable them to intervene effectively in problem situations. Now we look at the places where all of these come together—work settings. Social welfare agencies are concrete structures through which society expresses its social welfare mandate by providing the authority and resources to perform social welfare services. Drawing upon theoretical knowledge and practice wisdom, agencies organize objectives and resources so that services are provided. Agencies differ considerably in their structure, their objectives, the resources available, their size, and in countless other dimensions. Consistent with our earlier discussion of organizational factors in the delivery of services, we would expect some discrepancies between agency objectives and agency functioning. For example, while the objective may be to provide services to those in need, most of the agency's resources may be spent developing procedures that may actually discourage applications for help. Therefore, a basic task facing the social welfare professional is deciding which work context offers the kinds of experiences and opportunities he desires. This chapter is an attempt to look at some of the factors that should enter into that decision.

Before looking at these contexts of practice, brief consideration of educational preparation for various types of positions will be helpful. There are four basic educational levels to which jobs are related: high school, Associate of Arts (junior college), Bachelor's degree (four years of college), and Master's degree (graduate study). There are no countrywide, uniform standards governing the educational level required for particular jobs, but there are some generalizations that are more or less commonly accepted. Jobs requiring only a high school degree are few and tend to be those that utilize the worker's actual life experience in a certain social context. For example, a streetcorner worker who has contacts with juvenile gangs in a target neighborhood could be hired with only a high school degree (sometimes even less). Opportunities for advancement are quite limited, and pay scales generally low, although the New Careers Program is an attempt at the federal and state levels to provide high school graduates with reasonable career opportunities. At the Associate of Arts (AA) level, there is generally a technician focus. Such persons do relatively routine work under close supervision. There are increasing numbers of technician programs at the AA level in such areas as mental health, social work, and nursing, but actual available jobs are lagging behind the proliferation of such programs.

The Bachelors (BSW) level has traditionally been the one from which most social welfare personnel are recruited. The BSW-level practitioner usually has a mixture of routine and judgment-type work, and in some cases carries the major part of an agency's workload. In the past, the BA graduate with any major could move relatively easily into social welfare related jobs. Specialized Bachelor's-level programs, in such areas as social work, criminology and law enforcement, and counseling, are now developing. As they develop, educators, practitioners, and students have begun to exert pressure on social welfare agencies to give preference in hiring and salary level to graduates of such programs. The Master's-level graduates typically hold the positions of most responsibility, authority, and pay, and have the greatest choice of positions. The majority of the professional leaders in such social service professions as social work, teaching, and criminology will no doubt continue to have Master's-level training. Naturally, this simple breakdown of educational levels does not easily accommodate some specialized training programs, such as medicine and law, but has general applicability to the social welfare field. Exhibit 8-1 provides data relating education levels to job types.

FACTORS AFFECTING OCCUPATIONAL ORGANIZATION

Social welfare professionals practice in a wide range of agency settings, performing an equally wide variety of occupational tasks. There is no simple way of organizing the large, complex web of agencies, occupations, and activities. The factors to be discussed in this section are not mutually exclusive—any specific agency will be some combination of many of them. However, they do represent factors that can affect worker opportunities, activities, and restraints, and are worthy of consideration when attempting to chart a career or make a specific job selection. After looking at these general factors, the public social service agency will be looked at in some detail as an example of how these factors come together.

An occupational context with a long history in certain social welfare professional areas, such as medicine, but which is relatively new to others, such as social work, is private practice. The private practitioner establishes her own office, sometimes sharing an office with other private practitioners. This person is free to establish areas of specialization, intervention practices (within general professional limits), and details such as fees, appointment scheduling, and so forth. As private practice increases in popularity, professional licensing assumes greater significance. It represents a way for users to have some confidence in the qualifications of a person representing himself as a medical doctor, psychiatrist, or social worker. Private practice has also stimulated some controversy in the area of third-party payments, payments from an insurance plan to a professional on behalf of a client. As more and more people have increasingly comprehensive medical and social insurances, having an arrangement whereby various social welfare professions are included in that insurance coverage is desirable. It enables users to seek a range of help without worrying about how they will pay for services received, and it assures the professional of payment without having to worry about the client's financial resources. In other words, both professional and user are free to concentrate on the problem. Developing an appropriate interventive plan and developing a sound helping relationship are foremost, rather than considerations of whether the help that is needed can be afforded.

In some respects private practice is a misnomer, since no professional works in isolation. Even though the professional may be free to establish her own place and conditions of work, the systems nature of human behavior makes it impossible to isolate social treatment from the social environment. Professionals normally depend on a network of professional relationships to use in their work. Medical specialists consult with each other about each other's patients, and refer clients back and forth as appropriate. Social workers consult with psychologists, doctors, school teachers, and many others in trying to understand the problems brought by the person seeking help. They may also work closely with social workers in agency settings, such as those in departments of social services, in order to have access to needed resources. Again the professional model becomes important. All professionals must have access to other professionals, for stimulation, for consultation, for support. In an agency setting, this contact is usually a part of daily functioning. The private practitioner must find opportunities for this kind of contact through informal discussions, attendance at professional meetings, or structured working relationships with others. A commonly used solution to this need is for the private practitioner to work concurrently, part-time, in an agency. This is readily possible, since time in private practice is structured by the individual practitioner.

EXHIBIT 8-1

The Maryland Social Welfare Picture—January 30, 1971

To give some idea of a typical proportion of jobs at various educational levels in major social welfare professions, the results of a census of social welfare jobs, undertaken by the Health and Welfare Council of Baltimore, Maryland are shown on pp. 284–85.

Tables from Health and Welfare Council of the Baltimore Area, *12,000 Welfare Jobs: A One-Day Census of Social Welfare Jobs in Maryland, January 30, 1971—Part I* (Baltimore, Maryland: June 1971), pp. 24–25. Used by permission.

Categories of Social Welfare Jobs by Level of Education Required, from Less Than High School Diploma through the Doctor's Degree

Occupational Category	Less Than High School		High School Diploma		Special Training		Some College (No Degree)	
	No. of jobs	Percent of category	No. of jobs	Percent of category	No. of jobs	Percent of category	No. of jobs	Percent of category
Supportive Aides	2638	83.6%	400	12.6%	72	2.3%	17	0.5%
Social Workers	—	—	—	—	1	—	2	.1
Correctional Workers	1	—	1876	74.6	—	—	—	—
Employment Workers	3	.3	158	14.8	—	—	22	2.1
Community Workers	46	5.7	243	30.2	122	15.1	64	7.9
Financial Asst. and Benefit Workers	—	—	98	16.6	—	—	278	47.8
Administrators	2	.4	7	1.3	—	—	135	28.0
Youth and Recreation Workers	6	1.2	12	2.5	—	—	5	.9
Health Related Workers	3	2.1	7	5.0	1	.7	1	.7
College Teachers of Social Welfare Subjects	—	—	—	—	—	—	—	—
Total	2,699	22.1%	2,800	22.9%	196	1.6%	523	4.3%

The private practitioner has some distinctive advantages and disadvantages in comparison to the professional working in a structured agency setting. There is considerable professional autonomy in deciding upon the kinds of clients and the types of problems to be worked with. There is also considerable flexibility in selecting interventive approaches to be used. For example, the private practitioner is free to experiment with a problems-focused approach at will, to try new interventive roles such as social action, or to use techniques not commonly used in most agencies, such as behavior modification. This kind of professional freedom can be stimulating and enriching for the professional. Private practice can also be convenient and lucrative, since private practitioners may work out of their homes, and can establish their own fees.

On the other hand, the private practitioner can become isolated from the mainstream of professional activities, and lacks support in difficult and perplexing interventive situations. An additional potential problem is that the private practitioner's resources are limited, so one is dependent on agencies

Associate Degree		Bachelor's Degree		Master of Social Work Degree		Any Other Master's Degree		Doctor's Degree	
No. of jobs	Percent of category	No. of jobs	Percent of category	No. of jobs	Percent of category	No. of jobs	Percent of category	No. of jobs	Percent of category
10	0.3%	11	0.3%	4	0.1%	—	—	—	—
10	.3	1900	65.6	834	28.8	148	5.1%	—	—
—	—	639	25.4	—	—	—	—	—	—
—	—	864	81.2	—	—	17	1.6	—	—
9	1.1	249	31.0	46	5.7	27	3.3	—	—
—	—	208	35.6	—	—	—	—	—	—
2	.4	257	50.0	170	32.7	72	13.9	2	0.4
8	1.7	311	64.6	1	.2	8	1.7	—	—
15	10.7	113	80.7	—	—	—	—	—	—
—	—	—	—	31	50.0	2	3.2	29	46.8
54	0.1%	4,551	37.3%	1,087	8.9%	274	2.2%	31	0.3%

for certain resources, and it is sometimes difficult to establish workable ties to them. Doctors, for instance, must have relations with hospitals so that their patients can obtain beds. In many areas, there is considerable competition for the inadequate number of beds available, and the individual doctor may have difficulty obtaining the hospital resources needed. In a parallel situation, a social worker in private practice working with troubled families may need agency resources if it is determined that a child should be removed from an explosive family situation.

Moving now into factors related to working within an agency setting, the distinction between host and autonomous agencies bears a relationship to some of the issues in private practice. An autonomous setting is one in which a profession, such as social work, dominates the work of an agency. A family-service agency would be an example. It is composed primarily of social workers, although it may also have other professionals on a full- or part-time basis, such as a psychologist who performs testing and consultation. A host agency is one in which there is a high level of sharing between the several professions that perform the on-going work of the agency. A residential treatment center for the mentally disabled child would be an example. Such an agency would generally have social workers, psychologists, psychiatrists, and psychiatric nurses on its staff, as well as a range of paraprofessional staff persons.

Working in an autonomous agency can be a reasonably comfortable and supportive experience, since the worker most commonly interacts with others who share similar professional training and beliefs. This can create real strength in a group of people whose work is mutually supportive. Each performs part of collectively formulated tasks in agreed-upon ways. On the other hand, this kind of strong professional support can result in isolation from different professions. This can be accentuated if the dominant professional group begins to see the other professionals that are occasionally used as less important than themselves. For example, hospital social workers sometimes complain that medical personnel, who dominate in most medical settings, use social workers to carry out predetermined plans rather than involving the social worker in planning as well as implementation. In general, though, increased experience with interdisciplinary planning and sharing is helping to minimize such dominant-subordinate problems.

The host setting offers a rich, multidisciplinary approach to problem-solving, which can be much more effective and comprehensive than the more limited perspectives likely in an autonomous agency dominated by a single profession. This can be enormously stimulating to all of the members of the interdisciplinary teams. In some cases, however, members of a given professional group can feel isolated from their profession. While it is exciting and stimulating to interact with professionals from other disciplines, sometimes interaction with and support from "one's own" can be comforting and helpful. Here again, the increasing use of interdisciplinary teams of professionals is helping to minimize feelings of isolation and loss of professional identity.

Another factor in evaluating agencies is whether an agency is public or private. To summarize briefly the points discussed earlier, public agencies—that is, those receiving public monies and administered by publicly elected or appointed officials—generally have a mandate bestowed by public participation through the political process. The services provided form the backbone of the society's social welfare structure, and, while funding is sometimes inadequate for the objectives identified, it is far greater than would be available without public funds.

Public agencies depend on public decision-making for their mandate, and often work within rules that are complex and inflexible. Since public agencies may be attempting to meet several societal objectives at once—provide financial assistance, employment opportunities for disadvantaged minority groups, and career ladders for those with little formal education, for example—they may employ persons whose professional training and identification is limited. This is accentuated by the fact that some public pay-scales are low, and working conditions are taxing—crowded facilities, old and deteriorated buildings, massive amounts of paperwork. Professionals with high levels of training and a very strong professional identification may look on public employment as a last resort.

Private agencies—that is, those supported primarily by privately contributed funds and administered by self-determined structures—generally have more flexibility than do public agencies. Private agencies tend to be smaller, avoiding some of the problems of excess paperwork and overcrowding. Since they can determine their own objectives and procedures, they may hire only those with advanced professional training, and provide services to persons whose lifestyles are familiar to the persons providing services. Pay-scales are often low, but are partially compensated for by generally pleasant working conditions and reasonably high levels of cohesion among the professional staff members. On the other hand, private agencies may have very limited resources, which can severely limit the scope and effectiveness of their treatment programs. The very pleasantness of their working conditions may reflect some disengagement from the more basic, complex, and unpleasant problems of a community and its residents. Interacting with other professionals may be pleasant and stimulating, but does not necessarily make a contribution to attaining professional goals of opportunity and equity for all.

Although the distinctions between public and private agencies are very real, it is unfortunate that they have been so important in the past. Many professional people instinctively react against working in a public agency, feeling that it is doomed to result in poor quality service because of frustration against a paper bureaucracy, inflexible rules, and loss of motivation. These are realistic concerns. However, there is little question that public social services will continue to grow in importance. If social welfare as an institution is going to have a major impact on this society, it will do so primarily through the public social services. This does not minimize the important contribution of private services. It is simply to say that there are major, probably unsolvable, restrictions on private services that are much less severe for public services. The social welfare professional of the future needs to think about how she can use her social welfare skills to help overcome some of the problems of public social welfare agencies. As will be seen when looking in detail at departments of social services later in this chapter, the services provided in the public sphere are far too important to be left to the least trained, least interested, or least competent professionals. Whatever the problems, there is no more important, diversified, or challenging area of social welfare practice than exists in public agencies.

Another distinction that can be made between practice contexts is between total institutions and community settings. Total institutions are those agencies which have total control over a group of persons who live within it. Examples include prisons, mental hospitals, juvenile correctional facilities, and certain types of medical facilities, such as sanitoriums for particularly disabling or communicable diseases. Access to total institutions is generally strictly controlled, with visitors having limited entry and residents having limited departure privileges. Community-based agencies generally have much less control and much freer access. For example, while a nursing home has total control over a group of persons who live within it, they elect to enter the home and may leave at will. They may also have persons visit them with minimal restrictions, and may leave the home for visits to others. Because total institutions are so highly restricted in terms of access, they are often located in isolated settings that further discourage visiting or other types of communication between insiders and outsiders. There has been a relatively recent increase in agencies that are, to some extent, between total institutions and community agencies—the halfway house. They are total institutions in terms of total control and reasonably rigid rules governing access, but are usually located in a community and have specified channels of communication between the community and their own residents. In many cases they are seen as a bridge between the total institution and autonomous community living.

Total institutions obviously have a high level of control over their (usually captive) client populations. This control may be necessary to protect the community, and to protect the individual himself. It offers opportunities to use treatment techniques that require such control—for example, many of the behavior modification techniques discussed earlier where reinforcements must be closely controlled. However, they create real questions in terms of whether a helping relationship is truly possible. Helping is not control. It may be necessary to control people, but any helping professional will want to think through the implications of such control for the helping relationship. The isolation that exists between the total institution and the community also tends to deprive the professional helping person of commonly used resources. It is sometimes difficult to help someone to function more effectively in the social world when that person is isolated from that world. The halfway house tries to deal with this problem, providing an intermediate step during which the individual can attempt to use new skills in a carefully structured community context.

Total institutional settings also tend to be very expensive. In terms of professional priorities and planning, allocating massive amounts of scarce resources to total institutions where problems tend to multiply and results tend to be minimal is open to question. Community agencies avoid many of the above problems, yet in turn have the problem of coping with the interlocking web of social relationships all at once. Sometimes client control seems necessary, and sometimes it seems handy—but each social welfare professional has to decide whether she can function where it is practiced.

The final factor to be discussed in distinguishing between types of agencies is whether an agency is problem-focused or client-focused. Any agency has the organizational need to identify its objectives. Given the broad range of social welfare objectives, this is not easy. One reasonably concrete way to do this is to focus on either meeting the needs of all persons or groups having a particular problem—such as poor health or housing. Another approach is to focus on a particular client population, dealing with the range of problems it might have—the aged, children, or migrant farm workers, for example. Not only does the adoption of one or the other focus help an agency to develop a set of goals, it also suggests an appropriate type of staff and interventive methods. An agency specializing in services to migrant farm workers may want to have a team of professionals on its staff— medical doctors to identify and treat illness, malnutrition, and related problems; homemakers to help with basic child care, the teaching of efficient home-care skills, and the provision of requested birth-control information; social workers to provide personal counseling, help obtain needed educational and financial resources, and provide assistance in planning for the future; and nurses to assist doctors and provide routine preventive health care and information. On the other hand, a family service agency that concentrates on personal counseling services for individuals and families would want to have a professional staff of social workers and psychologists.

The focus an agency adopts can have important implications for the range of activities the professional persons on the staff will perform. A client-focused agency is more likely to engage in a variety of activities related to the range of problems which any client group is likely to encounter. Although the agency may hire a variety of staff persons, each of whom specializes in the performance of certain professional functions, there are still likely to be some opportunities to engage in diversified interventive approaches. The social worker performing in the migrant farm-focused agency discussed above would most likely have opportunities for outreach, broker, planning, and advocacy activities, as well as performing more traditional casework roles such as care-giving and behavior-change. The social worker in the family service agency is likely to have a somewhat narrower range of interventive roles commonly used in the agency, focusing mostly on traditional casework and group work skills. Values and knowledge also enter into the equation, since some professional persons might prefer the diversity of working with a range of client groups—older people, teens, children, married couples—all in the same agency. Others might wish to focus on the multiproblem environment of one group, such as the physically handicapped.

Throughout this book there has been an attempt to encourage an active orientation to the study and practice of social welfare. Because values are involved, there are no simple answers. The answers to the difficult questions of what is social welfare and what it ought to be; how effective is the existing social welfare structure; what knowledge must be mastered if the social welfare institution is to be understood and effective interventive methods developed; and how intervention can best be conceptualized, are locked within each individual. Each helping person must grapple with the questions, and seek the skills to answer them, always functioning within his value framework. It would be strange if the process of selecting one's own work context were somehow excluded from this framework of individual choice and values. Each professional must know what she wants to do, and where that can best be done. For some, the intensive control of the total institution offers opportunities to manipulate environment and behavior, which makes possible exciting behavior-change techniques. For others, the constantly changing panorama of a community provides excitement that can be maximized through private practice. For yet others, a tight job market may make it impossible to obtain the kind of job most desired. For all, however, maximum effectiveness depends on an understanding of the work context—its structure, its objectives, and the interventive opportunities within it.

AN IN-DEPTH EXAMPLE: A DEPARTMENT OF SOCIAL SERVICES

The preceding discussion has been somewhat abstract. To make it more meaningful, this section will look at a typical department of social services in some depth, hoping that such an examination will help to illustrate some of the issues involved in personally choosing an appropriate work context. We can only look at a typical department because they vary from state to state and county to county. A department of social services is typically organized on a county basis, with general supervision through a state agency. The state agency is, in turn, supervised by the federal Department of Health, Education, and Welfare, which has established some uniform guidelines that all departments must follow if they are to receive federal funds. The Guilford County Department of Social Services in Greensboro, North Carolina may be used to exemplify the major characteristics of such an agency.

In terms of the categories used above, the typical department of social services is a public, community, problem-focused, autonomous social welfare agency. It employs social workers (including paraprofessionals, and sometimes consulting psychologists) to deal with a range of financial and social problems that may be experienced by persons of many kinds—infants, children, teens, adults, and older adults. It is community-based, often having branches at several points throughout a county, and typically has an extensive network of relationships with other social services in the community, such as hospitals, health departments, schools, the police and the courts, facilities for the aged, alcoholism treatment centers, state employment offices, and the like. The agency is part of the public social welfare system, being supported by federal, state, and county funds, and being accountable to a publicly elected or appointed body—in Guilford County, the County Social Services Board whose members are appointed partly by the County Commissioners (who are elected) and partly by the State Board of Social Services (whose members are appointed).

Services in a department of social services are divided into two parts: financial services, helping directly or indirectly to meet the financial needs of persons seeking help; and social services, meeting the nonfinancial needs of applicants. Previously, financial and social services were provided by the same workers in the agency, so that a family seeking Aid to Families with Dependent Children, a financial service, would automatically receive personal counseling, a social service. This is no longer the case. Today workers specialize in providing either financial assistance or social services. Some of the reasons for this separation are described in Exhibit 8-2.

EXHIBIT 8-2

Understanding the Separation of Financial and Social Services

In 1972, states were required to reorganize their departments of social services to provide for the separate provision of financial and social services. No longer did someone seeking financial help have to accept social services, such as personal counseling or homemaker services, and no longer was the image of the agency to be first and foremost the provision of financial aid. Now someone seeking just social services would be encouraged to apply. The actual separation has been slow and sometimes grudging—it is hard to change bureaucratic structures rapidly, and to reorient persons who have developed work habits and a professional identity based on an earlier model. However, the separation is now reality. The information in this exhibit is taken from HEW's *The Separation of Services from Assistance Payments* (1972).

The objectives of separation are itemized below.

1. *To eliminate confusion about the relationship of the two functions to each other.* The public, welfare staff, and clientele are confused about the distinct purposes of the two functions. This stems mainly from the fact that policies are adopted which use financial assistance to achieve ends other than its principal purpose—meeting economic need. Persons who need, want, and are entitled to services sometimes refrain from applying for or accepting them because of the stigma they may attach to financial aid.

Referral sources see the welfare agency as relief-giving only. They do not consider it as a source of help in the solution of social problems of current, potential, or former recipients. This image must change if the agency's purpose is to be achieved. Statutory goals cannot be realized unless there is widespread awareness of the availability and utilization of services before, during, and after periods of assistance.

Separation will provide a framework which will promote clarification of the different goals of the functions, both in policy-making and in practice.

From HEW, *The Separation of Services from Assistance Payments* (Publication SRS 73-23015; Washington, D.C.: Government Printing Office, 1972), pp. 5–8.

2. *To assure, to the greatest extent possible, freedom of choice in seeking, selecting, and accepting individualized services, except in situations where protective services are necessary.* Under policies adopted by welfare agencies, assistance recipients theoretically may accept or reject services as they see fit. Experience, however, demonstrates that in reality the client feels obligated to participate in any exploration the agency may wish to make of his social situation and to accept any service offered as a part of his recipient status. This option—his under policy in most instances—cannot be exercised under an integrated system. Although the objective of a completely voluntary service program cannot be achieved under the present law because of the many interrelationships which it establishes, separation will enhance the client's opportunity to choose freely without implied or assumed coercion.

3. *To achieve a higher quality of administration by attention to adequate planning, staffing, and financing for each component.* Where the same staff has carried the combined responsibility for income maintenance and service functions, the compelling necessity of providing individuals and families with the means to meet their needs has meant a certain continuing diversion of effort—away from providing services and toward the determination of eligibility. Both functions thus have been somewhat

impaired. In each there is a blurring of the need for staff on the one hand, and financing, on the other. Essential continuity in both administrative and case-planning activity has been interrupted by this confusion: A fiscal crisis during the 1970–71 increase in caseloads resulted in suspension of services by some states and deployment of staff to determining eligibility for assistance payments.

When the two functions are administered through separate systems ("separate lines of authority" as required in the federal regulation), it will be possible to adopt program planning and financing methods which will preserve the integrity of each.

4. *To utilize staff more effectively by the creation of a structure which can make use of a wide range of personnel.* One of the most persistent problems plaguing public welfare has been the high rate of staff turnover. In the traditional public assistance operation, each worker, acting in both the investigative and service role, has had to perform a wide variety of tasks calling for many different skills.

Therefore, the educational and experience qualifications are set at the level required for the most difficult tasks. Separation will require the restructuring of positions and staffing patterns, so that many tasks now dubiously performed by social workers can be reassigned to persons with skills specifically related to those tasks.

5. *To make possible determinations of the costs and effectiveness of social services and income maintenance.* Under the present system, with the activities of staff inextricably entwined in carrying out the functions of assistance and services, it has been impossible to factor out the time and effort expended on either. In a separate system of service delivery, a variety of measurements can be established which can form the basis for sound program and fiscal planning, making accountability, in terms of "results," a reality.

The Social and Rehabilitation Service has underway two major projects directed toward this objective. One is conducting a cost analysis of social services under the public assistance and child welfare titles of the Social Security Act, and has, as one of its purposes, the provision of a basic foundation for future improvement in cost reporting and program budgeting. The other will produce a definitive blueprint for the periodic acquisition of data by which to judge the effectiveness of state and local social service programs.

6. *To facilitate the broadening of the scope of needed social services, including the development of service resources, by the development of a separate service operation.* Studies consistently show that the urgencies of financial assistance not only have overwhelmed the provision of social services; they have retarded the growth of new and different service. Moreover, where staff have adequately identified the need for a variety of services, the development of service resources has been slow, serving to discourage staff initiative. Although the law mandates the maximum use of other agencies in the delivery of social services through contractual arrangements, there has been comparatively little use of these resources. The creation of a visible entity of a social service unit or agency, with the allocation of identifiable staff resources to it, with the capability of working independently with other agencies, will preserve and promote the services program.

There is a range of specific services that are provided in the typical social service department. The following discussion is based on those provided by the Guilford County Department of Social Services, and is adapted from its brochure, "Services Available from the Guilford County Department of Social Services," issued in September 1972. Financial services may be broken down as follows:

Money Payments. Receipt of such payments is based on financial need as determined by state and federal policies and guidelines. Need must be demonstrated through an application process. The only direct money payment remaining in the department of social services is the Aid to Families with Dependent Children program, which provides financial aid to children under the age of 21 who are "deprived of parental support and/or care." In the past, social services departments also administered money payment programs for the destitute aged, the needy blind, and the needy disabled. However, these programs have now been taken over by the Supplemental Security Income program, which is federally administered.

Direct Assistance. These are programs that directly affect the financial resources of recipients, but are not direct money payments to them.

Food Stamps. This is a program that increases the food purchasing power of needy persons by enabling them to purchase stamps whose value is greater than the amount paid. The amount of stamps an individual may purchase, and how much they will cost, is determined according to state and federal guidelines. All persons who receive Aid to Families with Dependent Children receive or are eligible to purchase Food Stamps, but others who may not meet the criteria for AFDC may also qualify for Food Stamps—the elderly, college students, single persons, and so on.

General assistance. This program makes payments to landlords, utility companies, grocers, and others on behalf of individuals or families in need of temporary assistance—usually under emergency conditions. This program is funded and operated locally. Levels of assistance are generally low, and it is only intended to provide temporary help until a person can begin to receive assistance from some other more stable program.

Medicaid. This program makes payments to medical professionals for services rendered to the financially needy. Those receiving AFDC automatically qualify for Medicaid help, but non-AFDC recipients who cannot meet their medical needs may also be helped by this program.

Indirect Assistance. There are several programs that indirectly affect the financial resources of individuals and families. This would include programs such as foster care for adults and children, where adults or children that cannot remain in their own homes are placed in the homes of others who care for them. Foster parents or caretakers receive modest payments, to cover the costs involved, from the department of social services. Indirect assistance may also include programs such as day care, where payments are made to persons who care for the children of working parents that cannot afford to pay for such care, and family planning, where birth-control devices may be provided by the agency at no cost to the needy recipient.

Looking at the work implications of financial assistance programs for a moment, it is easy to see why they are often operated by paraprofessional personnel. The major tasks involved include the completion of forms, the fair and uniform application of regulations, the explanation of procedures, and the processing of applications. There are very few professional decisions that need to be made when carrying out these tasks, since regulations are usually very detailed and specific. The worker does interact with the appli-

EXHIBIT 8-3

A Typical Social Services Agency Organizational Chart

This chart is taken in modified form from HEW's *The Separation of Services from Assistance Payments* (1972). It shows a typical social services agency's organizational structure, including the result of separating financial from social services. Naturally there will be some variation between states, but this model is reasonably representative.

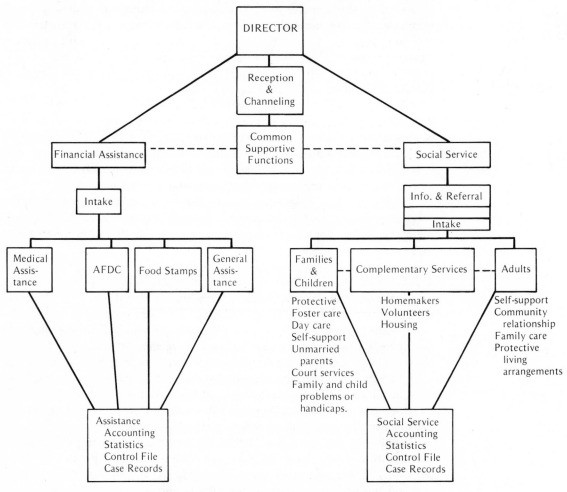

From HEW, *The Separation of Services from Assistance Payments* (Publication SRS 73-23015; Washington, D.C.: Government Printing Office, 1972), p. 98.

cant during the application process, and when eligibility verification is necessary, but the nature of the relationship is primarily informational. Interviewing skills are especially important, as is knowledge of forms and procedures and skill at extending personal support while completing the application process. However, empathy and the use of a variety of interventive skills are usually not important for the completion of these tasks. Consequently, highly trained professional social workers are generally not employed in the financial assistance section of a social services department, and typically find it a frustrating experience if they are.

Social services are many and varied, some focused primarily on adults, and some concentrating on the needs of children or the aged. In all cases, the provision of social services requires higher levels of professional skill than do financial services. Because of the many services offered, each will be only briefly summarized below (see also Exhibit 8-3).

1. Adoption services, which includes the investigation of applicants wishing to adopt a child, matching of prospective parents with children, providing informational and helping services related to child-rearing, and follow-up services to verify that the adoption is successful.

2. Employment counseling, job placement, and referrals to job training.

3. Help in locating adequate housing, which may include outreach and advocacy functions focused on identifying areas of inadequate housing and the provision of more adequate housing.

4. Homemaker service programs, which involves helping homemakers to obtain or further develop necessary skills related to cooking, home care, proper nutrition, child-rearing, and community participation.

5. Referrals to vocational rehabilitation programs.

6. Certifying eligibility for clinic services at the health department, and providing psychological assessment and testing services.

7. Disaster relief.

8. Cooperating with other agencies by providing information and referrals as appropriate. Agencies commonly worked with include other social agencies in the community (health department, private counseling and recreational agencies, public schools, and the like), local corrections personnel, the courts, other county departments of social services, and residential treatment centers in the state (such as mental hospitals).

9. Cooperating with out-of-town agencies needing information or verification of facts. Departments of social services are often contacted by an agency like Traveler's Aid, a branch of which may have been contacted by a client when experiencing difficulty far from home. This agency may need assistance in verifying facts and ex-

ploring available resources as part of developing the most appropriate interventive plan.

10. Adult services, such as protective services for vulnerable adults (the aged, the physically handicapped, and those with mental handicaps, for example), providing birth control and sterilization information when desired, and supervising adult group care settings (such as nursing homes).

11. Services for children. These are varied and include issuing work certificates for children between the ages of fourteen and eighteen (ages vary in different states), and processing applications for children needing specialized treatment such as that provided in schools for the deaf or blind. As noted earlier, foster care services are provided, including the finding and licensing of homes, and supervising children placed in homes. An increasingly important function of child-care workers is the proper supervision of children lacking it in their own homes (juvenile delinquents, for example) and the protection of children reported as neglected or abused (called protective service).

In the course of performing the many social service functions of the department of social services, the professional person has many opportunities to enter into a helping relationship with the persons seeking help. There is considerable room for the exercise of professional skills, and many opportunities to interact with a range of other community professional helping persons. Since it is impossible to predict how helping relationships will develop, the professional has considerable freedom to use individual judgment when working with a client. For these reasons, paraprofessionals are rarely used in providing social services except in certain cases where the tasks to be performed can be carefully structured in advance—homemakers, for example. From the professional person's point of view, the typical department of social services can be exciting and stimulating, offering a wide range of interventive and learning opportunities. Indeed, there are few agency settings that offer as many opportunities.

Against these advantages must be weighed the fact that social service departments are often large, impersonal, inadequately funded, and housed in crowded and depressing facilities. An additional drawback is that society's hostility toward social welfare values finds a generalized target in departments of social services—after all, aren't they the ones that support the indolent poor at Cadillac standards? In addition, these agencies often deal with persons who have no other recourse, no other resources. This makes the task more difficult, since there are few supports to build on. It often creates a hostile client, desperate for help, yet fearful and defeated. Like any work context, the typical department of social services has advantages and disadvantages that must be weighed carefully.

To conclude this chapter, Exhibit 8-4 presents "The Social Welfare

Career Packet." It provides some basic information helpful to the person seeking to learn more about the work of social welfare. The social welfare institution is rich with work settings, each having its own distinctive blend of strengths and weaknesses. There is no substitute for assuming the responsibility for finding out about the work contexts possible, both through literature and through visits. Better yet, volunteering to work a few hours a week in an agency that seems interesting provides the inside view—the best view of all.

EXHIBIT 8-4

The Social Welfare Career Packet

Materials presented in this exhibit are part of mimeographed handouts provided by the Health and Welfare Council of Central Maryland, Social Work Careers Service, Baltimore, Maryland. Although compiled a few years ago, they remain one of the best pictures of social welfare careers compiled to date.

SOCIAL WELFARE WORKERS AND THEIR WORK

What Does the Social Welfare Worker Do? The social welfare worker is concerned with society and its social problems. He deals with the causes, the prevention, and the treatment of such problems. The social welfare worker may work with individuals, with groups, and/or the community. He may also work with adults, with teen-agers, with children, or with all three.

At the present time our society is seeking new approaches to the increasingly serious questions of poverty, sickness, inferior education, urban ills, and racial injustices. Such new approaches are affecting, and will affect, the role of the social welfare worker. The student considering social welfare as a career, therefore, needs to know that if he enters the field he will become part of a dynamic but rapidly changing scene: new services are being offered and new methods are being developed to meet today's problems.

What Qualities Should the Social Welfare Worker Have? Social welfare needs those who are willing to accept the challenge of working in a field that is searching for ways to become more

effective in solving the problems of an increasingly complex society. Social welfare requires individuals who have drive, imagination, intelligence, understanding, patience, and a genuine commitment to do the job. For those who are able to accept the challenge, for those who are willing to invest in further educational preparation, this can be a most satisfying and rewarding career.

What Jobs are Included in Social Welfare? As stated above, social welfare encompasses a wide variety of jobs and job titles. Each category may or may not include workers on all educational levels from below high school through the Master's degree. The examples of job titles listed are representative samples only and by no means include all titles possible. Although there is considerable overlap with other fields and some lack of clarity in the structure of the jobs, most social welfare jobs fall into the categories listed below:

1. *Social Workers*—Includes social work and social work assistant positions. (Examples: Social Worker, Social Work Assistant, Psychiatric Social Worker, Medical Social Worker, and School Social Worker.) Community workers and group workers can be

included in this category or in the appropriate category below.

2. *Financial Assistance and Benefit Workers*— Includes positions of those workers primarily responsible for determining eligibility for benefits including welfare, medical assistance, social insurance, veterans' benefits, etc. (Examples: Public Welfare Interviewer, Eligibility Technician, and Claims Representative.)

3. *Community Workers*—Includes positions of those working in social welfare planning and research (Examples: Community Organizer, Planning Assistant, and Researcher); those working at the neighborhood level to improve or stabilize conditions (Examples: Neighborhood Development Assistant, and Community Organizer); and race relations workers (Example: Assistant Intergroup Relations Representative).

4. *Employment Workers*—Includes positions related to job development, job counseling, vocational rehabilitation, and staff development. (Examples: Vocational Rehabilitation Counselor, Staff Development Assistant, Employment Counselor, and Job Developer.) Excludes personnel officers and school guidance counselors.

5. *Youth and Recreation Workers*—Includes positions of those whose duties primarily consist of working with groups for purposes of recreation or youth development. (Examples: Group Worker, Youth Worker, and Recreation Leader.)

6. *Correction Workers*—Includes positions both in the field of adult correction (Examples: Correction Officer and Correctional Classification Counselor), and juvenile correction (Examples: Youth Supervisor and Juvenile Probation Worker). Excludes those who are primarily law enforcement workers such as policemen.

7. *Specialized Health Counselors*—Includes positions of counselors working with specialized health problems (Examples:

Alcoholism Counselor, Family Planning Counselor, and Drug Abuse Counselor).

8. *Supportive Aides*—Includes positions which are usually, though not exclusively, entry level positions open to those with a high school education or less and which support or augment the services of the Associate, Master's, or Bachelor's degree worker. (Examples: Homemaker, Day Care Aide, Social Service Aide, Relocation Aide, and Psychiatric Aide.)

9. *College Teachers* of graduate and undergraduate courses in social work and social welfare. (Examples: Professor, Assistant Professor, and Instructor.)

10. *Administrators*—Includes all social welfare administrative positions above the rank of supervisor. (Examples: Executive Director, Assistant or Associate Director, Division or Bureau Chief, Program Director, Project Director, and Coordinator.)

EXPLORING A CAREER IN SOCIAL WELFARE

Is social welfare the career for you? Do you think it might be, but want to know more about it? Will you like the work? Do you really have an aptitude for it? It's well to ask these questions now and there are a number of steps you can take to help find the answers for yourself.

First, review all of the information you can about a social welfare career. Your college or public *library* contains pamphlets and books about social work, recreation, corrections, job counseling, community organization, and other related helping occupations within the broad field of social welfare. *Your college vocational or placement office* also has such materials. The counselor in the placement office, or your college adviser, can help you plan which courses you should take to prepare for this career. He can also tell you whom to contact for additional information.

Sources of additional written career information include:

1. Social Work—Social Work Information Center, National Association of Social

Workers, 1425 H St., N.W., Suite 600, Washington, D.C. 20005

2. Recreation—National Recreation and Park Association, 1700 Pennsylvania Avenue, N.W., Washington, D.C. 20006

3. Rehabilitation Counseling—American Rehabilitation Counseling Association, 1605 New Hampshire Avenue, N.W., Washington, D.C. 20009

4. Vocational Counseling—National Vocational Guidance Association, Inc., 1605 New Hampshire Avenue, N.W., Washington, D.C. 20009

5. Public Welfare—American Public Welfare Association, 1313 East 60th Street, Chicago, Illinois 60637

6. Child Welfare—Child Welfare League of America, 44 East 23rd Street, New York, New York 10016

7. Mental Health Careers—Mental Health Materials Center, 419 Park Avenue South, New York, New York 10016

8. Group and Neighborhood Work—National Federation of Settlements and Neighborhood Centers, 232 Madison Avenue, New York, New York 10016

Books, pamphlets, and information can help, but how do you really know if this is the career for you? How do you find out if you'll like the work; how will you know if you're suited for it? Career testing opportunities are needed to help you begin to answer these questions. *Volunteer work* is an excellent starting point—not just any volunteer job, however, but one where you can be involved with people; where you have a chance to see what a social service organization is doing; where you have an opportunity to talk with the workers in the agency; where you can have a small piece of the action yourself.

Volunteer work is available both for a few hours per week during the college year and for any time from a few hours to the entire week during the summer. Students can call any social agency in which they are interested to offer their services and inquire about the opportunities and requirements. Among those local organizations throughout the state that use volunteers are: community action

agencies; groups working with retarded children; state mental hospitals; county or city departments of social services; youth serving organizations such as YWCA, Girl Scouts, Catholic Youth Organization, and Jewish community centers; bureaus of recreation; and the American Red Cross.

Another means of career testing while still in college is through *paid part-time jobs in the field of social welfare.* The number of such opportunities available during the school year is limited and students who volunteer in or live near an agency often have a better opportunity of securing those part-time jobs which are available. In addition your college placement office may have some listings of such jobs.

If you have a particular *skill which you can teach* you may be able to find a part-time job during the week or on Saturday working in a *recreation or youth serving agency.* In the process of teaching the skill, you will learn about the work of the agency, and very importantly, about your own ability to relate to and work with people, perhaps including those of backgrounds other than your own. Some of the skills for which there is a demand are: arts and crafts, ballet, sports, music, and swimming. To inquire about such opportunities call youth serving agencies near your home or college.

Paid summer work experience in a helping profession is one of the best ways of preparing for a social welfare career, although such work opportunities are limited in most areas. Some possibilities are the following:

1. *Summer Camps* provide an ideal opportunity for students to gain experience working with children. A number of camps, including both day and overnight camps, hire college students. The salary varies considerably from camp to camp. Students interested in camp jobs should seek further information from their placement office or the American Camping Association, Bradford Woods, Martinsville, Indiana 46151. Public libraries also have listings of camps approved by the American Camping Association.

2. *Recreation Departments* often hire high school and college students to work in their summer programs. For example, Baltimore

City Bureau of Recreation hires students seventeen years old and up as day-camp aides, playground aides, portable-pool guards, leaders for the handicapped, and traveling play leaders. Apply between January and mid-March at your local recreation department.

3. The *VISTA* program provides another means of testing an aptitude for a social welfare career. VISTA, Volunteers in Service to America, recruits, trains and assigns volunteers to work for one year fighting poverty in urban slums, on Indian reservations, in Appalachia, in mental retardation programs, etc. Applicants must be at least eighteen years of age and have no dependents under eighteen. The volunteers are sponsored by state and local agencies—public and private—and are paid only a minimum subsistence allowance and a $50 monthly stipend. For further information, write VISTA, Box 700, Washington, D.C. 20506.

4. Some large cities have *Summer Jobs in Social Work Programs,* in which young people are hired by agencies specifically so they can experience social welfare work first hand. To see if there is one in your city, contact the local chapter of the National Association of Social Workers, the local health and welfare council, or the local department of social services.

In summary, both information and career testing are essential in making a career choice. After such exploration you may or may not decide that social welfare is the career for you, but you will have a sound basis for your choice.

SOCIAL WELFARE JOBS: MATCHING TRAINING WITH TASKS

The field of social welfare can be entered at all educational levels from less than high school graduation through the Master's or Doctor's degree. Below is information about jobs and salary ranges at each educational level. Jobs may be in governmental service at the local, state or federal level, or they may be in private agencies such as those supported by the United Fund or other voluntary sources.

High School Graduation. A person with a high school diploma (and sometimes less) may obtain a beginning job in a social welfare organization such as a community action agency, a bureau of recreation, a department of housing and community development, a day care center, a department of social services, a child-caring institution, or a health service agency of a hospital. The student should be aware, however, that many of such jobs are available only to residents of certain neighborhoods or to members of the client group which the employing agency serves. Beginning social welfare positions are quite varied, but the worker usually does some of the following:

1. Goes out in the neighborhood to explain the services of the agency and to encourage the people to use the services.

2. Follows up clients who have been receiving the services of the agency.

3. When necessary, refers clients to other workers in the same agency or to other agencies for further service.

4. Helps the professional working with a recreation, community or therapy group, or with an individual or family.

5. Keeps simple records and reports.

6. Cares for and supervises children and/or adults in an institution, recreation center, or their own home.

Most workers with a high school diploma or less start at a salary of $4,500–$6,000 and receive increases with experience and training. Some of the positions provide for career advancement following additional experience, training, and/or formal education.

Some examples of the titles or jobs one may hold with a high school diploma are: Neighborhood Development Assistant I, Recreation Assistant, Health Aide I, Homemaker, Community Worker, and Youth Supervisor I.

Associate of Arts Degree (two years of college). A person who has an Associate of Arts degree (AA) may be employed in interviewing and beginning counseling positions with employment and manpower agencies, county and city departments of social services, hospitals and clinics, mental hospitals, and other organizations. He can work as a recreation leader, housing relocation aide, administrative secretary in a social agency, or serve as an assistant in urban planning.

The worker with an Associate of Arts degree often does some of the following:

1. Interviews clients and/or examines written information in order to determine eligibility for service including financial, medical, or other benefits.

2. Provides some of the services of the agency including elementary counseling.

3. The following duties are similar to those performed by workers with a high school diploma. The AA worker, however, usually would be assigned to situations of a more complex nature than those assigned to the high school graduate.

    a. Goes out into the neighborhood to explain the services of the agency, and to encourage people to use the services.

    b. Follows up clients who have been receiving the services of the agency.

    c. When necessary refers clients, whose problems indicate the need for such referral, to other workers in the same agency or to other agencies for further service.

    d. Helps the professional in working with a recreation, community, or therapy group, or with an individual or family.

    e. Keeps simple records and reports.

The salaries are varied, but most workers with an AA degree start at a salary of $6,000–$7,000. Most of the AA degree positions provide for salary increases and career advancement following additional experience, training, and/or formal education.

Examples of the titles of jobs one may hold with two years of college are: Public Welfare Interviewer, Health Aide III, Relocation Aide, Beginning Casework Assistant, Mental Health Associate, and Intake Interviewer. Some of the above jobs require additional experience beyond the AA degree.

Bachelor's Degree (*four years of college*). The largest number of employees in the social welfare field are those holding a Bachelor of Arts or Bachelor of Science degree. Although one may obtain a job in the social welfare field with a college major in any subject, many employers prefer someone who has majored or taken courses in the social sciences (sociology, psychology, social welfare, economics, etc.). Most of the provision of direct services to individuals, groups, and organizations is carried out by persons with a four-year college degree.

The worker with a Bachelor's degree and no experience usually does some of the following:

1. Provides specific services for clients, such as placement of a foster child; preparation for parole; preparation for hospital release; location of jobs, etc.

2. Assists clients and families, both individually and in groups, in discussing their problems and in developing and making the most of their abilities.

3. Assists clients in using agency, hospital, or community resources to help them solve their problems.

4. Works with a community, recreation, or therapy group.

5. Determines financial or service eligibility.

6. Gathers information, analyzes material, makes recommendations, keeps records, and submits reports.

7. Keeps in close contact with other agencies and organizations; makes referrals when necessary; works with other agencies concerning community problems.

The Bachelor's degree worker with no prior experience usually starts at a salary between $7,000 and $8,000. Some examples of the titles of jobs one may hold with a Bachelor's degree are: Casework Assistant I, Street Club Worker, Employment Counselor I, Assistant Intergroup Relations Representative, and Juvenile Probation Worker. Some of the above jobs require additional experience beyond the Bachelor's degree.

As the Bachelor's level worker gains experience, his duties become more complex. With considerable experience and increased responsibility, some Bachelor's degree workers earn as much as $11,000 to $14,000.

Master's Degree. The Master's degree in social work (variously titled MSW, MSSA, MA, etc.) is often specified for positions in the social welfare field, although for certain jobs other Master's degrees are acceptable and sometimes preferred. The Master's degree in social work currently requires two years of college beyond the Bachelor's degree. Only a small percentage of employees in the field of social welfare possess a Master's degree. (In social work alone, only approximately 20 percent of all employees hold a Master's degree.)

The duties of the Master's degree worker may include the following:

1. Works with clients on more complex situations.

2. Develops and works with groups established for the purpose of therapy, personal development, and/or recreation.

3. Works with neighborhood or community groups to analyze their needs and develop plans to meet the needs.

4. Develops, coordinates, and evaluates programs and policies.

5. Supervises and trains staff.

6. Interprets the work of the agency through writing and speaking.

With experience, the Master's degree worker may advance rapidly either to the provision of direct service on a deeper level, to supervision, and/or to administration. In actual practice, outside of private agencies, very few persons with a Master's degree and experience are engaged primarily in the direct provision of services to clients. Advancement for Master's degree workers is almost always in the direction of supervision, staff development, planning, and/or administration.

Some examples of the titles of jobs one may hold with a Master's degree are: Social Worker I, Senior Community Organization Advisor, Counselor II, Juvenile Services Regional Supervisor I, Deputy Commissioner, and Assistant Administrator II. Some of the above jobs require additional experience beyond the Master's degree.

The Master's degree holder with no previous experience usually starts at a salary between $8,000 and $10,500. With increased experience and job responsibility a Master's degree worker may earn $12,000 to $25,000, and sometimes more.

STUDY QUESTIONS

1. In your community, visit a social welfare agency that interests you. What kinds of programs does it offer? What kinds of clients use its services? What kinds of professional and paraprofessional staff does it employ? What types of interventive methods are used in carrying out its programs? Would you enjoy working there? Why or why not?

2. Interview a social worker in your community. What frustrations and rewards has this worker experienced in his or her work? Would you find these frustrations tolerable? Would the rewards be adequate for you? Why or why not?

3. Make a list of the characteristics you would want in your ideal social welfare job. Then organize them in terms of the criteria used to analyze agencies in this chapter (for example, if you listed "working with children" you would put that under client-focused agency). Remember that the criteria are not mutually exclusive, so one of your characteristics might fit under more than one criterion. After doing this, what sort of agency seems ideal for you? Is there such an agency in your community? If so, visit it and see if, in practice, it seems as attractive as it does in theory. If there is not such an agency in your community, what kinds of compromises might you have to make in order to find a job in the "real world"?

SELECTED READINGS   The best sources of factual information about specific careers are those shown in Exhibit 8-4. The sources below are separated into (1) discussions of professional career issues; and (2) biographical-novelistic accounts of what being a helping person *feels* like. Many of these are available in paperback editions.

Collins, Alice. *The Lonely and Afraid*. New York: Odyssey, 1969.

Henry, William E. with John Sims and S. Lee Spray. *The Fifth Profession*. San Francisco: Jossey-Bass, 1971.

Lubove, Roy. *The Professional Altruist*. New York: Atheneum, 1969.

Richan, Willard with Alan Mendelsohn. *Social Work: The Unloved Profession*. New York: New Viewpoints, 1973.

Addams, Jane. *Twenty Years at Hull House*. New York: New American Library, 1960.

Beers, Clifford. *A Mind That Found Itself*. New York: Doubleday, 1948.

Crook, William H., and Ross Thomas. *Warriors for the Poor: The Story of VISTA Volunteers*. New York: Morrow, 1969.

Decker, Sunny. *An Empty Spoon*. New York: Harper & Row, 1970 (about urban education).

Densen-Gerber, Judianne. *We Mainline Dreams: The Odyssey House Story*. New York: Doubleday, 1973 (about drug addiction).

Fry, Alan. *How a People Die*. New York: Doubleday, 1970 (about native Americans).

Gell, Frank. *The Black Badge: Confessions of a Caseworker*. New York: Harper & Row, 1969.

Green, Hannah. *I Never Promised You a Rose Garden*. New York: Holt, Rinehart, and Winston, 1964 (about mental illness).

Greenberg, Joanne. *The Monday Voices*. New York: Holt, Rinehart & Winston, 1965 (about a vocational rehabilitation counselor).

Horwitz, Louis. *Diary of A. N.* New York: Dell, 1971 (about an AFDC child).

Hough, John. *A Peck of Salt: A Year in the Ghetto*. Boston: Little, Brown, 1972.

Milio, Nancy. *9226 Kercheval: The Storefront that Did Not Burn*. Ann Arbor: University of Michigan Press, 1970.

Thompson, Jean. *The House of Tomorrow*. New York: Harper & Row, 1967 (about unmarried mothers).

PART **IV**

Conclusion

9

Thinking Ahead

LOOKING AHEAD toward the future of social welfare in the United States, one must incorporate the perspective used throughout this book. While there seems to be little doubt that social welfare is a firmly institutionalized part of the fabric of American society, fundamental social and professional issues remain. They are by now familiar: How are services to be provided most effectively? How are they to be funded? What kinds of services will be available to which people? What roles will social welfare professionals play in social policy and social planning? How will the various social welfare professions resolve their own internal dilemmas and controversies? Looking ahead is always a risky endeavor, especially when dealing with an area of social life as volatile as social welfare. Still, there are some trends and issues that may suggest the future of social welfare in America. This chapter will look at several of them.

THE CHANGING SOCIETAL CONTEXT OF SOCIAL WELFARE

It is obvious that contemporary society is different from any that humanity has ever known, and that it continues to change with a rapidity that makes future predictions hazardous. These changes began in the Industrial Revolution, and have created a society whose complexity is staggering. People living in highly industrialized societies are presented with almost infinite choices and opportunities, but in return pay a price in the anxiety and bewilderment that often accompany such flexibility. Future demands placed on the social welfare institution can be expected to change as the needs of the people within society change.

There are several specific changes in the social structure which are likely to affect the provision of social welfare services in the future.[1]

A Shift from Relative Deprivation to Relative Abundance. The capacity of American society to produce goods and services has tended to raise people's expectations and aspirations. This has been accentuated by increasing success in eliminating some of the ascriptive barriers that previously kept certain groups from aspiring to much more than survival—racial and ethnic groups in particular. The mass media make it obvious that there is something available to gratify virtually every need and every whim. They further suggest that these items are available to all, or at least that everyone should aspire to have them. This society's emphasis on the biggest and best reinforces the belief that America has something for everyone; other countries may have scarcity as a way of life, but scarcity in this country indicates a problem of some sort rather than an inevitability. We expect to be comfortable, to have all of our needs met relatively easily, and to choose what we want when we want it. Sacrifice is no longer an accepted part of the vocabulary for the average American.

It has long been a goal of American society to provide "a chicken in every pot," and to some extent the society has attained this goal. Certainly the social welfare institution, with its emphasis on improving social functioning and minimizing suffering, seeks to help the society attain this objective. Still, abundance has its problems, and the social welfare system of the future can expect to deal with some of them. Abundance may be a way of life for some people, but many groups are still systematically deprived. As these groups are led to expect abundance and opportunity and reject deprivation and sacrifice, personal frustration, intergroup conflict, and individual and group-supported deviance can be expected. Aspiring to the rewards of abundance may also create a renewed interest in the legislative process as a way to redistribute societal resources more equitably. The social welfare practitioner of the future will no doubt be called upon to help individuals and groups participate in the political process as an interventive strategy.

There are other problems associated with abundance. A high level of personal affluence tends to use resources inefficiently—the American fixation on the automobile and convenience food takes a high toll in terms of poor energy utilization and the generation of waste. The costs of personal affluence must be borne by the society—a polluted river affects many people, and requires massive funding if it is to be cleaned. Social welfare will increasingly have as one of its responsibilities the monitoring of the use of social resources. Social planning that balances personal access and social costs is becoming essential. Furthermore, there is a tendency to equate abundance with the "good life." This may be true to the extent that people have enough to eat, adequate clothing and shelter, and access to a technology that spares them hard or dangerous work and personal discomfort. It is not the case, however, that affluence solves personal problems. Often the reverse is true. It is easy for a psychology of abundance to lead to greater and greater expectations for oneself and one's associates. The more one has and does, the more one wants and expects. Exploitative interpersonal relations can result, along with demands for personal freedom ("doing your own thing"), which make stable, mutually rewarding interpersonal relationships practically impossible.

Perhaps the greatest problem with abundance is that it facilitates goal displacement. When so much is possible it is easy to believe that affluence is not only desirable, but ultimately even necessary. The American automobile is truly an engineering marvel, offering swiveling front seats, coutourier designed upholstery, genuine Circassian walnut dashboards, and a rainbow of colors. But are these necessary? Do these features improve the value of the automobile for meeting the individual's needs in any fundamental way?

Is the car any safer or more economical? Yet people aspire to absurdly luxurious automobiles because they are available, and may feel quite unhappy if economic circumstances force them to accept a less fancy but equally serviceable car. The point is that abundance is only as desirable as it is useful. If it brings us comfort and convenience without alienating us from ourselves and others, it improves the quality of life. If it distorts people's views of themselves, their friends and families, and their goals, it creates problems instead of progress. Technology is infinitely tempting, and many people succumb to its charms. When individuals lose their way and abandon appropriate goals and means, the social welfare system will need to be ready to help them reassess their lives and make appropriate choices.

An Increase in Structural Complexity.   Industrial society is very complex. Each individual occupies many different positions, including those related to family, work, recreation, sex, and age. As was noted in Chapter 5, this multiplicity of positions can create conflicts and ambiguities which the social welfare system can help to avoid or mitigate. Since many positions are achieved (that is, chosen by the individual), the social welfare professions may also be needed to help people make choices among the various alternatives. This includes helping them to make their personal goals explicit, and analyzing the implications of various decisions. For example, the young person considering marriage while still in college can be helped to consider the possible effects on career choice and training, interpersonal rewards and strains, and obtaining needed resources. As always, the choice is the individual's, but the social welfare professional helps the person understand the sometimes confusing assortment of options and consequences.

Structural complexity also affects the provision of services in society, including social welfare services. The reliance on large-scale formal organizational structures and the use of computerized data collection, analysis, and retrieval methods can sometimes create service-delivery systems that are impersonal and inaccessible. If the marvels of technology are to be translated into useable services, the social welfare institution must help people to understand the services available to them, procedures for obtaining these services, and their rights as consumers. There are countless examples of the problems that can arise in a complex society—misunderstood and in some cases illegal credit practices; unintelligible food-dating codes; dealing with mistakes in computerized charge accounts, and many others. Even such basic rights as voting may be jeopardized by modern technology, as when an inexperienced person attempts to work a voting machine. Finally, of course, there are the procedures that make social welfare services themselves inaccessible—the complex eligibility requirements; exhaustive and highly detailed application forms; complicated insurance payment procedures; and centralized and isolated locations, to name some of the potential problems. Increasingly, the social welfare institution will have to be concerned with humanizing a highly specialized, efficient, but impersonal social world.

Human values must not be lost in a display of sophisticated technological hardware or blind attempts to achieve organizational efficiency.

The Knowledge Explosion and Shifting Values.   American society is increasingly a credentials-oriented society. Higher and higher levels of training are specified for many work positions, a natural consequence of increasingly sophisticated technological equipment and procedures. More and more knowledge is necessary to understand even the basic rudiments of everyday life—reading computerized printouts of books checked out of a library, or understanding food-dating codes, for example. Services previously provided by persons who would explain procedures if necessary are now provided by machines that permit no dialog. Increasingly, knowledge is indeed power. We depend on specialists, and learn not to question their expertise. We read in the newspaper about issues we cannot really understand—should society invest in space exploration? The supersonic transport? Nuclear energy? At best, we can develop expertise in only a few areas. For the rest, we have to trust others, knowing full well that sometimes they cannot be trusted.

The knowledge explosion can have the effect of eroding our sense of involvement in the world around us. It may seem useless to worry whether billions of dollars should be spent to send people to the moon rather than improve public education, since we obviously cannot even understand the complicated issues involved. When a specialist deprives us of our right to self-determination, or dehumanizes us with his sophisticated knowledge and technology, it seems futile to complain. In the welter of confusing daily activities, it sometimes appears that we have all we can do just to take care of ourselves. There is little energy left to use in worrying about the problems of others. After a day of frustrations in impersonal and unstable work or shopping contexts, we may seek only to gratify ourselves. Values of commitment to people and life goals, careful planning to achieve these goals, self-sacrifice and sharing, and honesty can appear useless in a social environment that threatens our integrity and challenges us to preserve ourselves in the face of bewildering procedures and seemingly endless changes. The social welfare system must once again help individuals to better understand their environment, and to maintain their dignity and freedom within it. Social welfare must also strive to have an input into the social system so that human values are preserved and social processes are humane. Knowledge must be used for people, not against them. Social change must help people to function more effectively, not desensitize and dehumanize them.

In the remainder of this chapter, some directions the social welfare institution is apparently taking in trying to cope with its changing environment will be explored. First, new approaches to meeting people's basic financial needs will be considered. This will be followed by a consideration of social services as a way to help people meet their nonfinancial needs. Finally, issues facing social welfare professions themselves as they attempt to meet society's needs will be presented. The unprecedented rate of social change in contemporary American society has created problems and potentials that are difficult to comprehend. Trying to create a viable social welfare institutional structure under such circumstances is a challenge with serious implications for the future of social welfare in America.

MEETING FINANCIAL NEED

Any attempt to revamp our procedures to meet people's financial needs runs head-on into some core questions: For whom is society responsible? To what standard of life is society committed, and do all groups in society have a right to the same standard? What groups have a responsibility to contribute to the needs of others? Who decides on the allocation of societal resources, and through what decision-making structures? Already some answers have been provided. Social Security has gradually been expanded in scope, and payment levels have been raised. Grants to the aged, blind, and disabled have been centralized and simplified so that recipients are helped with minimal harassment and uncertainty. Grant levels are more adequate than previously, but are still unable to meet a living standard of basic dignity. Grants to families with dependent children are still low, contingent upon complex and often degrading eligibility and application procedures, and subject to societal scorn. There is still no comprehensive program to meet the financial needs of *all* members of this society, in spite of the fact that the fragmented, specialized programs that do exist have been slowly moving in that direction.

As the limitations of the current programs to meet financial need have been recognized, alternative plans have been proposed. Already noted in Chapter 2, they are presented below.[2]

Children's allowance. This plan, used in numerous other countries, automatically pays parents a cash allowance for each child. Since the allowance is automatic, it reduces the stigma attached to the receipt of welfare payments. On the other hand, it provides money to those not in economic need, and as such is a poor utilization of resources (although changes in the tax structure could mitigate such effects). Some people question whether this type of plan would lead to an increase in the number of children per family. Even assuming this to be undesirable, experience in other countries does not support such an apprehension. This plan does, however, discriminate against those without children.

Negative income tax. The Internal Revenue Service (IRS) would pay those whose income falls below a certain level, just as it in turn is paid by those whose income is above set levels. This plan gets somewhat complicated by a work incentive, whereby low-income persons would have only a portion of their work income used in the computation of the payment they receive from IRS. There is some debate over whether the negative income tax still perpetuates the stigma of relief, and there is some societal resistance to payments without a work stipulation.

Social dividend. This plan would provide a universal payment to all regardless of income or status. It is the most costly of all plans, but insures equality of treatment to all and has no work provisions. It would be funded out of federal income tax revenues.

During the period 1969–1972, President Nixon and the Congress debated several possible pieces of national legislation to guarantee each American a base-level income. These attempts were made concrete in President Nixon's Family Assistance Plan, which was ultimately rejected by Congress. Since that time, aside from a draft bill by the National Association of Social Workers, there was little specific legislation proposed until Representative Martha Griffiths introduced her plan in 1974. This plan attempts to deal with some of the traditionally thorny problems involved in trying to unify existing programs and incorporate work incentives into a comprehensive income-maintenance program for all Americans. Ms. Griffiths's bill and an analysis of the issues it attempts to deal with are discussed at some length in Exhibit 9-1.

The history of America's attempts to meet its citizens' financial needs supports cautious optimism in looking toward the future. From the time of the Social Security Act in 1935 onward, there has been a slow increase in the number of income-maintenance programs available and the standard of maintenance provided. These programs have tended to focus on specific groups, and usually groups whose members are not able to care for themselves through no fault of their own—children, the aged, and the disabled. As postindustrial society begins to confront the reality of static or even declining national productivity, as well as the increasing automation of technical and service activities, it is confronting the reality of widespread and long-term unemployment as a normal characteristic of the industrial social system. As long-cherished cultural values of self-sufficiency and societal responsibility for its members clash, the humane thrust of the latter value is being reaffirmed. It seems reasonable to believe that some kind of guaranteed income level for all Americans will be assured in the near future so that everyone will be at least minimally protected from the economic uncertainties of postindustrialism.

Some level of guaranteed income has already been assured for the aged through Social Security or the Supplemental Security Income (SSI) programs, for the disabled through SSI, and for children through the Aid to Families with Dependent Children (AFDC) program. A national system of income security for all persons will, as illustrated by the Griffiths plan (Exhibit 9-1), unify many of these separate programs into a more comprehensive and less complicated national program. Income security would also be facilitated through pending national health legislation, since health care is one of the major sources of income insecurity for many, particularly the elderly. Medicare and Medicaid are already operating to help meet the health needs of the elderly and those receiving SSI or AFDC.* Private insurance plans are widespread, and help protect a large segment of the general population. A national health insurance plan will unify efforts to meet peoples' health needs, and simplify the many different, fragmented, and noncomprehensive health plans

---

*Coverage of patients on kidney dialysis under Medicare is the beginning of broad coverage for catastrophic illness.

that currently exist. In spite of continued resistance to national health insurance by the American Medical Association, some form will probably become reality in the next few years. When it and a guaranteed income program become reality, America will have taken major and badly needed steps to meet the basic financial needs of its people.

EXHIBIT 9-1

The Griffiths Proposal for Welfare Reform

Representative Martha Griffiths of Michigan introduced legislation to meet the financial needs of poor Americans in December of 1974, just before her retirement. At the time of this writing, no action had been taken on her proposed legislation, and it is difficult to predict its fate. However, it has been widely acknowledged to be a workable approach to welfare reform, and it raises and attempts to resolve the major issues that have tended to block welfare reform in the past. The material in this exhibit is taken from the *Washington Bulletin* (January 13, 1975).

Mrs. Griffiths was a close observer of the fate of the Nixon welfare reform plan and the issues it raised, especially in the Senate. She has designed a plan to answer, if not satisfy, the critics of welfare reform in the 91st and 92nd Congresses. The sticking points on welfare reform in that period were:

1. *The national standard.* It was set at $1,600 for a family of four in the first Nixon plan. This amount was deemed by many to be too low and by others to be either too high or likely to grow to that level. Thus both liberals and conservatives were doubtful about the plan.

2. *Increase in the rolls.* The Nixon plan would have increased the number of welfare beneficiaries by including the working poor, that large group of people now omitted from any federal cash benefit program who nonetheless earn less than the welfare level. Many critics did not think welfare "reform" should increase the rolls.

3. *The effect on work.* The proposal raised

From the *Washington Bulletin*, Vol. 24, No. 1 (January 13, 1975). Used by permission.

the question of whether there might be a diminished interest in work if there were an assured income under a welfare plan.

4. *The "notch" problem.* This refers to the relationship between and among the various income support programs of the federal government: food stamps, AFDC, housing subsidies, Supplemental Security Income, and Medicaid. Critics pointed out that these programs meshed so poorly that they represented a factor of disincentive for self-support.

Mrs. Griffiths' plan deals with these issues. She has designed a negative income tax plan which combines welfare benefits and tax reform in one package. Those with low income would get a benefit. Those with higher income, but still under financial stress, would get tax relief.

Mrs. Griffiths' plan faces the issue of the size of the benefit to be paid to the very poor by stating that the country cannot afford high support levels. Taking the figure of $5,400 for a family of four with no other income (a rallying point for the more liberal groups in the earlier welfare reform discussions), Mrs. Griffiths estimates it would cost $56 billion a year for a program of benefits, assuming a 50 percent reduction in benefits for each earned dollar. This cost is deemed prohibitive. Speaking directly to the issue, she said: "The theory of comparing what is given in welfare with what is needed is foolish. 'What is needed' is a phony standard set up by a paternalistic middle class. The real standard is what similar people earn, and how they are treated."

The Griffiths plan emphasizes work and the benefits to be derived therefrom. The plan makes it financially attractive and almost necessary for families to get into the mainstream of work in order to get full benefits. Thus the plan responds to the critics of the Nixon welfare reform proposal by supporting the work ethic and deemphasizing the basic benefit. Even so, the basic benefit of $3,600 for a family of four with no other income would be larger than under the Nixon plan. It is estimated that this would be above the level of welfare payment in about half of the states.

The increase in the number of persons to become eligible for aid under the Nixon reform proposal discouraged enactment. The Griffiths plan has the same problem, for it, too, would add to the numbers of beneficiaries in order to reach the working poor. The Committee report deals with this issue by stating that one must expect an increase if one is to accomplish the large goals of welfare reform.

The "notch" problem is dealt with by abolishing the food stamp, assistance to Indians, and AFDC programs and making modifications in the Supplemental Security Income program. Other benefits programs would be brought into the plan by taking account of the cash value of housing supplements and by modifications in unemployment insurance and federally financed day care.

Reformation of the Tax System. A major feature of the Griffiths plan is reformation of the tax structure. Everyone permanently residing in the U.S. and anyone else required to file a tax return would be entitled to a $225 annual per person tax credit against income tax liability. Unused credits would be paid to the filer. This would replace the current personal exemption provisions of $750 per person and the low income allowance which sets a minimum floor of $1,300 on the amount by which each tax payer can reduce taxable income through the standard reduction. The advantage of this proposal is that the $225 is worth something to every individual while the $750 personal exemption is of value only to those persons who have taxable income. The tax credits for the usual family of four would be $900 a year. It would be payable in full to those with no other income and would be proportionately less if there is income.

Allowance for Basic Living Expenses (ABLE). This would be a program of supplementary help to accompany the tax credit plan. ABLE would be available to everyone over age 18 or under 18 if head of a family.

The schedule of allowances in the starting year 1972 would be determined by subtracting a filing unit's offset income from its total allowances based on this schedule:

Members of Unit	Annual Allowance
a. Married couple filing jointly	$2,050
b. Head of household filer	1,225
c. Single filer	825
d. Dependent age 18 or over	825
e. 1st and 2nd child in filing unit, each	325
f. 3rd, 4th, 5th, and 6th dependent child, each	225
g. 7th and successive dependent children	0

Allowances would total $2,700 a year for a couple with two children ($2,050 plus $325 plus $325) or $2,325 for a divorced mother of four ($1,225 plus $325 plus $325 plus $225 plus $225). These allowances when added to the personal tax credit would comprise a federal floor under individual and family living.

The offset income is the proportion of income of the individual or the family specified in the plan. A 50 percent deduction is to be made for earned income less Social Security taxes paid. An 80 percent deduction would be made for the value of public housing subsidies. A 100 percent deduction would be made for veterans pensions, farm subsidy payments, and refunds from federal income tax. A 67 percent deduction would be made for all other income such as property income, public or private retirement benefits, child support payments, alimony and annuities.

The key is the deduction of 50 percent of each dollar of earned income. This portion of the Griffiths plan is designed to provide a reasonable incentive for work, to provide reasonable supplementation of low income, and to maintain a reasonable income differential between workers and nonworkers.

Illustration. The plan can best be understood by an illustration of a family situation. Taking a family of two parents and two children with the husband employed earning $3,000 a year:

Gross allowance (ABLE)	$2,700
Gross earnings	3,000
Social Security Tax (deduct)	176
Net earnings	2,824
One-half disregarded	1,412
Offset income	1,412
Net allowance	1,288
Tax credits	900
Earnings	3,000
Total income (earnings, ABLE, tax credit)	5,118

The net allowance would amount to $690 if the family received $3,000 in Social Security benefits:

Gross allowance	2,700
Social Security benefits	3,000
(multiplied by 0.67 percent)	2,010
Deducting offset income from gross allowance	690
Tax credits	900
Total income (Social Security, net ABLE allowance, plus tax credits)	4,590

Relationship to Other Programs. Federal grants for AFDC would cease. States would be required to make supplementary payments to AFDC families already on the rolls in amounts sufficient to keep total family income from being reduced under the plan. Mandatory supplementation would include 80 percent of the cash value of the families' food stamp bonus, if any. This protection would be required for two years. States could voluntarily supplement the payments for new cases and for all cases beyond the two year required period. There would also be a "hold harmless" provision to assure states that for two years after enactment they would not be spending in excess of their share of expenditure in a base period, proposed to be 1976. The Subcommittee assumes that this "hold harmless" provision would not be much used for various reasons including the fact that there is so much turnover on the AFDC program that the number of persons to whom the states must make payments would reduce rapidly. Thus the assumption and, to a certain degree, the pressures are against, state supplementation. The plan does not profess to be "adequate" in its basic amounts. The plan depends on earnings to build up family income.

The new Supplemental Security Income program initiated in January 1974, would also be modified. An SSI recipient or one receiving a state supplementation under the SSI program could not be counted as eligible for ABLE or get the income tax credits as provided under the Griffiths plan. It is proposed that dependents, including spouses and children, be included under SSI, that the disabled and the blind recipients under age 18 be transferred to ABLE family units, and that the assets test for SSI (now $1,500 in liquid assets) be liberalized.

The food stamp and commodity distribution program would terminate with the enactment of the Griffiths plan. No changes are proposed for Medicaid on the assumption that it will be replaced by health insurance by 1977.

Housing subsidies will be reflected in the ABLE grant by a deduction equal to 80 percent of the value of any housing subsidy (defined as the difference between a unit's fair market value and the tenant's rent payment). This proposal is a direct reflection of the "notch" problem. It is designed to avoid the high combined benefit-loss rates which discourage work effort. This would narrow the differential between poor families who receive public housing and poor families who do not, and the net effect would be to have the public housing programs increase the amount of low-cost housing and not just increase family income.

The framers of the new program had some difficulty in projecting the relationship of the plan to Unemployment Insurance. The alternatives were to exclude UI beneficiaries from ABLE or to count the benefit as a 100 percent deduction from ABLE benefits or to permit a duplication of benefits. A compromise was worked out along these lines: UI eligibility requirements should be tightened by limiting UI to those workers with substantial work experience; UI benefits should be limited to only 26 weeks or less, and ABLE should fill the needs of the long-term unemployed; UI dependents allowance should terminate; UI benefits as a percentage of former net wages should be raised for the high-income workers but should be limited to no more than 50 or 60 percent for all workers; and ABLE should impose a 67 percent benefit loss on UI benefits.

Federally aided day care centers would be prohibited from using a fee schedule related to income. Instead modest fixed fees should be charged to everyone. Special earnings deductions to be allowed under the income tax for a one parent working head of household and for the two earner families would help low-income workers to pay the modest fee (or babysitter charges) and would substitute for current child care deductions in the tax code.

Cash payments to Indians on reservations would be replaced by the new program, and grants to students under the higher education assistance program would be offset dollar-for-dollar by any cash supplements they receive under the new program.

The Plan and Its Administration.   There are a series of details about this plan and its administration which are of interest:

1. *Resources.*   No set ceiling would be placed on resources in order not to discourage savings. Assets will be valued once a year in $10,000 units. An amount would be imputed to assets, and the actual interest or other earnings would be deducted from the assumed amounts. Assets up to $10,000 would have no imputed earnings, but actual income would be taken into account. Assets from $10,000 to $20,000 would have an imputed income of $100. This figure rises steeply from larger resources.

2. *Administering agency.*   It is recommended that the plan be administered by the Internal Revenue Service and fully integrated with the income tax system.

3. *Accounting period.*   It is proposed that there be a monthly retrospective accounting system for ABLE with a twelve-month carryover provision (first-in, first-out). This suggestion is based on the experience of the income-maintenance experiments of recent years which have shown the difficulty of recouping excess payments if such payments are made on a monthly basis. The Subcommittee feels that a short accounting period providing a

"cushion" against income loss will serve as a disincentive to work. Thus there would be no help for seasonal workers, irregular workers, and those who lose their jobs if their income over a period of a year is calculated to have given them a "surplus" which they should have saved in preparation for a period of less productive employment or unemployment. There would be a constantly shifting period of calculation, taking into account earnings over a year's time.

4. *Emergency assistance.*   Recognizing the fact that emergencies could not be accommodated within the proposed plan, it is recommended that the social services provisions which would continue to be administered by states be redefined to include emergency assistance. Since there is no proposal to recognize this as an increase in state cost, emergency assistance expenditures would have to be financed out of the states' share of the overall $2.5 billion social services funds. The state share of this expenditure is 25 percent.

5. *Work requirement.*   There would be no work requirement under the Griffiths plan. The Committee gave careful consideration to the experience under current provisions with respect to enforced requirements for registration for work, acceptance of training, etc., and found these experiences unsatisfactory and difficult to enforce.

Evaluation of the Plan.   The income security plan proposed by the Subcommittee of Fiscal Policy is the most thoughtful and comprehensive proposal made by a U.S. legislative body. It is bold as well as imaginative, for it attempts to deal with the intermesh of several of the many income support programs now in existence. The conclusion of the Committee's work is certainly worth careful study and evaluation.

Advantages.   It would improve the living standard for many needy people including the working poor in many states, the welfare recipients in many states in which payment level is below the $3,600 level for a family of four, single people, childless couples, and others who are now excluded by the rigid dimensions of the present categorical structure of aid. It would "cash out" the undesirable and obsolete relief-in-kind food stamp program. It clearly separates work programs and requirements from an income-maintenance program. It combines tax reform with income support and will help people in the low-income classification even though they may be above the payment level of the assistance aspects of the program. The Subcommittee estimates that people with income up to near $25,000 a year will benefit from the overall proposal. It is a program which could be administered with greater dignity than the current welfare programs because it does not involve issues of morality, judgments of who can work, or relatives' responsibility. A program that would put an additional $15 billion dollars a year into the hands of low-income people must be regarded warmly, if not enthusiastically.

Disadvantages. It takes a hard attitude toward those persons with little or no income. While the payment level is higher than in any previously proposed welfare reform plan, it is lower than the assistance level in half the states. Its dependence upon work and jobs to help people to higher income has a cutting edge. The intention is to push the lowest-income people into any available job so that they will increase their total income. This could decrease wage standards. Elimination of the food stamp program would end the only federal program which reaches the working poor and the one program which responds to the increasing need of that group. While food stamps imply less dignity than cash aid, the stamps might be preferable to cash benefits which have a lower ceiling. The plan is obviously incapable of responding to emergencies, and the proposed accounting period will make life difficult for people who earned a small "surplus" early in the year and used this "surplus" before applying for ABLE at a later time of need. An assumption behind the plan is that there will continue to be a "welfare program" operating in the states and localities. Inasmuch as no specific financing is arranged for such a backup necessity, one cannot be sure it will be there when it is needed.

THE PROVISION OF SOCIAL SERVICES

Meeting people's financial needs is basic to their security, but it does not necessarily insure a satisfying level of social functioning. A society that truly meets the needs of its members must help them to function effectively in the wide range of personal and interpersonal behaviors which comprise a complex, industrial society. Whereas financial security has increasingly been delegated to the public social welfare network, social services continue to be provided both publicly and privately. Certain types of social services have been traditional—child welfare services, such as adoption, foster care, and protective care; vocational rehabilitation; physical therapy; personal and psychiatric counseling; recreational services; marriage and family counseling, and many others. In Exhibit 8-2 the separation of social services from financial services in public assistance was described, and it represents one current attempt to emphasize society's responsibility to meet its members' financial and social service needs. The Title XX amendments to the Social Security Act signed into law in January 1975 (analyzed in Exhibit 6-2) operationalizes this responsibility even further by providing for a variety of social services to a much wider range of persons than were previously eligible to receive such services in public agencies.

An issue of some importance in the provision of social services is the future of private social services. Title XX provides for cooperation between private and public agencies. As noted in Chapter 3, private agencies have increasingly contracted with public agencies to provide social services. Also previously mentioned is the leveling off of contributions to United Way campaigns, of necessity reducing the funds available to private agencies. It is reasonable to expect that private agencies will increasingly develop cooperative arrangements with public agencies so that the resources of each can be used to develop an effective network of comprehensive social welfare services. Social services are inherently more complicated than financial services, since they depend on an understanding of human behavior and effective mechanisms to change it when necessary. Meeting people's financial needs may encounter value obstacles, and may become enmeshed in technical questions of how best to achieve a certain financial objective, but it is a much less complex problem than changing human behavior. Therefore, part of the future of social services lies in the future ability of social welfare professions to find more effective ways of understanding and changing human behavior.

THE FUTURE OF SOCIAL WELFARE PROFESSIONS

Obviously the social welfare institution is shaped by policy decisions made in political structures and in private agency board rooms. Yet the social welfare professions themselves also have a significant impact on the structure of social welfare. They train their members and develop standards to evaluate their work. They develop and support values that they seek to implement in the larger societal decision-making arena. They provide the daily, concrete social welfare services in ways that either help or do not help those in need. They interact with other social institutions and nonwelfare professionals to generate support for their goals. In a complex, competitive society, the social welfare professions are responsible for fighting for more adequate attainment of social welfare objectives. In order to carry out all of these functions, the social welfare professions themselves must be strong and must have clearly defined objectives and methods. The future of social welfare includes the future of the social welfare professions, and there are several issues that can be identified in trying to foresee the future of these professions.

Changing Models of Professionalism.   In the past, increasing professionalism was thought to lead to better professional service, but that assumption is now being questioned.[3] Professions have always claimed the right to be relatively autonomous. Working from the assumption that they were dedicated to public service, they claimed the right to formalize their own values, to identify their own objectives based on these values, to codify a specialized knowledge base, and to translate this knowledge into specialized practice principles and techniques. This emphasized the profession as self-monitoring, thereby protecting it from intervention by outsiders not oriented toward public service, or not knowledgeable about the complexities of providing helping services. By creating a group of cohesive, organized professionals, professions could become countervailing forces to work for changes in social policy that would improve the quality of life for America's citizens. The American Medical Association is often used as a model professional organization—strong, politically active, and effective in controlling standards of medical training and practice.

Against these advantages, some significant disadvantages of the professional model must be weighed. Highly organized professions can become elite groups with the power to protect their own interests. The same countervailing power than can be used to fight for needed social change can also be used to resist it if it threatens the profession's power. The American Medical Association has been heavily criticized for resisting national health insurance, for example. The Association argues that it will reduce the quality of medical service. Others argue that it may weaken the Association's power over what is currently a virtual medical monopoly, thereby improving service but weakening the organization. The point is that professional power can be used in many ways. If the assumption of public service turns out to be incorrect, professional power may be used to generate or perpetuate professional and personal privilege rather than improved social welfare services. Even the assumption of a public-service function has been questioned. Who should have the right to decide what is "public service"? Should a public assistance recipient decide what services he needs, or should a skilled professional make that decision? Should the medical profession decide that life should always be preserved as long as possible, or should each individual decide that for oneself? Should psychiatrists decide when a person is mentally healthy, or should the individual have some say in that determination? The power vested in professions to make very important decisions about what people ought or ought not do, what services ought or ought not be available, what groups should receive services or should be excluded, obviously affects the access that people have to social welfare services. If powerful professions are trying to protect themselves rather than concentrating at all times on service to the public, then their right to make these decisions should be questioned.

Even the professional's right to select knowledge and develop interventive methods based on that knowledge has been questioned. Some would question the validity of social science as a basis for understanding human behavior, for example. Movies portraying scientifically grounded behavior modification as an uncontrollable monster with inhuman effects raise this point. Being objective in dealing with people's problems has also been criticized as a dehumanizing approach to helping. Providing helping services in large, centralized bureaucratic settings has generated resistance and resentment. Most important of all, accusations have been made that social welfare professions simply attempt to control people so that they will accept the existing social system, rather than attempting to change the system itself so that it is more responsive to human needs.[4] Here again, professional autonomy is at issue. Should people participate in decisions about the kinds of service they are to receive? Should there be free clinics and neighborhood service centers rather than huge, isolated service structures? Should social welfare professionals be avowedly in the business of societal reform? Who does control the social welfare professions, and whose interests do they really represent?

The issues are reasonably clear, but the solutions are much less so. The historical development of social welfare has shown that providing helping services to people requires much more than good intentions. It requires training, resources, and societal support. It also requires a commitment to helping, and a set of values that supports this commitment in practice. Professions are structures to provide such training, to obtain and effectively utilize resources, and to develop ways to operationalize commitment effectively. A profession must have some degree of self-protection simply because there are many competing structures in society fighting for the same social resources. The question becomes one of finding a level at which the profession can protect itself and still be open to input from the users of its services. It must not become so preoccupied with its own interests that it becomes disengaged from the needs of those it serves. Some strategies for doing this were discussed in Chapter 3, but the task has only begun.

It is naive to want professions and professional organizations to be totally responsive to users, and to have as their primary mission the reform of society. The professions and their users are much too dependent on society's mandate and resources to be able to challenge directly the existing social structure. However, professional commitment requires a more just society. This suggests that the professionals of the future must be astute political actors, who can work within the existing social structure to utilize available resources, and still find and use opportunities to affect social policy. They must also live their democratic values by involving the users of services in decision-making about those services. Yet they must continue to use their specialized training to have their own input into decision-making. As has been said many times earlier in this book, the social welfare professional of the future will have to be involved in far more than a peaceful 9-to-5 schedule of client interviews in an office.

Specialization and Integration.   Two trends seem to emerge from current thinking about the future of social welfare practice. As noted earlier in this chapter, when looking at the changing shape of society itself, there is an increasing need for integrative kinds of services. Society has become so large and so complex that people can easily be lost within it. At the same time, there are many kinds of services available to help people function more effectively. The problem becomes one of helping people to find the services they need, and to help them understand the procedures necessary to obtain these services. This calls for a general integrative function within social welfare. This function includes many more specific functions, such as outreach, brokerage, mobilization, advocacy, and support. All help to individualize social welfare services. Services exist to be used by people. If they dwarf people, if they are inaccessible to those who need them, or if they are unknown to potential user groups, they are useless.

A basic professional skill is to help society more adequately meet the needs of its members. Services must be comprehensive so that all major needs are met. They must be accessible and known to users and potential users. They must be coordinated, so that the individual is treated as a whole person rather than an eccentric collection of specific needs.

At the same time that the professional seeks to create an integrated network of useful and accessible services, there is increasing belief that some problems are so complex that they require highly specialized practitioners.[5] The issue of generalists and specialists is one that has been broached in social work education, and in other parts of this book. Traditionally such education has opted for a generalist model, in which all trained practitioners had a wide range of skills that enabled them to work in a variety of settings. In medicine, the general practitioner is something of an analogy. The generalist is well-suited to perform integrating functions as described in the previous paragraph, and therefore is a vital member of the professional team. However, as medicine discovered some time ago, there is also a need for specialists to deal with certain kinds of especially difficult and complex problems. Social work education appears to be moving in this direction by beginning to identify two levels of training: generalist training at the bachelor's level, and specialized training at the graduate level. A specialist might deal with something like services to the deaf, in which the ability to sign (that is, use manual symbols in place of speech) must be learned, as well as a great deal of highly technical knowledge about the causes of deafness, levels of deafness, and the relationship between levels of deafness and levels of social functioning. A generalist might assist a specialist in making use of the range of services available to a deaf family in a community (schooling, recreational services, vocational rehabilitation, and so on), and might make contact with significant nondeaf persons such as teachers and neighbors. The specialist would provide the major on-going service to the deaf person or family being helped.

The issue of specialized and integrated services can be related to the earlier discussion of models of professionalism. Service structures that combine generalists and specialists may maximize the professional's specialized training at the same time that it maximizes professional involvement in and awareness of user needs. As generalists seek to identify and develop services to meet needs, and deal with the problems of coordinating many kinds of services in a community, they are sensitized to issues in service delivery and have contact with a range of user groups. They can provide a valuable mechanism for organizing users so that they may have input into professional decision-making. At the same time, the specialist draws upon knowledge and skills identified by the profession as appropriate for specific problem areas. Hopefully the specialist is working toward the profession's model of appropriate service, while the generalist is helping users to evaluate that model. While this potential exists, it will not be easy to attain if the relationship between general practitioners and specialists in medicine is indicative of the current ability of professions to utilize these two types of professionals creatively and for maximum benefit of the needy.

EXHIBIT 9-2

Social Welfare Priorities for the Future

In looking toward the years ahead, basic general priorities are needed to help us chart our course. The following list is taken from John B. Turner, *Development and Participation: Operational Implications for Social Welfare* (1974).

- Many government and welfare leaders are more aware of, concerned with, and will work harder to solve the problems of balancing economic with social interests. They recognize the astronomical increase in the power of government, as well as large private institutions—power to influence, intentionally or not, every facet of an individual's life, almost on an hour-to-hour basis.

- More effective welfare programs are not likely to be forthcoming until citizens and politicians alike recognize that structural problems in a society are a major source of family and individual troubles, many of which require public solutions that offer useful incentives to individuals and families.

- Gains in women's rights will continue, particularly in employment and politics. Gains for migrant workers will quicken as the total number of workers is reduced, largely through mechanization of the industry. But many will face unemployment problems elsewhere. Progress for minority groups is harder to predict. It will probably depend on a more disciplined use of the political system. This in turn will depend on developing the internal strength of the minority communities to a far greater degree.

- There will be a much greater effort on the part of regional, state, area, and local governments to collaborate with each other and to sponsor human services. This development will usher in a greatly expanded era of collaboration among voluntary and governmental agencies.

- How to keep citizens informed on the one hand and provide the opportunities and structures for involvement on the other will continue to be a central issue in social development. Participation will increasingly come to be seen not as a solution, but as one condition for better solutions.

- For a while the unease about the increasing attention given by professions to advocacy vis-à-vis service functions will continue. It may even grow. However, when one remembers that the demand for advocacy is not limited to social work, it seems likely that new, more creative and more effective ways of helping people help themselves—to become their own advocates—will develop across the range of the social professions. Recognition and use of the ombudsmen is likely to grow.

- Professional training and experience are well on the way to routine inclusion of curricular materials on how to involve consumers and citizens, work with paraprofessionals, and work with related disciplines.

- Efforts to develop better research tools and capabilities will expand, and efforts will surely be made to coordinate basic areas of research exploration and development. Even though there is general agreement that government should have a more directive role in supporting research geared to social policy-making, important questions remain: What levels of government should spend the social policy research dollar, and what groups should carry out the research?

Professional Priority-Setting. However the issue of professional autonomy versus user input is resolved, the professions must not lose their ability to affect social policy. The social welfare professions are intimately acquainted with human need and problems in the structures developed to meet those needs. They must constantly provide data to support the need for more adequate services, and participate in the political processes out of which societal decisions emerge. America can become a welfare state in the best sense of that term—a society in which all members have opportunities to develop fully and function effectively, with services available to assist them when needed and desired. It is a basic responsibility of the helping professions to make sure that America's priorities are human priorities. Society's primary function is to provide services and resources for its members. Society must serve, and social welfare professionals must help it to understand and achieve the most effective ways of serving by participating in decision-making at the national, state, county, city, and neighborhood levels. Without a societal decision to give priority to social welfare needs, the social welfare professions will not be able to function effectively to achieve their objectives. In this basic sense, the future of social welfare must lie in societal priorities that make comprehensive social welfare services possible. Exhibit 9-2 looks at the form that appropriate priorities might take.

CONCLUSION   Achieving changes in social values sometimes seems a hopeless task. Although there is no question that the social welfare structure is solidly institutionalized in the United States, this book points out that adequate services are still needed in many areas. Certain basic social values must be changed if these needed services are ever to be feasible. The perspective of history is encouraging. When one thinks of the centuries it took to achieve the breakthrough of the Social Security Act, the lesson is clear—social change is slow and tedious. This country has made progress in social welfare. We do care for others in ways and at levels unthinkable not too many years ago. Yet we as a society still value individualism, discrimination, and laissez-faire capitalism, and these values often conflict with social welfare goals. Any projection that attempts to predict the resolution of this conflict would require a prediction about the future of the society. This is an impossible and perhaps sterile task. What the issue of value change in the future does suggest in a practical way is that all of us citizens will affect the values of the future. Values are made and can be changed. If we as human beings, citizens, and social welfare practitioners believe in certain values, we must fight for their adoption. It is a worthwhile project for the future of each of us.

It always comes down to us. We are society. We are the social welfare system. We are human beings. We make our own decisions. The study of social welfare is so wonderful because it calls to us to assume the responsibility of our human heritage by using ourselves to make the life of everyone better. It involves us totally: our feelings, our values, our ability to think, learn, and reason. It can be a life-encompassing task, or a part of other tasks.

But it is there. The future? I hope that here, at the end of this book, the future presents itself to you in a different way from before. I hope that you see it as rich with many opportunities, theoretical and practical. Most of all, I hope you see it as an active challenge to assume the responsibility for making everyone's social welfare a part of your life.

STUDY QUESTIONS

1. Make a list of what you think the major problems facing members of American society will be in the next ten years. For each, list the social welfare services currently available to meet these needs. What areas of need remain unmet, if any? What predictions could you make about the future of the social welfare institution on the basis of this exercise?

2. Consider that the average college student has an active work career of approximately 40 years to look forward to. How do you assess the kinds of changes that seem likely in the social welfare professions over this time span? Does this affect your career planning? Why or why not?

3. Let us assume that circumstances made it impossible for you to enter a social welfare profession as a career. What would be your second choice for a career? How could you work to affect the future of social welfare in that career, and as a citizen of the United States?

REFERENCES

1. Many of the points made here are also dealt with in Edward R. Lowenstein, "Social Work in Postindustrial Society," *Social Work* 18 (November 1973): 40–47.

2. For more detail, see John Romanyshyn, *Social Welfare: Charity to Justice* (New York: Random House, 1971), pp. 258–90; and the President's Commission on Income Maintenance Programs, *Working Papers* (Washington, D.C.: Government Printing Office, 1969), Part III, pp. 407–55.

3. Much of this discussion was stimulated by Jeffry Galper, "Social Work as Conservative Politics," Module 55 (New York: MSS Modular Publications, Inc., 1974), pp. 1–33, esp. pp. 3–9.

4. Frances Fox Piven and Richard Cloward, *Regulating the Poor: The Functions of Public Welfare* (New York: Pantheon, 1971).

5. Scott Briar, "The Future of Social Work: An Introduction," *Social Work* 19 (September 1974): 514–18.

The Case File:
Two Illustrative Cases

*T*WO CASES are presented here for use by instructors and students in seeing how the values, knowledge, and skills discussed in the text manifest themselves in real social welfare situations. The cases are presented in their entirety and with no notes or supplemental material so that instructors may use them in whatever way they wish. As an aid to students, a paragraph highlighting some of the major issues raised in each case is presented below.

The first case illustration, Mrs. R, focuses particularly on a systems approach in working with a family. In this case, the way in which problematic individual behavior may have its roots in and have an effect on the behavior of other individuals and groups is clearly illustrated. By using a systems approach, the worker utilizes many interventive points as she attempts to identify problems and resources and develop a helping strategy. Her efforts go far beyond Mrs. R as she looks at the individuals, groups, organizations (including professional social welfare organizations), and societal values and structures that impinge on the person for whom help is sought.

The second case illustration, 165 Howell Street, is an extended account of a community organization project. It clearly illustrates how one-to-one, small group, and community contexts fit together in the development of an effective interventive plan. A problem approach is also illustrated as the worker and his clients use such strategies as care-giving, behavior-changing, mobilization, advocacy, community planning, and education. As with the case of Mrs. R, the importance of a systems approach in professional problem-solving is demonstrated. Finally, 165 Howell Street shows how the community serves as a context for individual and group behavior.

CASE
ILLUSTRATION 1:
THE CASE OF
MRS. R

Mrs. R, a black, forty-two-year-old, obese mother of ten children, was admitted to a state mental hospital. Prior to admission, Mrs. R, who has an eighth-grade education, resided with her husband and children in a six-room apartment in a deteriorated old building in a ghetto neighborhood. The family received a maximum AFDC grant, and Mrs. R earned a small income from steady night work. The family managed poorly as their income pro-

From Ben Orcutt, "Casework Intervention and the Problems of the Poor," *Social Casework* 54 (February 1973): 85–95. Use with permission of Family Service Association of America.

vided only basic necessities. (They would be currently categorized as the "working poor.")

Mrs. R was diagnosed as a chronic schizophrenic, undifferentiated type. She was hospitalized at the request of the family court when at a court hearing both she and her husband were charged with child neglect. Her bizarre delusional responses led to recommendation of hospitalization. Mrs. R spoke of being unable to take care of her ten children, ranging from two-year-old twins to a fourteen-year-old daughter on whom she relied. Her child care was erratic, and at times she could not feed, change, or train the twins, nor could she touch or acknowledge any of the children. She refused to prepare her husband's meals and refused sexual relationships, fearing pregnancy. She used a contraceptive preparation which had been ineffective. Mr. R had withdrawn from her verbally and emotionally, and generally was away from the home. He had deserted her four years before, but returned when ordered by the court to face a jail sentence or return home.

Mrs. R is essentially nonverbal; her voice has a strained, unnatural sound. She distrusts people and is aloof and withdrawn. She complains of the heavy strain of family responsibility. Mr. R does not see himself as a helpmate and does nothing to maintain the family or marital relationship, nor does he give physical care to the children. Clinic appointments, school appointments, household chores and management, and discipline are left to Mrs. R. She says she resents this and her husband's criticism of her being a poor housekeeper, but she does not speak out about it. She tends to withdraw and appears apathetic.

The six school-age children all have learning difficulties and are in special classes at public school. One child, age ten, is severely retarded and cannot dress herself. All the children in the family are functioning below normal expectations. Little is known of Mrs. R's early life beyond the fact that she was the youngest of nine children and was born on a farm. She moved to the city with her mother during her teens after her father died. She worked in factories, was self-supporting, and lived with her mother until age twenty-six, when she married her present husband. Her mother has subsequently died, and there is no extended family in the city. In the hospital, in addition to appearing isolated, she evidences some delusional ideas.

This case illustration is similar to a magnitude of cases known to hospitals and to voluntary and public agencies that serve people from low-income groups in areas of a central city.

At the outset, one sees a family system in chaos and in transaction with a range of interlocking systems in the environment. The primary focus, as discussed here, would not be simply on Mrs. R as a new patient in the state hospital with an identified diagnosis of schizophrenia. The focus would be on Mrs. R as a component of her family system and the interlocking social systems, such as the hospital, the family court, Department of Social Services, the ghetto neighborhood, and public schools—and indirectly with the work system, where her husband is a structural part.

The unit of attention may shift with diagnosis and intervention, but primarily the focus is on the family in trouble. There is no attempt to minimize the fact that Mrs. R has a severe emotional illness. Her personality system is disorganized, with an overwhelmed ego that cannot successfully mediate the intrapsychic and environmental forces. Her individual dynamics should be assessed in concert with the dynamics of her family system and the transactions with other linking systems. With this focus, intervention is aimed at family equilibrium, differentiation, and growth in the family system. This practice does not imply that the R family system is seen and treated only as a family group, with help to Mrs. R accruing as residual to shifting the family dynamics in an improved equilibrium of the system.* It is important, however, to focus on change of functioning in the family as a dynamic, interactional unit, as well as change in the dynamics of Mrs. R's individual functioning. Intervention is aimed at both the family and individual systems. Treatment may be individual or family group treatment, or both.

The social caseworker who applies systems theory as a frame and focuses on the family unit, with Mrs. R as a component, will intervene in the following directions.

1. Build a trusting relationship with Mrs. R (person system) through regular contact, as a caring, dependable object whose quality of communication and tangible help can stimulate effective contact, a sense of trust, and self-worth. Dealing with her reality, its burdens, and a more realistic appraisal is aimed at improving her reality testing and expansion of ego-functioning.

2. Encourage Mrs. R, in dealing with ward and hospital systems, to participate and enlarge her object relationships and general functioning in her patient role.

3. Intervene in the hospital system to mediate problem situations, including access to knowledge of family planning, and serve as interpreter or advocate for the client in order to reduce stress and support hospital input for nurturance and change.

4. Involve Mr. R (family system) in a greater role of leadership as the sole parent in the home, as is consistent with his capacities and as the family transactions permit.

5. Intervene with the Department of Social Services agency system in the provision of a homemaker (paraprofessional) on a long-term basis and bring routines into the home by which child care can be brought up to standard, without displacing Mr. or Mrs. R but by encouraging their support and accrediting parental strengths.

*The system purists are described by Christian Beels and Andrew Ferber, "Family Therapy: A View," *Family Process* 8 (September 1969): 296.

6. Intervene with housing authorities to provide adequate housing.

7. Intervene with the school system to mediate, interpret, advocate, or plan with school for children to maximize learning. The ten-year-old severely retarded child, who remains in the home, will need special planning depending on her functioning and the extent of care required.

8. Intervene with the family court to mediate and interpret family difficulties and enlist support for the family as a structural unit.

9. Intervene with the family as a group in assessment of family dynamics and with family group treatment as appropriately timed. The aim in treatment is to improve interpersonal relationships, facilitate appropriate communication and role-carrying, and shift the affective supports within the system to meet individual needs for growth and mastery of developmental tasks.

10. Enroll Mrs. R, as diagnostically indicated, in a formed group aimed at socialization and introduce the other family members who can benefit to community services offering group experience.

The social caseworker's diagnostic assessment of the individual/family and environmental transactions guides the intervention at varying depths in all of the linking systems to achieve reduction of frustration and to increase the supplies of energy and information that will stimulate exchange that is restorative and growth-producing. Systems concepts aid in depicting the fluid, interactional relationship within the person/family systems and those that interlock to form the environment for Mrs. R and the family. The functioning of Mrs. R as a component of her family system is conditioned by and conditions that of other members of the family. The homemaker who enters the family system must also be taken into account in the transactional processes. Serving as a dependable mother surrogate, the homemaker can be responsive to deep and feared dependency needs in Mrs. R's personality system which affect the entire family transaction.

The casework practitioner thus orchestrates a range of services combined with a therapeutic approach not only to strengthen Mrs. R's ego functioning, in individual work, but also to modify the functioning of the family unit. . . . The practitioner has responsibility to contribute from his knowledge of broad client needs to policies and development of a range of services, with delivery patterns that serve to prevent problems and to restore individuals and families, whose maladaptations are associated with substandard living. The aim must be to make available appropriately trained manpower, equipped to render direct helping services in a service network with sufficient resources. Professional knowledge, competence, and skill are basic requirements for the wide responsibilities of social casework practice at the hub of the wheel, especially aimed at poor, dysfunctional families alienated from the mainstream.

Part 1: Introduction

The Project. The School of Social Work received a training grant from a federal agency and, in cooperation with the Southside Community House, assigned six graduate social work students to service tenement dwellers in the area. The tenements to be serviced were selected on the basis of past tenant participation in agency programs; this is not to say, though, that all tenants had a past relationship with the Community House. The number of tenants who had a past relationship varied from building to building. One of the selected buildings had been serviced in like manner for a few years previous to the initiation of this project by the agency itself, and its experience and interest were important to the decision as to which agency the school would cooperate with in the implementation of the proposal.

Though the original plan was to have one first-year student and one second-year student service a particular building, prior to the commencement of the work a decision was made to extend the service to six dwellings; and therefore, each of the six students was assigned to a separate dwelling. The basis for each tenement assignment was unknown to me; that is, I do not know why I was assigned the tenement I worked in rather than one of the other five.

Other factors were also important in the selection of these six from the many tenements that existed in the area. In each there were recognized multiple and complex social problems. These included poverty, overcrowding, discrimination, family disorganization, out-of-wedlock children, poor and deteriorating health, and emotional disturbance. In most of those selected there also were problems of mental illness and narcotics addiction, but I did not find such to be extensive in my tenement.

Social work servicing was to take the form of a generic approach with particular emphasis upon developing a tenant group in each building. Participation of all tenants was to be striven for, but this objective or goal would be subject to modification after more was learned about the building and the tenant system. Specific goals could not be formulated until more was learned about each tenement complex, but basic or broad goals were formulated prior to the initiation of service. The tenants in these buildings were recognized as having experienced oppression, defeat, disillusionment, and despair. They were therefore in need of assistance in learning how to negotiate the complex bureaucratic structures which influenced them, in need of developing a stronger sense of community, in need of recognizing their true worth and abilities, in need of personal enhancement and development, and in need of developing a more positive image of the wider community and realizing their place in it.

From Louis Lowy, Leonard M. Bloksberg, and Herbert J. Walberg, *Teaching Records: Integrative Learning and Teaching Project* (New York: Council on Social Work Education, 1973), pp. 85–107. Reprinted by permission of the Council on Social Work Education.

The Agency. As previously mentioned, the Southside Community House, an established agency with a long history of service to the community, embarked on such a program six years before this program began when it recognized that several disturbed youngsters using its program resided in the same building. The idea of working with all the families as a tenement social system was explored as an alternative to the more traditional plan of trying to work with each family as an isolated unit. Though the tenement program was funded from outside sources, the original program was undertaken at agency expense. Since the inception of this plan, graduate social work students have serviced the one particular building selected.

The Tenement. The building was a five-story walkup with three apartments on each floor except the ground floor, which had two. All apartments facing front had three rooms, while those in the rear had five. Three years earlier, title of the building was transferred to the City Department of Real Estate, and at that time the building was partially renovated. Cockroaches were to be found in abundance throughout the building. Rats showed themselves infrequently. There was usually garbage in the halls, but not to any great degree.

The exterior and halls, though in need of paint and plaster, were in fairly good order. The complaints usually involved poor plumbing, holes in the floors and walls, defective utilities, and difficulty in getting anything fixed— from the front door lock to the rear room window sashes.

The Group. One must understand that all the tenants were viewed as the client system to be serviced. The group which was formed not only was used to enhance the lives of those who actively participated, but was the vehicle used for reaching out to the others. Hopefully, the development of the group would have a positive effect on even those who were not participating members. Therefore, the group was not closed or limited; it was open to "other members." I personally preferred to view those adult tenants who had yet to participate, as members who would one day become active participants, rather than as possible members. This must be clearly understood, for it was important in my approach at all times. I have lost sight of the children, teenagers, or "visiting" adult males, but a focus was necessary and I decided to work with the strongest and most influential members of the entire client system: the mothers. For the purpose of this discussion, then, "the group" refers to only those who actively participated in group sessions.

Most of the members were there because of urban renewal and felt cheated that they had been displaced because of the building of housing projects and yet had been rejected in their many attempts to gain admittance to one. The large majority were dependent on the Department of Social Services for their economic needs, and all were dependent on the Department of Real Estate for their housing needs. In the tenement they had to cope with the lack of concern of the building agent; they had to watch what they said and did that might come to the attention of the DSS caseworker; they had to worry about what to do when someone became ill. The tenement is where they were, but all felt despair and defeat in being there.

The stresses which they had to endure came from almost anywhere. They could come from a large complex bureaucracy or from one's own child. They could come from inorganic as well as organic sources. Each tenant learned to deal with these stresses in his own way, but no one seemed to be able to get out from under. Seemingly, whenever one problem was solved, two others took its place. Assisting these people in understanding and developing skills in handling these stresses could not be done as swiftly as one hoped; it is a long process but a necessary one if these people are to be helped.

The History. Initially, I discovered that there were two major opposing family-based groups, friends of each group, and a few who had little or nothing to do with either group. These two groups comprised half of the tenement population. I decided the focus initially should be to bring these two factions together, and later to bring in the others.

During the early weeks neither group would meet with members of the other. I would hold two meetings on the same day. At one o'clock I would meet with the Waters group, then at two o'clock I would go up and meet with the Wards. Then both sides agreed to get together. On the day of the scheduled meeting everyone was either out shopping or sick. I then decided to concentrate on the mother-leaders, and they agreed to meet even though their daughters refused. Both mothers found something else to do at the time of the scheduled meeting, but it was finally held that day on fairly neutral territory: Olympia's third-floor apartment. Mrs. Ward went down two floors, and Mrs. Waters went up two. Then another meeting was set, but no one was at home on the planned day.

During the following week, Mrs. Ward contacted her best friend, Mrs. Moore, and Mrs. Moore told me she wanted to be included. One must note that Olympia is Mrs. Waters' best friend. The next meeting would be composed of the two mother-leaders and their respective best friends. Something happened before this meeting was held, though.

For almost three weeks the tenants had been without heat. Installing the new heating system was supposed to take five days, but unfortunately was dragged out to fifteen. On Monday, I received an "emergency call" from Edna and went to the building to learn that everyone was now angry enough to forget differences and do something. Mr. Ward agreed to go around with a petition and got almost everyone to sign. We then took it to a Community Council Legal Unit lawyer; I met him there after again calling Mr. Tubb, who "guaranteed" it would be taken care of that day. After speaking with the lawyer, Mr. Ward and I returned to the building to await the man who was supposed to finally okay the installation. For several hours Mr. Ward and I waited together in the doorway, to keep out of the rain and cold. Finally, the heat and hot water were restored.

When Wednesday came, all four came to the meeting at Olympia's, and Mr. Ward also joined us. When we attempted to relate the action he'd taken Monday, Mrs. Moore cut him off and said she didn't care to hear; she was there for other reasons. Gradually an argument developed and Mr. Ward left, cursing at Mrs. Moore. At the conclusion of this meeting I explained that I had asked the lawyer to talk with us at a next meeting. Mrs. Moore offered the use of her apartment.

Throughout all this beginning effort to get together, there was constant complaining about the building and its agent. There was a stated goal to meet with the man, and he had already agreed to it, but I felt the group needed further development before such a meeting could take place. The CCLU lawyer was part of this development. I met with him a couple of times before the meeting and agreed to what he would talk about, the questions I would ask, and his fostering of a group spirit.

At that meeting Mr. and Mrs. Ward, Sally, Mrs. Moore, Mrs. Waters, Faith and Olympia attended. They left this meeting stating they had to get together and stick together; "there can be no loose ends." The next meeting was also scheduled to take place in Mrs. Moore's, but a couple of days later I learned the Waters subgroup refused to return there because of Mrs. Moore's intoxication and insulting of Olympia. An agreement was reached to switch the meeting place to Edna's; even Mrs. Moore agreed, though I did not fully explain why the others wanted to switch. In this conflict the Wards stated they'd meet anywhere and saw justification for the others' not wanting to meet in Mrs. Moore's. This was quite a change of attitude for them.

The next meeting was held with the new DSS caseworker. I spent a few hours with him before the meeting, and he was very willing to help and understood what I hoped to accomplish. At the meeting he too fostered a group spirit and cohesion, but cautioned them about how to handle themselves with the building agent. He offered his support in their planned confrontation with the building agent, and he promoted good feeling between the tenants and himself.

Here I must restate one objective: to help the tenants negotiate the complex systems they are faced with. I tried to focus always on cooperation and communication. On one hand the meeting with the caseworker was intended to prepare them for the meeting with the building agent; but at the same time it was the big initial step in better communication and cooperation with DSS.

The meeting with the building agent was one big "if"; no one even had a hint as to how it would turn out. In the two previous fairly formal meetings I felt secure about the outcome beforehand because of my contacts with the "guest speakers," but I had no lengthy discussion with the building agent beforehand. He was coming only because he felt "sorry" about the lack of heat in December. Neither the tenants nor I expected anyone other than Tubb, and they were even doubtful he would show his face.

Throughout this period of time I was developing relationships with the tenants. Since the day we waited in the cold and rain I had spent much more time with Mr. Ward; he had bluntly stated he wanted no responsibility, but would help me when he could. Primarily, I was trying to enhance his self-image and to "educate" him as to how we should deal with key persons. Previous to this he had usually cursed at me and treated me as part of the hated establishment.

Mrs. Moore was none too friendly from the beginning either, but we had a working relationship. Though she drank heavily, I responded to her as I would do to any other and would discuss the details of situations with her, though I was extremely doubtful that she could comprehend one word. I always had a sense that there was very strong racial feeling involved on the part of Mr. Ward and Mrs. Moore, but I believed I could not confront it until something was stated outright and a positive relationship of some kind had been developed.

Edna and Mrs. Waters were always friendly, but had long since learned "not to get too involved" if someone came to help. Be nice to him or her, get what you can, but don't stick your neck out. The most fearful of any risk or conflict, though, was Olympia. Only after constant reassurance did she permit the first meeting to be held in her place, and as soon as the group was growing and things were happening, she flatly told me she was afraid and didn't want her apartment used. She was almost terror-stricken whenever someone mentioned "taking on" the building agent. She and Faith were the only two participating members who paid December rent even though all had agreed to stick together and not pay. That risk was too much for her. Our relationship was rather well established and she had found some support in me, enough to finally enable her to disagree with her subgroup prior to this meeting.

I had met individually with Helen only once prior to this session, but that talk was enough to change the image I had had of her when she was in the company of her mother and sisters. I was struck with her intellectual ability, her ability to understand her situation, and her methods of coping with it.

Mrs. Taylor was almost an unknown to me. Previously she had been so intoxicated that she didn't understand anything I said. I had asked Mr. Ward and Olympia to speak with her and try to motivate her. They succeeded, for she did finally come to the meeting with the DSS caseworker. She came to that session thinking I was the lawyer others had told her about. I finally convinced her otherwise.

The Members. I will discuss only those who attended this session, but one must remember that there were other tenants and I did consider them as clients and, in a way, definitely part of the group.

Waters Subgroup.—*Mrs. Waters* lived in Apartment 1A, was the mother of Edna, Helen, and Faith, was a middle-aged Negro Methodist, was very religious. Her "adopted" children—Joe (12) and Vera (15)—lived with her. Her son, John, was the superintendent of the building, and the apartment actually belonged to him. She received DSS assistance for Joe and Vera. She declared a "Charleston divorce" from her husband years before, and he lived nearby with John. She could not read or write. Olympia was her best friend. Mrs. Waters had a bad heart and switched apartments with Helen (5C) because of this.

Our relationship was quite friendly, and she asked others to be as honest and truthful with me as she was. She found great comfort in her religion, did not promise and wanted to avoid conflict. She provided warm mothering to her daughters, and one by one they returned to her dwelling. Initially she was very much the sole leader of the group, but a sharing developed, especially with Edna.

Edna lived in Apartment 2A, was the twenty-nine-year-old mother of three small children, was a Methodist, was married but did not live with her husband, and received DSS assistance for the children. She recently had been hospitalized twice, yet she was the type who couldn't rest or relax. The diagnosis was yet to be made, but they thought she had heart trouble and she was taking medication. Her apartment, since her illness, was the hub of Waters activity.

Prior to her emergency call she was polite and cordial, but there was little strength to our relationship. After that call our relationship blossomed and she began to take more of a leadership role with the subgroup and the overall group as well. Of all of those in her subgroup, I felt she was the most interested in a group and wanted everyone to be friendly. She thought very much in terms of the group and influenced the others to think this way also.

Faith lived in Apartment 3B, was the mother of an eleven-year-old daughter, was in her mid-twenties, and was also a Methodist. Her husband lived with her, yet she received DSS assistance for the child. She just recently had moved into the building (four months before) to be closer to her mother, Mrs. Waters.

For the most part she was quite independent, spent most of her time in her own apartment cleaning, and appeared cool toward the others. She began to change, though. At the meeting with the lawyer, she came for herself; at this one she was more a part of the group. She had often said she wanted nothing to do with the group, but she was changing.

Helen lived in Apartment 5C, was the mother of one son, had just turned thirty, and also a Methodist. Though not as religious as her mother, she was the most religious of the daughters. Her male "cousin" was usually seen in the home and I became friendly with him after this session. She was very much attached to her mother and was rarely in her own apartment. She received DSS assistance for her child and had discussed a desire to return to work; she formerly had been a Youth Corps enrollee at the Alliance. Our relationship was good and I contacted the building through her [telephone]. She was willing to help and would participate, but was pessimistic about the outcome. As long as the group appeared together she would participate, but if conflict arose (which was the case) she retreated and said she would rejoin the group when the troubles were straightened out.

Olympia lived in Apartment 3C alone (her Egyptian husband had been deported four years before) and was a middle-aged, overweight Negro Catholic. Until her husband's deportation she worked as a domestic; she received DSS home relief assistance. We were trying to change her category, though, since she too had heart trouble.

She was highly dependent on others for everything, and avoided conflict for fear of losing friendship. She always kept her front door ajar for fear of dying and not being found for weeks. Any legal-looking paper threw her into a dither. Our relationship was good, but had been better in the past. I felt she was jealous because I had also developed a good relationship with others. She and Mrs. Moore had been the best of friends, but this turned into almost continual conflict, which was made-up two days after. She seemed to get involved in these arguments because the Waterses didn't like Mrs. Moore and she felt she must oppose Mrs. Moore in order to be "in" with the Waterses.

Ward Subgroup.—*Mr. and Mrs. Ward* lived in Apartment 5A and had eight children and two grandchildren living with them. Two daughters, Sally and Bonnie, lived in separate apartments with their own children; two other children were institutionalized. They had been receiving DSS assistance for almost twenty years. Both were middle-aged Negroes. Mr. Ward worked (and probably still does, part time) as an electrical draftsman until he was laid off. Then his heart went bad. He had just about attacked every caseworker up until that time. The previous caseworker said she hated the family and would go out of her way to give them as little as possible.

The Wards disliked the Waters group because they were not New Yorkers, yet got things the Wards couldn't get. To them the Waters family were newcomers making out better than they were. They saw the Waterses as snobbish and pretending to be better than they, yet John Waters was responsible for Bonnie's child and also her new pregnancy. Mr. Ward had always been called upon in case of extreme emergency, by everyone, including the Waters group. He apparently had been able to put aside his feelings when a real crisis hit, and everyone realized this.

Sally lived in Apartment 5B, right next to her parents. She had two very young children and was about twenty years old. She received DSS assistance for the children and also was a Youth Corps enrollee at the Community House.

She was extremely aloof and hard, and until recently hadn't spoken with her father in many months. She considered herself better than all the others in the tenement, had a "cousin" who provided her with fine clothes, etc., and saw herself getting out of the tenement as soon as possible. She demonstrated no liking for anyone, even her mother, and was very cool to me. Our talks were formal and fairly sophisticated—at her desire.

Mrs. Moore lived in Apartment 4B, next door to Bonnie. She had three sons, but only one was at home and she was then arranging to have him institutionalized. The eldest son, twenty-seven, had raped her daughter (then nine), ten years before and the girl had died in the hospital. The middle son was in "boarding school" in South Carolina. Her youngest son she accused of stealing her welfare checks. She was twice married and divorced and spent most of her time with her boy friend, Jack. She continued to receive DSS assistance for the children. Except for Mr. Ward, she was the only high school graduate of the group. Only once did I see her when she was not intoxicated.

Our relationship was conditional on my willingness and ability to help her with personal complaints. Through what happened in group sessions, though, we were very honest and frank. Every other tenant had verbalized that she had an inferiority complex and they pitied her, but she was not well liked, even by some Wards. From the beginning she was desirous of a working relationship, yet definitely not a friendly one. She never brought up the subject of race, but I felt that she had deep, strong negative feelings toward whites.

Mrs. Thomas lived in Apartment 1B with her three teenage sons and received DSS assistance for them, was almost deaf in one ear and had had four operations on her leg, was a middle-aged Negro, and was considered by all to be the one who drank the heaviest. One could almost always find her in the company of four or five drinking companions.

She was generally liked by all, and they believed she had suffered so much that she broke under the strain. Her son had been imprisoned with the Ward boy about the time her leg was injured. Before that she had been a hard worker, energetic and kind to everyone. Mr. Ward was one of her drinking companions, and he and Olympia stated that they felt the group was a success, for at the very least it had gotten Mrs. Thomas on her feet again and active as part of the group.

Outsiders.—Mr. Tubb was the building agent for the building. He was unwilling at first even to talk to me. Then we talked a few times on the phone, but still he refused to meet with me. Eventually he came to this meeting, though reluctantly. He refused to discuss the meeting beforehand and said nothing about the fact that his superior was also coming.

Mr. Ryder was Mr. Tubb's superior, and I knew nothing of him until the meeting.

Rocky was one member of a two-man team which did the small repair jobs around the building. I did not know he would attend either.

Part 2: Group Meeting—January 16, 1968.

This meeting was to be the climax of the group's movement toward unity; it was to be a show of strength and solidarity. I also hoped to have the group members realize some of their potential and ability, see that they could assert some independence, and plan their next moves with as little intervention on my part as possible.

Though they had long asked to meet with the building agent, I doubted their stated actions once they would actually meet with him. All had said they would believe it only when it actually happened. On the one hand, they wanted to really let loose with him, and on the other, they feared the situation. It was an unknown and a risky one at that. Behind them lay the experience of a friendly outsider who met with them, then the DSS caseworker who represented that "machine" they hated and felt was always looking over their shoulders; and now they were to face the representative of the organization which aroused their most negative feelings.

Had they learned from these experiences? Had they fostered the feelings of security and competence that I intended they should? Were these enough to help them face today, realize their situation, and grow from it? I didn't know for sure, and my anxiety was showing. I went so far as to suggest an early lunch to my co-workers so I could get to the building early, urge a high attendance, check on their readiness, etc. At lunch I realized my own feelings and saw that such action would be contrary to what I hoped would result from the meeting. If the meeting was to stimulate greater independence, then that is what I would have to foster right from the start.

I arrived at Edna's apartment a few minutes before one o'clock, which was the time set for the meeting. She was well dressed and very anxious since no one else had come yet. If dress were any indication, I would say she felt the meeting was the most important to date. At earlier informal sessions she wore nightgowns, at the meeting with the lawyer a house dress, with the DSS caseworker a dress, and this time it looked more like evening wear or her Sunday best. As time went by her mother, Mrs. Waters, came with Vera, who took the children downstairs. (This pattern was now well established and working well.) Soon after, Olympia came, followed shortly thereafter by Faith. "Where is everyone else?" was the common question. I suggested that, if they were worried about it, one of them should check on the others. (This would no longer be my function but theirs.) No one moved. Mr. Ward came in, asked for his wife, then went to get her. They continued to verbalize their anxiety about the others not being there. I remained silent, but I think I was just as anxious as they were. Finally, Edna took it upon herself to check on the others.

Meanwhile, Mrs. Thomas arrived and was helped in by a middle-aged man who quickly left after she was seated. She began jokingly yelling at me because of the postcard I'd sent. "I can get upstairs by myself, it's the getting down I can't do," she remarked. We all laughed and I realized she was "just what the doctor ordered." She was slightly intoxicated, and her remarks were very humorous. This light touch was what was needed at that point, and everyone took the opportunity, including myself, to release some of the anxiety through laughter. Edna returned with Helen and they joined in the fun. Now present were Edna, Helen, Faith, Mrs. Waters, Olympia, Mrs. Thomas and myself.

Mr. Tubb arrived, paid no attention to the tenants, came over to me, and, after a brief exchange of names, asked, "Are you going to hold the meeting?" His manner was more than abrupt, and I suggested his eyes speak for themselves. "Is this all?" he quipped. "We expect some more . . . that's what we're waiting for," I retorted. He then said his superior was waiting outside in a car and he went to get him. The tenants were extremely anxious at this point and began to move about. They said they couldn't believe it; "His boss too?" they asked. Edna rubbed her hands in delight about her chance to really tell them off. I reminded them of last week's session and what they said they would say today. Mrs. Waters and Olympia wondered where Mr. Ward was: "What's keeping him anyway? He should be here," said Mrs. Waters. I then asked about the other tenants. Yes, they had contacted the Puerto Rican families but no one could come. Also Mrs. Roland was out looking for a new apartment in the Bronx. "What about Mrs. Moore?" asked Edna.

I tried to reassure them, but they remained very anxious. I couldn't even reassure myself. Laughter worked before so I tried it again; I talked about the room, and they joked about the difference between "Charleston people" and other Negroes. Mrs. Thomas's remarks were beautifully funny, but then again anything probably would have seemed funny at that point. We all needed a good laugh.

Mr. Tubb returned and introduced me to his supervisor, Mr. Ryder, and the handyman who usually did the work in the building, Rocky. I then introduced them to the others. Olympia was still muttering, "Where's Tom?" I suggested we wait a few minutes for the others; Ryder said he was a busy man and either we begin or he'd leave; the others knew what time the meeting began, and the Department of Real Estate men were punctual. I began by explaining my interest, agency affiliation, and why we were holding this meeting. Mr. Ryder seemed not to be listening and asked, "Where's the lawyer?" I explained that he wasn't here, nor was he supposed to be, and strongly reiterated my point that he was here to talk with the tenants, not a lawyer or myself. "All right, all right, what's your problem?" he asked as he pointed at Mrs. Thomas. She was numb. I interrupted and told him this was no interrogation. "I know it isn't," he retorted, and pointed at Olympia and asked, "You got a complaint?" She almost fainted. I pulled his arm down and told him he was acting like a Gestapo officer and that he was here "to talk with" these people and not to yell at them. He said he didn't realize he was acting like that, but if that's how it looked, he'd stop. Then he asked me to "watch that I don't do it again." Then he put his hands under his legs to demonstrate his change of approach.

Again the harsh questions, but this time without the pointing. No one answered; they seemed perched on the limb of a tree. Then he loudly said, "See, this is a waste of time. They know they're treated right, they've no complaints, see for yourself!" He stood to leave. I sat way back and told him he was a "load of bullshit" and again told him the stupidity of his actions. I also mentioned that the tenants were doing the right thing in not talking. "Not until you really show a willingness to talk should they speak out." Then he asked if I were blaming him, and I said I was.

He sat down again and asked how he should act. I explained the difficulty of the situation because he'd already acted the way he had, but possibly he had now convinced the tenants that he wished to talk. I asked if anyone cared to say something. Dead silence. I suggested, in an asking way, that I relate Mrs. Moore's complaint since I had received her request to do so if she weren't present. I told the story. "Where is she?" Ryder quickly asked. I told him that this was not the point and asked if he'd really come to talk. "If so, explain it, not ask where is she," I told him. He looked at Tubb, and Tubb now had a quantity of official-looking cards in his lap. He sorted through them, then said three times his men tried to correct the situation but she was never at home.

This irritated Edna and she said that was a lie. Olympia supported her; they were finally talking. I decided to restrict my intervention from this point on. Then they all began to yell at once about these "supposed calls" with no one at home. Ryder turned to me "Now who do I believe?" he asked, holding his hands over his ears. Rocky yelled out that the tenants were wrong, and he was almost assaulted. Ryder intervened and told Rocky to keep quiet. "Where do we go from here?" Ryder asked. I refused to answer, quite loudly, and suggested he pose this question to the tenants. At this they resumed order.

As he began to ask them, Mrs. Moore came in. They all tried to fill her in at once. Mr. Ryder introduced himself. She took the floor and began to go over her complaint time and time again. Mr. and Mrs. Ward came in during this talk. Ryder promised to take care of it by Friday, but this didn't end her talking.

The others were getting annoyed at her. Mr. Ward was asked to talk by the others. Still Mrs. Moore would not stop; she was very drunk. We all sat painfully through this; at times I was asked to intervene, at others, Mr. Ward; side talks started. I continued to look at Mr. Ward, asking with my eyes that he intervene.

I was being torn apart inside, but I couldn't intervene. This was Mr. Ward's chance and I wanted him to seize it. He tried, he yelled at her, but still she continued. Then he made a motion to leave. Mr. Ryder pulled him back when he realized how much the others were pleading with him to stop her and not to leave. I felt sick to my stomach.

Then Mrs. Waters screamed at Mrs. Moore and told her everyone wanted Mr. Ward to speak. Mrs. Moore became silent. Mr. Ward began by thanking Mrs. Waters, then Mrs. Moore started in again. The others were almost out of their seats by then, but Mr. Ward gave her a dressing-down that quieted her. Then he began to relate his feelings. Mrs. Moore started in again; this time Olympia put her hand over Mrs. Moore's mouth and Mr. Ward continued. When he finished he looked questioningly at me. I said he had stated the problem very well but it might help if he gave some examples that would refute Mr. Tubb's records. In a low voice, "Give me some help . . . get me started," he asked. (Or was he telling me what to do? I'd like to feel it was the latter.) Then after I said, "the exterminator bit," he gave example after example.

Ryder then turned to Tubb and said he was taking control of the building "until I get to the bottom of all this." Mr. Ward was proud, very proud, and everyone could see it. I was jumping inside. He had taken that big step. Totally unlike him, he didn't use one curse, even at Mrs. Moore. At times he stood there like a meek lamb, worried, scared, unsure of himself. But he finally came through and provided the strength the others needed. I felt that no amount of "talking" about his position could have done for him what today's meeting was doing. I'd assist as I saw fit, but I would at least hesitate in interventions; I felt even more certain they could really declare some independence. In short, I was relieved.

Then Mr. Ward and Mr. Ryder began to go over the details of repairs and equipment. The list grew so long that Mr. Ryder promised to have a team of his men go through the entire building and fix everything and write down anything needed that they couldn't do. This brought responses from Mrs. Thomas, Edna, Mrs. Moore, and Olympia. Olympia really let loose. She refused to let his men in her apartment because they only "make things worse." Then she said Rocky did sloppy work. All the others disagreed and said his partner was a jerk, not him. Olympia stuck to her guns, stood yelling, and grabbed at Rocky. Edna and Helen tried to restrain her, but she quickly put them down verbally. Each had had a say, now she was having hers and she really brought this point home. They retreated and Olympia concluded her complaints. I had seen her angry before, but her taking on the whole group was almost inconceivable. Three times during her excited statements she remarked about her "bad heart" and "high blood pressure," but these remarks only affected Mr. Ryder; the others were now used to them.

Mr. Ryder said he would stay with his team and they wouldn't leave until the work was done to the tenants' satisfaction. Olympia then accepted his proposal and the others quickly followed. Then they began to praise Mr. Ward and talk among themselves.

While this was going on, Mr. Ward leaned over and whispered, "Should I bring up the rent?" and I winked in response. Then he stood in the middle of the room and told the story of no heat and no hot water in December. He concluded by asking where they [the tenants] stood on the rent. Mr. Ryder looked to Tubb and Tubb explained about the 33 percent. Ryder said, "Well, where's the problem? You're getting a 33 percent cut . . . I see no problem about the rent." Mr. Ward briefly spoke about the hardship it caused and concluded by emphatically stating that he wouldn't pay one cent of December's rent and that he'd only accept a 100 percent cut and nothing else. This really irked Mr. Ryder, and he suggested a 10 percent cut instead. I could not believe my ears, nor could Mr. Ward. Mr. Ryder went on to say they couldn't have everything they asked for and began to tell how expensive it was to keep up a building. With this, Mr. Ward pushed his way out. As the others attempted to bring him back, I talked with Mr. Ryder. I said 33 percent was already offered and saw no reason for lowering it. Then his attitude got the best of me and I lost my cool. I literally blew my stack and let him know how Tubb strung us along and how only the tenants suffered, while everyone else made money on the deal. Regaining control, I asked Helen to try to clear the air. I asked her because of her abilities and the way I thought she'd react.

She began by explaining what a good paying tenant she was and that she had no major complaints, but she couldn't permit the rent situation to be left as it was. In a low but firm voice she told of illnesses and hardships of the tenants, and then she too placed much of the blame on Tubb's faulty handling of the situation. When she finished, I added a few facts about specific attempts to correct the situation. It now became apparent that Mr. Ryder had not been told all the details, as Tubb had said he would do earlier.

Ryder was moved by Helen's talk and looked angrily at Tubb, then he asked if 50 percent would be acceptable. I said that the tenants would have to decide, and, as I told Tubb, the decision would be made at our get-together after this meeting. I then asked the tenants if they wished a change in plans. They did not and felt we should stick to our original plan.

Then he told us this 50 percent figure was not assumed; he'd first have to get permission, but in light of the situation, he felt he would get that permission. Mr. Ryder rose to leave, but I stopped him and we summarized the agreements reached today for all to hear. The primary ones were: He'd have an answer on the 50 percent cut in a few days; he and his team would go through the building next week; no punitive action would be taken against any tenant; the building agent would meet with us once a month and would have to report to Mr. Ryder on each session; Mr. Ryder would also visit some apartments today at the request of those tenants who wanted it.

I reminded everyone to come back for the get-together and thanked Mr. Ryder for coming, and then he assured me of his cooperation. As Rocky passed us he commented, "Now they like me . . . now they like me." Ryder laughed.

Informal session. I helped Mrs. Thomas downstairs and she said she could be told later about our get-together. She didn't want to go upstairs again after Mr. Ryder left. I rejoined the others in Edna's.

When I returned, I discovered that Sally had come down. This was the second time she had come after the meeting for the informal session. Edna, Helen, and Faith filled Sally in and seemed happy with the results. Then they began to discuss Mrs. Moore and verbalized their dislike of her coming intoxicated. Sally was laughing at their accounts; I was in the kitchen, but I could hear.

When I came back they asked me to talk about the meeting. I suggested we wait for the others before making any decisions, but we could begin to talk in the meantime. Helen asked if I felt things were really going to change. I said they already had and began to explain what it had been like in the building a few months before. Some interrupted with supportive statements and concluded with Edna's "Now we're really together . . . it's real . . . but we gotta stick together." Olympia started talking about the meeting.

I began to get back to Helen's question and explained our gains, but cautioned about what the actual results might be. We couldn't hope for too much, and a bumpy road lay ahead; but we had communicated, we had let them know we had a group that was concerned and willing to take action; we had gotten together. I reminded the Waters girls and Sally about their earlier feelings about each other, and how their mothers tried to get together because they possibly saw the merits of friendship. "You know, I don't hear any more remarks like that," I said, commenting on their previous refusals to see each other.

Then Mrs. Moore came back, listened a minute, then interrupted. She began by calling us all a bunch of nothings. "You're nobodies talking about nothing. You just talk; it doesn't mean nothing." I asked if she was angry with me and she said she wasn't. I said I was angry at her because I thought we'd reached a stage where we could talk frankly and I felt she was angry with me. She replied, "I'm not really angry with you. It's us. Why the hell do we need you? Who are you anyway, coming here? If we need you that only proves we're nothing, you're a white man. (The others cut her off and I asked her to continue.) I'm really mad at us. Why can't we hold a meeting without you?" she concluded.

I said that Mrs. Moore and I had talked about this before and that I wholeheartedly supported her views. "Why can't you hold meetings without me?" I asked. Olympia and Faith felt that they couldn't. Olympia said, "We're not strong enough yet, don't you see that?" Faith said I had the power to get things done and without me they were "lost." Mrs. Moore objected and began to repeat that I was white and she was a "Negro female." I began to respond when Olympia blew her top and said such remarks were out of order and called Mrs. Moore a drunkard. Mrs. Waters supported Olympia, but the others wanted to hear my reply. Olympia quickly left in a frustrated state. Only Mrs. Waters tried to stop her. I was tempted to also, but felt it best not to do so. Such action at the very least could be damaging to the group, particularly at this crucial point.

Then Mrs. Waters asked me to return to the earlier discussion about the meeting with Mr. Ryder. I said I felt it best to deal with Mrs. Moore's remarks instead and told them that just as we asked the white caseworker to spell out his philosophy, so too I should do the same today. "I'm white and you're all black. Now it's said out loud. Does it change anything? (Mrs. Waters pleaded for me to stop.) Maybe now that it's said we can talk more frankly. I don't know, sometimes I feel I don't belong here, and at others it's more like a second home. The thing is, you're a group now. I helped, but I, a white guy, shouldn't be in the front. You have to develop your own leadership. A black person should be your leader, not me. Let's face it, there's a hell of a lot happening these days, and if I stayed in the front, I'd be hurting you, all of you, and me too. I think you've got what it takes, you're ready. Just think about it a minute."

Edna broke the silence by yelling, "But Jack, you're our leader." Her mother, almost in tears now, said just about the same thing. Helen hit on another point I had hoped to get back to. She said this was a risky business and today they'd all stuck their necks way out. She wasn't prepared to do it again without me. She commented that I almost lost my cool a couple of times, but I'd gained control, something they couldn't do. She remarked, "I was watching you. I saw you struggling to keep calm. You warned him he was getting you hot under the collar. You realized what the risk was. I don't know if everyone here really knows even now."

I said a big part of this I'd failed to say; I wasn't going anywhere. I suggested I continue as I had been doing, but with a new twist. "From now on your leader will tell me what he wants from me. I'll help him or her all I can, and I'll remain available to all just as in the past."

Now Edna changed her view and began to praise Mr. Ward for both today's action and past ones. Helen played up the point that they also were crucial to today's success. Yes, I was needed, but they were gaining strength and should begin to realize this and do for themselves. She felt meetings should be held without me, so they could discuss things in their own way. I'd be told of the results, but not all that was said or how it was put.

Edna took the leadership and they began to formalize my future role as they saw it. Each had a say, even Sally, and gradually they defined specifically what I should do after they selected a leader. I would consult with "him." I'd continue to come to the more formal meetings, speak when I saw fit, but wouldn't lead it. After such meetings I'd tell them what was right and wrong and give them any information I thought they should have. I would also continue to see them individually and help in any way I could. I was pleased that they based many of these suggestions on their experiences with our group meetings. Edna, for instance, said it was a good idea to have me explain things after a meeting because it was working well. This was the third time we'd done this. I praised them on what they'd just done, explained what they'd done in moderately sophisticated language, and said I totally agreed with their decisions. Everyone was happy except Mrs. Moore.

She had more to say. She knew they were all talking in terms of Mr. Ward as the leader and she didn't like this. "Why him?" she asked. "I'm the one who got Jack—Mr. Benton—to come here. I'm the one who went around asking for help. You'd be no place without me. We wouldn't even be together here today if it weren't for me." Olympia came back as she was talking, and Olympia told Mrs. Moore to keep her mouth closed. The others giggled and Olympia looked at them sternly but proudly.

Helen asked how everything looked. I pointed out the great steps forward they'd taken, but again cautioned about bad days ahead. I'd be there to help, though, and they shouldn't feel too bad if I was asked to take a more active role. I hoped the situation would not arise, but if it did, they

should remember it would only be temporary. They couldn't expect themselves to be a well-organized, sophisticated group overnight. They'd have to
learn to deal with internal problems and conflicts, and if individuals had a
fight, they'd have to stick with the group—even if with the persons in the
room who had just fought with them. Faith and Olympia emphasized that
either they would be a group or they would return to their "old ways" and
live in their own separate "cat holes."

Then I asked Mrs. Moore if she had anything to say. She replied that
she'd been told to be quiet. I said, "Well, if you think you should." She began to talk again about the leader. Edna interrupted and said they'd decide
that later, not today, "since Tom ain't here now." Edna looked at me and
explained that Mr. Ward was involved in "personal business" today, had
come a long distance to be here for the meeting, and had had to get back.
"That's why he left when he did, really." I acknowledged this.

Then Edna asked me about an earlier comment of mine concerning
MacMahon Clinic; she wasn't sure what I'd said and felt we should discuss
it before we ended the meeting. I said I would, but before I did, I just wanted
them to be thinking about the rent decision. "This should be discussed too,"
I said.

Edna said she was concerned about her children's health. Helen felt the
situation at the clinic was very poor, and Edna disagreed and related a recent
incident. With that, Mrs. Moore jumped up and screamed that her daughter
had been "murdered" there. This drew immediate silence. Edna broke it by
first sympathizing with her and then explaining that things were changing
now. Sally supported Edna, and Mrs. Waters asked that I speak.

I began by saying I felt the doctor who was used by most of them was
unfit. I was amazed at their approval of this statement; I thought they liked
him. I then went on to explain that someone from MacMahon Clinic was
coming to talk with us and we should hear him out, even if we had strong
feelings against MacMahon. Mrs. Waters pressed for my particular stand.
I said, "If right now I was faced with only the two choices, I'd have to select
MacMahon as the better one." This apparently satisfied them. Then they
decided to hold off on the rent decision since Mr. Ward had a big voice in
this and shouldn't be left out.

In concluding, Edna suggested that they adhere to the idea of moving
the meeting place around. Mrs. Moore's offer was turned down since she'd
already held one. Faith's offer was accepted and they remarked about gradually getting Mrs. Thomas to exercise more. Next time she'd have to make it
up to the third floor.

Next, Edna suggested that from then on they have coffee and snacks
at the meetings. "Coffee for Jack and snacks for me. How about it? Let's
have some eats too. If they're really our meetings we should be able to do
what we want at them—and have what we want at them too." Everyone
agreed except Faith, who said she couldn't fix coffee. Edna said she'd take
care of it. "Then it's fine with me," Faith concluded.

There would be no planned guest speaker at the next meeting; instead they would choose a leader, decide on what to do about rent, and plan following meetings. They began to leave one after the other, and I spoke to most individually before they departed. The general trend of each of the comments was how much of a success they felt the meeting had been.

Part 3: Early Contacts with Olympia—November 1, 1967

As I knocked on Mrs. Waters' door (receiving no answer) a short, very heavy Negro woman with very sharp and pleasant features walked down the hall and inquired, "Are you Joe?" I said I was and added, "But are you sure I'm the right Joe?" She smiled and asked if I was the one she was told to expect. "Aren't you going around meeting all the tenants?" She explained that Mrs. Waters had told her to expect me and expressed her desire to talk with me.

She explained that Mrs. Waters was around somewhere in the building and was about to help me find her when I suggested we talk. "Well, not out in the hall, I hope; that's not proper. Let's go up to my apartment," she said in response.

As we reached her apartment (3C) she stood rather motionless and seemed to be trying to catch her breath. I asked if she was feeling ill and she explained her poor health. "I just have to take my pill and then I'll be fine," she said as she opened the door. At her suggestion I went to the living room and waited for her to take her pill. The layout was the same as Mrs. Roland's apartment (the bathroom a few feet from the front door, then an open kitchen area, then the living room, and, at the far end, the corridor opening into the bedroom).

A few seconds later she joined me and had apparently undergone immediate transformation. Now she was alert and revitalized completely. (I thought this rather strange.) I complimented her on the appearance of the apartment and she thanked me, explaining that such cleanliness was proper. She added that possibly because others had children it was harder for them to keep things clean. I agreed but felt she meant me to think she was trying to be nice to the others but was really better than them. (At this point there was just an inkling, but I felt this definitely was the situation as our conversation continued.)

We then made the appropriate introductions and I explained my hopes of organizing a tenant group. Her name was Olympia. She said she should be glad to take part but doubted that many would participate. I explained who I had already seen and said they had reacted in a positive way for the most part. "Oh, Mrs. Thomas is interested?" she asked. I asked if there was a particular reason for her questioning tone, and she stated, "It's just that she's one of those I wouldn't think would want to, but I guess she can really use help. I'm glad to hear she's at least trying."

Then she changed the subject to her health and explained that she had an enlarged heart. She spoke of her Egyptian husband, who had been deported four years before (he had been deported four times), and said he had tuberculosis. When they discovered this about him they ("doctors") also made her take an X-ray and discovered no TB, but did discover an enlarged heart.

A number of times I attempted to get her to discuss any problems in the building but each time she changed the subject back to herself (her husband, her past life, her health, etc.). The talk was pleasant and rather frank, and I felt convinced she wanted me to like her and feel sorry for her and at the same time applaud her for what she had been able to do under difficult circumstances.

Under no circumstances would she tell me of other tenants, saying, "I can't speak for them. That wouldn't be right, would it?" Concerning her feelings she would only say, "I wouldn't want to give you a wrong notion. I think you should meet them and make up your own mind after you've talked to them." And when I asked who lived in a particular apartment (part of a stream of conversation), she said, "Oh, look at me, I never give out information and here I am talking to you this way. But I wouldn't want to give out any information like that, it wouldn't be right."

I felt that a rather positive relationship could be established without much difficulty and that she could very possibly be a great help to me and the others in a group. Though the conversation for the most part received its direction from Olympia, I was able to learn a great deal about her, her relationship with certain other tenants, facts about the building and its internal system. In a sense I felt as though we were playing a game. To any question, she would first have to maintain the privacy of others, then I'd rephrase it, then it would be permissible for her to answer (after I had first seen that she was a proper person and that it was customary for her not to talk about others).

November 3, 1967. For a while I didn't know which way to turn; Olympia wanted to control the conversation. At numerous points she revealed some of her needs; for instance, when we were talking about certain foods Mrs. Waters eats and makes, Olympia looked at me and said, "Now, you and I don't eat such stuff—do you?" They asked if I drank; I said I did. Olympia quickly added, "But not like they do around here; white people know how to hold their liquor. That's what you mean, ain't it?" I said that I had gotten plastered a few times, but she was right, it wasn't a habit with me (they howled with laughter). Olympia added, "The same with me. I don't drink no cheap wine, and I know how to hold it, and went into a long story about the many "fine restaurants" she drank in and didn't get drunk.

I had a constant feeling she was trying to play up to me. She wanted me to recognize her as being better than the others and a fitting person to socialize with "white folk."

November 8, 1967. We both came to the door (opposite sides) at the same time and I startled her. I explained about Mrs. Waters's absence and

Olympia said she couldn't attend the meeting anyway. She was ill with "an extremely bad cold." On invitation I went into her apartment and she fixed a cup of coffee for me. As happened at our first meeting, she set up a TV table in front of her living room chair (she suggested I sit there), then came the cup of coffee, two spoons and a creamer. A second later she came with sugar. "You know, I'll bet I'm the only one here with this kind of sugar (cubes.)" I thanked her, but said I took my coffee without sugar. She replied, "Oh, I do too, sometimes. You know some people just can't take it that way." When she came back she sat at the dinette table. I got up, moved everything over to the table, returned the creamer to the kichen, came back, and sat at the table with her.

She began to discuss her cold and how she and Mrs. Waters had gone to the clinic the day before. I felt the conversation was strained and commented on this. She replied, "It's just what I told you; you can't help these people. Look, even Mrs. Waters—she couldn't have forgotten." I explained that quite a few days had passed since we had planned this meeting. She said I should have come by and reminded people. I explained my earlier intent and said that something had come up at the office. I said, "Well, I guess it is a bit more than just partly my fault." "That's not it, it's the people here."

As we continued to talk I learned some of her true feelings. She explained how she had been dispossessed from her apartment on City Street in Brooklyn. The people in that tenement were warm and friendly. "But over here it's cold." I asked what she meant. Instead of answering she asked, "Is it like this all around the neighborhood?" I said she probably knew more than I about that, and asked in a leading but empathetic manner, "Is it everyone that's cold?" She spoke of Mrs. Waters in particular. "Even though we're best of friends, there's still something there, a coldness. Do you know what I mean? In Brooklyn we all cared for each other. If something happened to one of us, it happened to all. We helped each other and really loved each other. It was family, real family, not like here. Everyone here only cares about himself. They'll be friendly, but not real friends. Do you really understand what I'm saying?"

I said I had experienced a similar situation, but that it was even harder for her because she couldn't get away as much as she might like. I offered, "Probably sometimes you even feel trapped. But I think you have done a good job of making the best of things." That, she then explained, is what keeps her going. "Everyone needs a purpose. These people have children and the kids give them a purpose for living. But me, sometimes I wonder. But I do the best I can. That's my purpose, and to me its just as important. Everyone needs a purpose, right?" (She was deeply serious.) I said she was correct and added, "I think a big thing, though, is that we can all find much purpose if we just look around and maybe a little inside. It's there; I'm really glad you feel it, and I think you are being great. You know, I see you are one of the strong people here."

She then explained about some of the others and how even though they had children they didn't even try to help themselves or become better people. She asked very pointed questions, like "Whose fault do you really think it is?" and in a sense we argued. She felt most in the building were responsible for their own condition. "You can't blame the government or other people. Hell, it's them, it's their own damn fault." I explained that I couldn't find it in me to blame them. "It's just that some are stronger and able to take it, like you. And then some others are missing a little something, I don't know what. It's probably even different for each one. I can understand how you feel; after all, you live here and I don't. It's easy for me to say I'd rather understand than blame, but someone who lives here would really have to be a great person to be understanding and not get angry." Continuing after a pause, "You know, I think if I lived here I'd feel hurt—like the others are letting me down. I mean, they're human and so am I; they should care."

She then wanted to know if I felt hurt about the meeting's "falling to pieces." I said I'd be a damn liar if I said it hadn't bothered me; it had, but it "wasn't catastrophic." She asked, "What does that word mean?" I said, "In other words it's not the end of the world. It's a setback, but it's not a very bad setback. I didn't expect it, but I'm not going to give up. I'm like you. I'm going to keep on. You can't expect people to trust and like you right off the bat. They have to take their time, see what's happening first."

"But they should realize they have to do something too. The thing is that they don't even want help, some of them," she added.

The talk went on for some time and she revealed one great theme—her loneliness. She always spoke around the subject, and would probably not admit it if a direct question were put to her. I saw two major factors which I had to deal with: her health and her loneliness. It goes without saying that there were many tangentials to each area.

In discussing a meeting I suggested a change of strategy. I asked for her opinion about having only Mrs. Ward, Mrs. Waters, and herself meet with me the first time, instead of trying to get more tenants to the first meeting. She asked why I included her. She could understand about the other two, but not herself.

I explained that I felt she had much to bring to the group. As we continued she was hesitant about making any commitment. She realized Mrs. Ward's position without my saying anything and would permit her apartment to be used for the meeting. Other meetings including the other tenants would have to be held elsewhere. She didn't mind meeting with them, but she didn't want all of them in her apartment. She doubted that Mrs. Ward and Mrs. Waters would come to her place—"They never come in to see me, I always have to go to them"—but if I spoke to them and they agreed, it would be fine with her. We then went down to Edna's again.

I told them I'd come again next Wednesday, and went back upstairs with Olympia to get my coat. When we got upstairs we began to talk again.

The discussion was serious and meaningful. The major point I wanted to make was to have her tell me she couldn't sleep at night. She said it wasn't that she was afraid of dying; it was that she is afraid of dying and not being found for weeks. She related a story from her past and explained that a friend had died and she had discovered it two weeks later. "I said goodnight to her and she must have just gone in and dropped dead." She screamed this last part and seemed to be in a trance. I tried to be sympathetic and reminded her of her friends. She said they really weren't friends and they wouldn't even bother coming up to her apartment. She then related a few instances when she was sick and no one had come to her aid. But she always kept her door ajar so she could "feel closer" to the others.

I said I wouldn't be by every day, but at least a couple of days a week, and I cared and would always stop in at least to say hello. She was apparently happy, but commented, "Why should I have to rely on you? They should care; they live here; people who live together should care about one another." She went on to say I must have a lot of things to do rather than be concerned about her—real important things. I said she was my concern and was one of those real important things she was speaking of. Her reply was a warm, friendly smile. I told her I'd be in again next Wednesday, collected all the data she had given me (her doctor, real estate agent, DW caseworker) as we talked, put on my coat, and let myself out.

November 10, 1967. After the meeting I went to Olympia's and she immediately asked about the meeting. I explained the "wait and see" situation. She quickly left that topic and began to talk about herself. Formerly she had been a maid and liked to work with rich people so she could have certain luxuries surrounding her. We discussed this at length, and our relationship became stronger with each talk.

At another point she explained that her doctor would not give her a note so that the Welfare Department would change her status from home relief to aid to the disabled. She told me of her "naughty" habit of using salt, though she was told not even to buy a shaker. As she put it, "Who can eat fried chicken without salt? That's just plain crazy." Also she confessed she should not be smoking—"doctor's orders."

We talked of her problem with the toilet and about her welfare check not coming—she had to go down on Mondays to pick it up in person. I explained my intention of contacting the caseworker and the building agent. She favored this, but impressed on me that they did their best and that both were liked by the tenants. "The last welfare person was just a horrible man. Don't do anything to get her [present worker] changed or mad at us," she commented. I reassured her and explained in detail of my intentions.

There were times during this talk when we laughed and joked. The feeling was friendly and I believe she saw me as an informal professional. I could relax and laugh, but the job of helping and organizing a group never left me and she realized this. I didn't come just to comfort and befriend her; I was there to get things moving on the path of organized self-help.

Part 4:   Summary, February 1968–May 1968.

1. Though no tenant left the building, there were two cases which were important in this respect.

Kathy Waters, daughter-in-law of Mrs. Waters, moved from the Bronx to stay with Mrs. Waters. With the help of Miss Tegran of the CCL Unit, Mr. James of the Martin Welfare Center, and Mr. Collins of the Southside Welfare Center, we were able to relocate her in a five-room apartment in Brooklyn. She then contacted her assigned welfare center in Brooklyn.

Delores Watson, a friend from Charleston, came to stay with Edna because of her family situation. She came with her four children. With the help of Mr. Collins and Mr. Curtis of the Southside Welfare Center, we were able to temporarily relocate her in a three-and-a-half room apartment in the area.

Both parents and their children frequent the building and in this respect, the Waters subgroup had expanded to include Edna (or Gertie), Helen, Faith, Olympia, Delores, Kathy, John Waters, and Mrs. Waters. As you can see, it was now a rather sizable grouping.

2. The group's contact with Mr. Tubb and Mr. Ryder of the Department of Real Estate proved fruitful during this period. The halls were painted and patched, toilet facilities were repaired for many, holes in apartments were patched, radiators were fixed, and those who requested them received new stoves and refrigerators. Much remained undone, though. Windows still had to be fixed and apartments were in need of painting.

A very positive working relationship was developed between the group and Mr. Collins of the DSS. Also, Mr. Curtis, unit supervisor, had a positive feeling toward the 165 Howell Street group and was helpful and ready to extend himself.

The group went through a very trying period, and Mr. Ward's leadership was challenged. As housing and welfare problems diminished in scope and intensity, the group turned inward and conflict was apparent in almost every meeting. Mrs. Moore was seen by the group as a destructive element in their quest for progress. Though all agreed she could be acceptable and helpful when sober, no one wanted any part of her when she had been drinking.

The Waters grouping grew in strength and number, but did not seek formal leadership. They felt it was a man's job. Joe Thomas was able to demonstrate some of his ability in leadership and was to be looked to in this respect. Mr. Ward, though the formal leader, lost the esteem and respect of the group and angered the others to the point where they no longer really wanted him as a leader.

Olympia began to speak out much more and confronted Mr. Ward a few times. She went outdoors more often and generally opened up quite a bit. The group provided her with a vehicle to grow and become more active and involved with others.

Faith, because of a number of specific actions, gained much respect, and possibly even Mr. Ward feared her ability and its recognition by the others.

Mrs. Cole of 193 Howell Street, a friend of Mr. Ward and Mrs. Thomas, became involved in the group and was a very active participant. Her relationship with the group did not rest solely with Mr. Ward.

3. *Goals:* (a) Though there had been some improvement in their living conditions, improvement as a concrete goal was not yet fully realized. (b) The goal to involve all tenants never crossed the racial barrier. There still remained two Puerto Rican families to be involved and the Ross brothers in Apartment 2B. Their involvement was open to discussion. Perhaps it would be better to focus on individual family problems instead, including these three families, and view the present group as a secondary force; maintain the group, but focus on *all* families; possibly then, these others would join the group. Note: There was a problem of drug addiction in the Acevedo family. (c) Constant contact, even if not in person, was advisable. Other workers, too many others, came and went, with gaps between. I felt the worker should impart the sense that he was there all the time, even though he wasn't. Possibly, too, more attention could be given to the children and teenagers— or, if desired, they could be the new focus.

4. *Agencies and contacts:* Ed Collins of the Department of Social Services was helpful in regard to the group as a whole, as well as to its individual members. He was particularly helpful regarding Mrs. Moore and Kathy Waters. Because of work pressures, he often got bogged down. A call to him was all that was necessary for him to react positively and, if possible, quickly. At last contact there were two caseworkers assigned to the building, but Ed would probably be the real contact person for a while, even if he was no longer assigned there.

It goes without saying that Mr. Tubb and Mr. Ryder were involved with all tenants, but as leader, Mr. Ward had much more contact with them and was recognized by them as the leader of the building.

Though CCLU was involved for a period around the no-heat situation, Miss Tegran continued to help at a later date, specifically in the case of Kathy Waters.

Other contacts were not as intense or involving but of possible concern would be two parole officers: the case of Nicholas Duke, the contact was Mr. Coshen; in the case of Mr. Ward, Jr., the contact was Mr. Femolo.

Glossary

Glossary items are provided for the major theoretical and practice concepts discussed in the book. Specific programs (such as Medicaid, Supplemental Security Income, etc.) are not included in the glossary, but may be located in the subject index. Readers wishing to restudy any glossary items should check the subject index and then turn to the page(s) cited there.

Accountability Demonstrating that social welfare programs are effective in meeting needs. This usually requires that program objectives be clearly specified.

Achievement of positions The assigning of positions on the basis of individual ability (students who get the highest grades receive honors, for example).

Action system That part of a behavior change effort which works with the change agent system and the client system to influence the target system.

Adequacy The effectiveness of a program in meeting the needs of the target population (that is, the people the program is intended to serve).

Administration The effective management of professional resources and responsibilities in social welfare agencies and structures.

Advocate role Part of an interventive strategy, advocacy involves helping clients obtain needed services. This may require the implementation of new services.

Almshouse A facility to house those considered legitimately needy in which basic life-sustaining needs were met.

Ascription of positions The assigning of positions without consideration of an individual's abilities ("a woman's place is in the home," for example).

Autonomous social welfare agency An agency in which one profession dominates decision-making and the provision of services.

Behavior-changer role Part of an interventive strategy, behavior change involves modifying specific parts of a client's behavior.

Behavioral psychology The branch of psychological theory which asserts that all behavior is learned in separate units (acts), that the units (acts) are related to each other, and that the units (acts) become established in the individual's behavior repertoire by means of external reinforcement.

Biopsychosocial whole Helen Harris Perlman's concept, which suggests that helping professions must understand the total person in his social environment. The helping relationship must include an awareness of the person's biological, psychological, and social characteristics and functioning.

Bread scale A subsistence level calculated according to food costs and family size, with welfare aid given if a family's income fell below that level. Public assistance budgets used today are a kind of bread scale.

Broker role Part of an interventive strategy, brokerage involves knowing services that are available and making sure those in need reach the appropriate services.

Bureaucracy A type of formal organization of people, tasks, and materials characterized by clearly specified goals and means and impersonal relations between those working in the bureaucracy.

Capitalist-Puritan value system The belief that people are responsible for themselves, and those who become dependent on others should be required to find ways to become self-sufficient.

Care-giver role Part of an interventive strategy, care-giving involves providing supportive services for those who cannot fully solve their own problems and meet their own needs.

Casework An interventive method that seeks to improve social functioning by concentrating on one person in depth, examining the individual's biological-psychological-social behavior within that person's social context.

Change agent A person who facilitates change.

Change agent system That part of a behavior-change effort that is composed of the change agent and the organization in or with which that agent works.

Charisma The personal qualities of an individual that enable that person to win the trust and loyalty of others.

Children's allowance The payment of a cash allowance to parents of children who are still minors.

Civil rights movement An ongoing attempt to achieve equal rights for all minority groups in American society. Most often this term refers to the attempts during the 1950s and 1960s to achieve racial equality for black people.

Classical (respondent) conditioning Acquiring a behavior by pairing an unconditioned stimulus with a conditioned stimulus.

Client A member of the client system; the person being helped.

Client-centered or nondirective therapy Developed by Carl Rogers, it adapts a psychoanalytic approach to focus on the client's perception of and feelings about her situation at any point in the life cycle. The helping person does not assume responsibility for and control over the person's situation in this therapeutic approach.

Client-focused agency An agency whose services are planned to meet whatever needs exist for a specified client population.

Client (user) participation The degree to which the persons who need and use a social welfare program have the opportunity to participate in program planning and evaluation.

Client system That part of a behavior-change effort that is composed of one or more persons who seek help or a change of some kind.

Collective bargaining The negotiation between a union and a business (or an entire industry) to establish mutually agreeable work contracts.

Collusion When several businesses agree to set prices or otherwise to jointly control the economic conditions within an industry. This interferes with normal market mechanisms, and increases the power of the businesses in the marketplace.

Community A spatially defined social unit within which there are identifiable patterns of social interdependence.

Community organization An interventive method that seeks to improve social functioning by using organizational and community groups to develop skills in identifying needs and organizing to meet these needs.

Community planner role Helping community groups to plan effectively for the community's social welfare needs.

Comprehensive neighborhood service centers Providing a range of social welfare services at centers scattered throughout a community. These centers are usually independently planned and operated, and are not usually under the control of a centralized administrative, bureaucratic structure.

Confidentiallity Insuring that information obtained from and relating to clients is only used professionally and with the permission of the clients.

Consultant role Working with other professionals to help them be more effective in providing services.

Counter-conditioning (reciprocal inhibition) Eliminating a behavior by reinforcing a behavior that is incompatible with it.

Countervailing power structures Structures that arise to check or balance a lopsided distribution of power.

Coverage The number of people actually participating in a social welfare program.

Creaming When social welfare agencies concentrate on those services and users with whom they have been successful in the past, in order to legitimate the agency itself.

Curative social welfare services Services provided to solve an already existing problem.

Data-manager role Collecting and analyzing data for decision-making purposes.

Decentralization of services Dispersing social welfare services throughout a community so that they are more readily accessible to persons who may need them. Decentralized services are usually operated by a centralized administrative, bureaucratic structure.

Diagnosis Interpreting information from and about a client to understand his situation and the problems in it.

Diffusion The borrowing by one society of cultural elements from another culture.

Discovery An innovation providing completely new information.

Disposable income The amount of money available to be spent by an individual, household, group, or organization.

Dividing the client Dividing a person's problems into specialized subparts and assigning different professional persons or agencies to deal with each subpart.

Economic institution The major social structure to distribute the resources needed to produce, distribute, and consume goods and services.

Ego psychology An adaptation of psychoanalytic theory that focuses on the present, and utilizes the personality's rational processes to understand the problems of the present.

Eligibility requirements The criteria used to determine who is eligible to receive services in a social welfare program. Eligibility requirements may include such factors as age, income, employment status, parental status, etc.

Empathy The ability to comprehend and sense another person's situation and feelings from that person's point of view.

Epigenetic principle of maturation Erik Erikson's theory, which asserts that each individual has a genetic timetable governing her physical maturation.

Equity The degree to which a program is actually available to the people in the target population. While in theory a program may specify a certain target population, in practice various characteristics may serve to exclude certain members of that population (lack of transportation to reach an agency to apply for service, for example).

Evaluative role Part of an interventive strategy, evaluation involves assessing needs and resources, generating alternatives for meeting needs, and making decisions among alternatives.

Extended family The form of the family comprised of three or more generations. It commonly also includes other blood-related persons.

Extinction Eliminating a behavior by not having it reinforced when it is performed.

Fiscal policy The government's intervention in the market to establish and implement economic policy.

Gaps in service When a social welfare agency or service network offers only part of the services needed by a person.

Grant programs Making a direct grant to a person to help meet the individual's needs (Supplemental Security Income, for example). Grant programs are usually funded by a combination of federal, state, and local tax revenues. Grants may also be in-kind, that is, providing a product (clothes, for example) rather than the money to buy the product.

Great Depression Starting with the Stock Market Crash of 1929, the Depression created massive unemployment, bank failures, and unprecedented need in the society. A series of programs were enacted to revive the economy and meet the human need created by the Depression. These programs comprised the "New Deal" of Franklin D. Roosevelt's administration, and included the Social Security Act in 1935.

Group dynamics Social behavior in small groups, including such factors as group composition, leadership, goal-setting, and cooperation or competition in group interaction.

Group work An interventive method that seeks to improve social functioning by using the small group as the context and process of change.

Guaranteed income Guaranteeing that the income of all persons or families reaches a predetermined level through a system of income supplements paid by the government to those whose income falls below this level.

Health Maintenance Organization A medical organization that contracts with persons to provide comprehensive health services for a flat fee. It is a type of health insurance.

Helping relationship The mutually desired

interaction between a person seeking help and a professional helping person that is based on trust, respect, sharing, and mutual involvement in the problem-solving process.

Host social welfare agency An agency in which there is a high degree of sharing between several professions that participate in decision-making and the provision of services.

Humanist-positivist-utopian value system The belief that it is society's responsibility to meet the needs of its members, and that most human breakdown is caused by societal malfunctioning.

Income-maintenance program A program that provides or increases the income available to a person or family.

Indenture Archaic practice of removing children from their own homes if their parents sought welfare help, and placing the children in more affluent families in return for the child's labor.

Indoor relief Providing welfare services to persons who reside in a facility for that purpose (originally almshouses, workhouses, and the like; today prisons, mental hospitals, rest homes, and so on).

Industrial Revolution Basic changes in the system of production in Western societies caused by the use of mechanical power in the production process in place of predominantly human or animal power. The roots of the Industrial Revolution go back to economic and social changes in the seventeenth century, with the main impact occurring in the eighteenth and nineteenth centuries. The revolutionary new use of mechanical power had far-reaching effects throughout the social structures affected.

In-kind payment Providing a person with a needed item (such as furniture) rather than the money to buy that item.

Institutional racism The comprehensive disadvantage created for members of a racial group by the systematic and cumulative discriminatory actions carried out within all of the major social institutions.

Institutionalized social welfare services Services that are an integral part of a social structure and are available to all societal members.

Interviewing Purposeful communication, including both verbal and nonverbal communication.

Invention An innovation created by useful new combinations of already existing information.

Judeo-Christian value system The belief that people have the right to make their own choices, but that society has the obligation to provide resources to help them do so and to aid them when the results of their choices create problems for themselves or others.

Laissez-faire capitalism First formalized by Adam Smith in 1776, the idea that minimal government regulation of the economic system promotes healthy competition and maximum efficiency. Most capitalistic societies of today have considerably more governmental economic control than that suggested by a pure laissez-faire system.

Life cycle The progression from birth to death through socially structured experiences related to chronological age. At each point in the life cycle the individual draws upon physical and social resources to solve problems and achieve gratification.

Lobbyist A person paid to represent the interests of a person, group, or organization in the political and legislative processes.

Management by objectives (MBO) A technique to measure program effectiveness by specifying concrete program objectives, analyzing data to assess whether these objectives have been obtained, and making decisions about program structure and functioning on the basis of these data.

Market The economic mechanism that relates consumer demand to producer supply.

Means test A test of eligibility for aid in which the applicant must demonstrate that her financial resources are below the level specified by the program from which help is being sought.

Methods approach to intervention Fitting a problem to a preexisting method (such as casework).

Mobilizer role Part of an interventive strategy, mobilization involves helping clients to utilize existing services more effectively.

Monopolistic social welfare services The lack of choice in social welfare programs. Often only one program exists to meet a need (Aid to Families with Dependent Children, for example), leaving the person in need no choice in where he can turn for help.

Modeling (observational learning) Acquiring a behavior by watching the behavior of others.

Negative income tax A tax system in which those whose income falls above a predetermined level pay an income tax, while those with incomes below this level receive a supplement.

Nonjudgmental attitude Separating attitudes about a person from attitudes about that person's behavior. Although the behavior may be unacceptable, the person continues to be accepted as a worthwhile, autonomous individual.

Norms Rules for behavior.

Nuclear family The form of the family comprised of two generations, parents and their children. Under special circumstances, other blood-related or nonblood-related persons may be regular members of a nuclear family.

Ombudsman A person or agency that reaches out into the community to identify need and help people in need make use of appropriate social welfare resources (or develop such resources if they don't already exist).

Operant (instrumental) conditioning Acquiring a behavior by having it positively reinforced when it is performed.

Outdoor relief The provision of welfare services to persons who are living in their own homes. This is the major form of welfare services provided in this country today.

Outreach role Part of an interventive strategy, outreach involves reaching out into the community to identify need and to follow up referrals to service contexts.

Parish In Tudor England, the local governmental unit providing for public welfare services and payments. Roughly equivalent to our present counties.

Personality The individual's distinctive and regular manner of confronting and dealing with persons, problems, and situations.

Pluralism Competition among major groups in American society, which encourages each to participate in the political process to fight for its own interests. Through this competition, it is assumed that coalitions will be formed based on compromises that allow each group to have its major interests represented in the legislative process.

Political institution The major social structure to allocate power through a system of government.

Policy The decision-making that utilizes the political and administrative processes to identify and plan economic and social objectives.

Position Named collections of persons performing similar functional behaviors.

Positive reinforcement Rewarding a behavior when it is performed.

Poverty Economic resources that are inadequate to provide the basic necessities of life as defined by a society. Poverty is both the objective reality that basic necessities are lacking, and the subjective reality that one lives on the fringe of society.

Power The ability of one person to influence others regardless of the wishes of the person being influenced. Bases of power include the ability to reward or punish, expertise, legitimacy, and identification (the ability to win the affection of the person being influenced).

Practice wisdom The understanding resulting from accumulated experience.

Preventive social welfare services Services provided before a problem exists, in an attempt to prevent the problem from arising.

Primary group A small group characterized by intensive, face-to-face interactions that permit the group members to express any aspect of their personalities.

Private income-transfer program Using monies voluntarily donated by one group for the benefit of other groups.

Private social service program A noneconomic social welfare service (such as birth-control counseling) supported with funds voluntarily donated.

Problem approach to intervention Developing a specific interventive strategy (method) in response to a specific problem.

Problem-focused agency An agency whose services are planned to meet the needs of any clients that have a specified problem or set of problems.

Problem-solving That part of the helping process that involves the gathering of information, defining problem situations, assessing helping resources and obstacles, formulating a plan of action to solve the problems identified, and evaluating the success of the plan after it is carried out.

Profession An organization of specialists characterized by an emphasis on the use of specialized knowledge and skills to serve the public, and close colleague relationships to insure competence in professional training and performance.

Professional certification Recognition by a governmental agency or nongovernmental association of the fact that an individual has met specified predetermined qualifications.

Professional licensing Legal regulation of members of a profession. Licensing may be of two kinds: (1) title licensing—legal regulation specifying the qualifications necessary to use a professional title (who can call oneself a social worker, for example); (2) practice licensing—legal regulation specifying that certain professional activities may only be performed by members of a particular professional group. Practice licensing usually includes title licensing.

Psychoanalytic theory A theory of personality development which asserts that the three major personality structures postulated by the theory—id, ego, and superego—result from the competition between the demands of society and the attempts of the physical organism to find gratification. This competition progresses through biologically related stages, with the main outlines of the personality structure established by adolescence. Sigmund Freud is the founder of psychoanalytic theory, although more recent neo-Freudians have further developed his ideas.

Public income-transfer program Using public monies collected from one group for the benefit of other groups.

Public social service program A non-economic social welfare service (such as marital counseling) supported with public funds.

Punishment Attempting to decrease the probability of a behavior's occurrence by removing a positive reinforcement or presenting an aversive stimulus.

Referral Sending a client to another social welfare resource when an agency is not able to provide the help needed. In some cases, clients may be referred to a more appropriate helping person within one agency. Referral involves the identification of a more appropriate resource and follow-through to insure that the client actually receives service as intended.

Rehabilitative social welfare services Services that are provided to solve an already existing problem, and to prevent its recurrence in the future.

Repossession When a store, bank, or credit company takes back an item purchased on credit because one or more payments have been missed.

Research The collection and analysis of data in order to assess the effectiveness of interventive efforts and the operation of any part of the social welfare institution.

Residence requirement Making the receipt of welfare benefits contingent upon residence in a specified geographic area for a specified period of time.

Residual social welfare services Social welfare services that are provided only to those who can prove need and who

qualify by meeting restrictive eligibility requirements.

Revenue sharing Providing local communities with federal funds and allowing them to decide how they should be spent. Part of President Nixon's "New Federalism," revenue sharing is an attempt to increase community autonomy by imposing less federal influence on the programs that must be operated by communities.

Role Norms associated with a position.

Role ambiguity A lack of clarity in the definition or teaching of appropriate role behaviors.

Role conflict Conflicting role expectations existing in one or more positions simultaneously.

Role set Complementary roles that are defined in relationship to each other.

Role theory The study of how tasks are organized and distributed in society.

Rural community A community characterized by small population size, low population density, a relatively homogeneous population, and relative isolation from other communities.

Secondary group A group characterized by relatively impersonal interaction focused on the performance of specified tasks.

Separate but equal The provision of separate facilities, which are said to be of equal quality, for members of different (usually racial) groups. Most often used in maintaining racial segregation, and struck down as unconstitutional by the Supreme Court in 1954.

Settlement house A community facility to help residents meet their social, recreational, educational, and collective action needs.

Shaping Acquiring a behavior by the use of differential reinforcement and extinction to move from a spontaneously performed behavior via successive approximations to the new behavior.

Social change Change within a part of the social structure, without destroying the structure's identity.

Social Darwinism An extension of Charles Darwin's biological concept—survival of the fittest—to social life. Social Darwinism maintained that those who were needy were less fit than those who were not, and therefore should not be helped since the society would only be preserving defective individuals who could never be self-sufficient.

Social dividend A cash payment to all members of society regardless of income.

Social differentiation Socially defined distinctions between groups on the basis of ascriptive criteria (age, sex, race, and the like), or achieved criteria (income, occupation, education, and so on).

Social history Obtaining background information about a client that is then the basis of diagnosis and problem-solving.

Social institution A cluster of positions, roles, and norms organized so as to meet a significant societal objective.

Social insurance Programs to meet people's needs, which are funded by contributions these people have made during periods when they are not in need (unemployment insurance, for example).

Social stratification A type of social differentiation in which groups are ranked on a scale of superior, inferior, and equal.

Social system An organized interrelated group of activities, each of which affects the others. In its broadest sense, *the* social system is the organization of the parts of the structure of a society in such a way that the functional independence that results enables the society to survive. Within *the* social system are a number of subsystems that are internally cohesive, but also affect each other.

Social utility A basic service needed for people to function effectively in society, and the provision of which is usually heavily subsidized by society.

Social welfare Improving social functioning and minimizing suffering through a system of socially approved financial and social services at all levels in the social structure.

Social work A socially legitimated profession that seeks to help people singly and in groups to meet their needs and achieve satisfaction in their daily lives.

Socialization Learning the culture in which one lives.

Socioemotional leader The main person in a small group who promotes group interaction and helps to maintain a cohesive interpersonal network within the group.

Starting where the .client is Beginning the helping relationship at the point where the client feels the need for help. Intervention may ultimately shift to other areas, but this decision must be made in consultation with the client.

Separation of powers The organizing principle underlying the federal political structure, which provides a system of checks and balances to prevent one branch of the government from having controlling power over the whole structure of government.

Target system That part of a behavior-change effort composed of those people whose behavior must be changed if the goals of the change-agent system and the client system are to be attained.

Task leader The main person in a small group who helps the group achieve its goals.

Tax allowance Allowing an individual, group, or organization to exclude certain income from the total income on which tax is calculated.

Total institution An agency with total control over the clients who live within it, and somewhat isolated from the community in which it exists.

Urban community A community characterized by large population size, high population density, a heterogeneous population, and extensive ties with other communities.

Warning out The practice of refusing residence to persons seeking residence but who were judged by the community as likely to become dependent on welfare in the future.

Workfare The belief that those persons receiving financial aid should be required to work in return for this aid. Since the majority of financial aid recipients are incapable of working, for a variety of social and physical reasons, there is an inherent contradiction in this concept.

Workhouse or house of correction An archaic facility that housed those considered shiftless (illegitimately needy), in which the basic life sustaining needs were met in return for forced work.

Dentler, Robert, 188
Depression, the Great, 51, 170
Desegregation, 68, 69
Diffusion, 197
Disabled, aid to, 59
Discoveries, 197
Discrimination, 68, 69, 176
Disinhibition, 163
Dix, Dorothea, 47
Dobriner, William, 190
Drive state, 158
Dunbar, Ellen, and Howard Jackson, 93, 99
Dunham, Arthur, 108

Economic Opportunity Act (1964), 69, 70–73
Economic institution, 215
Economy, structure of U.S., 215, 218, 220–21
Education, for jobs, 281–82
Ego, 145
Eight-hour workday, 48
Eisenhower, President, 68
Elizabethan Poor Law of 1601, 38, 39
    See also Poor Laws
Empathy, 238
Environment:
    effect of, on groups, 256
    influence of, on behavior, 142, 156–57, 164, 170
Epigenetic principle of maturation, 147
Equality, *see* Inequality
Equity, 116
    See also Social welfare
Erikson, Erik, 143, 147–48, 154
Ethnocentrism, 185
Extinction, 161

Factories, public, 39
Family:
    early groups, 39
    extended, 37
    nuclear, 37
    primary group, 137
    small-group characteristics of, 185–86
    social institution, 37, 97, 185
Faubus, Gov. Orval, 68
Federal Emergency Relief Fund (FERA), 52
Federal Reserve Act, 48
Federal Trade Commission, 48
Ferguson, Elizabeth, 31

Financing relief, 49–50
    See also Funding; Funds
Food Stamps, 98, 111, 293
Foster grandparents, 184
Free-enterprise system, 225
Freedman's Bureau, 44
Freud, Sigmund, 143–45
Friedlander, Walter A., 18
Funding, 59, 60, 113, 114–15
    problems of, 225
Funds, welfare, 39, 59–60

G.I. Bill, 64
General Education Board, 51
Goals:
    professional, 102
    societal, 308
Government:
    allocation of power in, 205–206
    separation of power in, 205
Griffiths, Martha, 312, 313–15
Gross National Product (GNP), 48
Group dynamics, 184–88
Group(s):
    awareness of, 122
    as recipients, 47, 110, 112
    contemporary, 170
    early, 36–37
    effects on individual, 170, 187
    flexibility of, 171
    politics of, 213
    problems of small, 184–87
    structure and function of, 137, 256–57
    task- or process-oriented, 186, 256
Group work, 251, 255–57
Guaranteed income, 312

Habits, 156
Hall, Richard N., 89–90
Hardcastle, David, 77
Head Start, 70, 71, 177, 229
Health programs, 69, 117–19, 312
Health Maintenance Organization (HMO), 76
Helping relationships, 237–38, 239–41
HEW, *see* U.S. Department of Health, Education, and Welfare
Hippocratic Oath, 93
Hoover, President, 49

Morrill Act, 44
Mothers, aid for, 50, 112, 209

Nader, Ralph, 213
National Association for the Advancement of
    Colored People (NAACP), 50
National Association of Social Workers (NASW),
    2, 5, 6, 9, 90, 91, 207
    code of ethics, 94–95
National Child Labor Committee, 50
National Conference on Charities and Correction,
    47
National Conference on Social Welfare, 47
National Labor Union, 47
National Tuberculosis Association, 50
National Welfare Rights Organization (NWRO),
    75, 112, 120
Needs, of society, 171
Needy, 38, 39, 41, 44
    See also Poor
Negative income tax, 311
Neo-Freudians, 147, 148
New Careers Program, 281
New Deal, 51
New Federalism, 77
New Left, the, 75
New York Association for Improving the
    Conditions of the Poor (AICP), 44
New York Society for Prevention of Pauperism,
    44
Newman, Edward, and Jerry Turem, 104
Nisbit, Robert, and Guy Swanson, 196, 197
Nixon, Richard, 75, 312
Nonjudgmental attitude, 240
Norms:
    defined, 170
    roles as, 171
Note-taking, in interview, 246

Observation, 247
Observational learning, 158–59
Office of Economic Opportunity (OEO), 70–74,
    116, 122
Old Age and Survivor's Insurance (OASI), 52
Old Age and Survivor's Disability and Health
    Insurance Program (OASDHI), 53, 60
Ombudsman, 100, 213
Operant (instrumental) conditioning, 157–58

Outdoor relief, 38, 40, 41, 44
Outreach role, 266

Pangloss Mental Health Association, 95
Parish, welfare in, 38–39
Parsons, Talcott, 253
Paternalism, 111
Pavlov, I. P., 157
Perlman, Helen Harris, 136, 252
Perlmutter, Felice Davidson, 121
Personality:
    defined, 137
    Freudian theory of, 145–47
Personnel:
    education of, 281–82
    self-awareness of, 164
    See also Professional; Workers
Phillips, E. Larkin, and Daniel N. Weiner, 154
Phillips, Wallace, and Alexander B. Pierce, 249
Pincus, Allen, and Anne Minahan, 22
Pluralism, political, 206
Policy, social welfare, 50
Poor:
    aids for, 223
    as consumers, 221, 225
    attitudes toward, 38, 39, 41, 44, 45, 51
    early categories of, 38
    participation of, 122
    problems of, 223, 224
    work ethic for, 39
    See also Needy
Poor Law:
    Elizabethan (1601), 38, 39, 41
    New (1834), 40
Poor People's Campaign, 75
Positions, social, 174
Positive reinforcement, 159, 160–61
Poverty:
    attitudes toward, 39, 41
    causes of, 40
    current, 221, 222–23
    War on, 30, 70, 115, 122
Power:
    bases of, 187
    political, 205–206
Practice wisdom, 135
Practitioner (social welfare), 266
Pre-casework, 252
Primary-group satisfaction, 185

1 2 3 4 5 6 7 8 9 10